Enough Said

What's Gone Wrong with the Language of Politics?

Enough Said

WHAT'S GONE WRONG WITH
THE LANGUAGE OF POLITICS?

Mark Thompson

THE BODLEY HEAD
LONDON

Grateful acknowledgement is made for permission to reproduce extracts from the following: *Four Quartets* by T. S. Eliot, published by Faber and Faber Ltd; 'Pressure' by Killer Mike, lyrics written by Michael Render, published by Aniyah's Music, all rights reserved, used by permission; *Hamilton*, written by Lin-Manuel Miranda, copyright © Lin-Manuel Miranda, used by permission of the author.

1 3 5 7 9 10 8 6 4 2

The Bodley Head, an imprint of Vintage,
20 Vauxhall Bridge Road,
London SW1V 2SA

The Bodley Head is part of the Penguin Random House group of companies whose addresses can be found at global.penguinrandomhouse.com

Penguin
Random House
UK

Copyright © Mark Thompson 2016

Mark Thompson has asserted his right to be identified as the author of this Work in accordance with the Copyright, Designs and Patents Act 1988

First published by The Bodley Head in 2016

penguin.co.uk/vintage

A CIP catalogue record for this book is available from the British Library

Hardback ISBN 9781847923127

Typeset in India by Thomson Digital Pvt Ltd, Noida, Delhi

Printed and bound in Great Britain by Clays Ltd, St Ives plc

Penguin Random House is committed to a sustainable future for our business, our readers and our planet. This book is made from Forest Stewardship Council® certified paper.

MIX
Paper from
responsible sources
FSC® C018179

For Jane

Contents

1 Lost for Words

Don't Retreat, Instead – RELOAD!

Sarah L. Palin, Twitter, 23 March 2010[1]

Public language matters. Words are free, and every politician and journalist and citizen can draw on an unlimited supply of them. But there are days when the right words are all that counts, and the speaker who can find them determines what happens next. Over time, leaders and commentators and activists with empathy and eloquence can use words not just to exploit the public mood, but to shape it. And the result? Peace, prosperity, progress, inequality, prejudice, persecution, war. Public language matters.

This is hardly a new discovery. It's why public language and public speaking have been studied and taught and fought over for thousands of years. But never before has public language been as widely and readily distributed as it is today. Words hurtle through virtual space with infinitesimal delay. A politician can plant an idea in 10 million other minds before she leaves the podium. An image with an author and a deliberately composed meaning – a plane hitting a skyscraper, say – can reach the eyes of viewers around the world with an instantaneity no longer constrained by distance or mechanical limit. Once, and not long ago in human history, we would have heard a rumour, or read a report of it, days or even weeks later. Today we are all witnesses, all members of a crowd that is watching and listening in real time.

Now. It's happening now. He's saying that now. You're posting this now. I'm replying now. Listen to me. Look at me. Now.

We think of ours as the age of digital information, and so it is. But we sometimes forget how much of that information is conveyed in human language which is doing what it has always done in human societies: alerting, frightening, explaining, deceiving, infuriating, inspiring, above all persuading.

So this is also the age of public language. More than that, we are living through an unparalleled, still unfolding and uncertain *transformation* of public language. Yet when we consider and debate the state of modern politics and media – how policies and values get discussed and decisions are made – we tend to think of it only in passing, as if it is of interest only insofar as it can help us understand something else, something more foundational. It is the argument of this book that public language – the language we use when we discuss politics and policy, or make our case in court, or try to persuade anyone of anything else in a public context – is itself worthy of close attention. Rhetoric, the study of the theory and practice of public language, was once considered the queen of the humanities. Now she lives out her days in genteel obscurity. I'm going to make the case for putting her back on the throne.

We enjoy one advantage over earlier generations of students of rhetoric. The searchability and indelibility of modern media mean that it has never been easier to trace the evolution of the specific words and statements of which a particular oratory is constituted. Like epidemiologists on the trail of a new virus, we can reverse time and track an influential piece of public language from its pandemic phase, when it was on every lip and every screen, back through its late and then its early development, until we arrive at last at the singularity: the precise time and place it first entered the world.

*

On 16 July 2009, Dr Betsy McCaughey, the former lieutenant governor of New York, appeared on Fred Thompson's radio show to give her two cents on the hottest political topic of that summer: President Barack Obama's controversial plans to reform America's health-care system and extend coverage to tens of millions of previously uninsured citizens.

Fred Thompson, who died in the autumn of 2015, was a colourful conservative whose furrowed and jowly gravitas had taken him from a successful law career to the US Senate, not to mention several successful stints as a Hollywood character actor. After the Senate, he embraced talk radio, and in 2009 his show was one of countless conservative outlets on which Obamacare was being dissected and condemned.

There wasn't a better person than Betsy McCaughey to do just that. A historian with a PhD from Columbia University (thus entitling her to that medical-sounding 'Dr'), McCaughey had risen through sheer brain power from humble origins in Pittsburgh to become a significant public figure on the American right. And she was considered a specialist in health-care policy. She had been a forensic as well as ferocious critic of Clintoncare, the Democrats' failed attempt to reform the system in the 1990s. Obamacare, of course, was a rather different proposition – indeed, some of its founding principles had either been developed by Republicans, or even implemented by them. The policy bore a particularly inconvenient resemblance to Mitt Romney's health reforms while he was governor of Massachusetts. At the time of McCaughey's radio interview, Romney was already being touted as a possible candidate to take on Barack Obama in 2012.

But Betsy McCaughey was too forthright and ideologically committed to be discomforted by the intellectual genealogy of Obamacare. Nor was she likely to face a particularly testing cross-examination from her lawyer-turned-radio-host. American politics was polarising even before Barack Obama arrived in the White House, and the media discussion of that politics had polarised along with it. The paradoxical result was that, the more bitter the divisions became, the more likely it was that everyone in any given studio or political website would agree with one another. The people with whom they all *disagreed* were absent – indeed were probably all gathered in a different studio, making the opposite case in an equally cosy ideological cocoon where they faced the same low risk of contradiction.

On the face of it, then, nothing about this encounter – the political circumstance, the characters, the likely flavour and flow of the argument – was out of the ordinary. But on 16 July, Betsy McCaughey had something new to say. Deep within one of the drafts of the Obamacare legislation which was then making its way through Congress, she had stumbled on an unnoticed but alarming proposal:

One of the most shocking things I found in this bill, and there were
many, is on page 425, where the Congress would make it mandatory . . .
that every five years, people in Medicare have a required counseling
session that will tell them how to end their life sooner, how to decline
nutrition, how to decline being hydrated, how to go into hospice
care . . . These are such sacred issues of life and death. Government
should have nothing to do with this.[2]

There are two things to note about this claim. The first is simply
that it's untrue. The part of the bill which McCaughey was referring
to – Section 1233 – did not in fact call for compulsory 'end of life'
counselling sessions. Such sessions would have remained at
the patient's discretion. The intent of the draft section was to make
these *voluntary* sessions eligible for coverage under Medicare, the
federal programme which pays the medical costs of many older
Americans.

But the fact that it was untrue – and indeed was promptly and
definitively refuted by defenders of the bill – did nothing to stop it
from rapidly gaining currency. This is the second, and more intriguing,
point to note. Provision of end-of-life counselling had previously
enjoyed tentative bipartisan support, but in the days following
McCaughey's appearance, many of America's most influential conservative commentators and a number of prominent Republican politicians, including the then House minority leader, John Boehner, took
up her charges. And the claim began to be rounded out. The conservative radio host Laura Ingraham cited her 83-year-old father,
proclaiming: 'I do not want any government bureaucrat telling him
what kind of treatment he should consider to be a good citizen. That's
frightening.'[3] While a few commentators associated with the right
ridiculed the 'myth' or 'hoax' of Section 1233 – on MSNBC's *Morning
Joe*, Joe Scarborough joked about the 'Grim Reaper' clause[4] – most of
the discussion on the conservative side of the political divide was
predicated on the assumption that McCaughey's claim about the bill
was not a myth, but a straightforward statement of fact.

Then, on 7 August, Sarah Palin entered the fray with a posting on
Facebook which included the following passage:

The America I know and love is not one in which my parents or my
baby with Down Syndrome will have to stand in front of Obama's

'death panel' so his bureaucrats can decide, based on a subjective judgment of their 'level of productivity in society', whether they are worthy of health care. Such a system is downright evil.[5]

What followed is well known. Within a few days the freshly baked term 'death panel' was everywhere – on radio, TV, the newspapers, the Web, Twitter – spread not just by its author and her supporters but, unintentionally yet also unavoidably, by those who were frantically trying to debunk it. By the middle of August, an opinion poll by Pew suggested that no fewer than 86% of Americans had heard the term. Of those, 30% believed it was a real proposal – the proportion among Republicans was 47% – while another 20% said they weren't sure whether it was true or false.[6]

Despite all denials, a belief that Obamacare meant compulsory death panels remained stubbornly widespread, and a few months later the Democrats dropped the underlying proposal. When in 2012 the Obama administration again raised the possibility of covering end-of-life counselling under Medicare, the tag line threatened to take flight once more and the proposal was quickly dropped. In the summer of 2015, after extensive further research and consultation, Medicare announced that it did indeed intend to pay for end-of-life counselling. Predictably, Betsy McCaughey immediately took to the *New York Post* to announce: 'Death panels are back.'[7]

A phrase which exaggerated and distorted a claim that was itself false, and which in any event had virtually nothing to do with the central thrust of Obamacare, had changed the course of politics. In fact, it is probably the only thing that many Americans can recall about the whole health-care debate. As the veteran conservative firebrand Pat Buchanan remarked about Sarah Palin: 'The lady knows how to frame an issue.'[8]

*

Let's set aside whatever views we may have about the protagonists in this political drama, or indeed about health care and politics as a whole, and consider the phrase 'death panel' purely as a piece of rhetoric. What makes it tick? Why was it so successful in shaping the debate? And what, if anything, does it tell us about what is happening to our public language?

Part of its strength is obviously its *compression*. A powerful political point that can be expressed in two words is perfect for the world of Twitter – and not just Twitter. Say that at some point in the summer of 2009, you'd been walking through an American airport past a TV monitor. The words 'death panel' fit neatly onto the straps which all the cable news networks put across the bottom of the screen. You don't even know whether the person on the screen is arguing in favour or against Obamacare. What you see – and what you remember – is the two words.

We can break the compression down further. The phrase has the effect of a *synecdoche*, that type of metonym in which the part stands for the whole. We know when we hear them that the words 'death panel' don't just stand for Section 1233, they stand for the whole of Obamacare. Actually, they stand for everything to do with Barack Obama, his administration, his vision for America.

And the words are *proleptic*: they take an imagined future scenario and present it as current reality. Whereas Betsy McCaughey simply misrepresents the draft bill, Sarah Palin offers a political prediction which goes like this: the legislation the Democrats are proposing will give the federal government control over your and your family's health – control over life and death – and sooner or later they'll create a bureaucracy to decide who gets what. On the face of it, then, this is a slippery-slope argument – let them pass this law, and in the end the government will decide who lives and who dies. But of course it isn't a complete argument at all. It's a piece of rhetorical panache which leaps straight away to the dystopic end-state and brings it to life with vivid imagery. The power of the prolepsis in such that you may not even notice that the intermediate steps in the argument are missing.

The impact of the phrase is accentuated in the original posting by two inspired pieces of passing-off. Sarah Palin puts the phrase 'death panel' in quotation marks as if she's quoting from the draft bill; she also puts quotation marks around 'level of productivity in society', as if that too was Barack Obama's term rather than her own concocted phrase. This evocation of a dehumanised socialist/bureaucratic state seems to have been prompted by fellow conservative Congresswoman Michele Bachmann's lopsided interpretation of the views of the bioethicist Ezekiel Emanuel, one of the most fervent advocates of universal health care. It is of a piece, though, with attacks on US government attempts to reform health care stretching back over half a century and more; in the mid-1940s, the American Medical Association described President Truman's plans for national health insurance as Soviet-style 'socialised medicine'. But the words 'death panel' trigger even darker allusions: twentieth-century eugenics and euthanasia programmes, and the selections in the death camps, with Barack Obama and Medicare officials taking the place of Nazi doctors.

If we listen really carefully, though, we can hear something else. The mention of Trig, her Down's syndrome child, signals how far Palin has generalised and radicalised an argument that began with what now seems the relatively modest claim that the elderly were going to be badgered into refusing further treatment. Now it's about murdering the young.

And there's a broader implication. An American voter might reasonably conclude that there are two kinds of public policy question: those that go to the heart of religious, cultural and ethical differences – the debates about abortion and same-sex marriage are obvious examples – and those that are essentially managerial. How can we prevent another shock like Lehman Brothers? How can we best protect the United States from the Zika virus? You might further conclude that the question of health-care reform fell squarely into the second category.

Not according to Sarah Palin. Her previous public mentions of Trig had been in connection to her opposition to abortion, and for her Obamacare raises similar issues – this is a battle between the forces of good and evil. In referring to her Down's syndrome child, she's attempting to pivot the visceral, Manichean quality of the abortion debate into the battle over health-care reform. When it comes to abortion, the two sides believe there can be no compromise. The same is true of health care, she says. You can't compromise with people who mean to slaughter your children.

And that's the final point to make about the phrase 'death panel'. It's maximal: in all respects it states its case in the strongest possible terms. What Sarah Palin claims to be uncovering is nothing less than a conspiracy to murder. There is no presumption of good faith on the part of your opponent – this is a fight to the political death, a fight in which every linguistic weapon is fair game. It is a rhetoric which doesn't seek to dispel distrust of politicians, but to foment it. And it worked.

Perhaps the term 'death panel' leaves you cold. Perhaps you find the rhetorical conceit grotesque or comical, and you are amazed that anyone could be taken in by something so crude and exaggerated. But all rhetoric is designed for a particular time and place, and above all for a particular audience – it is a supremely tactical, contextual art – and the phrase probably wasn't intended for you. Given the context and the people likely to hear it, however, it was devastatingly effective, like a precision-guided munition punching its way through to its target.

And yet in one respect it is an utter failure. It is so tendentious, so abstracted from the real – and difficult – decisions and trade-offs which must be faced in any debate about health care, so purely partisan in intent and meaning, that it makes the real policy choices associated with Obamacare not easier to understand, but harder. Whether wilfully or not, explanatory power has been wholly sacrificed in the interest of rhetorical impact.

There is Great Anger

Across the political spectrum, there is a growing acknowledgement that something has gone awry with our politics and the way in which political questions are debated and decided in America, Britain and other western countries. Democracy is a rough business and disquiet about it is hardly new – read Plato or Thomas Hobbes. But there is substantial evidence to support the current anxiety.

'There is great anger. Believe me, there is great anger,' the American celebrity property developer Donald Trump told his followers on 15 March 2016, in a speech following his victory in Republican primaries in four more states. Whatever else you make of Trump, it's hard to argue with this observation. The Edelman Trust Barometer measures trust in government, business, media and NGOs in twenty-eight countries around the world. Its 2016 survey showed a fractional improvement in trust in government after the lows of the financial crisis, but it also suggested that the gap in the level of trust in political and other institutions expressed by elites (or the 'informed public'*), and that expressed by the population at large, had widened

---

* If you are between twenty-five and sixty-four, are college-educated, in the top 25% of household income for your age group, and consume a fair amount of general and business news, you meet Edelman's criteria for this group.

year after year, and indeed was the widest that Edelman has ever seen.[9] The three countries where the gap has grown the most over the past four years are France, the UK and the US.

In both America and Europe, near-term disillusion with mainstream politicians – caused by their failure to do anything about income inequality or to punish anyone after the financial crash, by rising anxiety about globalisation and immigration, and by the bitter residue of the war in Iraq – have exacerbated and accelerated adverse trends in our political systems which were already causing concern. In the US and other western countries, politics has become vituperative, the gap between left and right has widened not just among politicians but among the public, and the number of policy areas on which the mainstream parties are willing or capable of reaching an accommodation with their opponents has shrunk, in case of the United States close to zero. As a result, decision-making in many national and supranational political institutions has become sclerotic.

The low level of trust in established politicians has led many citizens to turn away from them in search of alternatives. These include old-fashioned left-wing radicals, like Jeremy Corbyn in the UK and Bernie Sanders in the US; anti-immigration and extreme right parties like the French Front National, which has polled strongly in recent elections and whose leader, Marine Le Pen, looks like being a serious contender in the 2017 presidential election, and Austria's FPÖ, or Freedom Party of Austria, whose candidate Norbert Hofer came within an inch of becoming president of that country in May 2016; new populist-radical groupings like Syriza in Greece and Podemos in Spain; parties centred on single issues, like Britain's UKIP and Scotland's SNP; and pure anti-politicians, like the Italian comedian Beppe Grillo, or Donald Trump. The success of these non-mainstream parties and individuals has tempted some politicians within the mainstream to ape their style and tactics. In their different ways, Ted Cruz and Boris Johnson are examples of this last phenomenon. As a result, established parties and political institutions are experiencing disruptive forces both from without and within.

But public apathy and lack of engagement with politics is at least as serious an issue as those of fragmentation and the rise of the populists. In many democracies, voter turnout is falling. The young are a particular concern: in the 2014 midterm elections only one in five American 18- to 29-year-olds voted. Both the supply and the consumption of serious news has been falling – and public trust in mainstream media, which is facing its own centrifugal forces as well as an existential economic crisis brought on by digital, is in scarcely better shape than that in mainstream politics.

The obvious question, of course, is why. Or to sharpen the point, recognising that (for reasons we will also explore) conspiracies have come to sound more credible to us than accidents nowadays, *who is to blame?* The good news is that a large team of detectives is at work on the case, and that they already have a number of suspects. The rather less good news is that the suspects are so numerous, and the detectives' theories so contradictory and difficult to confirm, that as yet it has proved impossible to charge anyone.

One group of sleuths wants to pin it on the politicians. That sounds straightforward enough, but even here there's a disagreement. Some want to blame individuals. Tony Blair's name comes up frequently, as does George Bush's, though some of the older detectives are still obsessed with Margaret Thatcher, Ronald Reagan and Bill Clinton. Their continental colleagues mention Silvio Berlusconi and Nicolas Sarkozy, as well as any number of Central and Eastern European leaders. Each detective makes their case with passion, but we can't help noticing that they only ever mention politicians whom they personally dislike and with whose politics they obviously disagree; left-leaning detectives only blame politicians of the right, and vice versa. We can't of course rule out the possibility that all of the ills of democracy in one country stem from the nefarious actions of one individual or party or ideological orientation, but it's hard not to conclude that these detectives are so emotionally involved in the case that they have lost objectivity.

Other investigators discern shifts in attitude and behaviour which go beyond individual politicians. In their cheerily titled 2012 book *It's Even Worse Than It Looks: How the American Constitutional System Collided With the New Politics of Extremism*, the distinguished political scientists Thomas E. Mann and Norman J. Ornstein examine a series of recent policy clashes to demonstrate the particular difficulties which the US political system – as compared to a European parliamentary democracy – has in coping with periods of strong ideological antagonism between its main parties. But its thrust is resolutely one-sided. The 'new politics of extremism' are entirely the fault of the Republican Party and one of the book's suggestions of how to put things right is as follows:

Punish a party for ideological extremism by voting against it. (Today, that means the G.O.P.*) It is a surefire way to bring the party back into the political mainstream.[10]

Vote Democrat, in other words. But blaming an adverse trend in political culture entirely on one party and then inviting your readers to vote for the other one is scarcely a recipe for reducing political division. Nor does it really address the issue of radicalisation and fragmentation *within* a party – fragmentation which, in the case of the Republicans, means that there is essentially no one at the controls, and no means of achieving consensus about any future direction for the party, whether towards the centre or away from it.

Perhaps we'll have better luck with Amy Gutmann's and Dennis Thompson's *The Spirit of Compromise: Why Governing Demands It and Campaigning Undermines It*. The book tackles the same problem – ideological difference leading to legislative and governmental stalemate – in a more even-handed way, looking for systemic causes rather than blaming any one party for it. For Gutmann and Thompson, the root cause is that political campaigning has become continuous rather than limited to set periods before elections, and that the behaviours that go with campaigning – in particular the need to distinguish yourself sharply from your political opponents – are inimical to successful government, and in particular to the eponymous 'spirit of compromise' on which they claim much practical political progress depends.

This is potentially a more compelling diagnosis, though exactly where it takes us remains unclear. The book ends with some practical suggestions for the reform of America's political institutions, but the central call is for something altogether more abstract, a new equilibrium between the dutiful and reasonable Dr Jekyll mindset of good governance and the riotous Mr Hyde of the campaign trail:

> The uncompromising mindset should not be eliminated even if it could be. Campaigning requires it. Campaigning and the uncompromising mindset are in the DNA of the democratic process. The democratically defensible aim therefore is to find a better balance between the mindsets. That balance is currently eluding American democracy, and it is increasingly at risk in other democracies.[11]

---

* 'Grand Old Party', i.e. the Republican Party.

Here too – notwithstanding Gutmann's and Thompson's specific recommendations for improved civic education and campaign finance reform – we find ourselves reading a prescription for a way forward that sounds suspiciously like a restatement of the problem. The whole point about poor Dr Jekyll is that he is destined never to find a happy medium, or even a *modus vivendi*, between the two halves of his character.

Nor do Gutmann and Thompson have an entirely satisfactory answer to the problem of political opposition. While governments govern, it is the nature of opposition parties to oppose (in the US system, parties are often governing *and* opposing at the same time in different branches of government or different houses of Congress), and opposition is inevitably a form of permanent campaign. The normal rules of campaigning therefore apply: opposition leaders are encouraged to attack as much of their rivals' political programme as they decently can, and to fight for even symbolic victories. Not to do so, not to kick against measures which you argued vehemently against at election time, but rather to help the other side achieve more in government than the barest minimum that the disposition of votes would allow them, can feel hypocritical and a betrayal of one's own supporters.

Gutmann's and Thompson's call for a return to the spirit of compromise thus runs up against a fundamental asymmetry, which is that compromise is generally more attractive and necessary for governments than for oppositions. Two and a half thousand years ago, the Athenians dealt with this problem by instituting ostracism, political exile, to prevent defeated would-be leaders from disrupting the orderly conduct of government. That is hardly an option for us.

And – although the authors never state this in terms – their conclusions could be taken to imply that the best policies are generally to be found in the centre ground between the ideological poles. Yet there are many examples of successful policy ideas which began their life on the radical left or right rather than in the zone of moderate pragmatism between them. We should also beware of assuming that the best politics is consensual in intent and docile in flavour. Often obstinacy and a noisy determination to be heard is the only way of getting bold new policy ideas accepted. High passion and loud argument can be the sign of a healthy as well as a sickly democracy.

I have chosen two books about American politics. If I had selected similar books about the state of contemporary European politics, they would have focused on political paralysis too – though probably the rather different stasis that can emerge from coalition politics in a parliamentary system, or from a deadlock of vested interests in an unreformed political culture. But many of the underlying themes would have been the same.

Behind these topical diagnoses are any number of academic theories about why our democracies are suffering their present tribulations. In his 2014 book *Political Order and Political Decay*, for instance, the political scientist Francis Fukuyama charted the rise and decline of institutions in western and other civilisations over centuries. The historian Niall Ferguson also focused on the role of institutions in *The Rule of Law and Its Enemies*, his Reith Lectures series for the BBC in 2012. But institutions – meaning our constitutional arrangements and political practices, our systems of law and order, and the structures and conventions under which economic, social and cultural activities take place in our societies – are only one place to start when a political scientist uses history to explain our current difficulties. Without even attempting to do justice to the different schools of thought on the subject, we might just note that we can usually place even these scholarly investigators on a political spectrum: those on the left warning that the contradictions of capitalist liberal democracy – essentially meaning inequalities of power and wealth – are finally coming home to roost; while those on the right see once-strong political and social cultures being undermined by the levelling forces of progressivism and political correctness.

But some of our detectives are on the trail of a quite different set of villains: the media. Here too they are divided between those who blame specific malign forces – Fox News, Rupert Murdoch, *The New York Times*, the BBC and the *Daily Mail* are names that might appear near the top of sample American and British lists – and those who cite structural changes, by which they mean the technological and commercial forces that have fragmented audiences, disrupted traditional media, introduced a 24/7 news cycle and, at least according to some, generally dumbed down and poisoned public discourse.

In fact, claims that our media is letting democracy down – and specifically that it is failing properly to explain political choices to the citizenry – long pre-date continuous TV news, let alone Gawker and

BuzzFeed. Over four decades ago John Birt, a future director general of the BBC who was then a TV current affairs producer of notable seriousness, wrote in *The Times* of London with his colleague Peter Jay that 'there is a bias in television journalism. Not against any particular party or point of view – it is a bias against understanding.'[12]

John Birt's thesis was that TV journalism's love affair with story, emotion and moments of eye-catching but ultimately insignificant impact meant that the serious choices of which real government and policy formulation consist were either not aired at all, or were so simplified or foreshortened as to be useless if the object of the exercise was to inform, rather than just to entertain, the public.

That claim, and others like it, have been repeated with increasing urgency as technology has changed the grammar of journalism and the way it is consumed. In 2007, Tony Blair described the media as a 'feral beast', arguing that the resulting competition between media outlets had led to a savage hunt for what he called (following Birt) 'impact journalism', in which responsible reporting was replaced by sensationalism and character assassination.[13] As a result, an honest and straightforward dialogue between political leaders and the public was becoming increasingly difficult. The journalist John Lloyd's 2004 book, *What the Media Are Doing to Our Politics*, painted a picture of a modern British media (very much including the BBC) which was so arrogant, so obsessed with competitive success, and so self-deceiving, that it risked losing any sense of civic responsibility.

Again, I have chosen examples from one western country. Had I instead picked critiques of the media in the US or continental Europe, the case studies and the institutions would have differed but the charge sheet would have been much the same.

Finally, there is the public. Some politicians and other members of our elites wonder – always privately, of course – whether the real culprits for the breakdown in trust, engagement and comprehension between voters and politicians aren't the populace themselves. Perhaps *they've* changed. Perhaps some combination of affluence and hedonism and the technologies that allow them to fill their heads with entertainment morning, noon and night have led them to become more shallow and selfish, less civic-minded, less able to concentrate.

There are dispassionate experts on tap here too, notably in the field of social psychology which has developed and broadened in recent years to include the strongly trending field of 'behavioural economics', which applies psychological, social and economic data and insights to understand how human beings make choices about what to buy or which services to use – and, by extension, what public policies to support, or even who to vote for. In fact, the conclusions of thought-leaders in behavioural economics like Cass R. Sunstein (the co-author, with Richard H. Thaler, of the influential 2009 book *Nudge*) tend to support traditional wisdom about human beings: that many of us prefer to avoid views we disagree with and, if confronted with them, may well become more, not less, fixed in our existing opinions; that we are far more likely to believe a rumour or a conspiracy theory like the *death panels* if it fits our world view than if it doesn't.

The politicians, the media, the public. You will have your own views about each of these explanations. I am sceptical of any theory which is predicated on the wickedness or insanity of any one political party or media organisation. I believe that social psychologists and others are making interesting and potentially significant empirical advances in our understanding of individual and collective human behaviour. But none of their work suggests that the public should be singled out for blame for the palpable deterioration in our political cultures. Indeed, that instinct to jump at once to blame; to turn individuals or parties or particular companies or institutions into pantomime villains or maniacs; to descry a plot behind every political or cultural development which runs counter to one's own preferences: this instinct seems itself in need of further exploration and explanation.

Nor do such theories explain why the same or similar trends are apparent in different countries with different political and media landscapes. I believe that the structural and behavioural changes we're seeing in media *are* relevant but, unlike Tony Blair, I believe they're only one part of the story and probably not the most important one. The same goes for the possible culpability of individual politicians and political parties.

We Have Lost the True Names of Things

Watching the global financial crisis unfold from the vantage points of the BBC and latterly *The New York Times*, I have been struck by how hard everyone – politicians, journalists, academics – has found it to explain *what* is happening and *why* to those who have been most affected by the shock. Remedies were proposed which politicians duly promoted or disparaged. Monthly economic data was released. Across the media, there was a super-abundance of news, comment and debate. But the disconnect between all of this and the public was palpable. It was not just that ordinary citizens found the crisis difficult to fathom – that, after all, was true of most members of the political and media elites as well. It was that many had given up even trying to understand what was happening. The jargon-filled arguments within the elites passed over their heads and, even if they hadn't, a growing number of people had come to doubt every word that came out of the mouths of politicians, business leaders and those whom they were told were experts.

The distress signals were manifold. In many democracies, they took the form of the dismissal of incumbent leaders and parties, regardless of policies or political orientation. In some, the rise of populism, xenophobia and racism. In some European countries, national strikes and civil disturbances. And almost everywhere – and so pervasively that it has become the background music to any discussion about the state of our politics – a growing, darkening cynicism.

Public incomprehension and distrust are measurable. One BBC survey in 2011 found that in the UK only 16% of those questioned felt confident about defining the term 'inflation'.[14] For 'GDP' the number was 10%; 'liquidity', 7%; 'credit default swaps', 'CDOs', 'QE', 'TARP', 'the EFSF' – not asked, but presumably off the scale. For most lay people, much of the theoretically 'public' discourse about the economic crisis might as well have been in Sanskrit. Ipsos MORI identified what they call a 'presumption of complexity' among a significant portion of the public, a default sense that certain public policy terms and issues are too arcane to even attempt to understand.[15]

And even for those lay people who felt it was worth the effort, there was deep scepticism about whether what they heard could actually be trusted. Even before the crisis, a 2005 MORI report suggested that 68% of the British public believed that official figures were changed to support whatever argument the government of the day wants to make; 59% felt that the government used figures dishonestly. In the UK and many other western countries, trust in many of the media organisations who relay and offer their interpretation of this official information was similarly low.

Is such deep public distrust justified? If you are a member of Edelman's 'informed public', your answer may well be no. Perhaps you blame our education system, or the zeitgeist, or the populists who congratulate their audiences on their lack of trust. Of course, it is one of the features of the current breakdown in trust that everyone thinks that someone else is responsible for it.

In this book I am going to argue that, more than the frailties of any one set of actors, what lies at the heart of the problem is language itself. I will not claim that rhetoric is some kind of prime mover of political and cultural change. As we shall see, rhetoric is itself constantly acted upon by other forces, many of which have been correctly identified by those diligent detectives. But rather than treat it as a by-product of other deeper factors, I want to place it in the centre of the causal nexus. As much as anything, our shared civic structures, our institutions and organisations, are living bodies of public language, and when the rhetoric changes, so do they. The crisis in our politics is a crisis of political language.

*

I began this chapter with Sarah Palin's 'death panel' because it seems to me to encapsulate some of the most troubling trends in contemporary political discourse. It achieves its impact by denying any complexity, conditionality or uncertainty. It exaggerates wildly to make its point. It is built on a presumption of irredeemable bad faith on the part of its political target. It accepts no responsibility to explain anything to anybody, but instead treats the facts as if they were a matter of opinion. It rejects even the *possibility* of a rational debate between the parties. With language like this, no wonder so many citizens turn away from politics in disgust.

The 'death panel' may be an extreme case, but we shouldn't pretend that its faults are rare. On the contrary, as we shall see in the following pages, they regularly feature in the language not just of those, like Sarah Palin, on the edges of politics but in the mouths of mainstream leaders, moderates as well as radicals, even august scientific bodies.

To take a single example, in May 2016 the Treasury select committee of the House of Commons[16] accused both sides in the bitter referendum campaign on the UK's continued membership of the European Union of misleading the public with irresponsible and exaggerated claims which they were presenting as 'facts', but which in many cases relied on hidden and highly questionable assumptions. 'What we really need is an end to the arms race of ever more lurid claims and counter-claims made by both sides on this', Andrew Tyrie, the committee chairman, told the BBC. 'I think it's confusing the public, it's impoverishing political debate.'[17] In this case, the two 'sides' included the entire political establishment of the country from the prime minister down.

A few weeks later the UK voted to leave the EU. It was a stunning reversal, not just for David Cameron (who announced his resignation the next day), but for Britain's traditional elites as a whole. Emotive language about immigration and dubious promises about 'taking back control' had won out over often wild warnings about the economic consequences of exit. The poor, the angry and the old had outvoted the prosperous, the better educated and the young. England and Wales had outvoted Scotland, Northern Ireland and London.

Nor are these trends restricted to words alone. As well as maximalised written and spoken language, the visual rhetoric of news and politics has become compressed into lapidary images, resonant, artful, tendentious. One way of thinking about 9/11 is as mass murder conducted to create a single piece of rhetoric, in this case a few seconds of news video showing aeroplanes flying into skyscrapers and the skyscrapers subsequently collapsing. The Twin Towers stand for western might and western values, their collapse for the possibility that that might and those values can be laid low. The flames, the sheering, falling walls, the billowing smoke and dust bring that hoped-for future's destruction into the present. Metonymy, prolepsis, maximality.

But there is more to the crisis than the problems of compression and exaggeration. Once science was afforded a privileged status in public discourse and its findings were considered fact. Today it is routinely treated as one more opinion. Fury and incomprehension have eroded even the barest standards of courtesy and mutual respect in debate, especially in cyberspace. We are increasingly reluctant even to try to find a common language with which to engage with peoples and cultures whose values differ substantially from our own. There is a growing intolerance for free speech, and a growing appetite to curb it, not just in controlled societies, but even in western countries that claim to venerate it. We will chart all of these developments in the pages that follow.

It is the argument of this book that these negative trends spring from a set of interlocking political, cultural and technological forces – forces that go beyond any one ideology, or interest group, or national political situation. A healthy public language knits public and political leaders together and, precisely because it succeeds in drawing ordinary citizens into the debate, ultimately leads to better and more widely supported policy decisions. But when public language loses its power to explain and engage, it threatens the broader bond between people and politicians. I believe this very process is taking place in our democracies today.

This is why the crisis in public language is so significant. For some, the cynicism, the leaching away of substance, the coarsening of expression, are essentially *cultural* disappointments – evidence of some wider dumbing down and failure of seriousness. For me, the critical risk is not in the realm of culture but that of politics and, in particular, democracy – its legitimacy, the competitive advantage it has historically conferred over other systems of government, and ultimately its sustainability.

To the critic who argues that none of this is new, I would reply yes and no. Some of the characteristics I discern in our rhetoric – like highly synoptic language or telling, memorable slogans and phrases – are as old as the hills. Let them eat cake. No surrender. The only thing we have to fear is fear itself.

Nor is this the first time that someone has stood up to claim that slogans, rhetorical tricks, savage ad hominem attacks and outright lies are replacing rational debate, or that extreme partisanship is rendering orderly government impossible. From Plato to George Orwell, the story of the West is littered with claims that the political language of the day is failing, and bringing the politics itself down with it. Indeed I will argue that we can learn a lot about the challenge we face with our own public language by studying these earlier critics and the crises they lived through.

There never was a golden age of public language, no Garden of Eden in which leaders and people once lived in perfect harmony, and politicians were unfailingly reasonable and courteous to each other. I will, nonetheless, make the case that there are specific accelerants that make our circumstances exceptional, in particular the way that the revolution in media and communications has interacted with our political cultures.

As I suggested at the start of this chapter, our first instinct today, if we sense a weakness in the way our politicians or our media communicate, is to work back to the root causes – the foundational economic or political interests, or the ideological forces – which we presume must lie beneath. We are children of the Enlightenment who have been taught that we must always dig below the surface to get at the truth, and that nothing is more of the surface than rhetoric, that slap of paint which politicians use to cover goodness knows what. So for us, causality always runs from underlying politics to language. But there have been periods, in modern as well as ancient history, when some observers have come to believe that the causality can flow the other way: that it's *when public language fails* and collective deliberation is no longer possible, that the wider culture goes south and the institutions of politics and the state begin to spiral down.

In Book III of his *History of the Peloponnesian War*, for instance, Thucydides adduces a change in language as a major factor in Athens' descent from dysfunctional democracy through demagoguery into tyranny and anarchy: people began to define things in any way they pleased, he says, and the 'normally accepted meaning of words' broke down.[18] In his account of the Catiline crisis of 63 BC in republican Rome, Sallust has Cato the Younger identify the misuse of language – specifically the scission of word and meaning – as the underlying cause of the threat to the state. Society, Cato says, has lost the '*vera vocabula rerum*', literally the 'true names of things'.[19] In seventeenth-century England, Thomas Hobbes lived through a civil war he believed had been caused in significant measure because a war of words about religion – spread through the pervasive pamphleteering which printing had made possible – had fatally weakened the linguistic common ground on which an ordered state depends.

Collapse of democracy, anarchy, civil war. These things seem vanishingly remote to most of us in the West – even if there is already an ugly and divisive mood in many of our countries, particularly about immigration, race and national sovereignty, or if some of the TV news pictures we have seen in recent years from Ukraine and Greece and elsewhere have reminded us how insecure civil order and the structures and conventions of a modern democracy can be. In Northern and Western Europe and the English-speaking world, we are still far from this kind of instability. Few would deny that our own divisions are growing, however, or that recent events – in particular the ongoing global financial crisis and all of the inequalities it has underlined, Brexit and our unhappy adventures in the Middle East – have revealed a gulf of incomprehensibility and distrust between decision-makers and the public at large.

Perhaps, in the event of an acute national threat, a language could once again be found, as it was in the Second World War, to galvanise and unify our nations. But consider instead a slow-onset emergency: an unstoppable tide of immigrants, or a looming crisis of social cohesion driven by growing income inequality, or a rate of global warming which turns out to be at the upper end of the climatologists' models. Do we have a rhetoric capable of supporting the process of debate and decision that would be required in that eventuality?

And there's another threat. Ever since Plato, critics of rhetoric have worried about instrumentality – the risk that eloquent but unscrupulous speakers will seek to convince not through the merit of their argument but by pressing the audience's buttons, in other words by using ideas, phrases and professional tricks which they've learned and tested over time to elicit a desired reaction from the people they're addressing now. We live in a world where these tactics are being rapidly mechanised. Which of two ways of expressing a marketing message – or a political thought – is the more persuasive? An A/B test, where the two are tested side by side with two segments of a given audience, will give you a definitive answer. Such testing is ubiquitous and significantly automated: whether you are aware of it or not, much of the public language to which you yourself are exposed is continually being algorithmically assessed and optimised. If human persuasiveness fails, it won't be replaced by a vacuum but by the persuasiveness of the machines. They knew in Athens 2,500 years ago how power gravitated to the most persuasive orator. The risk in the future is that power comes to lie in the hands of whoever has the biggest machine.

At the end of this book, I will turn to the question of solutions to the current crisis. If I am right and the causes lie deep in our culture and history, the answers won't come quickly or easily. But we had better start doing something. In the world of politics and public policy, words *are* actions, and they have consequences. Our public language is in danger of failing right now – and history tells us that, when that happens, bad things soon follow. The Lord of Misrule invites you to a dance.

2 That Glib and Oily Art

If there's one thing I can't abide it's rhetoric. I'm only interested in what needs to get done.

Silvio Berlusconi[1]

The word 'rhetoric' has several senses in English. The more widely known usage is negative, as in 'empty rhetoric'. Under this meaning, rhetoric is sweet talk, a crooked pack of verbal tricks which allows a shyster to turn a weak case into a strong one. It is 'that glib and oily art', which Cordelia detects in her sisters' false flattery of their father at the start of *King Lear* and which, she says, consists of speaking but purposing not – of a deliberate separation of language and reality. Suspicion of rhetoric defined like this runs deep in English-speaking culture and history. It seems to go with the famous no-nonsense empiricism and dislike of cant in which we take so much pride. As we shall see, though, it is more or less universal and has ancient precedents. But the word can refer quite neutrally to the academic investigation of public language, and the art of teaching it and mastering it as a practical skill. By extension, it is also often used as a synonym for public language itself. I'll use it like that in this book, unless the context makes clear that I intend one of the other meanings.

Rhetoric is a fact of life in all societies, but the more open the society, the more central rhetoric becomes. It is impossible to imagine a democracy without public debate and therefore competition in the mastery of public persuasion. One can accept all this and still believe that rhetoric is unimportant, that what really matters is the substance of what is being discussed – evidence, arguments, political ideas, moral and cultural values. But the reality is that, especially in democracies, the substance and articulation of policy are always tangled up, and to claim otherwise is itself to make a classic move in the rhetorical game.

It's what Mark Antony is up to when he says to the Roman crowd in *Julius Caesar*, 'I am no orator, as Brutus is; / But, as you know me all, a plain blunt man', in the middle of one of the most cunning displays of technical rhetoric, not just in Shakespeare, but in the English language. Silvio Berlusconi strikes the same pose with his remark about rhetoric at the start of this chapter.

Donald Trump's appeal as a presidential candidate depends significantly on the belief that he is a truth-teller who will have nothing to do with the conventional language of politics: a September 2015 Fox News poll found that 44% of a sample of US voters, and 62% of Republicans, agreed with the statement that 'he tells it like it is, and we need that now in a president'.

Of course, we shouldn't confuse anti-rhetorical 'truth-telling' with actually telling the truth. One of the advantages of this positioning is that, once listeners are convinced you're not trying to deceive them in the manner of a regular politician, they may switch off the critical faculties they usually apply to political speech, and forgive you any amount of exaggeration, contradiction or offensiveness. And, if establishment rivals or the media criticise you, your supporters may dismiss that as spin. Here's Florida voter Yolanda Esquivel, quoted by the BBC in November 2015, rejecting criticism of Donald Trump for his outspokenness: 'I'm looking at what candidates can do, not the picky little things they say that people want to make a big deal of and make into drama.'[2]

Across the West, anti-politicians from outside the mainstream, and those mainstream politicians who hope to use some of the anti-politicians' populist mojo to advance themselves within conventional political structures, are trying to strike this 'let's cut through the rhetoric' pose. But, whether or not they and their supporters are aware of it, anti-rhetoric is itself rhetoric – indeed, in the right circumstances, it can be the most persuasive form of rhetoric of all.

Despite its dismal reputation, rhetoric performs a vital role in an open society – which is to provide a bridge between the professionals, the political leaders, the civil servants and the experts, and the public at large. It is through an effective public language that average citizens can both understand and contribute to important questions and issues of the state. It is for this reason that rhetoric was considered so important in both Greek and Roman cultures. Indeed, for the Romans rhetoric was regarded as the most important of all the arts, more important even than poetry and literature – something more or less incomprehensible to us today.

So let's start at the top and listen for a moment to the statesman Pericles as the historian Thucydides imagines him describing the particular virtues of Athenian democratic culture:

> Our people are interested in the private and public alike and, even among ordinary working people, you'll find no lack of insight into matters of public policy . . . Unlike others, we Athenians decide public decisions collectively for ourselves, or at least try to arrive at a clear understanding of them. We don't believe that debate gets in the way of action – it's when you act without proper debate that you get bogged down.[3]

For the ancients, the concept of *freedom* evoked not our post-Enlightenment notions of personal liberty and freedom of expression, but the ability of favoured members of the population – citizens not slaves and, of course, men not women – to take part in deliberations about affairs of state. It is rhetoric, the language of explanation and persuasion, that enables this collective decision-making to take place. Someone who was unwilling or unable to engage in this way was considered an incomplete human being: *achreios*, 'useless', is the word Pericles uses for them. He himself, Thucydides says, was the most important man of his time in words as well as deeds.[4] Power comes from the mastery of public language.

Aristotle and Rhetoric

So what would the ancient Greeks have made of Sarah Palin's 'death panel'? A good place to start is the most systematic early account of public language, Aristotle's *Art of Rhetoric*. Like many classical philosophers, Aristotle was sceptical about the merits of *demokratia*, or 'people power' (literally, rule by the common citizenry), in part because he was alive to how readily rhetoric could be misused and perverted into demagoguery. But his *Rhetoric* is chiefly concerned with understanding how public language works and how it may be categorised and learned.

The ancients distinguished between those statements and arguments which could proceed to secure conclusions – mathematical operations, for instance, or scientific observations – and those which dealt with probabilities and opinions. They used the term *dialectic* to describe the careful reasoning which allowed philosophers like Socrates to probe difficult questions where certainty is impossible. Sometimes the process would lead to a clear and convincing finding, but often in the case of Socrates there is a different purpose – which is, by systematically questioning an opponent's argument, to expose inconsistencies in it. The result is *aporia*, a healthy kind of bewilderment in which a bubble of complacency is pricked and the interlocutor is forced to admit that they know much less than they thought they did. Often Socrates will admit that he too is perplexed, though he at least has some idea of what he does *not* know and has, through his questioning, managed to share his own valuable sense of ignorance and uncertainty with his opponent. Dialectic may lack the epistemic authority of, say, arithmetic, but it is a valuable tool with which to explore the many subjects of human inquiry which cannot be resolved definitively.

So where does rhetoric fit into this scheme? In the very first words of his work, Aristotle defines rhetoric as an *antistrophos* or 'counterpart' of dialectic. It too deals with probabilities rather than certainties, and does so in a manner which is intended to be comprehensible, not just to scientists and other experts, but to humanity at large. It is obvious, however, that although both use evidence and argumentation, rhetoric lacks the intellectual rigour of dialectic. How, then, does it make up for this deficit in persuasive power? Aristotle's answer is to introduce two further concepts: *ethos* and *pathos*.

Ethos is the broader impression that the speaker makes: it is the way they present themselves to us, and what we know of their character and history. *Pathos* refers to the emotions of the audience, the mood in which the speaker finds them and which she responds to and attempts to shape and satisfy. But those flat English words don't really do justice to what Aristotle means. In his 1920s lectures about Aristotle and rhetoric, the German philosopher Martin Heidegger translated pathos as *Stimmung,* a term for musical attunement as well as for generic 'mood'. It is the ability of a speaker to find and then sing in the same key as their listeners.

When I explain Pythagoras' theory to you, your opinion of my character and your mood are unlikely to influence whether you find my exposition convincing. If we listen to two philosophers debating a moral point, character and mood may hold greater sway, but we are still likely to accord more weight to what we take to be the objective strengths and weaknesses of their arguments. Aristotle's position seems to be that, in rhetoric, persuasive power is more evenly divided between pure argument (*logos*), the character and standing of the speaker (*ethos*), and how in tune the listening crowd is with both speaker and subject (*pathos*).

This account of how rhetoric works still feels compelling 2,500 years later. If we watch newsreel footage on YouTube of speeches given three-quarters of a century ago by speakers as different as Franklin D. Roosevelt or Winston Churchill or Benito Mussolini, the gauzy veil of history hangs between us and them. The arguments seem feeble, the language overwrought: it is hard to believe that anyone could have been swayed by them. What is missing, what is almost impossible to bring back to life knowing what we now know, is the felt context of the moment. In particular, it is the sense of a shared musical key, a dynamic harmony between speaker and crowd which explains how these remote figures were able to reduce thousands to tears or rage, or to instill calm and confidence in place of fear.

Aristotle makes another timeless observation about public speakers. They exaggerate. Indeed they *have* to exaggerate. No one goes to the funeral of a friend wanting to hear an objective list of their strengths and weaknesses, and no one complains if the speaker over-eggs the former and passes over the latter. No politician or prosecutor under-sells their own case or gives their opponent the benefit of the doubt. Aristotle calls this tendency to heighten statements in rhetoric *auxesis* or 'amplification'.

Very occasionally one comes across people who are not prepared to indulge in amplification. Cordelia, whom we met a few pages back, not only declines to join her two sisters in their false rhetoric of love, but refuses even to express her true feelings for her father Lear, for fear of seeming to exaggerate for public effect or personal advantage.

Perhaps this is what saintliness looks like – certainly it's something of which very few of us, and almost no politicians, have ever been capable. Aristotle is a realist and his *Rhetoric* is not just a treatise but a practical manual for rhetors. He treats exaggeration not as a fault, but as a fact of life and a reasonable weapon in the orator's arsenal, at least if used within bounds. Exaggeration was ubiquitous in the public language of Aristotle's day. You hardly need me to tell you that it's every bit as ubiquitous today.

Aristotle also notices how useful *maxims* and *fables* are to rhetors. By maxims, he means familiar sayings which encapsulate some piece of received wisdom. In the case of fables, the nugget of insight is revealed through the telling of a folk tale or fresh archetypal narrative. According to Aristotle, Aesop once saved a corrupt demagogue's life in the island of Samos by convincing the jury that, if they executed him, even more rapacious villains would replace him. He did it by telling them a story about a fox who refused to shake off the ticks on her back who had already fed on her blood, for fear of exchanging them for hungry new ones. Fables, Aristotle says, are 'comparatively easy to invent', whereas historical precedents – earlier factual instances which are close enough to the present instance to be a good guide to the right verdict or the right policy – are hard to find. It's no surprise, then, that rhetors often turn to imaginary stories, maxims or stock sayings rather than real-world examples to back up their argument.

Margaret Thatcher was one of many contemporary politicians with a taste for the home-spun common sense which a certain kind of traditional or fresh-baked saying evokes. It may be the cock that crows, but it is the hen that lays the eggs. Standing in the middle of the road is very dangerous: you get knocked down by traffic from both sides. You may have to fight a battle more than once to win it. Power is like being a lady: if you have to tell people you are, you aren't.

Set down coldly on the page, this is the stuff of Christmas crackers. But politicians use maxims for a reason – in the right context and delivered at the right point in a speech, they can make a given line of argument appear not just obvious but somehow self-evident, part of the natural order of things. They reach out beyond the closed language of the policymaker and the political partisan to something which sounds like the everyday experience of the ordinary listener.

Only politicians from certain rhetorical traditions – that of China, for example, or the American South – can still get away with fables of the fox-and-ticks variety to which Aristotle refers. But if we broaden the idea to include references to well-known narratives and stereo-typical characters and situations, then fables too are pervasive in modern public language.

Aristotle associates short sayings with another breakthrough he makes in his investigation into rhetoric. While philosophers may have all the time in the world to explore every branch of their argument in the interests of rigour and completeness, most rhetors are in a hurry. They want to get to the end of the trial, or to the vote in the Assembly; above all they do not want to bore, and thereby lose the attention and approbation of their audience:

> Rhetoric deals with the way we deliberate when we do it outside the formal rules of dialectic; and when we do it in the presence of an audience who will be unable to take an overarching view of a complex topic or to follow a lengthy chain of argument.[5]

So rhetors tend to cut corners. Instead of stating arguments in full, they offer incomplete dialectic in the form of partial syllogisms which Aristotle terms *enthymemes*, knowing that – as long as the rhetor has judged his audience correctly – the listeners will be able to fill in the gaps themselves.[6] The etymology of the word enthymeme suggests 'to the heart' or 'to the mind', perhaps implying that listeners are left with a missing piece of the argument to turn over in their hearts or heads. Aristotle tells us how this works in practice:

> For example, if you want to prove that Dorieus was the victor in a competition at which the prize was a crown, you just have to say he won a victory at the Olympic Games – there's no need to add that the prize was a crown because everyone knows that.[7]

If you define them as I intend to do, not just as incomplete syllogisms, but as any kind of argument which for rhetorical convenience or effect leaves the listener with work to do, enthymemes have come a long way since Aristotle's day and the question of crowns at the Olympics. 'Death panel', we recognise at once, is an enthymeme – the words might not mean much to a neutral observer, but they were all Sarah Palin's attuned supporters needed to fill in the missing parts of the argument to construct a complete critique of Obamacare. But now let's look at a more typical contemporary use of partial arguments in an example which brings together everything we've just discussed – exaggeration, the oblique use of well-known narratives and the compressed dialectical short cut – in a single rhetorical package.

In April 2013, a British man called Mick Philpott was convicted of manslaughter for killing six of his children in a fire at his house in a botched attempt to wreak revenge on a former lover. Philpott had become well known even before this tragic crime for a life involving multiple partners and no less than seventeen children, and lived largely, if not entirely, courtesy of the UK's welfare benefits system. After Philpott's conviction, the Conservative Chancellor of the Exchequer George Osborne had this to say:

> Philpott is responsible for these absolutely horrendous crimes and these are crimes that have shocked the nation. The courts are responsible for sentencing him. But I think there is a question for government and society about the welfare state – and the taxpayers who pay for the welfare state – subsidising lifestyles like that, and I think that debate needs to be had.[8]

As is often the case, the enthymeme does not present itself declaratively but it is there all the same, lurking in the words 'subsidising lifestyles *like that*'. In what sense *like that*? What argument does this comparison point us to?

The Chancellor is clearly inviting us to believe that the specific case of Mick Philpott has something to tell us which may inform the general debate about the welfare state, but what exactly is it? Is it (1) that paying people benefits is likely to cause them to kill their children and, if you reduce or eliminate the payments, fewer children would die? That's the strongest possible argument that the words *like that* might hint at, but it is manifestly absurd: millions of Britons receive benefits every year without harming their children. (1) is an example of the fallacy of arguing from the particular to the general. So let's try a weaker version of the argument, (2): that, while Mick Philpott's terrible crime is of course a one-off, the way in which the case revealed how the benefits system enabled – perhaps even incentivised – him to father so many children in so many failed relationships is a subject of legitimate debate and one which might cause public and politicians alike to contemplate reforms to the system. Unlike (1), (2) points to a line of argument which is generally regarded as reasonable and responsible, even by those who disagree with it, across the main political parties.

But the Chancellor's apparently casual remark could also give rise to a whole range of arguments between (1) and (2). We could make this claim, for instance (1.5): the welfare system and its free-and-easy payments encourage reckless behaviour which is all too evident in the lifestyle of Mick Philpott; of course no one would argue that this recklessness will lead, except in the most extreme cases, to manslaughter, but that does not mean that other forms of antisocial and negative behaviour – from abandoned children to substance abuse to minor criminality – will not often result. (1.5) avoids the absurdity and fallacy of (1), but still manages to imply that welfare benefits in the wrong hands can all too easily lead to antisocial behaviour and criminality and still hints at some connection, if only across a spectrum, between Mick Philpott and his terrible crime and other benefit recipients. This tactic is known as *guilt by association*.

To which of these variant arguments did George Osborne mean to gesture with the phrase 'lifestyles like that'? His political opponents quickly supplied an answer – at least (1.5) and quite possibly (1). In fact it is not clear which he meant and it is perfectly possible that he never determined which. In quantum mechanics, the principle of superposition holds that particles exist simultaneously in all the locations they could theoretically occupy until such time as they are actually observed. An open-ended enthymeme enjoys a similar quality: all its possible completions can remain simultaneously valid to some degree, unless and until the speaker tells us which they had in mind. If they never tell us, or if it turns out that they never decided in the first place, then this strange state of rhetorical superposition persists indefinitely.*

---

* Another contemporary rhetorical trope is actually named after one of the fathers of quantum mechanics. According to the *Urban Dictionary*, a 'Schrödinger's douchebag' is someone who makes sexist, racist or otherwise bigoted remarks and only decides whether they are being serious or 'just joking' when they see how others react.

But such modalities were not on the mind of George Osborne's then Labour opposite number, Ed Balls, when he responded to the Chancellor's remarks:

> George Osborne's calculated decision to use the shocking and vile crimes of Mick Philpott to advance a political argument is the cynical act of a desperate Chancellor.[9]

He made sure to add, however, that he too was in favour of 'a proper debate about welfare reform'.

This response also requires some unpacking. On the face of it, one politician criticising another for advancing a 'political argument' is like one carpenter accusing another of pursuing a cynical wood-working agenda. But here Ed Balls is using the word 'political' as a term of art. The case he is making is that there is a convention among responsible politicians that no one should attempt to make partisan capital out of a human tragedy and that, by saying what he did, George Osborne had broken this convention. This claim, we quickly realise, is also an enthymeme, in this case shrunk to fit within a single adjective.

What is surprising about Ed Balls' response is how close it is to George Osborne's original statement. Both politicians take care to emphasise how shocked they are by Mick Philpott's crimes: 'horrendous' for Osborne, 'shocking and vile' for Balls. Both also call for a debate about welfare reform. And simply by bringing it up in the context of the Mick Philpott case, Ed Balls acquiesces in George Osborne's essential intention, which is to establish a link between the two.

So what is going on here? First we should recognise the unseen presence of two background political narratives. Neither are mentioned but we can feel the way they pull and influence these two politicians' words:

> (A) Labour is soft on welfare and soft on scroungers like Mick Philpott. It's high time we reformed the system and forced the Mick Philpotts of this world to get a job and make some sensible decisions about their lives. Only the Conservatives can be trusted to do this.

> (B) The Tories are callous about the poor (and George Osborne is the most callous of the lot). Having failed utterly to turn the economy

round, they are now trying to distract attention by demonising benefit claimants, and trying to insinuate that all claimants are like Mick Philpott. Yes the system needs reforming, but the only party that can be trusted to balance toughness and compassion is Labour.

These two narratives go to the heart of each party's characterisation of the other and, though they might well deny it, it is reasonable to assume that the political objective of George Osborne's and Ed Balls' respective statements was to advance (and/or challenge) these narratives. But given the circumstances – above all, the tragic death of the children – the two narratives can only be referred to obliquely.

The closest George Osborne comes to (A) is saying 'that debate needs to be had', but that is enough for one of his own supporters (and perhaps, he might hope, a floating voter as well) to imagine how the parties would line up if such a debate actually happened: George Osborne and his fellow Tories making the case for cracking down on waste and abuse, Labour defending the system and the rights of claimants for tribal reasons.

In his brief response, Ed Balls attempts both to deflect (A) and to promote (B). First, he makes sure that everyone knows he is just as appalled by Philpott's crimes at Osborne, thus protecting himself from the charge that taking a less strident view than the Chancellor on welfare reform implies any level of sympathy or support for the child-killer or scroungers like him (contra A). Second, he attacks George Osborne's motives: Osborne's statement is 'calculated' – this is a premeditated language-crime – and 'cynical' (pro B). The immediate 'cynicism' is because Osborne is using the Philpott case as a diversion as the economy is going so badly, but the charge of cynicism is part of a wider and long-running critique of Osborne's character by Balls. Osborne is a 'political' Chancellor, according to Balls, again in the special sense that Osborne puts party advantage above the national interest. Notice the underlying assumption – ubiquitous in modern British politics and increasingly notable on the other side of the Atlantic – that there is an inevitable tension between party interest and national interest, as if our political parties couldn't care less about the country and were focused only on their own private agendas.

During his time as Shadow Chancellor, Balls used words like 'calculated', 'cynical' and 'political' constantly when he referred to

George Osborne to underline this line of attack. Often, as here, he found a natural, almost poetic rhythm with the stress falling firmly on the pejoratives: the 'political argument is the cynical act of a desperate Chancellor'. The use of the hostile adjectives in this instance means that, by the time he comes to agree with the Chancellor that a debate on welfare reform is necessary, Balls has already cast it as a battle with a politician whose intentions cannot be trusted.

What we have here is the small change of modern political discourse: two articulate and experienced players generating enthymemes on the fly and using words of apparently general meaning in the context of a specialised political language. The indeterminate character of the language, and its ability to summon up multiple possible interpretations, is of particular political value. Is George Osborne using the Philpott case to criticise a multitude of other benefit recipients? The conservative wing of his own party and in the country might think so and might applaud him for it but, as we have seen, there are other, milder interpretations, so he retains deniability. Is Ed Balls perpetrating the very crime he accuses George Osborne of, namely using the Philpott family tragedy to score tactical political points (for instance in deploying the word 'desperate' to attack Osborne for the poor performance of the economy)? Again, his supporters might think so and secretly cheer him on, but you would have a hard job proving it from the face value of his words.

A throwaway phrase which summons up an array of alternative arguments, each of subtly different political weight. Words which have a plain English sense, but also further latent meanings which only the politically initiated can fully understand. And a 'proper debate' which both parties say they want to see, but which none of their remarks serve to elucidate or advance.

A member of the public listening to this would certainly sense a moment of rough jostling, with two champion wrestlers each seeking the hold that will floor their opponent while striving to avoid the same fate themselves; when it is clear that no one will hit the canvas, the onlookers move on and the story passes out of the news cycle. The broad political context would probably also be clear to a non-specialist, the parties agreeing on the need for welfare reform, but divided on what shape that reform should take. Yet even a candidate answer to the substantive question – what, if anything, does this terrible case have to tell us about how the benefits system should be reformed? – is nowhere to be seen.

Two Types of Bewilderment

Aristotle and other ancient students of rhetoric can give us many of the insights and critical tools we need to unpick the public language of our time. Along the way they also remind us how little the fundamentals of rhetoric have changed over the years. Aristotle's picture of public language is so compelling because it is human-shaped, grounded in anthropologically sound observations about how we try to persuade others, and how we react when they try to persuade us.

But even as measured a thinker as Aristotle knew that public language could go wrong. And, as we saw in the last chapter, other Greeks – they included the altogether more purist and suspicious philosopher Plato, as well as the historian Thucydides and the brilliant comic playwright Aristophanes – came to fear that it *was* indeed going catastrophically wrong, not just in the mouths of a handful of troublemakers but across public life. For them, the language on which good governance and the stability of society and the state relied was becoming scrambled, and ordinary citizens were finding it harder and harder to distinguish honest public discourse from the excesses of extremists and schemers.

In *The Nicomachean Ethics*,[10] Aristotle warns us about two contrasting vices which can drive words and actions away from the golden mean of truth and virtue. The first is *alazoneia*, or 'boastfulness', and the second *eironeia* which, though it gives us the English word 'irony', in this context seems to mean bogus self-deprecation or excessive understatement. The two terms are associated with a pair of character types in the comic theatre of fifth-century BC Athens. The first character was the *alazon*, a brash fraud who struts about and brags about everything. Demagogues, soothsayers, priests and ambassadors were all dubbed *alazones* in different comedies. The second character is the *eiron*. He doesn't say too much but too little, and what he says is always crafty and not to be relied upon. He often gets the plot going, but you have to keep your eye on him. Sophists, the itinerant teachers of rhetoric and philosophy who were such a controversial feature of Athenian life, could find themselves being described both as *alazones* and *eirones*.

Aristotle also associated the word *eironeia* with Socrates himself, using it to describe his practice of affecting ignorance in order to draw his interlocutors out and demonstrate their own lack of knowledge. It's not clear whether Aristotle's negative characterisation of it in his discussion of truthfulness was intended as a criticism of this Socratic habit, but Aristotle emphasises that playing down the truth with *eironeia* is not as bad as replacing it with self-delusion or knowing falsehoods. He also concedes that, in moderation, *eironeia* can even be rather *chic*.

We can't know for sure if real-life braggarts and dissemblers contributed to the decline of public discourse in Athens and the ultimate collapse of its democracy. We do know that some of the greatest thinkers of the day thought that they did. We also know that the *alazones* and *eirones*, the blusterers and the dissemblers, the tellers of tall tales and of subtle untruths, are still all around us today. We will encounter many in this book.

Mahmoud Ahmadinejad, Iran's president from 2005 to 2013, is only one of many bombastic Holocaust-deniers spreading the politics of hate across the Middle East for reasons of his own. The response of Israel's prime minister, Benjamin Netanyahu? To retaliate with the puerile canard that the idea for the mass murder of European Jewry was given to Adolf Hitler by a Palestinian, the grand mufti of Jerusalem.

Some tall tales spring not from inter-communal hatred, but from cold considerations of state, and not from the *alazon*'s braggartry but from the slipperiness of the *eiron*. When James Clapper, the US director of National Intelligence, was asked whether the National Security Agency collected 'any type of data at all on millions or hundreds of millions of Americans', he replied 'No', a statement which the revelations of Edward Snowden showed to be, at least arithmetically, one of the greatest falsehoods in history. At first General Clapper patriotically defended his statement, then confided to an interviewer that it was the 'least untruthful' thing he could have said. Maybe so, but when the true answer to a yes/ no question is 'yes', your answer of 'no' is not just the least untruthful, but also the *most* untruthful it can be. In due course, the general would grudgingly describe his answer as 'erroneous' and a 'mistake'.

On matters of defence, diplomacy and real or imagined national security, modern western governments have regularly shown them-selves to be 'economical with the *actualité*', as the Conservative minister Alan Clark brazenly put it in the Matrix Churchill trial in 1992.* In general, however, public scrutiny in the form of parliamen-tary inquiry, whistle-blower leaks and investigative journalism, keeps the inclination to tell outright untruths within some kind of bounds. It's a different story in the case of societies where there is little history or expectation of openness and honesty in public language. Here is China's President Xi Jinping on the eve of a 2015 visit to the US:

> The Chinese government does not engage in theft of commercial secrets in any form, nor does it encourage or support Chinese compa-nies to engage in such practices in any way. Cybertheft of commercial secrets and hacking attacks against government networks are both illegal; such acts are criminal offenses and should be punished according to law and relevant international conventions.[11]

This is mirror rhetoric: everything which has a truth value of 1 on Planet Rhetoric has a truth value of 0 in reality, and vice versa. Here on Earth, the Chinese government takes part in hacking attacks on a monumental scale and doubtless also colludes in, and quite possibly controls, the extensive cybertheft operations which are conducted by Chinese companies, many of which are state-owned enterprises.

In February 2015, the Russian foreign minister Sergei Lavrov told a conference in Munich that his country's earlier invasion of Georgia and its annexation of Crimea were examples of international norms working well. 'What happened in Crimea was the people invoking the right of self-determination,' he said. 'You've got to read the UN Charter. Territorial integrity and sovereignty must be respected.' When these comments were greeted with open laughter, Mr Lavrov was defiant. 'You may find it funny,' he told the doubters. 'I also found many things you said funny.'[12]

---

* This was in the period during which the British were actively trying to *help* Saddam Hussein acquire weapons of mass destruction.

The whole world should laugh at Mr Lavrov, but after the numerous compromises which America, Britain and other western countries have made with the truth, many people (especially those in the developing world) have come to believe that the West's leaders are no better. It's hardly fair – western failings in the matter of public honesty are far more limited than those of the world's repressive regimes – but when rhetorical moderation and self-restraint are in short supply, and exaggeration and mendacity are no longer outliers, it is probably inevitable that domestic and international audiences should struggle to distinguish between occasional and habitual offenders.

Early in this chapter, we came across *aporia*, that moment of acknowledgement that the lazy assumptions you have been harbouring don't really stand up to scrutiny, that the apparently simple question is actually far harder to answer than you imagined, indeed that you don't have an answer at all. All this, Socrates believed, could be unlocked by a positive kind of *eironeia* and was the start of wisdom.

Today the public face a darker kind of bewilderment. It springs from distortions of public language which have been understood for thousands of years but which today, sped on digital wings, fly through our societies. In a world where you don't know who to believe, the braggart and the liar may be as persuasive as anyone – unless you shake your head and turn away from the whole thing.

How did it happen? Over the past three decades, I've watched the current crisis unfold and, in the coming chapters, I'm going to use my own experiences and observations to tell my version of the story of how we got here.

3 There You Go Again

The nine most terrifying words in the English language are: I'm from the government, and I'm here to help.

Ronald Reagan[1]

On Wednesday 28 March 1979, James Callaghan lost a vote of confidence in the House of Commons. His Labour government fell and the Tories won the subsequent general election under the relatively unknown and untested Margaret Thatcher. The Conservatives would stay in power for eighteen years and, even when Tony Blair led Labour back into power in 1997, his policies – like those of John Major before him, and Gordon Brown and David Cameron after him – would bear the unmistakeable influence of Mrs Thatcher. There was a crisp irreversibility about her. The same would turn out to be true of her ideas. We journalists love to declare *watersheds* and *tipping points* in an effort to bend the headlong rush of events into some kind of narrative shape. Surely this was one, probably the only significant one in the British politics of my time – at least until the fateful Brexit vote of June 2016.

But the spring of 1979 was a tipping point for me as well. I was twenty-one, an undergraduate in my final year at Oxford. I was interested in politics, though even then more as an observer than as a participant. Before it finally fell, the Callaghan government had lived for months on a parliamentary precipice – three-line whips, transient deals with minor parties, ambulances bringing dying MPs into the Palace of Westminster to vote. I was at home in Cumbria when that final vote took place but, a few weeks earlier, I'd come down to London in the hope of getting into the gallery to watch one of those previous close calls. I'd arrived at St Stephen's Entrance in what I'd hazily assumed would be good time, but it was hopeless, jam-packed already. So I hovered and chatted to some of the other loiterers for a few minutes, before heading back across Parliament Square to the Tube.

I had another reason for being in London that day. After taking the Tube to Oxford Circus, I strolled up Regent Street and dropped an application off at the BBC for one of the Corporation's training schemes. A life in broadcasting or journalism was not a long-standing ambition, or indeed anything you could call a plan; in fact, I had no idea what I wanted to do. But everyone I knew was applying to the BBC. So at the last minute I'd filled out the form and, too close to the deadline to rely on the post, ended up pushing it through the letter box of a sepulchral office building opposite Broadcasting House. Later – when I remembered how much TV I'd watched as a child; how much of an awakening Watergate had been for me in my teens; how easily I'd slipped into student journalism – this moment, the painstakingly typed form, the polished brass letter box, the letter which is in your hand one second and gone God knows where the next, would acquire a retrospective inevitability. At the time, it was just one possibility among many, and a remote one at that.

And then all at once I was there. My first day of work as a research assistant trainee, or RAT, was Monday 3 September 1979. Lord Louis Mountbatten, who had been blown up by the IRA in late August, was to be buried later that week. The monitors in one of the control rooms we traipsed through that first day were showing top-shots of Westminster Abbey, part of a camera rehearsal for the funeral. 'Good practice for the Queen Mum,' someone whispered in the reverent hush that I would soon come to associate at the BBC not with royalty, and certainly not with the Almighty, but with proximity to the divine presence of live TV.

The RAT was the lowest of the low, the most junior member of any given team, but paradoxically also somebody who everyone else knew had been chosen from thousands: a bright young thing, there-fore, and conceivably a future boss. Our reception – by turns friendly, suspicious, curious, dismissive, on rare and unsettling occasions respectful even – reflected all of that. The name was anything but an accident of course. This was the golden age of BBC acronyms: RAT wasn't bad, but it paled before the magnificence of that homage to Old MacDonald, EIEIO (Engineering Induction and Engineering

Information Officer), which some anonymous genius was said to have slipped through the system.

The scheme consisted of a twelve-month contract with BBC Television which, after a couple of weeks of basic training, would comprise four three-month 'attachments' on a series of different programmes. In theory, each RAT would be exposed to a range of departments and genres, from Sport to Children's to Drama, before – assuming all went well – settling on a chosen field. In theory we had a say in where we were placed. I told the organisers I particularly wanted an attachment in Current Affairs, and was promptly sent to Religion. Soon enough, though, I found myself on the daily evening magazine programme, *Nationwide*.

The day at *Nationwide* began with a Darwinian morning conference during which you had to pitch a series of suggestions in open compe-tition with every other researcher on the team. The editors weren't necessarily looking for new stories – most of the items were based on that morning's newspapers – but for imaginative, punchy angles and clever production ideas. If your suggestion was chosen, then so were you. You became not just researcher, but guest-booker, scriptwriter and producer, and ended the day standing anxiously in the control room behind the live studio director as your precious five minutes went out and were watched by millions. If not, you were condemned to spend the day running errands for another researcher – organising slides or cardboard graphics to put in front of the camera, say – or, worse, doing nothing and watching other more creative, more energetic, more skilful members of the team going frantically about their business.

Remembered nowadays, if at all, for its jokey end-items, *Nationwide* in fact offered its viewers a mixed diet which included reportage and debate on the day's major news events. I paid my dues with stories like the one about the world's fastest turkey-plucker – the turkey, alas, freshly throttled and still kicking when we cut to it – but quickly gravitated to the serious stuff: strikes, assassinations (Lennon, Sadat, attempts on Ronald Reagan and the pope), superpower diplomacy, Northern Ireland, but above all domestic politics.

The British left fractured after their 1979 defeat. The Labour Party took an abrupt radical lurch and a group of leading centrists split away to create their own new party, the SDP. We followed every twist and turn, as well as the lively story of the new Conservative government:

the battles between the 'wets' (One Nation Tories with qualms about the consequences of the government's economic policies) and the 'drys' around Mrs Thatcher; and the clash between the government and other powerful forces in the land, including Britain's miners, the Church of England, the educational establishment and the BBC itself.

So I was there when Neil Kinnock, a future leader of the Labour Party and then an influential left-wing MP, arrived in our studio in tears during the bitter 1981 battle for the deputy leadership of the party. I was standing next to the camera at the 1982 Conservative Party Conference in Blackpool when the BBC interviewer Robin Day called the Defence Secretary John Nott a 'here today, gone tomorrow politician' to his face, and Nott simply yanked the microphone from his lapel, got up and strode out of the studio. A few years later, I would be on the receiving end of nearly an hour of vigorous green-room persuasion from Mrs Thatcher herself as she sought to convince me and a handful of colleagues of the irrefutable wisdom of her plans to reform the NHS – plans which marked the starting point of a debate about health-care policy in Britain which, as we shall see, persists to this day along much the same lines.

Elections, budgets, policy debates, political crises: as a researcher, director, producer and ultimately editor, I was involved in covering scores of them, and met virtually every major British politician and public figure of the time. My days and nights were given over to the central preoccupation of every political journalist, which is to figure out what's really going on, what it means and what's likely to happen next.

I was bobbing in a sea of public language then – listening to it, cutting it, quoting it, deconstructing and reconstructing it. If I had thought about it at all, it would have been as *stuff*, the raw and undigested material of journalism, rather than as something which was worthy of consideration in itself. And yet, although I wasn't aware of it at the time, the language of politics – and the way in which I and other journalists sliced and diced that language before presenting it to the public – was already beginning to change.

The Age of Consensus

After the defeat of Germany and Japan in 1945, it was widely believed in the West – given the scale of the challenge of reconstruction and the confrontation with Soviet communism – that this was a moment to put the worst excesses of adversarial politics aside in favour of a consensual approach to public policy, inspired by the potential of science, technology and evidence-based decision-making to transform society.

It was not that internal ideological conflict would disappear – class differences and competing visions of the good society would persist and, in any event, democracy, the bedrock on which the whole western post-war project was built, continued to require at least a pro forma contest between parties of left and right. The hope was rather that some of the ideological energy that had torn Europe apart in the first half of the century could be focused and directed against the USSR, its proxies and sympathisers. Other differences could be downplayed as each country's leaders got on with the immense economic and social challenges in front of them.

The two objectives – the eventual triumph of western democratic capitalism over communism, and the economic and social transformation of western societies – were closely connected in many politicians' minds. The war had demonstrated the decisive role which superior scientific and industrial muscle could play in securing victory. Now the West would be engaged in a competition not just between rival world views and ways of life, but between scientists, engineers, designers, factory managers and workers. It would need a new hard-headed, practical politics to win the battle of materiel as well as that of ideology. And it would need a new rhetoric to help it do so.

In West Germany, Konrad Adenauer and his successors single-mindedly pursued the programme that the Chancellor laid out in 1949, to rebuild the economy on new technocratic principles and to address the 'great social problems' which that ruined nation faced, not least the challenge of providing homes and work for the 'flotsam millions' of Germans displaced by the war and its aftermath. Reunification would remain a long-term ambition, but for now Germany's foreign policy would align with NATO and the dream of a 'positive and viable European federation'.[2] Adenauer's Christian Democrat Party and their principal opponents, the Social Democrats, put electoral appeal and practical political considerations above partisan purity.

National reconstruction was also the top priority in France and Britain, and there too policy consensus was in the air. In France, the new parties of the fourth and fifth republics would still be clearly identified as left or right, but the policies they pursued in government were often indistinguishable. In the UK, the new National Health Service, which had been devised by a Liberal, was passed into law by Labour and supported by successive Conservative governments. A new word, 'Butskellism' – a combination of the surnames of the senior Conservative politician Rab Butler and one of Labour's leaders Hugh Gaitskell – was coined to describe an approach to politics which at least appeared to put a significantly shared national agenda above ideological difference. It was fully committed to social progress, in contrast to traditional Toryism; but progress achieved through demo-cratic means and a shared commitment to exploit the promise of technology, rather than through Marxist class struggle and authori-tarian centralism. The usual vituperation of British party politics – as recently as June 1945, Winston Churchill had warned Clement Attlee's Labour Party would inevitably 'fall back on some kind of Gestapo' if elected[3] – was somewhat muted.

America's case was different. It had not been bombed or invaded and, although the war had required sacrifices, it had left the US far more powerful than its allies. Nonetheless, faced with narrow (and soon to be overturned) majorities in the Senate and House, the Republican president Dwight Eisenhower also contemplated a different kind of leadership – and political discourse – which he explicitly contrasted with the pre-war partisanship of Franklin D. Roosevelt:

> People like to think of Mr Roosevelt as a leader; in the situation where his own party was delighted to hear a daily excoriation of the opposite political party, his methods were adequate to his time and to the situation. As of today, every measure that we deem essential to the progress and welfare of America normally requires Democratic support in varying degrees. I think it is fair to say that, in this situation, only a leadership that is based on honesty of purpose, calmness and inexhaustible patience in conference and persuasion, and refusal to be diverted from basic principles can, in the long run, win out.[4]

In its heyday, post-war consensus politics had a confident rhetoric of its own: it was heroic about the battle between the free world and communism, reasonable and resolutely modern about everything else. It was a rhetoric of the future, although its residual taste for a stately Edwardian turn of phrase reassuringly connected the listener with a past of shared values and settled social relations.

On the whole it was not a memorable rhetoric, however, and most of the famous sentences and phrases from that time give little clue as to the speaker's position on the political spectrum: JFK's 'ask not what your country can do for you, but what you can do for your country'; Harold Macmillan's 'the wind of change is blowing through this continent'; Harold Wilson's 'white heat of technology'.

Neil Armstrong's painstakingly engineered words from the surface of the moon in July 1969 typify its rather affectless optimism: 'one small step for a man, one giant leap for mankind'. Like ingredients in a hamburger, humanism and hubris, national pride and internationalism were carefully layered to create a sandwich which offered no resistance to the tooth, and which could therefore be marketed with confidence to consumers in every region of the blue and green planet slowly revolving above Armstrong's head.

Some Europeans hoped that the new technocratic approach to public policy and government might trigger a more profound break with the rhetoric of class and ideological division which had riven their countries in the past. In 1960s Italy, for instance, the Marxist film director Pier Paolo Pasolini called for the development of a language not just for Italy's ruling classes, but for all Italians. It would be a triumph of the reality of modern Italy (*Italia reale*) over the 'rhetorical' Italy (*Italia retorica*) of the traditional elites. To others, including the writer Italo Calvino, Pasolini's new 'technological' Italian was not a new national language, but a sinister non-language, an *antilingua*.[5]

There were also rhetorics of opposition of course, from the slogans of the 60s' counter-culture – by turns retro agit-prop and pop-iconoclast – to the measured solemnity of Nelson Mandela standing in a Pretoria dock in 1964 and reaching back to the cadence of seventeenth- and eighteenth-century English dissent and reform:

> During my lifetime I have dedicated myself to this struggle of the African people. I have fought against white domination, and I have fought against

black domination. I have cherished the ideal of a democratic and free society in which all persons live together in harmony and with equal opportunities. It is an ideal which I hope to live for and to achieve. But if needs be, it is an ideal for which I am prepared to die.[6]

Martin Luther King had drawn on a parallel, if more overtly passionate, tradition of Baptist homiletics in his 'I have a dream' speech in Washington the year before. Acceptance of the reality of conflict, defiance in the face of oppression, a determination to stand for one's principles regardless of the cost: now regarded as classic, at the time the voices of those who spoke for those who had so far been denied the benefits of the western post-war dream had an anachronistic, obdurate quality to them – beautiful old-fashioned structures at odds with contemporary taste, like Victorian churches standing in the path of the modern urban planner and his bulldozer.

At the 1964 Republican Convention, a dissident of a different stripe appeared to reach even further into the past to make his protest against the politics of consensus. Accepting the party's nomination, the radical small-government conservative Barry Goldwater responded to the 'false prophets' who had 'talked and talked and talked and talked the words of freedom', but whose endless compromises had undermined it. He defended his iconoclasm with words which his script-writers seem genuinely thought to be a quotation from Cicero – they certainly sound Ciceronian – but which were instead their own neo-classical invention:

> I would remind you that extremism in the defense of liberty is no vice. And let me remind you also that moderation in the pursuit of justice is no virtue.[7]

Liberal opponents dismissed Goldwater's assault on government interventionism and the New Deal as a dotty throwback; his campaign slogan 'In your heart you know he's right' was immediately met with the lapel-button riposte, 'In your guts you know he's nuts'. That judgement seemed vindicated when he was roundly thrashed by Lyndon Johnson in the subsequent election.

But Goldwater was speaking not for the past but the future. The spirit of consensus could not dominate indefinitely, and over the last third of the twentieth century it was progressively weakened: by buoyant new intellectual and political forces on both left and right; by the end of the Cold War which had given it much of its rationale; above all, by its own growing shortcomings. In many countries, voters – especially younger voters – came to see the politicians of the era of compromise not as high-minded and patriotic pragmatists but as members of a corrupt and unaccountable elite. Unaccountable because, when political parties seem to agree about most things, elections do not bring real change and, even though the constitutional machinery of democracy may be working perfectly, electors are effectively disenfranchised, and must either take to the streets, as some did, or turn to leaders committed to breaking up the cosy club.

Political pragmatism and a faith in technocratic policymaking would not disappear but, from the 1980s on, they would face constant challenge. As a result they would often go underground: they would continue to inform what political leaders *did*, but no longer what they *said*. In due course this growing gap between words and actions would magnify pre-existing suspicions both about politicians and about political language itself. That charge, however, was never laid at Margaret Thatcher's door.

Where There Is Discord

Let's return to that moment when Mrs Thatcher swept into power, and consider the political language of the time. It's a rhetoric in transition. Speeches, interviews, press reports and campaign messaging still owed much to the recent past: technocratic competence remained the gold standard, and politicians on all sides generally continued to appeal to reason and the facts as they strove to win policy arguments.

But Margaret Thatcher's radicalism extended beyond the realm of political ideas to the rhetoric in which those ideas were expressed, and gave it an unmistakeable quality – hard-edged, insistent, utterly sure of itself. She and her allies would be described as 'conviction politicians', the word 'conviction' suggesting a motivation which derived from character, or even faith, rather than cold-blooded rationalism.

The reaction from political opponents and from significant sections of the public was equally visceral, and the temperature and bitterness of the language employed by all sides quickly rose. Though the topics and targets have changed over the years, to a great extent that higher intensity has persisted in our public language ever since. Meanwhile, new and radical ideas began to be tested in the late 1970s in the field of political marketing and the handling of the media which point directly to our world and the gravamen of this book.

Take the most famous poster of the time, and indeed of modern British political history. Against a white background, it showed a long, snaking line of people waiting in a dole queue. The main caption read: LABOUR ISN'T WORKING. A second caption in smaller letters to the bottom right added: BRITAIN'S BETTER OFF WITH THE CONSERVATIVES.

The initial impact of the poster came not from its limited physical life – it was first put up in 1978 on a small handful of sites – but from the political row it ignited. The Labour government decided to go for it on two grounds. First, that it was fake: those people photographed in that long 'dole queue' weren't actually unemployed, they were Tory activists posing for the poster; and the photograph was a montage to make the queue look longer. Second, that the poster overstepped the line that separated political messaging from commercial marketing. A few weeks before the poster first appeared, Denis Healey, Labour's then Chancellor of the Exchequer, had accused the Conservatives of no longer trusting in their policies to appeal to the British public, but relying instead on the advertising agency Saatchi and Saatchi to market them with the 'same techniques' it used for Penguin biscuits, Quality Street and Fairy Snow.[8] He returned to the attack when the poster came out, and other Labour leaders would repeat the charge – that the Tories were attempting to sell politics like soap powder – again and again in the years to come.

The critique is of a piece with what became a broader pessimism on the left about even the possibility of a worthwhile public discourse about political choices. On this view, money from big business and a shadowy circle of rich backers had given Mrs Thatcher and her party access to a cynical image-making machine and the malign gifts of Charles and Maurice Saatchi, Tim Bell and other advertising and PR gurus. The object was to undercut and dumb down the traditional ideas-based debate between the parties. The right-wing press was already part of the conspiracy, and the rest of the media were too compromised or too supine to oppose it. In a perfect world, the BBC might have been an effective counterbalance, but that organisation was seen as craven when it came to powerful vested interests, and obsessed with preserving its reputation for impartiality at all costs.

This dichotomy between the politics of 'issues' and 'policies', and that of 'personalities' and other superficialities, and the lamentable tendency of the British media to focus on the latter rather than the former, had been a bugbear for the left for decades, but the arrival of Margaret Thatcher seemed to crystallise an essentially Marxist thesis: the public's inability to understand the truth about Thatcherism was the result of a *false consciousness* which the forces of reaction had managed to create by working their many direct and indirect levers of influence and control over the media. What Margaret Thatcher said was untrue – it was rhetoric in the most pejorative sense of the word – but her backers were able to ensure that she and her self-evidently destructive policies went largely unchallenged.

So much for theory. The practical effect of Labour's attack on the poster was to put it on the evening news and bring it to the attention of millions of voters who otherwise might have missed it entirely. It was a marketeer's dream: a small investment on paid-for media magnified a hundred or thousandfold through news coverage, commentary and the propagation and amplification which now takes place on social media, but which was then largely a matter of *word of mouth*. The poster struck enough of a chord that a follow-up version – predictably LABOUR STILL ISN'T WORKING – was deployed in the actual campaign the following year. Along with a second phrase – 'Crisis, what crisis?' – which James Callaghan was said to have exclaimed on his return from a foreign trip in the midst of the Winter of Discontent, the poster became a shorthand, not just for the reasons why Mrs Thatcher won in 1979, but for the moment when 'old' Labour – in other words, Labour as a mass democratic socialist party – lost the confidence of the British electorate, never to recover it.

Callaghan didn't actually say the words attributed to him: the conservative newspapers invented the remark as the kind of thing he *might* have said, and then headlined it as if it was an actual quotation. This is another technique which, in due course, would become standard practice for some journalists.

Puns are usually a bad idea in public language, but the pun in the poster works because of its seriousness and the precision of its irony. Isn't it strange, goes the thought, how the party which claims to represent the working class has presided over so much unemployment? They can't even look after their own heartland supporters. As with the 'death pancl', the phrase operates as a synecdoche: unemployment stands for a failed economy which in turn stands for a government which has also failed at everything else.

But the craftiest part of this apparently broad-spectrum message is the way in which it simultaneously targeted a critical segment of the electorate. To win a majority, the Tories had to persuade some voters who had previously supported Labour to change allegiance. Among them were members of the C1 and C2 socio-economic groups – junior supervisors, clerical workers, and skilled manual workers and their families. Many of these had been Labour supporters, but unemployment and the fear of unemployment were now their foremost concern. In 1979, a decisive number would indeed change sides, especially in southern England, and – much as the 'Reagan Democrats' would do for twelve years in the US – would keep the Conservatives in power until Tony Blair reclaimed them in 1997. The poster meant something to almost everyone, but it also spoke directly to the specific anxieties of these bellwether voters.

Much was made at the time and has been since about the role that advertising and image-making played in Margaret Thatcher's political success. She had chosen able media advisers and a brilliant advertising agency and, like British political marketeers before and after them, they had immediately flown off to America to discover and purloin the latest innovations there. There were the famous stories of the hair, the clothes, of Gordon Reece making her lower the pitch of her voice so that she would sound more authoritative.

In fact, Margaret Thatcher was intractable material for any image-maker to work with. She was what she was, and her strengths and limitations were immediately apparent to everyone from the moment she gained prominence. Unlike many other modern politicians, moreover, her views and her public persona did not change greatly between campaigning and governing, or over eleven years in office.

Like every British and American woman politician to this day, Mrs Thatcher was subjected to a continuous analysis of appearance, manner and mood. The media were also inevitably intrigued about her as a wife and mother, and the members of her immediate family soon became minor celebrities in British public life. But if she sometimes entertained questions about her home life, it was almost always with serious political purpose. Her enemies wanted the world to believe that her main ideological influences were outré Austrian and American free-market economists and the Svengali-like Sir Keith Joseph.* Her stories of her upbringing in Grantham, and her life with Denis and the children were intended to emphasise instead the role that family, patriotism and English thrift played in her make-up.

But she had no easy way of shifting gears from the public to the personal – indeed no real public language for the personal at all. Arriving at the door of No. 10 after her 1979 election victory, she reached for St Francis of Assisi, of all people, to express the spirit with which she hoped to govern – 'where there is discord, may we bring harmony', and so on.[9] But that came out sounding like an out-of-body experience, and when David Frost asked her, some years later, whether she had ever actually felt the presence of God in the room, she didn't really have an answer. Watching her on TV, one could sense a moment of puzzlement, the mighty mainframe whirring through its databases in search of a safe response. What she ended up saying was: 'I am very wary of talking about personal belief, because it could be so easily misinterpreted.'[10]

Both in office and in retirement, she sometimes appeared in the media in an informal setting – I shepherded her once for an evening when she appeared on the BBC telethon *Children in Need* – but essentially still in full formal public character. It is impossible to imagine her playing the saxophone on a late-night talk show like Bill Clinton, or hamming it up with Catherine Tate for *Comic Relief* as Tony Blair would do in 2007 while still prime minister. Boris Yeltsin's and Silvio Berlusconi's antics, and Vladimir Putin's pumped-up pecs, are emanations from a different PR universe altogether.

---

* Like several other members of her Cabinet, Keith Joseph was Jewish, a fact that did not go unnoticed by the British establishment or media. Veiled anti-Semitism, and the pointed presentation of Jewish public figures as 'other', remain a reality in the British media to this day.

Mrs Thatcher's oratory is best remembered today for a handful of phrases, especially those which her opponents believed could be used to demonstrate how out-of-touch and inhuman she was. Like 'Crisis, what crisis?', they were often 'improved' and taken out of context in the retelling. 'There is no such thing as society', 'they're frit, frit' and 'moaning minnies' all fall into this category. She was certainly capable of memorable outbursts and, as we shall see, deliberate phrase-making, but what is most striking about the speeches when one reads them today is their seriousness and willingness to delve deep into the detail of the underlying policies themselves.

Let's take her speech to the Conservative Party Conference in Brighton in October 1980. This was a difficult period for her government. The post-election honeymoon was definitely over, the economy which hadn't been 'working' under Callaghan showed few signs of recovery under the new regime, and unemployment was going up. Mrs Thatcher and her Chancellor, Sir Geoffrey Howe, were under acute pressure to moderate their economic policies, not just from the political opposition and elements of the media, but from some members of her own Cabinet. The point of the speech was to explain why that would be a terrible mistake. Mrs Thatcher gives her answer to these critics in the speech's most famous passage:

> To those waiting with bated breath for that favourite media catchphrase, the 'U' turn, I have only one thing to say. You turn if you want to. The lady's not for turning.[11]

This is characteristic of Mrs Thatcher's comic style – serviceable, delivered with brio, essentially leaden. The phrase 'that favourite media catchphrase' does double duty: it lets her audience know that she's not deaf, she *knows* there's a mounting public clamour for a change in policy; but, because both the words 'media' and 'catchphrase' suggest trendiness and shallowness, it also implies that not just the media speculation but the actual political idea of a major course correction is feckless and not thought through.

Then we get two puns in quick succession, the 'U' and 'You', and 'The lady's not for turning'. The first should be the better of the two. 'You turn if you want to' has an attractive snappiness, especially after the long preceding sentence, and its defiance is unexpectedly informal, saucy even. The second is based on the title of Christopher Fry's 1948 verse drama *The Lady's Not For Burning*, and really shouldn't work. The play is only remembered for its name, and many people haven't even heard of that; and anyway Fry's play has nothing to do with the point which Mrs Thatcher is trying to make. It's scarcely even a pun, more like one of those feeble titles one comes across in magazines which are generated by giving a familiar phrase a slight twist. But of course it *does* work: it's at once spirited and intriguingly loopy, especially in that turn to the third person. Yet even at the time it didn't really sound like Mrs Thatcher. It's a scriptwriter's line, one of a handful of mandatory jokes which she delivered like a trooper. Not really *ethos*, then, but pseudo-*ethos*. By contrast, 'You turn if you want to' sounds like the woman herself.

There are a couple of further, slightly painful efforts at humour – echoing a famous Heineken beer slogan of the time, she nods to her Foreign Secretary, Lord Carrington, as 'the peer that reaches those foreign parts that other peers cannot reach' – but the bulk of the speech is deadly earnest, a vast defensive fortification erected to protect the core elements of her young government's agenda: at home, monetarism, deregulation and a determination to pursue long-term growth despite immediate economic and social pain; abroad, a steely but not yet unfriendly approach to Europe, and steadfast opposition to communism and the Soviet Union.

It is generally closely argued and cogently expressed, sometimes with sophisticated technique. One of the potentially troublesome sections of the speech is the part that deals with unemployment. The problem is that Mrs Thatcher is speaking to two audiences: the Tory faithful in the hall and in the country, who believe that the Thatcher–Howe medicine is necessary and likely to work; and the general public, many of whom will be neither firmly for her or against her, and who will need to be convinced, not just of the merits of her policies, but also that she understands and has carefully weighed the human consequences. So with that second group in mind she starts by facing the issue head on:

Meanwhile we are not heedless of the hardships and worries that accompany the conquest of inflation. Foremost among these is unemployment. Today our country has 2 million unemployed.[12]

There. She's said it. It's a shocking number. But is it really such a shocking number? And has she really said it? Having apparently acknowledged not just that unemployment is the 'foremost' of the 'hardships and worries' which the public are facing, Mrs Thatcher at once begins to gloss both the number and the story.

However, she knows she has to be careful. Her many enemies will be looking for any hint of callousness, any overt attempt to belittle the suffering of the unemployed. So she makes use of a rhetorical tactic with elements of both *procatalepsis* and *apophasis*. The first (sometimes also called *prebuttal*) is when a speaker herself anticipates and answers a potential objection to her argument before anyone else has a chance to raise it. The second (sometimes also called *paralipsis*) refers to a family of techniques in which the speaker brings up a subject while apparently either refuting it or arguing that it should *not* be brought up: 'I've never paid any attention to what people say about the senator's private life, and I certainly don't intend to mention it in this campaign.'

What Mrs Thatcher attempts is a kind of converse procatalepsis with an apophatic flavour. She summons up an interlocutor (an anonymous 'you'), whom she imagines raising a number of qualifications to that bald '2 million' number. They are in fact qualifications she herself wants to make – and which her first audience will certainly want to hear – but she wants to distance herself from them as well:

> Now you can try to soften that figure in a dozen ways. You can point out – and it is quite legitimate to do so – that 2 million today does not mean what it meant in the 1930s; that the percentage of unemployment is much less now than it was then. You can add that today many more married women go out to work. You can stress that, because of the high birth rate in the 1960s, there is an unusually large number of school-leavers this year looking for work and that the same will be true for the next two years. You can emphasise that about a quarter of a million people find new jobs each month and therefore go off the employment register. And you can recall that there are nearly 25 million people in jobs compared with only about 18 million in the 1930s. You can point out that the Labour Party conveniently overlooks the fact that of the 2 million unemployed for which they blame us, nearly a million and a half were bequeathed to us by their government.

But when all that has been said, the fact remains that the level of
unemployment in our country today is a human tragedy.[13]

'You' can try to soften that figure in a dozen different ways but I,
Margaret Thatcher, would never attempt to do so. The prime minister
manages to enumerate all the reasons why she believes that the unemployment figures are actually less serious than they appear, without
actually *saying* as much herself. She presents herself instead as *listening*
to the points being made by someone else, sometimes reluctantly
having to concede that this insistent 'you' may have a point – 'and it
is quite legitimate to do so', she notes judiciously in a gesture of fairness to her imaginary opponent – but in the end returning to the
experiential/moral point she began with: 'the level of unemployment
in our country today is a human tragedy'. It's as if heart has conquered
head after all and revealed that Margaret Thatcher has far more
emotional intelligence than this admittedly very well informed but
rather chilly 'you' with whom she has been sparring.

This is rhetoric of some finesse, and it allowed Mrs Thatcher to
steer a safe course through tricky narrows. But it's a complicated
message – unemployment isn't as bad as our opponents say, yet I still
recognise how painful it is for those affected – and it didn't stand a
chance against 'the lady's not for turning'. It was the unflinching
resolve, not the sympathy, that made the headlines. *This* was what the
media expected. It was also what Mrs Thatcher and her speechwriters
doubtless intended. Despite its technical accomplishment, the 'human
tragedy' passage was never likely to make much impression.

But at least it was there for anyone who wanted to find it. It was
also likely to be reported, albeit towards the bottom rather than the
top of the story. In the early 1980s, British broadsheet newspapers
gave more room to extracts from political speeches than today, as
well as providing more detailed reports of parliamentary debates.
Parliament was not yet televised, but audio broadcasting had been
introduced and political reports on TV as well as radio included
extracts of speeches in sound, accompanied in the case of TV by a
slide with the speaker's name and photograph. Mrs Thatcher's 1980
conference speech was more straightforward: captured by outside
broadcast cameras in the conference hall and transmitted live, it was
recorded on the two-inch Ampex videotape machines in the BBC's

Lime Grove studios where passages could be selected, edited and ultimately injected into that evening's programme. I helped turn the clips of it around myself that night.

Typically, a researcher would be looking for two or three extracts from a major speech like this one. You'd certainly want the line that would grab tomorrow morning's headlines, but at least one other, more substantive passage as well; and you would expect to cover three or four other points in the presenter's script. The clips were known as *sync*, or *sync bites* – 'sync' standing for 'synchronised', a term taken from film meaning a shot or sequence in which the separately recorded audiotape and film had to be matched up. No such synchronisation was needed with videotape, but the name stuck. In practice, sync almost always meant speech or interview, which in current affairs meant public language. The 'bite' element was borrowed from American TV, where such clips were called *sound bites*.

Later, political aides and communications chiefs would obsess about generating exactly the right bite, but at this point it was generally a demand-side term, used by reporters and producers to mean something they hoped to extract from a given speech or interview. These morsels were seldom offered up to you on a plate; you had to search for them, watching the entire thing and drawing up a shortlist of candidate clips. You could only make the right choice, moreover, if you'd already reached an underlying editorial judgement about what was most important, controversial or memorable within the person's wider remarks.

I was one of the output editors of *Newsnight*, and on the ground in Moscow in 1986, when Mikhail Gorbachev gave the General Secretary's report to the 27th Congress of the Communist Party of the Soviet Union. Everyone knew it was a historic moment, but no advance copies of the speech had been made available and, apart from a brief conversation with a sphinx-like young man who claimed to be a Novosti correspondent but was obviously KGB, almost no guidance or spin was provided. There was nothing for it but to hunker down, listen to the simultaneous translation and (thankfully with the help of a couple of specialists) try to make sense of the thing in real time. Gorbachev spoke for hour after hour; when the English translation was made available late in the afternoon, it was the size of a short novel. We knew that somewhere in this endless thicket of language lurked suggestive hints about glasnost and perestroika and the rest of Gorbachev's programme of change. The challenge was to find them, analyse them and turn them into a coherent piece of television in the minutes we would have between his sitting down and our feed back to London.

Even in the 1980s, however, everyone in politics and the media knew that it was the headlines and the broad impression which a leader left that mattered most, and slowly but steadily Margaret Thatcher lost a rhetorical battle not at the level of *logos* – in straight argument she could give at least as good as she got to the very end – but that of *ethos*. The One Nation Tories she had swept out or marginalised might often have looked and sounded like grandees, stuffy and not quite of this world, but they were capable of expressing real empathy when the occasion required, empathy which was all the more effective because it was unexpected; Michael Heseltine's passionate response to the Brixton and Toxteth riots of 1981 was a notable instance. Whether they felt it or not, Margaret Thatcher and many of those closest to her, like Norman Tebbit (once described by Michael Foot, James Callaghan's successor as Labour leader, as a 'semi-house-trained polecat'), struggled to articulate it, even when they tried. And, as we saw in the case of 'the lady's not for turning', the few attempts at nuance they *did* make tended to be crowded out by the more strident passages which everyone expected from them.

But public expectations *were* changing – especially about the prerogative of the average citizens to be listened to. Ironically, Mrs Thatcher's strong sense of herself as an ordinary person, different from the mass of humanity only by dint of intelligence and ability, meant that she lacked the patrician's defensive radar, that moment in the interplay of *ethos* and *pathos* when a klaxon goes off inside your head to warn you that you had better say something to your audience right now to demonstrate that you understand them and feel their pain. This capacity is not limited to patricians of course: a handful of politicians are born with it – none more than Bill Clinton – and most learn to give a fair impression of it. Not Margaret Thatcher.

The public's growing disenchantment with her is often attributed to divisive policies, most notably the attempt to introduce the deeply unpopular Poll Tax. Those policies no doubt played a part, though it's worth noting that her fall was followed, not by electoral defeat for the Conservatives, but by another victory and seven more years of Tory rule. Other political leaders have been able to maintain the trust of the electorate through crises and conflicts greater than anything Britain lived through under Mrs Thatcher. More than her policies, what many members of the public – and many in her own party – had a problem with was *her*. It was a question of *ethos*, then, one which was closely entwined with the way she spoke. Perhaps she thought of her inability to bend and express softer emotions as a strength – she was clearly chuffed by all that Iron Lady talk. In fact, it was an ominous flaw. Those who hated her said (and still say) that it was a moral flaw. We could debate that until the cows come home. To me, as a practical matter, it was a flaw in her rhetoric.

In 1983, during the campaign that led up to her second general election victory, the prime minister made an appearance on *Nationwide* to answer live questions from voters in different parts of the country. I had left the programme to work on the BBC's new breakfast TV service, but I was in the BBC's Lime Grove studios on the day that Mrs Thatcher's small cavalcade swept in and, an hour or so later, swept out again. By then, I'd seen for myself what had happened.

These public grillings were not new. The BBC already had weekly programmes on radio and TV in which panels of politicians and other public figures gave their own views about current events and fielded questions from a live audience. During elections there were phone-ins involving the party leaders and other senior politicians. Nonetheless, a television Q&A with the prime minister was always an event, all the more so in the middle of an election campaign. In one significant respect, moreover, the format of *Nationwide* differed from a typical phone-in: rather than dialling up, the questioners were invited into the BBC's television studios around the country so that they could be seen as well as heard. This had the effect – which had never previously seemed important – of putting the questioner on a more equal footing with the politician in the studio.

And on this occasion, Mrs Thatcher found herself unexpectedly in the gladiatorial ring with a woman who, though scarcely a doppel-gänger, was similar to her in age and class and, more to the point, gave every impression of being as tough as she was. Diana Gould, a schoolteacher from Gloucestershire, pursued a closely argued line of questioning about the precise circumstances of the sinking of the Argentine cruiser the *General Belgrano* during the recent Falklands War. Mrs Thatcher's evasive zigzags – summary assertion, contradiction, condescension, attempted 'last lines' to shut the thing down – were as ineffective as the *Belgrano*'s had been, and the torpedo struck home. It was one of those public arguments in which the detail is obscure (for Mrs Gould, much hung on the precise bearing on which the *Belgrano* was sailing when it was attacked), but where the general viewer can still see who is gaining the upper hand.

There was a point of substance at the centre of the argument. Not only did Mrs Thatcher seem to have a less sure grasp of the facts than Mrs Gould, she never found a satisfactory answer to the other woman's question about why the *Belgrano* was targeted, despite the fact that it was *outside* the maritime 'exclusion zone', which the UK had declared around the Falkland Islands, and was sailing *away* from the islands when the British submarine HMS *Conqueror* sunk her.

But style was just as important. Mrs Thatcher tried several times to move from the particular to the general – 'My duty was to look after our troops, our ships, our navy, and my goodness me I lived with many, many anxious days and nights' – but these efforts sounded obfuscatory and self-serving. Her tone was courteous but imperious and, at a key moment, she managed to forget Mrs Gould's name. Quite understandable given the rigours of an election campaign, but something else which seemed to betray arrogance (she can't even be bothered to remember ordinary people's *names*) and lack of grip.

As is often the case, this memorable piece of television – which some in Labour fondly hoped would be a game changer – had no discernible effect whatever on the outcome of the election. Mrs Thatcher won handsomely and remained in power for many more years. But it had been a politician's nightmare: a well-prepared, articulate and tenacious challenger comes out of nowhere and suddenly the champ is reeling. At the time Mrs Thatcher was said to have been enraged and to have suspected that it had been a deliberate set-up; as she left the BBC's Lime Grove studios, people claimed she remarked that she would never set foot in the place again, and indeed she never did. But these are the kinds of stories which swirl constantly around the BBC, and the truth is that she sustained little immediate damage beyond embarrassment. Yet to some viewers the incident served to confirm an image of a leader who neither understood nor cared about them. As the years went by, that image became, like an iron mask, irremovable. By the end, it was the only public face she had.

Margaret Thatcher's speeches in office concentrated on policy and did so with precision and seriousness. Yet she allowed the media – sometimes even colluded with them – to create a version of herself which emphasised what she took to be her distinctive strengths but which came at a considerable cost: conviction and consistency ended up looking like monomaniacal inflexibility. This, taken with the growing compulsion of the mass media even then to simplify and simplify again, meant that it was the fiery eyes, the wagging finger and the sharp-tongued rejoinders, rather than the grand sweep of policy, which stuck in people's minds. By the beginning of the 1990s, the Conservatives believed they needed a leader who *sounded* more conciliatory if they were to avoid electoral defeat, and they concluded that, even if Margaret Thatcher were able to get the appropriate words out, if they came from her lips no one would listen anyway.

Despite her immense conviction and all her barrister's skills, despite the tutelage of brilliant marketing minds – some of whom showed by their work that they understood how political messaging needed to adapt to address a changing audience and a changing media environment – she lacked the rhetorical range and suppleness necessary to keep control of her own narrative. As a result, she could not prevent herself from becoming, or seeming to become, the thing her enemies said she was.

There You Go Again

On 5 July 1983, just a few weeks after Mrs Thatcher's appearance on *Nationwide*, I arrived in America for the first time. I landed at JFK and took a yellow cab into Manhattan. Although I'd only got there at lunchtime, it was still a reasonably full day. I unpacked and set up shop in a midtown apartment, was introduced to everyone in the BBC office where I would be spending the next eight months, watched the evening news shows go out, helped edit a couple of TV packages for the overnight satellite back to London, attended a performance of *42nd Street* on Broadway, and met my future wife.

My job was to produce short news reports and general features for the new *Breakfast Time* programme. One of the problems any British morning show had to grapple with in those days was where the news was going to come from. The London news cycle was geared to meet the deadlines of the national newspapers and early-evening TV news bulletins, so most 'planned' news had happened by 6 p.m. The House of Commons sat on into the night, but even then rarely produced much in the way of stories. The *Breakfast* New York team – the veteran BBC foreign correspondent Bob Friend and a producer, which I had now become – were meant to fill the gap. The American news cycle was similar to the British one, but the time difference meant that the US was still producing news long after the UK had gone to sleep.

So we would comb the CBS and NBC evening news programmes for fresh stories which might resonate with a British audience and would then repackage and re-voice them. We would also find, shoot and edit features of our own. All of the above would then be put on a late-night satellite so that it would arrive in the UK just in time for the following morning's show. And *Breakfast* wanted everything: hard news, US politics, events at the UN, business stories, social stories, Brits-in-America stories, art, fashion, movies, books, music, celebrities, food and every stripe of general and particular American wackiness.

The differences between American and British TV news were stark. The network evening news programmes were much shorter than their British equivalents once the many ad breaks were taken into account, and the amount of time which the executive producers were prepared to devote to serious subjects within that smaller compass was itself much less.

One academic study comparing the TV news coverage of the 1983 general election in the UK with the 1984 US presidential election found that the BBC's main TV news bulletin spent an average of nineteen minutes a day on the election during the main twenty-four-day campaign. By contrast, during the equivalent period in the presidential campaign, NBC devoted an average of five minutes a day to the election, CBS four minutes, and ABC just three minutes.[14] The typical duration of individual stories was also shorter. The same study found that the average length of an individual election item on the BBC was 2'07", while on CBS it was 1'35", on NBC 1'30", and on ABC 0'54".

Similar differences in editorial priorities and in durations applied during non-election periods. The gap would grow wider with the relaunch of *The Nine O'Clock News* in 1988; after that, the duration of the lead stories and the overall amount of time reserved for serious news on the BBC's main TV news programme actually went *up*. But the far more concise American style would increasingly become the norm on most channels in most western countries. Together with the idioms of short-form tabloid print journalism, it would be a decisive influence on the way news would one day be packaged on the Web, smartphone and social media.

The cadence of US network news also differed sharply from the British style. The packages were cut much more aggressively. Individual shots were shorter, sometimes as short as two seconds, so that there were often many more shots in their shorter reports than in our longer ones. There was usually no attempt to combine shots to create sequences or to smooth out sudden jumps in sound. The result would be a rough, fast, often rather exhilarating visual montage. This was of a piece with the pace and syntax of much of the rest of US TV, and especially of some of its new cable offerings like MTV, which had been launched two years earlier.

There was no attempt on these programmes to find a second or third quotation from a given speech, or to allow the clips to extend to thirty or forty-five seconds. It was rare for anyone to get more than one bite, and frequently the speaker – even the president – would be cut off mid-flow. Voiceover was breakneck and wall-to-wall. Picture was generally cut to words rather than the BBC tradition of cutting the visuals carefully together first, and only then asking the reporter to write and deliver their words against them.

Urgent to the point of brutality, it was a style of editing which could deliver TV news of panache and immediacy. It lacked the stuffiness of British broadcast journalism and that air of a cosy club of politicians and correspondents from which the viewer was excluded. Yet it also prefigured some of the concerns of this book. The compression of actuality and language saved time and increased the intensity of the viewing experience, but it came at a price: everything had to be shortened and simplified. There was no room for conditional clauses or other qualification. There could only ever be two sides to any given argument, and even they would be presented in fleeting summary.

The other thing that was obvious, even in 1983, was how far the *coverage* of political news in America had already come to influence the *generation* of that news. In the UK, Whitehall departments and political parties still tended to issue press releases, hold press conferences and offer interviewees on their own timetable, one which was probably fixed in Tudor times and was largely limited to weekday office hours. In America everyone *lived* the news cycle. Appearances in front of the live cameras outside the Capitol, big revelations in major running stories, coy phone calls to tell the guest-booker that so-and-so would, after all, consent to be interviewed by Jane Pauley and Bryant Gumbel – pretty much everything that was intended to make a splash was aimed at the morning or evening peaks of the cycle, while stories which the politicians and press secretaries wanted to bury were carefully timed to avoid them.

Things were about to get even more intense. CNN had launched at the start of the 1980s, and its coverage of the series of major stories which unfolded over the coming years – the shuttle disaster of 1986, Tiananmen Square in 1989 and the first Gulf War in 1991 among them, all stories which took place beyond the control of press departments or media executives – paved the way for a new 24/7 news cycle. The Internet then made it normative. The 24/7 cycle still had peaks and troughs, but the most important thing about it was the most obvious: it was on all the time, and the gaps which had provided reporters and editors with their thinking time in the past were simply abolished.

By the end of the decade, I was the editor of the BBC's main TV news programme and ran most of the BBC's coverage of the Tiananmen Square crisis from Beijing. Many of the accoutrements of the emerging digital era were already to hand – cellphones, lightweight video cameras and editing kit, the ability to broadcast from the middle of the square around the clock. So too the inevitable corollary of the cycle, which was an explosion of demand for journalism: every BBC outlet, radio and TV, wanted a fresh report every time anything happened, no matter at what time of the day or night. In one 24-hour period, we fed more than two dozen radio and television edited packages, as well as offering up countless 'two-ways' and live updates. I remember looking at the pile of cassettes that day and thinking, this is new.

Whether you were a political leader, a press officer, a reporter or an editor, the new news cycle was a monster which had to be continually fed. If you couldn't find anything else to feed it, there was an unnerving sense that it might end up eating you. The benefits were astonishing immediacy and relevance; the risks – given that editorial thinking time was being compressed sometimes into seconds – superficiality, distortion and error.

Making TV in the US of the mid-1980s differed from my first years at the BBC in other ways. The place was wired – we could feed tape or go live from more or less anywhere. And everyone you interviewed seemed to know exactly what to say. Attempt a vox pop* on a British street at this time, and most people would either turn away in alarm or stare sheepishly at the camera. Here they would immediately adopt a recognisable TV persona and deliver short, crisp statements of shock, amusement, anger or whatever else the given piece called for.

This knowingness about the ways of TV and the rest of the media would spread to the UK and the Continent. Soon Brits who had never been in front of a camera would talk with the relaxed confidence of old pros. In the 1990s, the limitless resource of TV-savvy citizens would lead to the development of essentially new television genres which are now collectively referred to as *Reality*. The new formats – doc soaps, format documentary, *Big Brother*-style observation, factual entertainment – were created for the most part in the UK and Holland and then shipped in bulk freighters to the United States and the rest of the world.

The flavour of Reality – demotic, articulate, capricious, maudlin, by turns brazen and confessional in tone – was partly drawn from tabloid journalism, but would soon return the compliment and became a major contributor of material to, and influence on that journalism itself. Eventually, it would also provide much of the tone of voice and subject-matter for the new wave of digital publishers.

The public's increasingly sophisticated awareness of how language and character played out on TV and other media would have another effect. It would break the spell that had, until then, given the public

---

* A now largely (and mercifully) discredited TV technique in which the journalist tries to convey some version of public reaction to a news story by splicing together snippets of interviews conducted with random passers-by in a public place.

language of political leaders some measure of protection from the extremities of ridicule and contempt. Soon the audience would extend no special favours to the politicians, or indeed to anyone else.

★

The politics of the America I was now living in was dominated by one man: Ronald Reagan. Both then, and later when I was back in the UK working on *Newsnight* and *The Nine O'Clock News*, his face and voice were everywhere – at home on TV, on the monitors in the office and the control room, in the edit. Forward, stop. Backwards, stop. Come in *here*, cut away *here*.

Much of my time in the US was spent outside New York and Washington, shooting the short, generally light features which were such a big part of the job. It meant that I met dozens of ordinary Americans, black and white, rural as well as urban, rich and poor. In the liberal citadels of the north-east, Reagan was a mystery, a long-standing joke who had incomprehensibly won a presidential election. But many of the people I met had voted for him and revered him.

Reagan is often mentioned in the same breath as Margaret Thatcher. There was certainly plenty they agreed on: the need to roll back the state and make way for the creative power of the private sector, tough-mindedness when it came to the USSR, and so on. But he was a politician, and above all a rhetor, of a quite different feather.

As we have seen, there are elements in the Thatcher story which smack of the rhetorical future, but she never really stepped over the threshold which separated the stately old world of public language from the one we now inhabit, and which was then just beginning to be discernible. In this respect, she remained a conformist, a woman who had always been determined to be taken seriously, and who had always assumed that the best way to achieve that was to speak seriously.

Ronald Reagan was a prophet of the future. He had an unrivalled command of every register of modern oratory, from the most informal and subversive to the most grandiloquent, and he could move from one to another in a trice. His political intent was just as serious as Margaret Thatcher's, but he could present it playfully, dramatically, emotionally – whatever the mood of the occasion required. He could sense the media's mood too, knew their appetites and their little ways and, until his faculties began to fail him in the last years of his presidency, he could mesmerise them like a cobra.

By the time Reagan took office in 1981, the American version of the rhetoric of the post-war consensus was giving out. Failure in Vietnam, the 1973 oil shock and stalemate in the Cold War meant that foreign policy had become a fraught topic. Economic instability and recession had shaken confidence at home in the promise of a Great Society which combined prosperity driven by technology with enlightened social policy delivered by an active government. Presidents no longer felt able to channel Churchill or FDR: the vocabulary of traditional grandiloquence, of *swords* and *destiny*, had come to sound not just dated, but phoney. They knew they still needed to aim high, but had lost the rhetorical means. Here's Richard Nixon giving the State of the Union address to Congress in January 1970:

> But let us, above all, recognise a fundamental truth. We can be the best-clothed, best-fed, best-housed people in the world, enjoying clean air, clean water, beautiful parks, but we could still be the unhappiest people in the world without an indefinable spirit – the lift of a driving dream which has made America, from its beginning, the hope of the world.

And there it is – an American exceptionalism that transcends the materialism and consumerism of which America is often accused. But the expression? Nixon's speechwriters first tell us that the spirit is 'indefinable' and then immediately attempt to define it: it's 'the lift of a driving dream'. The intention was presumably to convey the elements which make up the American spirit – lofty idealism and unstoppable energy – using everyday words; 'lift' like the Saturn rocket which had just taken men to the moon, 'driving' hinting not just at US momentum in industry and technology, but at the collective certainty and will-power of a nation.

Alas, 'the lift of a driving dream' would soon be held up as a classic example of Nixon's gracelessness as a speaker. 'Lift', 'driving' and 'dream' have literal as well as figurative meanings and, put together, the literal meanings are sharply dissonant. 'Lift' suggests vertical movement, while 'driving' suggests horizontal. But worse is 'driving dream'.

Dreams can be many things – kaleidoscopic, ethereal, photo-realistic – but has a dream ever felt as if it was about to put its foot down on the accelerator? Alliteration can give a phrase a tight phonetic logic, but it's got to be just so. In this case, it sounds like a shot in the dark from a man who's never had a dream in his life.

And then along came Ronald Reagan. 'It's morning again in America' was a line in a 1984 TV ad for Reagan rather than in a speech, but it accurately conveys his ability to express political abstractions and airy ideals in evocative everyday phrases. Like Mrs Thatcher, his great moment arrived at the end of the 1970s. And like her, he benefited from a broader turning of the cultural tide. But, even if 1980 was the year when it finally made sense to a majority of Americans, Ronald Reagan's rhetoric was not itself a product of that moment. He'd always spoken like that or, to put it more cautiously, we can hear the relaxed mature Reagan in some of his earliest political utterances.

His opponents naturally focused on his history as a Hollywood actor and – just as we saw their counterparts doing with Margaret Thatcher in Britain – dismissed him as a puppet, in his case an actor brilliantly delivering words which he was obviously not intelligent enough to have written himself. It wasn't true. Reagan was not just an exceptional performer, but an exceptional creator of rhetoric. Later on he used speechwriters, as every president does, but their work was based on a pre-existing style. It was his style. In fact, it was him.

Let's join him early on. It's October 1964 and the general election is only days away. Lyndon Johnson, who has been president for less than a year, will shortly achieve that annihilating victory over Barry Goldwater. Reagan, who will claim in this notable speech to have 'spent most of my life as a Democrat', but who is now a fervent Goldwater supporter, is thus about to speak up for a cause which he must already know is headed for defeat. Mindful of that Hollywood career, he is careful to emphasise right at the start exactly who is responsible for the material:

Thank you and good evening. The sponsor has been identified, but unlike most television programs, the performer hasn't been provided with a script. As a matter of fact, I have been permitted to choose my own words and discuss my own ideas regarding the choice that we face in the next few weeks.[15]

'The performer hasn't been provided with a script' is a pre-echo of the wry, confident humour of Reagan's heyday a couple of decades later. 'My own words' and 'my own ideas' reinforces the point that this is not just a celebrity endorsement. Ronald Reagan does indeed want to endorse Barry Goldwater but, believe it or not, he has some thoughts of his own.

What follows is a full-throated attack both on specific Johnsonian policies – on agricultural subsidies, the extension of social security, his alleged 'appeasement' of communist Russia – and on the central themes of the 'Great Society' and the 'War on Poverty'. Much of the speech works this way: Reagan presents his listeners with a series of quotations or semi-quotations from Democrats and others on the left, offered out of context and often in summary form or without attribution, and then keys off them into an indignant response. Senators Fulbright and Clark have, he claims, been revealing the Democrats' true ambitions; the first describing Johnson as 'our moral teacher and our leader' and the Constitution as 'this antiquated document'; the second defining liberalism as 'meeting the material needs of the masses through the full power of centralised government'. This is Reagan's reaction to the Aunt Sally he has just carefully set up:

> Well I, for one, resent it when a representative of the people refers to you and me, the free men and women of this country, as 'the masses'. This is a term we haven't applied to ourselves in America. But beyond that, 'the full power of centralised government' – this was the very thing the Founding Fathers sought to minimise. They knew that governments don't control things. A government can't control the economy without controlling people. And they knew that when a government sets out to do that, it must use force and coercion to achieve its purpose. They also knew, these Founding Fathers, that outside of its legitimate functions, government does nothing as well or as economically as the private sector of the economy.[16]

Reagan's quotations from the two senators are artfully chosen to make them sound like thorough-going communists: the word 'leader' in 'our moral teacher and our leader' is made to sound like the equivalent of the Russian word used of Josef Stalin, *vozhd*, while 'the material needs of the masses' and the 'full power of centralised government' transports us in a flash to downtown Moscow with Gosplan on one side of the square and the KGB on the other. Scarcely what the two senators had in mind, of course, but Reagan has manipulated their words to give character and colour to an otherwise familiar pair of arguments: first, that excessive government involvement in the economy inevitably leads to totalitarianism; and second, that, in almost all fields, the public sector is nothing like as effective and efficient as private enterprise anyway. With the first, we're back on that same old conservative slippery slope (unchecked, those farm subsidies will lead straight to communism), while the second is a free-market article of faith presented as if it was a clause in the Constitution.

But listen as Reagan extracts a kind of rhetorical logic from his bundle of found objects. 'This was the very thing the Founding Fathers sought to minimise.' Essentially true, but not principally for the reason Reagan suggests. 'They knew that governments don't control things.' Well, governments do actually (borders, nuclear weapons, the currency). 'A government can't control the economy without controlling people.' This is the big leap in the argument, but he presents it as if it was just another logical step. Controlling the economy includes an array of things, many of which (maintaining a tight monetary policy to restrain inflation, for instance) Reagan would himself become a strong advocate of, and all of which can be gradated – the imposition of taxes or regulations to safeguard competition doesn't have to add up to Soviet-style central planning. But Reagan makes it an absolute and then equates it with 'controlling people', which is also to be taken absolutely and which means robbing the citizenry of all their freedoms. He then claims that the Founding Fathers foresaw all of this, which is why they erected protective walls against it in the Constitution, walls which those devious Democratic senators and their 'moral teacher', Lyndon Johnson, are now intent on demolishing.

If you suspend all sense of proportion and probability, it fits together admirably. We might dismiss it as what rhetoricians once called an *argumentum ad captandum vulgus*, an argument to beguile those non-existent American 'masses', if it wasn't for the fact that the speaker so clearly believes it himself. But Reagan expresses it deftly, more deftly than most of the speeches uttered by incumbent leaders with teams of writers to help them, and – despite the elisions and exaggerations – at least leaves us in no doubt about his own conviction. And some passages are striking:

> No government ever voluntarily reduces itself in size. So governments' programs, once launched, never disappear. Actually, a government bureau is the nearest thing to eternal life we'll ever see on this earth.[17]

Both this and the preceding passage depend on a definition of government to which Reagan would hold true throughout his career: not government, in Lincoln's words, of, by and for the people; but government as a self-protecting, self-aggrandising, essentially anti-democratic organism, an enemy that must be confronted and cut down to size. Even in 1964, Ronald Reagan is finding ways of turning the tables, of making mainstream assumptions about the role of government seem weird and threatening, and his own critique of them the most normal thing in the world. You didn't have to be a Goldwater supporter to suspect that Reagan was on to something about the creep of government and of entitlement; and, though it's not that funny, that government bureau/eternal life punchline is a memorable one.

Perhaps influenced by the memory of the harangues of the European fascists and communists, many people in the late twentieth century assumed that, while centrists were likely to speak calmly and rationally, radicals – and especially conservative radicals – were bound to reveal themselves by rolling their eyes or frothing at the mouth. The left seized on the admittedly eccentric rhetoric and persona of Reagan's hero, Barry Goldwater, with exactly this implication. But Ronald Reagan himself was living proof that the assumption was wrong. He was neither a moderate nor a 'nice' politician, but an ideologically committed conservative radical. He held America's prevailing political establishment in contempt and he meant to expel and supplant it. Far from hiding his intentions, he spelled them out with utter clarity. But he didn't shake his fist or chew the carpet. He sounded sensible, human, charming, funny.

None of that made him soft. Here he is slipping a dagger into President Jimmy Carter during one of the television debates in the 1980 presidential campaign. A rather glassy-eyed Carter has just delivered an answer on his plan for (our old friend) national health-care reform, in this case a proposal for a universal insurance scheme not unlike that originally proposed by Truman, or the one ultimately made into law by Obama. It has been weighty and detailed and Carter concludes it with the words: 'these are the kinds of elements of a national health insurance, important to the American people. Governor Reagan again, typically, is against such a proposal.'[18] Reagan will go on to answer the point but, before he does so, he looks at President Carter with a long-suffering smile and murmurs four words almost under his breath: 'There you go again.'

It's a perfect modern refutatory enthymeme. This is of a piece, it seems to say, with everything you stand for, Jimmy Carter. Your answer to any question is more government, more control, higher taxes. Reagan doesn't attack the policy as such – he knew that Medicare, the existing entitlement that guaranteed health cover for older people, was popular with many prospective Republican voters – but rather his own imputed version of Carter's philosophy of government. But it's also a character study in a phrase, or rather two character studies: Carter is the swot who talks knowledgeably about inpatients and outpatients and catastrophic care; Reagan the honest scallywag at the back of the class, the boy with the guts to say that the emperor has no clothes and, worse, is really rather *boring*. It's not remotely gracious – this is a gladiatorial lunge, openly disrespectful of a sitting president, intended to maim – but Reagan makes it sound like a rueful long-suffering jibe between friends.

Like anyone hoping to make a romantic conquest, every modern statesman or woman needs a semblance of humour and, as we saw in the case of Margaret Thatcher, your speechwriters will duly provide you at least a simulacrum of it no matter how devoid of levity you happen to be. In Reagan it was obviously real and ran deep in him, but he used this abundant natural resource throughout his presidency for a specific political end: to lift himself rhetorically out of the persona of the politician into something altogether different – a vicarious ordinary citizen who has unexpectedly found themselves in charge of the nation, but who remains both amused and bemused by the antics of the professional politicians and steadfastly refuses to stoop to their level.

The 'you' of 'There you go again' is not just Jimmy Carter, but *all* of you: lobbyists, special interests, unions, the whole monstrous machine of big government, not just in Washington, but in every city and state capital. This isn't far from the rhetorical position of today's anti-politicians, but Ronald Reagan wasn't one of them either. He lacked their reckless fury and vainglorious self-righteousness, and managed to come across as an outsider and a safe pair of hands at the same time.

When he became president himself, the overt vituperation diminished, the generosity increased and the wit was polished until it sparkled like wisdom. Commentators would put much of his political success and enduring popularity down to the *optimism* he was able to project about America's future, a belief in the possibility of a clean slate and a new beginning. In the context of conservative politics, he also managed to achieve a more particular rhetorical victory.

Both before and after Reagan, the central problem of expression for the small-government right has been negativity. The best lines (that 'death panel') and the greatest heat and passion have been associated with what they are *against*, the tone disbelieving, censorious, sometimes near paranoid; they can come across as *der Geist der stets verneint*, like Goethe's Mephistopheles, the spirit that always denies. Reagan's criticisms of corporatist government and the welfare state were as trenchant as anyone's, but he made his proposal to roll back government sound like progress and something based on sound insights into human nature rather than ideology as such.

Reagan's genius for seizing the moment encompassed many rhetorical styles. There is the old showman at the Brandenburg Gate in 1987, using repetition and progressive simplification to move from the language of diplomacy to something much more human:

> There is one sign the Soviets can make that would be unmistakeable, that would advance dramatically the cause of freedom and peace. General Secretary Gorbachev, if you seek peace, if you seek prosperity for the Soviet Union and Eastern Europe, if you seek liberalisation: come here to this gate. Mr Gorbachev, open this gate. Mr Gorbachev – Mr Gorbachev, tear down this wall![19]

The first sentence is nothing special: 'dramatically' is feeble (as it always is) and breaks the rhythm of the sentence; the phrase 'the cause of freedom and peace' is doughy, pious. But the next sentence and that series of *ifs* makes us think – hello, now we're in the world of real rhetoric, we're building up to something. And then the three *ifs* are matched with three suggested actions, or rather three steps which add up to one big action: the Soviet leader is to *come* to the gate, then he's to *open* the gate – no, more than that, he's to *tear down* the entire Berlin Wall (which was just a few feet from where Reagan was speaking). The repetition of Gorbachev's name, especially that final 'Mr Gorbachev – Mr Gorbachev' is masterly, rollicking bravura combined with something which feels genuinely personal, a real call from one human being to another. Reagan was a Cold War purist, a builder of missiles and missile shields, and he was playing not for a draw but a win. Yet he finds a language which instead implies the possibility of reconciliation. Notwithstanding St Francis, it was a language that always eluded Margaret Thatcher.

Eighteen months earlier, the loss of the *Challenger* space shuttle presented Reagan and his writers with a different challenge. There is no argument to win here, no *logos*, rather a moment of national *pathos* to capture and express. The opportunity is to speak for all; the risk that you sound as if you're just going through the motions, saying the things that people always say on these occasions. Their noble sacrifice. Our hearts go out. We will never forget. Did not die in vain.

As luck would have it, we have a benchmark against which to compare Reagan's rhetorical answer. At the end of the 1960s, Richard Nixon's speechwriter William Safire prepared a statement in case the Apollo 11 astronauts were unable to return from the lunar surface:

> In their exploration, they stirred the people of the world to feel as one; in their sacrifice, they bind more tightly the brotherhood of man. In ancient days, men looked at stars and saw their heroes in the constellations. In modern times, we do much the same, but our heroes are epic men of flesh and blood.[20]

'Their sacrifice', 'the brotherhood of man', 'we do much the same'. It would have sufficed if it had ever been needed, but it is as lifeless as the dead astronauts it mourns in this defunct alternative universe. Now listen to this:

> There's a coincidence today. On this day 390 years ago, the great explorer Sir Francis Drake died aboard ship off the coast of Panama. In his lifetime the great frontiers were the oceans, and an historian

later said, 'He lived by the sea, died on it, and was buried in it.' Well, today, we can say of the *Challenger* crew: their dedication was, like Drake's, complete.

The crew of the space shuttle *Challenger* honored us by the manner in which they lived their lives. We will never forget them, nor the last time we saw them, this morning, as they prepared for their journey and waved goodbye and 'slipped the surly bonds of earth' to 'touch the face of God'.[21]

The address was written by Reagan's special adviser and speech-writer Peggy Noonan, who claimed that there was a fierce argument about that final sentence which quotes two fragments from the poem 'High Flight' by the American aviator John Gillespie Magee Jr (who was himself killed in a crash during the Second World War). According to Noonan, a member of Reagan's national security team tried to get it replaced with a more general line about 'reaching out and touching someone'. Presumably they feared that Magee's heightened and obviously poetic language would come over as distant or old-fashioned, perhaps also that talk about God is always trouble – safer surely to suggest that the American people give each other a comforting hug. Reagan showed in his exquisite delivery why there had never been anything to worry about. By pacing and expression, he managed to suggest subtle inverted commas around the two quotations and thus to convey that Magee's words were, like the death of Drake at sea, a way of placing the dead *Challenger* astronauts within a wider history of heroic endeavour.

*

At the time neither the left nor the majority of the media knew quite what to make of Ronald Reagan and the way he spoke. Unlike Mrs Thatcher, who usually sounded as if she was spoiling for a fight and was easily typecast as a Cromwellian figure, fierce and uncaring, he pursued combative policies at home and abroad and argued for them as relentlessly as anyone, but was somehow able to express them in a way which seemed above and beyond confrontation.

If you are ideologically committed, you may find it impossible to believe that the rhetoric of a successful political opponent can ever be genuine: since the Greeks, there have always been people who were only prepared to recognise something as great oratory if they agreed with the sentiments expressed, and who have regarded all other rhetoric as trickery or rubbish or both. For some on the left, there will always be something phoney about Ronald Reagan's down-home fluency, just as many on the right could never warm to Bill Clinton's unique ability to weave policy wonkery and heart-on-the-sleeve emotionality into rhetorical wholecloth. But such critics were a lost cause anyway. Reagan and Clinton were too astute to waste time or words on them, or on those voters whose ideological orientation was such that they could never be won over. Their aim was to move beyond their own heartland to the uncommitted centre of the nation and it was here that their gift for attunement came into its own.

It is reflected in their reputations to this day. While Mrs Thatcher has remained a divisive and widely detested figure even in death, Reagan is by a wide margin America's most popular recent president: while his average approval rating in office was unexceptional (at 53%, less than both George H. W. Bush and Bill Clinton,)[22] a CNN/ORC poll gave him a rating in late 2013 of 78%. That other great empathiser, Bill Clinton was close behind at 74%, while George W. Bush trailed behind at 42% and Nixon at 31%. Of modern presidents, only the assassinated Kennedy was ahead of Reagan at 90%.[23] That figure implies support and affection for Reagan not just among Republican voters and independents but among many Democrats – this despite the deep current polarisation of the country.

It's hard to put this stark difference in public attitude towards Mrs Thatcher and Ronald Reagan down to policy or achievement. They may be lily-livered by the standards of today's Tea Party, but at the time Reagan's policies were every bit as radical and divisive in an American political context as hers were in a British one. The outcomes – economic success gained at what was, for many, a troublingly high social cost – were much the same. Some will argue that the different political cultures of the two countries are a factor. For me, although I don't know how one would set about proving it, the critical difference is in the way these two political leaders *spoke* to their countries. No one could deny Margaret Thatcher her intellect and fighting spirit but, as we've seen, she was a prosaic and intractable rhetor whose words and style were easy for her enemies to target and use against her. Reagan's tonal range and suppleness meant that it was only in his last fraught years in office that his opponents even began to get the measure of him. No subsequent western leader would be so lucky.

But we should note what has been gained and lost. Ronald Reagan's strengths in *ethos* and *pathos*, character and attunement, achieved brilliant results with both media and public. Instead of a handful of memorable one-liners in a political career, he and his team seemed to deliver them every week and on every conceivable occasion ('I hope you're all Republicans,' he said to the surgeons in 1981 after being shot). *Logos*, argument, which for a democratic leader principally means the exposition and advocacy of public policy proposals, is certainly still present, but is given less space and prominence and is almost always cast in strongly partisan terms. We saw how, even in Britain with its drier political tradition and a far more rhetorically conventional leader, a good line like 'the lady's not for turning' could crowd out much if not all of the substance. In 1980s America, against that constant stream of alluring and characterful one-liners, serious policy didn't stand a chance.

A trend had begun. Soon other forces of change – the challenge of political differentiation after the fall of the Berlin Wall, the full professionalisation of political marketing, the arrival of the Internet and the deepening revolution in news media – would accelerate and intensify it. As a news editor and then as an editor-in-chief, I would find myself in the middle of all of it.

4 Spin and Counter-Spin

Far from being calculated, his words spring from his spontaneity and are a mark of his great sincerity.
French education minister Luc Chatel on Nicolas Sarkozy, 2010[1]

Over the three decades since that night when Ronald Reagan sat in front of the camera in the Oval Office and memorialised the crew of the space shuttle *Challenger*, the centre of gravity of American conservative rhetoric has shifted. As we've seen, the language-world that he inhabited could be muscular, wry, unexpectedly demotic, but it still aspired to a conception of measured eloquence which stretched back to the Founding Fathers and before. But it has lost ground to a very different kind of informal, studiedly 'non-political' form of political discourse. This has its own antecedents in previous outbursts of American populism (for instance, George Wallace's 'I say segregation now, segregation tomorrow, segregation forever'[2]), and we can detect other rhetorical influences in it: the stylised hyperbole of reality TV, the knowing comic beats of the late-night talk shows. Yet in many ways it still feels novel in the context of mainstream US politics. It is not that it has wholly replaced the pre-existing language of politics – much of the time we hear a mixture of the two – but rather that it is seriously challenging it.

Recently we've had a chance to experience it at full industrial strength. Here is candidate Trump addressing a stadium of supporters in Dallas in September 2015:

I made a beautiful speech. I thought it was wonderful. Everything was fine. A week and a half later, they attacked me. In other words they went through – and then they lied. They made it up. I'm talking about illegal immigration . . . We have to stop illegal immigration. We have to do it. (*Cheers and applause*) We have to do it. Have to do it. (*Audience*: USA! USA! USA! USA!) And when I hear some of the people that I'm running against, including the Democrats, we have to build a wall, folks. We have to build a wall. All you have to do is go to Israel and say how is your wall working? Walls work.[3]

We can deconstruct this like any other public language. The super-short sentences emphasise certainty and determination, but build up layer upon layer, like bricks in a wall themselves, towards a conclusion and an emotional climax. It's a style which students of rhetoric call *parataxis*. This is the way generals and dictators have always spoken to distinguish themselves from the cavilling civilians they mean to sweep aside. Wikipedia aptly quotes Julius Caesar's famous summary, not of his invasion of Britain, but of his victory in the Battle of Zela – '*Veni vidi vici*', 'I came, I saw, I conquered' – as a classical example of parataxis. Today listeners are more likely to associate it with the successful entrepreneur or CEO.

Donald Trump's style of parataxis is almost infinitely compressible, as his intuitive mastery of the micro-rhetorical world of Twitter shows:

Lightweight Marco Rubio was working hard last night. The problem is he is a choker, and once a choker, always a chokker [*sic*]! Mr Meltdown.[4]

'Lightweight', 'choker', 'Mr Meltdown' – this is personal in every sense of the word, and written personally on the spur of the moment or dictated on the fly to a harassed staffer, if that last miskeyed 'chokker' is anything to go by. But it contains no less than three different summaries of the Trump view of Senator Rubio, each of which is immediately and eminently retweetable.

Alliteration, repetition, rhythm have been the tools of English poets from the author of *Beowulf* to Gerard Manley Hopkins. The bricks of Trump's imaginary wall in the Dallas speech are 'w's: '<u>w</u>e have to build a <u>w</u>all, folks. <u>W</u>e have to build a <u>w</u>all. All you have to do is go to Israel and say how is your <u>w</u>all <u>w</u>orking? <u>W</u>alls <u>w</u>ork.'

The passage represents a total rejection of the conventions of political discourse. It's off the cuff, or at least intended to be heard as

such – the last thing Donald Trump wants is for his audience to think
he is reading from a prepared script. At this stage in the campaign, he
was generally holding notes but seldom referring to them. The notes
themselves were headlines, not prose, handwritten in large letters.
Many political speeches sound like the work of a committee. This is
undeniably, truculently first-person.

And it's fluid, the words following a still-emerging train of thought.
He starts an idea – 'In other words they went through . . .' – presumably intending to say something like *they went through my speech and
twisted what I said and presented it out of context*. But this is exactly the
kind of whiny complaint which conventional politicians make, so
halfway through he drops it in favour of the far punchier 'and then
they lied'. Isn't lying what these political and media enemies are all
about? Cut to the chase. 'And when I hear some of the people that
I'm running against, including the Democrats' sounds like we're about
to get a paragraph attacking other would-be Republican nominees,
or the Democratic contenders, or both. But Donald Trump doesn't
want to waste time pointing out the different ways in which Jeb Bush
and Hillary Clinton are defective candidates. In fact he doesn't sound
very interested in other candidates at all. So he simply leaves it out
and jumps, mid-sentence, to the main thing on his mind: 'we have to
build a wall, folks'.

The passage is punctiliously immoderate. Professional politicians
have traditionally wanted to be seen as wise counsellors; mastering
the detail and carefully weighing up the options before making a
policy proposal; at least seeming to listen to serious objections made
to them by opponents. Donald Trump speaks as if the truth and the
right policies were blindingly obvious, and the so-called wise counsellors who claim that the world is a complicated place, and that policymaking needs to take account of that complexity, are idiots or in
somebody's pocket. Saying the 'unsayable' is the clearest possible way
of signalling this contrary stance. But for Donald Trump, stomping
on political correctness is not just effective positioning. He's found a
wanton ecstasy in it, a joyous spasm of indignation in which supporters
are only too happy to lose themselves.

The Trump style eschews any kind of rhetorical cleverness. There
are no cunning mousetraps like the 'death panel'. The shocking statements are not couched in witty or allusive language. His campaign

slogan – Make America Great Again! – could hardly be less original or artful. Everything is intended to emphasise the break with the despised language of the men and women of the Washington machine. There is a wall between them and you, Trump seems to say to his audience, but I am on *this* side of the wall alongside you. They treat you as stupid, but you understand things far better than they do. The guarantee that I see the world as you do is the fact that I speak in your language, not theirs.

When Donald Trump repeated his ideas about how to tackle illegal immigration in a later debate with some of his rivals, one of them, the Ohio governor John Kasich, rounded on him, saying 'little false little things [*sic*], sir, they don't really work when it comes to the truth'[5]. But polling suggested that many potential Republican voters thought that Kasich himself had been too aggressive in the way he had taken on Trump, and Trump's numbers continued to rise.

Earlier in this book, we met the Greek Old Comedy stock character of the *alazon*, or braggart. Donald Trump has the aura not just of this but of other, quintessentially American, fictional figures. Indeed it sometimes feels as if one of David Mamet's characters, say, had stepped off the stage and into what we must continue to convince ourselves is real life.

But, as the 2016 campaign has demonstrated repeatedly, it is a mistake to dismiss Candidate Trump's rhetoric out of hand. If he is a braggart (and he might wear that badge with pride), he is one with an astonishing ability to listen to and respond to the mood of his audience. He has single-handedly revolutionised political messaging, issuing statements and rebuttals and simply emoting around the clock. He has communicated ten times as much as his more guarded, more 'professional' opponents, filling the political battleground with his noise and drowning out their more carefully rationed utterances. The sheer volume of communication and Trump's willingness to immediately exploit what works, and ditch what doesn't, allow his to be an experimental rhetoric. He has been in the market testing words and ideas much more aggressively than his rivals, and learning and adapting more quickly as well. The most erratic and idiosyncratic presidential candidate ever, lacking the organisation, resources and self-discipline considered essential for success, Donald Trump has nonetheless rewritten the rulebook of American political language.

He may be a one-off, but the fundamentals of Trumpian rhetoric – the explicit rejection of the decorum and moderation of traditional political discourse, its replacement with anger, shock tactics and radical policy simplification, the fetishisation of tell-it-like-it-is 'honesty' as the only value in public language – can be heard in the speeches and slogans of populists and anti-politicians across the developed world. In the US, the Republican right has been experimenting with inflammatory, extremist rhetoric at least since the birth of the Tea Party, though many of those responsible for it now claim to be aghast at where it has led. Once this new rhetoric of rage would have been political suicide. Today it resonates with tens of millions of Americans, while – to them, but not just to them – the cadences and tropes which used to hold sway at elections have come to sound evasive, stuffy and remote.

British politics used to be more restrained but, in the run-up to the 2016 referendum on Britain's membership of the EU, the Brexiters adopted some decidedly Trumpian tactics. Immigration was their ace card and they exploited it ruthlessly, including with a poster showing a sea of refugees that was worthy of Goebbels himself. On their 'battle bus', they plastered the deeply misleading claim that the UK sends the EU '£350 million a week'. They dismissed warnings about the risks of exit from Barack Obama, Angela Merkel and other world leaders, not to mention the overwhelming majority of economists and central bankers, as hot air from hated 'elites' to whom no one should pay attention. Donald Trump endorsed their campaign – and cheered their victory.

Not that the Remainers were blushing violets either. War, economic disaster, the collapse of the NHS and the ten plagues of Egypt were promised in the event of a vote to leave. With every fact debated and every source of independent expertise rubbished, the public were left to cast their vote largely on the basis of emotion and a gut judgement about which politicians they trusted more – or distrusted less. In the end, the Leave campaign was able to tap into deep wells of anger and alienation in the towns and smaller cities of the English regions and Wales, and add many blue-collar Labour voters to the ranks of the traditional, mainly Tory, Eurosceptics. That was enough.

For the UK's elites, it was an almost unthinkable reversal and terrifying evidence of how far the country had lost faith in their world view – and their political language. Even some of the victors looked taken aback by what they had unleashed.

In the next few chapters, I will attempt to chronicle how, across the West, politicians began to abandon the formality and restraint of traditional political rhetoric and to experiment with styles which were much closer to everyday language, more direct, often more pungent, but less capable of sophisticated expression. We'll look at two critical interactions: the increasingly fraught relationship between the politicians and a media which has itself been experiencing headlong change; and the growing divergence of the language of politics from that of policymaking. But first let me set the political scene by introducing the heirs of Reagan and Thatcher.

A Good Day for Bad News

In the last chapter, we heard Ronald Reagan declaiming in front of a very real wall in Berlin in 1987. Two years later, on 9 November 1989, that wall was breached and within weeks Soviet rule in Eastern Europe came to an end. Soon the Soviet Union itself would break up. The Cold War was over and the West had won.

Germany got down to the task of the reintegration of its formerly communist eastern lands with trademark focus. Elsewhere on the Continent, victory in the struggle against the USSR did not bring a new unity, but rather an acceleration of the centrifugal political forces that had already made themselves felt in the last years of the Cold War. In Italy, the investigation known as Mani Pulite ('Clean Hands') precipitated the final collapse of the venal and discredited political structures of the post-war era. The arrival of the Second Republic in 1994 did not bring stability, however, but further fragmentation of left and right and a window of opportunity for one of the first of the new populists, Silvio Berlusconi. In France, the fiercely anti-communist socialist François Mitterrand remained president until 1995. His reputation was to suffer in subsequent years as the extent of his instrumentality and cynicism as a political operator came to light, not to mention questions about his activity in Vichy France and his government's collusion in the 1994 genocide in Rwanda. In office Mitterrand quickly abandoned his socialist agenda for the country in the face of economic headwinds. Long years of gradualism followed, including two spells of *cohabitation* when he was forced to govern with a parliament controlled by the right. Mitterand was succeeded by a conservative centrist, Jacques Chirac, who campaigned on a platform of reducing government spending and lowering taxes, but as president soon found himself cohabiting as well. He achieved few of the reforms he had promised. The next president, Nicolas Sarkozy, had been a controversial and outspoken interior minister, cordially disliked by the left. He too promised significant economic and social reform but, especially after the global financial crisis erupted in 2008, backed down and governed much as his predecessors.

Unlike America, but in common with most European countries, Britain began the 1990s still feeling the sharp effects of recession. The political execution of Margaret Thatcher and the selection of a far less forbidding successor in the form of John Major enabled the Tories to hang on for most of the decade, but the bitterness and hatred of the Thatcher years remained, especially in the Midlands, the North of England, and in Scotland and Wales. She entered folk memory as a horror-movie bogeyman, while the Conservatives found that, for much of the UK they had become 'the nasty party'. Politics and the coverage of politics became nasty too, and remained nasty even after the long economic boom began with the UK's ejection from the European Exchange Rate Mechanism (a precursor to the euro) in 1992. Like one of Shakespeare's unhappy English monarchs, John Major struggled with one political rebellion after another, and off-the-record disloyalty – Tories claiming that honesty or their conscience required them to stab their own colleagues in the back rather than attack the opposition – became the norm.

That opposition was becoming much more professional. Tony Blair was elected Labour leader in 1994. The party had already been out of power for fifteen years and was desperate to get back into government. Their new leader capitalised on the progress made by two predecessors, Neil Kinnock and John Smith, and convinced it to move to the ideological centre. Old differences were put aside for the time being. Tony Blair tried to give this new positioning the mark of permanence with one of the simplest rhetorical expedients of all: he renamed his party. From now on, it would be New Labour, the word 'New' suggesting youth, freshness, open-mindedness, modernity (all words which the public might well associate with the young Mr Blair himself). Implicitly, however, the new brand also condemned 'old' Labour whose failed policies and dated class-based messages had cost it the previous three general elections.

New Labour was an exercise in what, around this time, Bill Clinton's sometime adviser Dick Morris started to describe as *triangulation*. Here he explains it in an interview with the PBS programme *Frontline* in 2000:

> Take the best from each party's agenda, and come to a solution some-where above the positions of each party. So from the left, take the idea that we need day care and food supplements for people on welfare. From the right, take the idea that they have to work for a living, and that there are time limits. But discard the nonsense of the left, which is that there shouldn't be work requirements; and the nonsense of the right, which is you should punish single mothers. Get rid of the garbage of each position, that the people didn't believe in; take the best from each position; and move up to a third way. And that became a triangle, which was triangulation.[6]

That phrase 'move *up* to a third way' is significant. The triangulator sees him or herself at an Olympian point *above* the two old positions. This was exactly what Tony Blair had in mind: to combine Margaret Thatcher's faith in markets and in the reforming power of deregula-tion with a leftist's concern for social justice and inclusion. Conservative disregard for the less well-off and old Labour pipe dreams about compulsory egalitarianism could both be consigned to the recycling bin.

In the mid-1990s, the electoral advantages of this 'third way' were overwhelming in both Britain and America. But triangulation has a weakness. For all their faults, the two old positions – in Britain, free-market conservatism and traditional socialism – are ideologically settled. Each has its literature, its dyed-in-the-wool supporters, its own robust internal logic. The triangulator's eyrie high above them has none of these. From it, he seeks to command politics by driving a wedge through the ideological middle, but is vulnerable from both left and right. And like any exercise in splitting the difference, the policy choices can feel arbitrary – why strike the balance *here* rather than *there*? In the mid-1990s, against the backdrop of economic success and a manageable international scene, triangulation looked like the politics of the future. A decade later, many voters would ask themselves if it had ever added up to anything more than tactical opportunism.

Triangulation was a more radical challenge to the divisiveness of purist left–right democratic politics than Butskellism. If that had been pragmatic and transient – an echo of the government of national unity which had won the Second World War – this was an attempt to supplant the politics of ideological division and push them permanently to the edges of national life. The Blairite 'third way' had a genuine policy agenda, but we can also think of it as an attempt to replace one rhetoric – the acrimonious and futile wrangling of the Thatcher years – with another. Instead of insults hurled across an unbridgeable ideological gulf, the triangulator's synthesis would be made real for the public by a new way of talking about policy. There is no better example than that early rhetorical *coup de main* by Tony Blair, that a future Labour government would be 'tough on crime, tough on the causes of crime'.

This sophisticated new note was hard to strike consistently, however, and for traditionalists it could sound suspiciously like dalliance with the enemy. Tony Blair and his team had observed the disastrous result of mixed messages both for their own party and for the Major government, and had witnessed the glee with which the British media seized on anything which could be interpreted as a sign of party disunity. They also knew that – notwithstanding triangulation – in office they would face an overwhelmingly hostile conservative press.

So they decided to take a new, far more tough-minded approach to communications. From now on, there would be a comms strategy and a grid – a chart plotting everyone's speaking calendars so that they could be compared and coordinated. Every political message, whether offensive or defensive, would be conceived and refined to further the government's overall strategy. It would then be dropped into the optimal spot in the grid, so that the words came from the right lips in the right place at just the right moment. The room for manoeuvre in communications which individual politicians and government departments had historically enjoyed would be curtailed. And there would be sanctions: anyone who spoke out of turn would not just lose the political backing of No. 10, but would also find themselves being actively briefed against and, if necessary, despatched to the outer darkness of the back benches. To enforce the new regime, Tony Blair appointed Alastair Campbell, a former tabloid political editor, as his head of communications and strategy. He would do the job with brilliance and an air of savage righteousness.

In opposition and in the early years of government, the Blair–Campbell approach was astonishingly successful. Tony Blair and his political partner Gordon Brown ran circles around John Major's battle-weary troops. In 1997, Tony Blair arrived in Downing Street amid great public optimism and, in those first few months in power, displayed a preternaturally confident touch with the media. He negotiated the tricky aftermath of the death of Princess Diana ('the people's princess' he called her on the morning of her death) with delicacy and grip. Then he and his advisers decided to stake his personal political prestige on direct involvement in peace talks in Northern Ireland, previously an elephants' graveyard of British political reputations. The graciousness and generosity with which he negotiated and promoted the Good Friday Agreement positioned him perfectly as a statesman who could soar above the political fray and reconcile the irreconcilable. He had another memorable (if unintentionally hilarious) one-liner ready when the Agreement was finally reached: 'A day like today is not a day for sound bites really, but I feel the hand of history on our shoulders.'[7]

Yet over time the way in which he and Alastair Campbell sought to choreograph the story of the government *became* the story. This was not the first regime to endlessly re-release good news, kowtow to newspaper proprietors, or ruthlessly sacrifice its own ministers when a damaging story ran for too many news cycles. But the weird combination of professionalism and paranoia with which the Blair government sought to guard its narrative felt new and decidedly alien, a break with a – now misremembered and romanticised – tradition of impromptu heartfelt eloquence, dazzling wit and endearing British fallibility.

Blair's people believed, and said quite freely if one challenged them, that the new tactics were the only credible response to an unremittingly hostile media environment. That claim was hard to dismiss. Unfortunately the effect was to make, not just the conservative newspapers, but more or less the whole of the media doubt every word they said. The new government's response to that mounting scepticism was to redouble their efforts to control the message.

An incident in 2001 crystallised the feeling that official news management had taken on a disturbing life of its own. On the day of 9/11, Jo Moore, an adviser to one of Tony Blair's ministers and a former chief press officer of the Labour Party, sent an email to the press team in the ministry responsible for transport, local government and the regions, saying: 'It is now a very good day to get anything out we want to bury. Councillors' expenses?' Given the thousands of innocents who were losing their lives at that moment in the World Trade Center, it was a grotesque suggestion, one which seemed to speak of a loss of moral bearings, not just by a single political operative, but by an entire government.

Spin was the term used to describe this. It's an American word which originally referred to one particular form of media manipulation – proactive off-the-record briefings by so-called 'spin doctors' to encourage journalists to adopt the preferred interpretation of a given political statement or event – but it came to be associated with the whole bag of tricks. Many of the techniques were as old as the hills. Political discourse has always been manifold, the official speechifying accompanied by a quiet word in the right ear, the planting of the right rumour or joke. But the obsessive and hostile coverage of Blair-era spin meant that many members of the public became fully aware of it for the first time.

The new approach to communications might irritate the media and trouble the public, but not enough to blight New Labour's upward path. Tony Blair won a second election easily in 2001 and moved confidently into another term. At this point, observers could have been forgiven for asking themselves why such a successful government felt it needed to spin quite so hard.

But then 9/11 happened, Britain joined the American-led war against al-Qaeda and the Taliban in Afghanistan and, by the middle of 2002, it was clear that Tony Blair's government was also contemplating joining the United States in a second war to unseat the dictator Saddam Hussein in Iraq. The government justified the war on the basis of evidence about Saddam Hussein's supposed weapons of mass destruction (or WMD) which famously turned out to be false.

Insensitive emails are one thing. Invading a country on the basis of unjustified claims about non-existent security threats is another. Once the gulf between the government's claims about Saddam and the reality became apparent, Tony Blair and his colleagues suffered a loss of credibility from which they would never recover. It was characteristic of this astonishingly focused and energetic team, however, that they would never stop trying to do just that. One of the countermeasures that Alastair Campbell and the prime minister's political strategist and marketing guru, Philip Gould, now deployed in earnest was an unconventional approach to TV appearances by the prime minister which they had first experimented with in the noisy run-up to the Iraq war: the *masochism strategy*.

This was a response to the realisation that the bond of trust between leader and audience (the bond of *ethos* and *pathos*) was at breaking point, specifically because the public had come to believe that Tony Blair was so set on his course that he was no longer listening to them and was incapable of course-correction. It was a conviction that this process had passed the point of no return that had prompted the Conservatives to replace Margaret Thatcher as prime minister in 1990. The masochism strategy aimed to forestall such an outcome by offering up Blair for a confrontation with critical citizens on live TV where he would have no choice but to listen, and to be seen to listen. If the masochists had been around in the early 1980s, they would have regarded Mrs Thatcher's *Belgrano* confrontation on *Nationwide* not as a PR mistake but as a heaven-sent opportunity. By Tony Blair's final election campaign in 2007, masochism had become a central communications doctrine. Here's one of Blair's biographers, Anthony Seldon:

> A key campaign strategy was to expose Blair to as much media publicity as possible and show him confronting his critics. The party's 'war' book, the bible on how the election should be fought, said that 'TB must connect with the electorate, particularly with the hard-working majority, and make it clear he is not abandoning them' . . . opportunities were positively sought for him to appear on television and admit 'we've made mistakes, we can do better and I'm aware of that'. Campbell and Gould thought it important for him to be seen to be 'taking some hits'.[8]

During the campaign Tony Blair repeatedly found himself under fire on live TV from members of the public on topics ranging from Iraq to the NHS to income inequality. He patiently defended the detail of government policy, but the purpose of the exercise was at least as much about *ethos* as it was about *logos*. Here is a leader, his presence seemed to say, with the courage to stand up to his critics, and the humility to listen as they read out the charge sheet. He took great care throughout to look people in the eye, to let them speak without excessive interruption, to find a way of responding without belittling them or suggesting superior intelligence. He never forgot anyone's name.

The pop psychology may be straightforward, but this is sophisticated political messaging which adds a layer of soft subliminal rhetoric – the gutsy but empathetic leader willing to take the heat in his effort to understand and convince the public – to the traditional layer of policy advocacy. 'Winning' is no longer just, maybe not even mainly, about winning the argument as such, but about re-establishing a mood of sufficient mutual trust that the argument can at least begin to be heard: *ethos, pathos, logos* in that order.

You can debate which you prefer: the angular, patronising but unselfconsciously authentic voice of Margaret Thatcher talking to Diana Gould on *Nationwide* in 1983, or the carefully composed humility of the listening Tony Blair a generation later. But you cannot deny that the second represented, for good or ill, an innovation in the marketing of political leaders or, to use a term coined by Vladimir Putin's sometime media adviser, Gleb Pavlovsky, an advance in *political technology*. Today it features as a defensive tactic in communications playbooks across the western world. When President Obama decided in January 2016 to use his executive powers to introduce new gun controls without congressional support, it was inevitable that a few days later he would make himself available to be grilled on live TV by gun supporters – indeed, he criticised the National Rifle Association for refusing to take the opportunity to face him down in front of the cameras.

But counter-spin, which is what the masochism strategy adds up to, is really just a variant of spin, based on the same research techniques, the same marketing insights, devised by the same experts. It speaks to the absence of manipulation – look, no hands – but is of course itself exquisitely spun. For that reason, it can succeed in dispelling press and public scepticism about government messaging only in specific political circumstances, and only momentarily.

The masochism strategy was predicated on another bleak conclusion by the comms experts – that conventional media had become so hostile that they should take every opportunity to circumvent it entirely. Better to be confronted by a group of angry but still biddable members of the public than by one of the broadcast media's professional hit men. In the UK, this instinct to circumvent the media whenever possible would survive the Blair and Brown governments. Before he became prime minister, David Cameron said to me that he could no longer see why any public figure agreed to be interviewed by the BBC *Newsnight* anchor, Jeremy Paxman; it had become a 'snuff movie for politicians'.

But the attempt to re-establish trust by establishing a direct dialogue with the public went much wider. Town-hall formats, more or less choreographed, became increasingly popular in election campaigns. Even between elections, governments and opposition parties would attempt to draw the public into discussions about policy choices, in exercises like Tony Blair's 'Big Conversation', a roadtrip during which he and other ministers were supposed to listen to citizen perspectives on public policy. Petitions – now e-petitions – which for centuries had been an informal part of political life became officially sanctioned with the guarantee that, if a certain threshold of names was reached, a parliamentary debate would follow.

When David Cameron came to power in 2010, his director of strategy Steve Hilton arrived in No. 10 with a fresh set of ideas about how to draw government and people closer together. Instead of traditional policy levers and paternalistic public information campaigns, ministers would use insights from social psychology and behavioural economics to help drive meaningful progress on such intractable issues as poverty and unhealthy eating: a Behavioural Insights Team – immediately and inevitably dubbed the 'Nudge Unit' – was quickly set up in Downing Street. The government would also release vast quantities of data and make it freely available to the public on the Web. This new transparency would not only drive efficiency and innovation in public sector organisations, but promote citizen engagement and personal, social and corporate responsibility. Hilton's 'post-bureaucratic' plans to replace big (and distrusted) government with reform to be led and carried out by the people themselves called for the mobilisation of social entrepreneurs, hundreds of thousands of community activists and an army of connected citizens.

The army never materialised. Indeed little of this came to pass, and none of it – nor the incessant tweeting and posting, the websites and the YouTube videos – seemed to have the slightest effect on public trust or engagement. A somewhat frustrated Steve Hilton left No. 10 in early 2012. The Cameron government soon settled into a middle-of-the-road approach to communications, experimenting in the digital space, but placing much store by its inevitably more cordial relations with the conservative press. As for spin, while avoiding some of the wilder excesses of the Blair years, Whitehall and David Cameron's No. 10 quietly incorporated most of the techniques pioneered by Alastair Campbell and co into their own playbooks. Toned down and domesticated, so familiar now that people seldom remark on it, spin became routine.

The Clown and the Secret Policeman

In several respects, the story of spin in Britain is unique. It arrived abruptly – or at least that was how it appeared. It became a significant focus of political attention itself. It felt more of a breach with tradition than it did, for instance, in the United States where political communications had been professionalised much earlier. As a result, many members of the public took it personally.

But in truth, spin became standard operating procedure among mainstream parties virtually everywhere in the western world. Most continental European countries avoided significant involvement in the Iraq War and did not feel betrayed over the *casus belli* as many in Britain did. But the global financial crisis which unfolded from 2008, and the painful recession and public sector cutbacks which followed it, seemed to cast just as much doubt on what their elites had been telling them. Cynicism about politics is hardly new, but by the end of the decade, attitudes were hardening and anger was rising throughout the Continent and the English-speaking world. Citizens across the West who, a few years earlier, might have been prepared to put their scepticism on hold and give at least some of the politicians the benefit of the doubt, now refused to believe any of them. Even before that, however, in some countries challengers had emerged who sought to distinguish themselves by the way they spoke and to reject the carefully constructed and focus-grouped language of the incumbent parties in favour of something more earthy and immediate.

Let's return to Italy. In the last chapter, we heard Pier Paolo Pasolini calling for a new unifying technological public language for the country. In his book *Language and Society in a Changing Italy*, the academic Arturo Tosi charts what actually happened to political rhetoric in Italy in the last years of the consensus and in its chaotic aftermath. Traditional orotundity and abstraction increasingly gave way not to a dispassionate language of plain facts and rational policies but to the vivid and the demotic. Political statements became more direct and less coded. Slogans, typically pugnacious and memorable, often took centre stage: 'Thieving Rome, the [Lombard] League will not forgive you.'[9] Bloodcurdling, if faintly camp, military metaphors began to abound, especially on the right ('We're oiling the Kalashnikovs' was one contribution from Umberto Bossi of the Northern League[10]), while an argot based on Italy's national sporting obsession became popular with politicians of every political stripe:

I'm still warming up on the edge of the field, with my kit on. (Silvio Berlusconi)

In my opinion our position is not offside. (Fausto Bertinotti, Neocommunist Party)

They've put me into reserve, off the pitch and that's where I'm staying. (Giulio Andreotti, Christian Democrat, former prime minister)[11]

This is a public language aimed at the common man and woman, though scarcely as Pasolini imagined it: it is the language of the TV blaring in the corner of the living room or behind the bar; the language of supposed popular authenticity; and, at least in the mouths of male politicians, of clicheic Italian virility.

More than any other modern Italian political figure, Silvio Berlusconi typified the new rhetoric. Admirers would sometimes compare him to Reagan and Thatcher, the brave free-marketeer with the courage to take on and sweep aside a corrupt generation of trimmers. But in truth he lacked their commitment to reform, their zeal, their strategic consistency. Silvio Berlusconi appeared on the scene as a quintessential para-politician, a Trump before the fact: populist, changeable, instrumental – and with a rhetoric to match. From his first appearance on the political stage, he was a predictable and assiduous fan of football and military metaphors, both of which fitted comfortably with his central presentation of himself as the masterly but plain-spoken businessman sent to Italy by God.

He had a brand marketeer's touch when it came to naming the many parties and coalitions he assembled over the years: Forza Italia ('Come on Italy!'), Polo del Buon Governo ('Pole of Good Government'), La Casa Delle Libertà ('The House of Freedoms') and so on. But in other ways his political discourse was more novel. Tosi (writing in 2001) identified several curious tics, including Berlusconi's habit of dropping courtly and consciously old-fashioned phrases into his speeches (*mi consenta* – 'if you'll allow me') and his unnerving use of the honorific when referring to himself in the third person (il Signor Silvio Berlusconi). Then there are the jokes. 'I am the Jesus Christ of politics.' 'Ah Barack Obama. You won't believe it, but the two of them sunbathe together, because the wife is also suntanned.' 'When asked if they would like to have sex with me, 30% of women said yes, while the other 70% replied "What, again?"'[12]

Whether the man himself would ever have admitted to a 'Berlusconi rhetoric' is another matter. For Silvio Berlusconi, the words 'rhetoric' and 'rhetorical' were always an insult – something associated with the old political culture he was trying to sweep aside. When he sued *La Repubblica* in 2009 over the ten hard-hitting questions about his conduct which that newspaper had repeatedly printed, he claimed that the questions were not just defamatory but 'rhetorical', when in fact that was the one thing they were not.[13]

So what is going on here? For many Italians, especially on the left, Berlusconi's erratic rhetoric was idiocy and nothing more. Many foreign observers might have been tempted to agree – especially as tabloid headlines and legal entanglements came to define both the man and the era. The phrase *bunga bunga*, used by the media to refer to the orgies in which *il Cavaliere* was alleged to delight, grew into a kind of maximal enthymeme itself, a world of pantomime hypocrisy and colour-saturated excess.

But one could make the case that what Berlusconi was in fact doing – with some craft – was to employ a heterogeneous toolkit of words and rhetorical gestures with the specific aim of forging and then maintaining a grand tactical alliance of the Italian right: at one moment echoing a lost politeness that might still speak to some older conservatives, switching next to the suave and modern managerialism of the billionaire entrepreneur, then to the voice of the strong man with its dog-whistle hint (always deniable) of the age of Mussolini, and finally to the language of the terraces of AC Milan – the old, the young, white collar, blue collar, big business, small business, the hard-liner, the semi-detached.

Even the jokes have a knowing, postmodern quality to them. Berlusconi resembles a stand-up comedian of the old school who has discovered that he can use his well-worn schtick successfully with a new, younger crowd who interpret his material as an entertaining and teasing attack on the boundaries of political correctness, the more risqué the better, while his original audience can still laugh along at the same blue jokes without being aware of the wink and the quotation marks.

And, despite the incomprehension and disgust of political opponents and the wider world, this linguistic concoction worked well enough for Italians to give Silvio Berlusconi two spells as prime minister. But it is a purely political public language, optimised for the briefest of sound bites and the bluntest of posters, and only capable of delivering the broadest of messages. As a means of helping voters to understand the choices facing the country, like the language of the 'death panel', it too turns out to be an *antilingua*, not an aid but a stumbling block in the path of understanding.

Silvio Berlusconi is often talked about as an isolated aberration but, as anxiety about immigration and Islamist extremism grew across Europe, other conservative leaders started reaching for similarly crude rhetoric. Perhaps we shouldn't be surprised that Geert Wilders, the leader of the Dutch anti-immigration Party for Freedom, should have taken to describing the Prophet Muhammad as a paedophile and a murderer. But by the 2012 presidential election cycle, even Nicolas Sarkozy, the sitting president of France, was stating bluntly that there were too many foreigners in his country. The left had been attacking the crudeness of Sarkozy's language on immigration and other issues for some time. In 2010, one of his ministers, Luc Chatel, had defended the president's rhetoric by saying that in these complicated and difficult times, the president was right to 'speak straight and true', and to refuse the kind of 'convoluted style and syntax' which loses both 'listener and citizen'.[14] The irony of suggesting that the right response to greater political complexity is less sophisticated language seems to have been lost on both Luc Chatel and his boss.

Russia's brief flirtation with something approaching open democracy ended in what one British Foreign Secretary called the 'drunken shambles' of Boris Yeltsin's presidency which ran from 1991 to the end of the century. From the start, his successor, the young and politically inexperienced former KGB lieutenant colonel Vladimir Putin, was determined to show what a different animal he was. Here he is in a 1999 press conference three months before he became president, laying out his strategy to eliminate the threat from Chechen terrorists:

> We will track down terrorists everywhere. If they are in an airport, then it would be in an airport. I beg your pardon, but we WILL hunt them down and blow them away even if we find them in the shitter. End of story.[15]

The pungency of the key phrase (*my ikh i v sortire zamochim*), which means 'we'll "wet" them even in the shithouse', made this one of the new president's most noted early remarks. As Rémi Camus, an expert in Russian grammar and linguistics, wrote in a 2006 article, the family of words denoting wetting and wetness, including the verb *(za)mochit* – 'to wet' – have been used by criminals and police since tsarist times to signal the spilling of blood.[16] *Mokroye delo*, 'wet business' or 'wet job', originally meant a violent robbery or murder. In the golden age of the KGB, it was slang for a clandestine operation involving an assassination. Svetlana Boym, who until her death was professor of Slavic and comparative languages at Harvard, told me that she thought there might be something else behind the phrase: a reference to a specific kind of hazing in the army and the prison system, in which Muslim recruits and prisoners are forced to defile themselves by being made to clean filthy toilets.

This is hardly parliamentary language, but that of course is the point – the new power in the land assuring his fellow citizens that he has the state security expertise and unlimited capacity for violence to get the job done. The fear of causing offence ('I beg your pardon', like Berlusconi's 'if you'll permit me') is for show only; *I know this*

world and I know what works is the real message. No one had ever
talked like this before. It cut through the conventional political rhetoric
of 1990s Russia like a knife. In future, the taste for brutality would
be more veiled. The air of menace would remain.

It tells us just how debased our attitude to public language in the
West has become that Vladimir Putin's rhetoric has often been favour-
ably compared to that of our own leaders. Why can't Barack Obama
speak with such clarity and muscularity, some conservative politicians
and commentators have wondered aloud. Perhaps they base this
suggestion on the altogether more guarded language President Putin
uses when he is talking to external audiences, remarks which are
blandly translated and lack the ambiguity and dark allusiveness of the
Russian he uses for domestic consumption. His critics in Russia believe
one of his greatest skills is the way he is able to deliver quite different
messages to audiences at home and abroad without the latter even
being aware of it.

Back in 1999, Vladimir Putin's rhetorical register was altogether
narrower. The president of a country must be able to strike a wide
range of notes, however, and so the circle around him, including
that self-proclaimed political technologist Gleb Pavlovsky, got
down to business. They were watching developments in political
communications in the West with interest, in particular the experi-
ments we discussed a few pages ago in what Putin's team started to
call *direct democracy*. How much better if, instead of the tainted, unruly
wrangling which characterised debate in the Duma, the Russian people
could enter into an unmediated dialogue with their leader! Accordingly
and to this day, President Putin regularly makes himself available for
multi-hour live TV programmes during which Russian citizens can
ask him questions on a host of different topics.

It's unprecedented – a Russian leader so confident, so open that he
is prepared to expose himself to anything the public can throw at him
and for far longer than Mrs Thatcher or Tony Blair, or any American
president, ever attempted. Nor, unlike those western politicians, does
he ever duck and dive. He listens attentively to the question and then
just comes right out with a thoughtful answer. Really the only difference between *A Conversation with Vladimir Putin* and Mrs Thatcher on
Nationwide is that President Putin controls the questions as well as

the answers. He controls the TV channels and radio stations which broadcast the programme too. The 'conversation' is better described as a dramatised monologue, the leader deep in dialogue with himself and finding much he can agree upon.

This is the form of accountability without the substance, the masochism strategy without the pain. When we contemplate the dysfunctional relationship between politicians and the media in our own countries, it's always worth remembering what the alternative looks like. You can watch it right now on YouTube.

Vladimir Putin tapped into distinct features of the Russian political scene – understandable terror of anarchy after the chaos of the immediate post-Soviet years, suppressed national anger at their country's defeat in the Cold War and subsequent marginalisation. But in other countries all sorts of would-be political insurgents were taking a demotic axe to the discredited rhetoric of the mainstream: nationalists and single-issue agitators like Nigel Farage of UKIP; hardline anti-immigration/racist parties of the right like the French Front National and the Greek Golden Dawn; new popular groupings of the radical left in Greece and Spain; protest movements like the Stop the War Coalition. All would tell their supporters that they had been lied to for years by the political establishment. All would claim to be speaking with a new plainness and candour.

But by now the public were hearing a similar message – about the need to replace deceitful spin with words of simple truth – from many mainstream politicians too. Over the two decades between the fall of the Berlin Wall and the global financial crisis, the public presumption of good faith between opposing parties and factions evaporated in many western countries. Established politicians got into the habit of calling each other liars and phoneys with almost as much vehemence as the insurgents. They didn't seem to realise that, as far as the public were concerned, they weren't just talking down their immediate opponents, but damning an entire profession – one of which they themselves were members. The fringe politicians and the extremists took up the cry from outside the tent. The media faithfully reported it all. No wonder that more and more voters came to believe it.

The near universal trashing of the regular language of politics creates perfect conditions for the true demagogue, by which I mean the politician for whom populism is not a means to an end, but an end in itself. In the shape of Donald Trump, it has become a central fact in the 2016 US presidential election.

Demagoguery has erupted many times before and has often sputtered quickly out again. Perhaps that will happen again, but we shouldn't count on it. The public fury which is driving the present surge of populism may be disparate and incoherent, but it is real and continues to grow. Political elites hope that the anger is transient, and that the normal service will be resumed soon. Yet the language they would once have used to calm things down is the very thing which has failed – and which now sets the public's teeth on edge. They've pressed the emergency button several times already, and nothing has happened.

Can the media ride to the rescue by exposing the difference between responsible rhetoric and the wild distortions and contradictions of the extremists? The Fourth Estate might like to think so, but for those who have already turned their back on the rest of the establishment, the journalistic mainstream presents not as an honest broker or a credible witness, but as another part of the problem.

5 Why Is This Lying Bastard Lying to Me?

Is.it becoming worse? Again I would say, yes. In my ten years,
I've noticed all these elements evolve with ever greater
momentum. It used to be thought – and I include myself in
this – that help was on the horizon. New forms of communication would provide new outlets to bypass the increasingly shrill
tenor of the traditional media. In fact, the new forms can be even
more pernicious, less balanced, more intent on the latest
conspiracy theory.

Tony Blair, 2007[1]

In 1970 the French philosopher Paul Ricœur used the phrase the
hermeneutics of suspicion to describe a particular feature of modern
thought. 'Three masters,' he wrote, 'seemingly mutually exclusive,
dominate the school of suspicion: Marx, Nietzsche, and Freud.' All
three, in Ricœur's account, detected a layer of falsity and deception
in human consciousness and utterance which must be torn away before
the truth can be revealed:

All three clear the horizon for a more authentic world, for a new reign
of Truth, not only by means of a 'destructive' critique, but by the
invention of an art of interpreting.[2]

The specific 'art of interpreting' and the nature of the unmasking
varied. For Nietzsche, it meant finally putting the moral and

intellectual legacy of religion aside and confronting the reality of human existence after the death of God. For Freud, it consisted in psychological theory and the use of analysis to penetrate beneath the conscious mind to the unconscious truth. Marx prophesied a mass political awakening in which the scales would fall from the eyes of the world's urban proletariat and they would recognise the struggle between the classes for what it was. According to Ricœur, the underlying narrative is the same. The truth is hidden. People are deluding themselves and each other. The seeker after truth must develop a way of interpreting, and thus seeing through, the layers of deception.

The relevance to journalism is obvious. What is a story? In the mid-1980s, an older BBC colleague told me the answer that every young journalist sooner or later hears: a story is something that someone somewhere doesn't want you to report. The quotation which forms the title of this chapter – 'Why is this lying bastard lying to me?' – smacks even more of Ricœurian hermeneutics. Over the past twenty years it has been widely cited in the debate in Britain about journalistic cynicism, and is often attributed to the famously scornful BBC interviewer Jeremy Paxman. In fact the line, which originally referred specifically to the risk of being manipulated by a politician offering a non-attributable briefing, was first used in the UK by the London *Times* journalist Louis Heren, who in turn claimed to have heard it from an unnamed American newsman. It calls for its own 'art of interpreting'. Ask yourself why this politician is giving you this 'story' at this moment. Explore motive, dig deeper, get underneath the words.

But the presumption in the quote that the politician is a liar – not just in this, but in all instances – gives the game away. The phrase is not a dispassionate piece of professional advice, but a declaration of permanent war between journalists and the political classes. By the end of the century – and whether you warmed to it or regarded it as evidence of a moral crisis in British journalism – it had come to stand for a relationship in crisis.

The hermeneutics of suspicion is not based on fantasy. Even those politicians, probably the majority, who avoid outright lies do often offer an incomplete or partial version of the truth. Many are also capable of what feels like a suspension of disbelief in which they seem genuinely to be able to forget early statements or actions which contradict the policy or image they now want to project. Donald Trump seems to have attained a unique Zen state in which random and rambling invention is truth, and the actual truth is a litany of lies cooked up by the pygmies who oppose him. And companies and institutions really do hide and distort things. They may be rarer and messier than in the movies, but sometimes real conspiracies take place. The journalist's instinct to challenge and investigate is a necessary one.

Even before the arrival of spin, however, the presumption of bad faith – as if we lived in, and had to report, a world where no politician ever told the truth and nothing could ever be taken on face value – had gone far beyond this for many British journalists. It had become a fundamental orientation, one so ingrained and unquestioned that they had ceased to be conscious of it. No doubt this extreme and eventually almost involuntary scepticism was more pervasive among journalists than the public at large, but there too a shift was taking place. In 1993 the author David Foster Wallace diagnosed that our culture had become permeated by

> sarcasm, cynicism, a manic ennui, suspicion of all authority, suspicion of all constraints on conduct, and a terrible penchant for ironic diagnosis of unpleasantness instead of an ambition not just to diagnose and ridicule but to redeem . . . It's become our language; we're so in it we don't even see that it's one perspective, one among many possible ways of seeing.[3]

You can decide for yourself whether Wallace is right about our culture as a whole. But I'm certain that this passage is an accurate picture of the professional world view of many of the journalists I worked with – not always individually or privately, but collectively and publicly, because to argue openly against these background assumptions was, and still is, to risk being taken for a dupe or worse.

A Bias Towards Understanding

Towards the end of the 1980s, I played a role in one of the most determined efforts ever made to push back against this prevailing journalistic wisdom. I was still at the BBC, and by now had returned to London and become a senior editor on *Newsnight*. This was a period when the relationship between the BBC and Mrs Thatcher's government had more or less broken down. A flawed 1984 *Panorama* investigation into extremism in the Conservative Party ('Maggie's Militant Tendency') had led to a messy and, for the BBC, disastrous libel action. A year later, the Thatcher government attacked a BBC documentary – *Real Lives: At the Edge of the Union*, which featured the IRA commander Martin McGuinness – as a threat to national security. Next her ministers argued that the BBC's reporting of a 1986 American bombing raid on Libya, which had received British support, had been inaccurate and partial.

To the government and other critics, these incidents suggested a journalistic culture which was arrogant, sloppy and shot through with left-wing bias. The BBC refused to accept that there was any systemic problem at all. The truth was more nuanced. Some of the attacks were preposterous, in particular the crass government assault on *Real Lives* which, disgracefully, the BBC's own governing body abetted. Nor was the charge of deliberate political bias true of the over-whelming majority of BBC journalists. But the editorial oversight of investigative journalism had been erratic, and there were occasions when, in the absence of an effective political opposition, the attempt in Current Affairs to scrutinise and challenge the Thatcher government came across as hostile. BBC News – which at this point was separate from Current Affairs – took its responsibility for accuracy and impartiality seriously but, particularly on the television side, its agenda often had a mid-market flavour (with the Royal Family looming large), and there was a lack of editorial depth and distinctiveness in much of what it did.

By early 1987, the chairman of the BBC governors, Marmaduke Hussey, had had enough. The director general and editor-in-chief, Alasdair Milne, was fired and the job was effectively split. Michael Checkland, a formidable administrator but neither a journalist nor a programme-maker, would be known as DG, but would in reality be a CEO charged with modernising the Corporation and delivering the efficiency savings which the government had demanded. As his deputy, the governors appointed John Birt, the ITV programme executive whose campaign to end 'the bias against understanding' we discussed in Chapter 1. His first task, in their minds, was to address the BBC's troubled journalism, and he became de facto editor-in-chief. For Birt, this was a chance to put his ideas about a new approach to news and current affairs into practice in one of the world's largest and most influential journalistic institutions.

A few months after he arrived, I was asked to move from *Newsnight* to the BBC's main television newsroom. Shortly after that, John Birt appointed me editor of *The Nine O'Clock News* with the brief to turn this flagship TV news bulletin into a model of the new journalism. I was thirty. If he was the leader of a revolution in news and current affairs – and both he and his critics agreed that, for good or ill, revolution was the right word to use – then this was its first call to arms.

And so with two close colleagues – Mark Damazer, another refugee from *Newsnight*, and Richard Sambrook, a rising star in the newsroom itself – I got down to work. From the start, we decided that the *Nine* would have a different agenda from every other BBC news programme. I wanted it to compete not with that night's news on ITV, but with the following morning's broadsheet newspapers. There would be more international stories, more and better reporting about economics and business, and no more royals, unless they were part of a real news story. The BBC had always had a few specialist correspondents. Now John Birt was prepared to invest in a regiment of them, including in new fields like social affairs. Critically, the big stories would be allocated much more *time* – not just a brief video report of the events of the day, but a second, sometimes a third package which would attempt to put the immediate news in context or to explain the underlying policy question. All of that might then be followed by a live interview. The idea was to do in the grammar of television what the most serious newspapers, and magazines like *The Economist*, had always tried to do – which was to go beyond the slavish reporting of events and to try to make sense of it. To accommodate all of this, and at a moment when every other broadcaster was trying to *reduce* the space devoted to news and current affairs, the whole programme would become longer.

The new version of *The Nine O'Clock News* was launched in late 1988 to a mixture of amusement and consternation both inside the BBC newsroom and beyond it. Christopher Dunkley of the *Financial Times*, one of the most distinguished TV critics of the day, wrote a scathing assessment under the headline 'The Nine O'Clock News

Goes Serious'. Far from welcoming the move upmarket, Dunkley worried that the 'more solemn, more austere, more didactic' tone would fail to satisfy either sophisticated viewers (who wouldn't need the 'Janet-and-John lecturettes') or the public at large. He also detected something inhuman in the new approach: '. . . the tone is not that of a friend passing on information. There is, rather, a sense of the tablets being handed down from some superior being to the hoi polloi.'[4] To Dunkley, in aspiring to meet the expectations of elites who already had access to their own appropriate sources of news (like the *FT* itself), the new programme was turning its back on its true audience, the mass of ordinary citizens whom the BBC was meant to serve.

In the event, the relaunch of *The Nine O'Clock News* coincided with a stream of exactly the kind of news events which best suited our new approach. Lockerbie, Tiananmen Square, the death of Ayatollah Khomeini, the fall of the Berlin Wall and the end of the Cold War all took place in the year after the launch and, with the time and resources now at its disposal, the *Nine* acquitted itself well. To everyone's amazement, the audience figures for the programme went up, not down. Partly as a result, the core recipe – specialist journalists, analysis alongside reportage, an agenda closer to the broadsheets than the tabloids, disproportionate airtime for the top stories – became the norm across the BBC's main news programmes and remains so to this day. John Birt's clarity of purpose and determination had achieved a permanent improvement in the quality and seriousness of one of the world's great news providers.

The critics had a second and more pointed line of attack against *The Nine O'Clock News* and the rest of 'Birtism'. In its most extreme form, this argued that John Birt had been inserted into the BBC by a hostile government with the express purpose of emasculating the Corporation's journalism, and that he planned to do so by replacing challenging reporters and presenters with harmless automata. The counterclaim by the most outspoken advocates of Birtism (which included some of the colleagues he had brought with him from ITV) was that this supposedly 'tough' and 'challenging journalism' had in fact been self-indulgent and intellectually incoherent.

Behind this debate, we can see two different ways in which a journalist might seek to get at the truth. We can call the first *forensic*. It relies on some blend of detection and cross-examination, which in the context of the BBC of the 1980s meant investigative reporting on programmes like *Panorama*, and kinetic interviewing on Radio 4's *Today* programme, *Newsnight* and the like. It is intrinsically adversarial, psychologically as well methodologically: it is prone to see the subject of a certain kind of story as the *target*, and to pursue them accordingly. The second is *analytical*. It gathers facts, data, opinions and processes them dispassionately into a rational account of our current knowledge of the story, the range of options facing the protagonists, the likely outcomes, and so on. This second approach had been John Birt's trademark at ITV, and was indeed now his central ambition for journalism at the BBC as well.

Of course, there was never any doubt which was the more glamorous of the two. The romance of the investigative journalist was well established by the 1960s – think of the courageous young reporter in Costa-Gavras's film *Z* – but it was real-world events, the Pentagon Papers and Watergate, that brought it to a peak. By the 1980s, if you thought of investigative journalists, the faces that came to mind were those of Robert Redford and Dustin Hoffman. And note the ideological orientation. Although in real life conservative newspapers like the *Sunday Times* and *the Wall Street Journal* had their own strong investigative traditions, in popular culture the prevailing narrative became one of liberal journalists uncovering the nefarious doings of right-wing governments. If you were a young journalist and you had a black leather jacket and a Nikon or an Arriflex with a telephoto lens, you too could uncover a crypto-fascist. (I'd had a crack at that myself in the very first piece of investigative journalism I took part in for the Oxford University magazine *Isis* in 1977.*)

Was it ever part of the Birtist agenda to undermine investigative journalism? It was certainly never part of mine. I came to *The Nine O'Clock News* believing it needed more, not less, original reporting. When I became editor of *Panorama*, I put all the money and resources I could into the investigations, which I thought were the *raison d'être* of the programme.

During John Birt's early years as deputy DG, when his confidence in the professionalism of the investigative teams was low, there were

---

* A 28-year-old Christopher Hitchens was our mentor.

occasions when I thought his approach was overcautious. But soon he came to trust front-line investigative reporters like John Ware and Peter Taylor, and editors like me, and continued to back investigative journalism when he became director general in 1993. Although his critics could never bring themselves to admit it – the rhetorical battle lines and personal enmities were too fixed and bitter for that – the ultimate result was, if anything, to strengthen the BBC's hand in original journalism.

Other trends were at work too. The character of the investigations changed. The stories required more specialist knowledge and became increasingly analytical themselves. Rather than running down a street with a camera crew in pursuit of some villain, the reporters now spent more time in the office sifting through mountains of documents. In due course, outstanding reporters arrived at the BBC – Robert Peston was a striking example – who were patently capable of delivering major scoops *and* delivering authoritative explanation and judgement on important running stories, and the whole premise that there was a necessary opposition between the Birtist focus on expertise and analysis on the one hand, and a full-blooded commitment to courageous investigation on the other, ended up looking shaky.

It was a very different matter when it came to the other main expression of forensic broadcast journalism, the adversarial political interview. The issue was never resolved during John Birt's period at the BBC, nor subsequently, and it remains a point of contention to this day. It also reflects one of the questions at the heart of this book.

We've already heard the case *for* aggressive broadcast interviews. Under this view, the public statements of politicians and other public figures are automatically suspect. The interviewer's central task is to puncture the interviewee's rhetoric and uncover the truth. If that's too big an ask, then at least the interviewer can expose inconsistencies, or a refusal to answer a question, so that the public can draw the appropriate conclusions. Seen like this, political interviewing becomes a heroic and manly form of journalism. (More or less literally manly, by the way, because in those days in the UK – though not in the US where such encounters tended to be less gladiatorial – the task of interrogating politicians was traditionally only rarely given to women journalists.)

But there is a case against the aggressive political interview as well and, a couple of years after he succeeded Michael Checkland as DG, John Birt delivered it in a set-piece public assault on what he called the 'disputational approach' and

> the ritualistic encounter which is little more, normally, than a brief opportunity to bicker, to exchange insults and to assign blame. Such encounters add little of substance to general understanding, and irritate our audiences.[5]

In this speech, which was given in Dublin in 1995, Birt went on to say that 'politicians have a higher claim to speak for the people than journalists'. Given the particular legitimacy which democratic elections confer on successful candidates, that statement might seem unobjectionable. But in the strained climate of the late twentieth-century BBC, it and the rest of the Dublin speech confirmed to the old guard, and to many media commentators, that John Birt was a better friend of the political establishment than to their conception of 'proper' journalism.

John Birt's call for a drawing back from the 'disputational approach' had no discernible effect on interviewing at the BBC. Indeed his claim that it irritated audiences was only true of some of them; there were plenty of viewers and listeners who thoroughly enjoyed a good dust-up first thing in the morning on the *Today* programme or last thing at night on *Newsnight*. Indeed, when asked in surveys about their attitude to the way BBC interviewers treated the politicians, far more said that the Corporation was too soft than too hard. A gap had opened up which would widen greatly over time. On one side of the divide was an elite who thought that the aggressive style was discourteous and damaging to public life, because it prevented politicians from talking directly to the people, and because it favoured heat over the light of meaningful policy discussion. On the other were most journalists, but also a significant slice of the population whose level of trust in that elite was already such that they thought that the politicians on the receiving end of those nasty interviewers deserved everything they got. Over the next two decades, this sentiment would grow.

I've described a set of trends that were already much in evidence, within but also far beyond the BBC, *before* the official arrival of spin.

That of course only served to intensify the atmosphere of distrust and vituperation between the press and the politicians.

Meanwhile, much the same story unfolded in the United States. During the period after 9/11 when an understandable spirit of national solidarity prevailed, most American newspapers and broadcast media accepted the Bush administration's claims about Saddam's weapons of mass destruction with too little scrutiny and scepticism. When they came to realise how badly they had misled their audiences, they decided never to fall into the same trap again. Those associated with the left gave George W. Bush no quarter in the final years of his presidency, while conservative news sources decided to pay the next president, Barack Obama, the same compliment. In common with their counterparts in most other western countries, they have all been living the life of maximal distrust ever since.

The news media famously likes to think of itself as a separate estate within our democratic polities, distinct from and thus able to challenge the political establishment. But more and more people – at the edges of politics, in protest groups, in the now rapidly expanding blogosphere – were beginning to wonder aloud whether mainstream media weren't themselves part of that elite. A growing number of citizens on the right had come to suspect that political correctness was causing the main news providers to suppress or distort coverage of immigration and crime, while many on the left thought they couldn't be trusted on big business, the economy and the environment. Add to this emotionally charged news stories like Israel/Palestine, with increasingly uncompromising and media-savvy advocates for both sides complaining almost daily, and it is unsurprising that a generic hostile narrative began to gain currency: the media claim to be impartial but in fact have any number of agendas; they accuse the politicians of saying one thing and doing another, but that's what they do themselves. In Britain, public confidence in the media – and especially in the popular press – had always been low, but now it underwent a further slide. Even the supposedly more high-minded public service broadcasters found themselves routinely in the firing line.

It had also become clear that we faced a paradox, not just about how best to conduct political interviewing, but about the wider challenge of doing justice to modern politics. Confront the politicians too little, and many listeners and viewers would conclude that we were in cahoots with them, and their faith in the politicians would fall further. But confront them too much, and we might also stoke public cynicism and disillusion. In theory, it should be possible to find a sweet spot between the two. As I discovered myself, however, when in 2004 I took on the job of editor-in-chief of the BBC myself, defining that sweet spot and guiding the institution's colossal journalistic machine towards it, was by no means easy.

Howlround

It's difficult to pinpoint the start, but at some point in the last twenty years of the twentieth century journalism entered its own permanent revolution. The story of media is the story of the age, and the drivers of change were the same. Digital technology greatly expanded consumer choice in news and other forms of content and, through new devices and distribution networks, made that choice available whenever and wherever audiences wanted it.

The cost of making and distributing many forms of content tumbled and in journalism, along with many other content categories, the barriers to entry came down. Digital also triggered a complex convergence between what had once been the largely discrete activities of content consumption and social communication. As a result of all these things, the business models of many legacy media were severely weakened or destroyed, while the conditions were created for new and quite different content companies to spring up and succeed.

For the most part, policymakers encouraged this direction of travel and declined to erect the regulatory obstacles which might have slowed the revolution down. The threat to traditional media jobs was immense, but the unions were in retreat and would focus more on getting the best exit deals for their existing members than on how many posts there would be in the future. It became easier to get a toehold in journalism or television – at the BBC, it no longer depended on the long odds of one of those graduate trainee schemes – but much harder to plot a career. More open, more casual, less secure and often – at least at the front line – lower paid: jobs in journalism and the media began to feel less like those of an industrial elite and more like other creative careers – trying to make a go of it as an actor, say, or a novelist. And disruption increased competition not just between newspapers, magazines and TV channels but within them. This competition between members of a more transient workforce, often with less training and less knowledge of, or allegiance to, traditional professional values, would lead to problems of its own.

But the most important effect of both the new technology, and the opening up of the media industries, was to put far more power into the hands of the public. In the era of constrained choice, TV controllers and schedulers had immense influence on what the public watched. With relatively few channels, even less intrinsically popular programmes could command significant viewing figures; indeed, schedulers could help such programmes by *hammocking* them, in other words by placing a less audience-friendly piece – a brand-new comedy, for instance, or an arts documentary – between two tried-and-tested hits in the hope that inertia would lend it viewers it might otherwise not have received. If hammocking was a tactic, the strategy was *bundling*. Both newspapers and TV channels proceeded on the basis that consumers would accept a package of many different kinds of journalism and programming, including much in which they had no interest, and which they would simply doze through or flick past, as long as they could find enough that they did value.

Bundling is still central to the strategies of many media companies, but from the 1980s onwards, first multichannel TV and then the Internet began to erode it. It became increasingly easy for people to find precisely what they *did* want and to avoid what they *didn't*. Now you could watch music videos all day long if you wanted, or never, keep abreast of the news 24/7 or avoid it altogether.

All this posed a question which has troubled cultural theorists for centuries: just what will the audience choose to read, watch and listen to when they can choose anything? By favouring the consumer, the new balance of power also presented newspaper editors and TV bosses with a dilemma. Should they accept that the world had changed, and abandon any hope of badgering refractory readers or viewers into consuming worthwhile but initially unappealing fare? Or should they stick to their guns, even if that meant losing much of what was once their audience? Or was there a sustainable position somewhere in the middle, a new form of hammocking or some new contract under which the public would accept a little of what they didn't want along with a lot of what they did? Would they notice the drop of medicine in the sugar lump?

Media editors, managers and proprietors were being forced to confront the same difficult choice as the modern rhetor: to give a more empowered, more restless audience what it wants to see and hear; to hold true to some pre-existing set of principles and objectives; or to venture out into the middle ground in search of some new equilibrium. The questions sound abstract, but the disruptions of digital made them real and much of my time as an editorial leader was spent wrestling with them and watching other media organisations doing the same.

The answers which individual editors and chief executives gave to these questions drove a wedge through the western world's journalistic institutions. On one side were public organisations like the BBC and America's public radio which were constitutionally required, and in some cases funded, to continue to offer high quality impartial journalism to their audiences. Joining them were a relatively small number of commercial enterprises – *The New York Times* was one – who took their mission to report the news 'without fear or favor' and with adequate resources just as seriously as the public media organisations, and shared their determination to consider the political, social or cultural *significance* of a given story alongside its likely *popularity* in deciding their news agenda.

On the other side were profit-maximising media companies, some of whom had once been able to cross-subsidise serious, but less audience-friendly categories of news like international, science and arts reporting, but who now felt compelled to concentrate on the content most likely to attract eyeballs and advertising revenue.

Sometimes the results were stark. The American broadcast networks had a strong tradition of international reporting. I saw them in action myself during the Tiananmen Square crisis and the first Gulf War. In those days they arrived on the scene of a large-scale news event like an American carrier group, scores of people, squadrons of cars, rows of phones open around the clock to New York. By the time of Benazir Bhutto's assassination in December 2007, it had all changed. She died in Rawalpindi, Pakistan but several US TV news organisations reported the story out of Baghdad for the simple reason that the continuing conflict in Iraq was one of the few foreign stories the networks *had* to cover. The *mise en scène*, the palm tree and the Kevlar jacket for the piece-to-camera, looked in keeping even if it wasn't actually the right country.

The news divisions had been under pressure to cut costs and, in any case, were shifting the agendas of their main evening news shows towards domestic news and human-interest features. Many newspapers in both the US and the UK were doing the same. Around the world, the foreign press clubs began to empty. The head of one US network rang me not long after the Bhutto assassination to ask if the BBC was interested in supplying virtually all of their needs in international news. When I asked why foreign stories had become less of a priority, he told me that there wasn't much call for them anymore: nowadays Americans tended to find the news from abroad dispiriting.

The story of newspapers was more varied in detail but essentially similar. Brutal competition was not new to the British national newspaper industry and, even before the Internet began to take its toll, 'quality' newspapers had started to prune the detailed reporting of political debates, religion, science and culture and the ranks of the specialist correspondents began to thin out. Once print advertising began to flee to digital and circulation decline steepened, these trends accelerated.

The structure of the American newspaper business is different with less than a handful of national titles and a tradition of strong 'metro' papers serving the country's major cities and regions. These metros had historically enjoyed near monopoly power in print advertising and many of them used the generous revenue which resulted to fund outstanding national and international, as well as local, journalism. But by the 2000s, their economics were heading south and, in most cases, their proprietors made savage reductions to their newsrooms. They relied more on stories from the wire and syndication services. Investigative journalism – which is both time-consuming and expensive – wasn't wiped out entirely, but it became rarer.

The newspapers launched websites but discovered that in the digital environment they wouldn't enjoy either the same reader engagement or the same advertising pricing power that they had in print, and consequently that revenue was going to be much harder to come by. They faced a multitude of new rivals on the Web, and their dwindling investment in journalism meant that they would struggle to compete with the best of the upstarts even when it came to quality.

With local variations and at different speeds, these structural forces played out across continental Europe and the rest of the developed world. The result has been a set of trends in the journalism and broader factual and cultural content that most people read or watch. Headlines, brief summaries, lists and other formats which can be absorbed in seconds have all become prevalent. Across most of journalism, stories themselves have on average got shorter. Partly for this reason, partly also because of greatly increased competition for attention, stories also typically tend to the maximal; the strongest accusation, the most baleful statistic, is the one that makes it to the first paragraph or the anchor's intro. Nuances and qualifications are likely to be pushed down the story or – because the stories are now typically so short – out altogether.

Across the media, moreover, *logos* has given way to *ethos*: in other words, the exploration of character – what the words, appearance and actions of famous people tell us about who they really are – has expanded, while the presentation of facts and arguments, even the arguments made by those same famous people, has shrunk. And, even within the realm of *logos*, there has been another discernible tilt.

To use Plato's distinction, *doxa* has gained ground at the expense of *episteme*. *Episteme* is Plato's term for true knowledge and understanding. For him, it belongs to science and philosophy and is grounded in the facts and well-formed argument. *Doxa* is opinion, common belief; it is what ordinary people believe, or could be made to believe, but without the same underpinning of evidence or structured argument. *Doxa* belongs to the world of rhetoric – it is the currency in which rhetors trade – and Plato's objection to rhetoric is based on his belief that it promotes *doxa* and denies or disables *episteme*. *Doxa* is also an inescapable part of democratic debate, and is therefore at the heart of Plato's objection to democracy too.

But in the context of modern media, *doxa* has powerful advantages. Opinions, especially strong opinions, appeal to the heart as well as the head, whereas *episteme* is a wholly cerebral affair. More importantly, opinions and opinion-formers can be a point of differentiation in a crowded market. Economics is not an ownable science and the *episteme* associated with economics, such as it is, can be accessed by any digital or physical news provider in the world. But, all things being equal, only one newspaper can have Paul Krugman as an exclusive columnist. And if Professor Krugman's opinions on economics and politics are of interest to many readers – as indeed they are – then they confer a competitive advantage on *The New York Times* which its rivals will not easily counter. It's not surprising, then, that opinion plays a larger part in the offer of many news outlets than it used to, nor that in some cases – for instance US cable news – it has to a significant extent *replaced* news as the core proposition.

Not of course that today's would-be opinion-former is limited to conventional news brands or settings. Facebook, Twitter and the blogosphere have created a limitless marketplace for *doxa*, a public arena in which your ability to get your opinion across is no longer constrained by the limitations of old media (the *Financial Times* and the *Washington Post* can only hire so many columnists), but simply by the challenge of being heard in the midst of a multitude in which everyone else is shouting too. Your fame or lack of it may count (*ethos*), as may the originality or pungency of your ideas (*logos*), but the power with which you are able to express them is everything. It may not look like rhetoric traditionally defined but in this new digital market place of opinion, the art and craft of persuasive public language matter more than ever. But what if you lack eloquence? Never fear – as we shall see later in this book, there is now an entire machine-world which can come to your aid.

It has been my fortune to work exclusively for organisations which have set themselves against these tides. As we saw, the leaders of the BBC took a decision to make its news more serious-minded in the late 1980s, and the institution has maintained that commitment ever since in its new digital services as well as on TV and radio. Meanwhile, during a period when other US newspapers have savaged their newsrooms, *The New York Times* has broadly maintained its journalistic strength.

It has more foreign bureaux than ever. Most newspapers, including such bastions as the *Wall Street Journal* and the *FT*, have reduced the average length of their articles, perhaps in the belief that, in the middle of a breathless modern life, even weighty news needs to be served up with what the hospitality industry calls *portion control*. *The New York Times* has moved in the opposite direction. Articles are longer than they used to be, sometimes much longer. When in 2012 the journalists working on *Snow Fall*, a multimedia feature about a skiing tragedy in the Cascades, presented their first draft to the executive editor, it was 17,000 words long. She still asked for additions. The editorial section of *The New York Times* is full of opinions, but the newspaper's sustained commitment to the presentation and explication of the unadulterated facts also marks it out, especially in fields like science, medicine and social policy.

Yet *The New York Times* is an exception to the general downward trend among legacy publishers. Nor, despite assiduously marketed claims to the contrary, have many of the new digital publishers invested significantly in original serious journalism. Most have taken their journalistic cue from the gossip columns of the tabloids and from the world of comedy and entertainment. Some of the work, for instance on BuzzFeed, is witty and fresh and speaks authentically to aspects of our culture, but news is hardly a priority. When they do cover serious stories, the new players generally commandeer the raw material from traditional media and rewrite it with more search-engine-friendly headlines and, of course, without the caveats and the conditional clauses.

Watch the enterprising young reporters of the digital and TV media brand Vice and you could imagine we are living through a new golden age of democratised investigative journalism and foreign reporting. Then hear the morning alarm on your smartphone and wake up again. Like BuzzFeed, Vice has real energy and creative flair, but it is first and foremost a sophisticated marketing machine paid for by legacy programmers and commercial brands, all desperate to demonstrate to bosses and clients that they can connect with millennials.

Most of the young people who work for the new publishers find themselves not knee-deep in a war zone or with the time and resources to pursue a heroic long-range investigation, but locked in a digital sweatshop, ripping off other people's work, making lists and chasing clicks, racing to keep one step ahead of the scything blades of Facebook's unforgiving algorithm.

Digital has had another effect, namely to accelerate and intensify the news cycle. People react instantly to news on Facebook, Twitter and other social media platforms. Having initially been baffled by this phenomenon, legacy publishers quickly became obsessed by it. The result has been a noisy feedback loop, the phenomenon which the sound engineers call *howlround*. A news event happens and, within seconds, digital space is full of reactions and opinions. Old media reports these opinions as if they carried real weight and then that old media verdict is itself propagated across the social platforms. When continuous television news arrived, stories would be 'called' – in other words, a settled view would emerge of the rights and wrongs of the matter – in hours rather than days. Spin was in part a reaction to this increase in news velocity. Now the time frame is often minutes.

Surrender to the feedback loop was based on a false premise, namely that the early signals emanating from the social media platforms were likely to be representative of public opinion as a whole. Unfortunately, as anyone who has had to moderate online comments will tell you, the opportunity to offer one's opinion on the news (and on people you disagree with) tends to attract a disproportionate number of the angry, the extreme and the mentally ill. The effect of ignoring the skewed nature of the contributors and treating them as if they were a statistically valid sample of the public at large often has the effect of exaggerating reaction and sentiment. That is then fed back into the loop where it provokes yet more reaction.

We will return to the question of Internet rage later in this book. For now, suffice it to say that the language of (often anonymous) unbridled hatred which the digital platforms have enabled has damaged public discourse in other ways. It often triggers an equal and opposite response so that an entire debate descends into vitriol. And it sets a new dark standard for the expression of strong opinion, which some politicians and commentators are only too happy to meet.

The Internet has also given the public unprecedented access to accurate information about their world and the issues we all face, given the will and the discriminatory powers to find it. The dream of a digital journalism and of an army of citizen reporters holding the state and society to account is not dead yet. But it is currently hard not to agree with Tony Blair's grim conclusion in the passage from his 2007 speech quoted at the start of this chapter: that when it comes to public discourse, digital has so far proven to be a false dawn. It was meant to make things so much better. When it comes to public language and constructive democratic debate, so far on balance it has only made them worse.

6 An Unhealthy Debate

Suffer or pay – the same old choice in a two-tier Tory NHS.
We've got to wake people up to what is happening now. These
are the first steps towards an American health-care system, [with]
English hospitals now asking for credit cards before they give
care.

Andy Burnham, Labour Shadow Health Secretary, 2013[1]

When we talk about public language and the health of our democracies, the significance of the politicians and the media is obvious. Democracy is a conversation between leaders and people and, whether we like it or not, it is the politicians who generally break the ice. Because only a tiny fraction of citizens ever hear politicians speaking face to face, journalists play a critical role in mediating the dialogue. They do not enjoy a monopoly – the Web means that anyone can read a policy document or political statement and broadcast their opinion about it to the world – but even the most gung-ho digital insurgent must admit that, for the time being at least, professional media conditions much of the political discourse that actually reaches the public: both *what* they hear and *how* they are likely to hear it, through the way it is filtered, framed and (depending on your point of view) distorted by political bias or some other overt or hidden influence. But I want to turn now to a third group of people whose interaction with the first two is also an important part of the story. I mean the *technocrats*.

Over the course of the nineteenth century, the social, economic and military ambitions of advanced western governments grew, and so did the scale and complexity of the duties they undertook. They also came to believe that, at least in principle, public administration should be carried out to a new standard of legality, rationality and accountability. They would need much larger government departments, and those departments would increasingly be filled not as of old with the untrained beneficiaries of patronage, but a new tribe of professional civil servants.

It was the German sociologist Max Weber who, early in the twentieth century, first developed a systematic account of the *bureaucratic state*, by which he meant an administrative system in which responsibility for devising and implementing public policy was put in the hands of specialists, with each expert working on policies and activities where they could best bring their particular knowledge and skill to bear.

The term 'technocrat' is often used to describe the experts in Weber's model. The word summons up an image of highly trained advisers and implementers, but I want it to apply to a broader group of people. Contemporary political office is itself largely managerial and requires ministers and other elected officials to master the language and the ways of the technocrat, even if they have never had the training which a 'pure' technocrat would have undergone. In modern democracies, policy formulation – and the language in which the resultant policy is expressed – is typically the product of work by politically impartial policy experts, ideologically committed policy advisers, and generalist politicians. In this chapter, I will generally use 'technocrat' to refer to politician-managers as well as experts, though I will distinguish between the two where necessary.

All contemporary policymaking in the West takes place in the shadow of two centuries of astonishing social progress. At first in Great Britain, other Northern European countries and North America, but ultimately across the western world, policymakers achieved feats of development and societal improvement unprecedented in history: population health transformed through clean water, better nutrition, medical advances and the building of community-wide health services; transportation, energy and communications infrastructures conceived, designed and constructed; universal education mandated and delivered; economic and monetary frameworks and institutions devised and implemented; basic pensions and welfare benefits provided for the old and the poor; and so on.

Problems remain, of course, as well as challenges which are either new, or at least give that appearance – cyber security is an example of the first, and climate change of the second. But the contemporary technocrat does her work with both the benefit and burden of knowing that, in most areas of public policy, vast strides have already been made. The benefit is the ability to build on prior success. The burden is that further progress is much harder to make. The law of diminishing returns applies and the net benefit of a new investment or intervention is likely to be more marginal than what went before. And, because in most western countries the level of taxation and the percentage of GDP devoted to the public sector are themselves live political and economic issues, departmental budgets are already stretched and in much of the developed world are actually shrinking; as a result, the absolute amount of money available for new initiatives is limited almost everywhere. Different public policy goals are often in tension with one another, moreover, and the trade-offs between them loom larger as the prospective incremental benefits shrink.

It was easier to make the case in the mid-twentieth century that London needed a major airport in the first place, than it is today to convince the public that that airport needs an additional runway. Now the rival demands of economic growth, noise pollution and wider concerns about the environment pull in contrary directions. The effort required to bring this second policy decision to a conclusion – the scale and cost of the research, the regulatory hurdles, the levels of political and public disquiet and opposition, the political capital required, the sheer length of time before a resolution can be achieved – is far greater than it was when the first, far more significant decision was reached.

To make progress, those who formulate public policy must therefore gather data and marshal their arguments with great thoroughness. Across the West, policymakers now strive to assemble empirical evidence and test hypotheses against it in the manner of formal science. But this evidence-based policymaking means that anyone who truly wants to understand the issues in a given area of potential reform must master vast tracts of information and argument. Since the 1950s, public policy development, and the task of training future policymakers, has become a major industry spanning universities, research institutes, think tanks and NGOs, as well as government and political parties, and it has given government departments the legions of economists, scientists, planners, statisticians and lawyers they need to march across the fitness landscape and identify, in each policy area, the precise grid reference which – at least in theory – represents the optimal trade-off between all the competing considerations.

Technocracy has its own language too, drawn mainly from the social sciences and the law. But mastering this tongue requires at least a nodding acquaintance with statistics, probability, cost/benefit analysis and accounting, not to mention a willingness to endure the weirdly affectless and dehumanised style in which many public policy documents are written. There are exceptions – the final report of the 9/11 Commission is a model of limpid, sensitive prose[2] – but most public policy documents remain impenetrable to the public themselves and, despite freedom of information legislation and ever greater 'transparency', the gap between the illuminati and Pericles' 'ordinary working people' has grown steadily wider. And yet precious few technocrats seem to regard the explanation of policy as part of their job.

Many were never trained how to do it, and even those who were may doubt whether their listeners would be capable of understanding them, given how intricate the issues have become. As their world and that of popular political debate have diverged and they've come to realise that few politicians are prepared even to *raise* the question of hard choices and painful trade-offs, some must have concluded that to attempt such explanation is a hiding to nothing. If the public are bewildered, then surely it is the duty of someone else – the media, academia – to put it right, while they get on with the serious business of working out what needs to be done. Not that many politicians are in favour of civil servants speaking directly to the public either; as far as they're concerned, communications is first and foremost a *political* matter best left to their own good instincts and yet another group of specialists, the PR professionals.

Cato the Elder defined the rhetorical ideal as '*vir bonus dicendi peritus*', the good man speaking well. But what does 'speaking well' consist of? Within and around government today there are two competing answers to that question which resemble the two different approaches to journalism we have just discussed. The modern technocrat aims to use data and logic to formulate and debate policy in the most empirical and logically coherent way possible. The politician wants to frame those same issues in as sharp and politically compelling a way as he can. While the first sees no rational need for ideological differentiation – just follow the facts – the second is understandably obsessed with it. Both may regard public understanding of the issues as a good thing in principle, but neither is likely to see it as an over-riding priority. When urgency is high and the potential for partisan advantage low – following acts of God, say, or when dealing with new diseases or other population health emergencies – technocratic and political priorities may align around simple, clear information and advice to the public. But such moments are rare.

There is a further important complication to introduce. When a politician enters office, they are liable to find themselves shifting from an approach which emphasises partisan persuasiveness to the exclusion of almost all else, to a position somewhat closer to that of the pure technocrat. Now our once bold campaigner has complex policies to propose and defend, statistics to marshal, above all problems and limitations to confront and excuse. As a result, and even if they continue to try to score partisan points where they can, their language tends to become more like the language of the professional drafters of those same policies, less vaunting, more expert, more circumspect. We can think of the language of a given politician zigzagging between the campaigning/opposition mode to the governmental/technocratic and back again as their career unfolds.

I am close here to Gutmann's and Thompson's idea of the 'compromising' and 'uncompromising' mindsets which we came across in Chapter 1, though note that I am contrasting two modes of political discourse rather than two states of mind, and suggesting that each mode arises from different rhetorical needs. The crowd listening expectantly to the candidate require one kind of public language; the audience of experts discussing an arcane matter of policy quite another. Politicians respond differently to each, not because of a given 'mindset', but rather because they are professional communicators and it is clear to them what the context and *pathos* of each occasion demands.

And so it is that even successful contemporary politicians find themselves trapped between two rhetorics. Often it is not their opponents' language, but their own words which seem to mock them. How easy is it to limit immigration or to reduce the inequality between rich and poor? During the campaign or in opposition: simple! In government: not so much. The pressure of modern politics and 24/7 media means that the temptation to promise the earth grows even as the room for manoeuvre in the tough world of real policy choices narrows. Those politicians who insist on sticking to the possible are inevitably accused of 'lacking vision' – thus Mario Cuomo's celebrated dictum that 'You campaign in poetry. You govern in prose.'[3]

Barack Obama is perhaps the most obvious example of the two rhetorics, *the change we need* giving way almost overnight to tight-lipped and sometimes testy managerialism. The word-worlds of Obama the campaigner and Obama the president turned out to be so different that it was almost as if they were twin brothers with contrasting personalities – the electorate voting twice for the passionate rebel, yet each time finding themselves stuck with a professor who, despite his undoubted intelligence and command of the issues, seemed somehow to have mislaid the unbounded sense of possibility and hope which had made him so attractive in the first place.

But the same cycle – brave promises followed by glum disappointment – recurs in all western democracies. It's not new, indeed it has arguably been the narrative of most executive political careers since Pericles. But the character of modern politics – the competitive bidding on emotive policy issues, the intense pressure to oversimplify to get the headline, the sheer complexity of government, the furious media scrutiny which greets any shortcoming – seems to have increased the amplitude, by which I mean the distance from the peak of expectation to the trough of disillusion.

When we think of political failure, we tend to think of failed *actions*, the policy that didn't work or the economy that didn't revive. But much of today's sense of betrayal is focused on politicians' *words* and the gap that often opens up between those words and reality. And when the public finally tire of all those broken commitments? They are likely to turn from the discredited incumbents in search of fresh faces and voices and a new promise of change. The cycle begins again.

But something important is getting lost in the wash. It is the public's ability to understand exactly what a given policy proposal consists of, how long they will need to wait before they see results, and how they should judge its success or failure. I want to illustrate the problem by returning once again – this time in a different political cultue – to the rhetorical challenges involved in introducing, debating and explaining health-care reform.

Health provision in most western countries is under strain. The burden of meeting the medical needs of an ageing population and of affording the cost of new drugs and procedures, the debate about whether health care should be provided universally and, if so, to what standard – these questions exercise health professionals, policymakers and politicians almost everywhere. The character of the debate varies widely, however, given the differences in provision and political expectation in different countries.

Twitter and Twist

In Chapter 1, we witnessed a battle by conservatives to prevent universal 'socialist' health-care provision coming to the United States. Now we will explore a British debate in which the political polarity was reversed. Britain already has a universal health-care system in the form of the much-loved NHS. The attempt to reform it was led by a Conservative health minister, Andrew Lansley, who was a member of the Con–Lib Dem government that took office after the 2010 general election. The reforms were opposed by the Labour Party, health-sector unions and some health-policy academics and specialists. But the same pressures were at work on public language as they were in the US, albeit not yet to the same degree; and these generally leftist British opponents of health-care reform would face a very similar rhetorical challenge to that of their right-wing American counterparts.

First, the policy area is fiendishly complex. To have entered fully into the debate, one would have needed to know how the current NHS system of commissioning and providing health services functioned; what the perceived strengths and weaknesses of this system were (itself a deeply contentious subject); the range of possible reforms or alternate systems and structure (to include the approaches adopted in other countries); the details of the Lansley proposals; and the evidence and main lines of argument with which to assess the Lansley proposals against both the status quo and the other alternatives. I asked one of the leading experts at the King's Fund health-care think tank (a 'pure' technocratic institution) how long it would take an intelligent layperson to understand the issues behind the 2012 Act and she replied: what sane person would even try? The task would become harder as amendments stacked up. There would be more than a thousand by the time the bill became law.

Second, just as in the States, some of the critics would find themselves having to argue against ideas and positions which were in important ways similar to ones previously promoted by their own political side. For years successive British governments of left as well as right had concluded that the best way to improve the quality and allocation of resources within the NHS was to inject greater choice and competition into the commissioning of health services – though, to respect sensitivity on the left about anything that smacked of marketisation, the word 'competition' was often replaced by the term 'contestability' when Labour was in power.

Betsy McCaughey and Sarah Palin had seized on Section 1233 and their spurious claims about end-of-life counselling because, even though it was peripheral to the Obama plan, it was easier to understand than the world of individual mandates and health-insurance exchanges, and therefore easier to distort. Better, it could be made to speak to wider – and more emotive – ideological differences between liberals and conservatives, and to what McCaughey and Palin claimed were the true intentions of the Obama administration. All in all, it was a much safer way of discriminating between the two political sides than the central proposals of Obamacare.

In the same way, the opponents of Lansleycare knew that, while the finer points of GP-commissioning as a replacement for Primary Care Trusts might provide hours of delight for MPs, peers and the charmed circle of health-policy experts, they were unlikely to catch fire with the public. So they too were on the lookout for aspects of the draft legislation which – even if they were at the margins – could be used to reveal what they took to be the Tories' *real* agenda.

In their view that agenda was privatisation pure and simple. So their goal – at once rhetorical and political – was to convince a significant proportion of the British public that *privatisation* was the true meaning of the Lansley bill. For them, it was a battle over a single word.

I want to look at one of the tactical battles in this wider war. This revolved around not an argument, nor even a word, but a number: 49%. The trigger for this debate was Clause 163 in the emerging draft bill[4] which read:

> [an] NHS Foundation Trust does not fulfil its principal purpose unless, in each financial year, its total income from the provision of goods and services for the purposes of the health service in England is greater than its total income from the provision of goods and services for any other purposes.

In other words, a Foundation Trust cannot make more money from non-NHS – presumably private – sources than it does from the NHS itself: commercial income in any given year cannot exceed 50%. In the shorthand of the debate, that quickly became 49% and it was this 49% limit on commercial income which, although never actually mentioned in the bill itself, spread like wildlife on Twitter and the Web.

But what does the 49% actually *mean*? It is hard to believe that a raw percentage, that basic building block of the technocrat's art, can have multiple meanings, but in reality numbers can carry a cargo of meaning every bit as rich as words.

To a Conservative, the 49% might indeed be seen as a long-term stake in the ground for the economic liberalisation of the health service – though, given that the bill maintained the universal right to NHS care, it was unclear where the new army of private patients to consume that 49% of health resources was ever going to come from. To a Liberal Democrat, the 49% was unintelligible in isolation from the system of checks and balances which they claimed they had won from their coalition partners. In reality, they claimed, Foundation Trust hospitals could not increase their private income above 5% without a vote from their governing body, not to mention scrutiny from the regulator. The 49% was just a backstop that in practice would never be needed.

But to Labour and many of the other opponents of the reforms, the 49% was of great significance. On 8 March 2012, under the expansive headline 'The Tories are disembowelling the welfare state – sheep-like, decent Lib Dems can only watch' – the noted columnist and social affairs expert Polly Toynbee wrote in the *Guardian*:

> On Thursday Shirley Williams led her erstwhile rebels into the government lobby to vote for hospitals' right to use 49% of beds for private patients.[5]

Polly Toynbee has simplified Clause 163 into a new 'right' which hospitals are being granted and she's reified the 49% and brought it to life by making it 49% *of hospital beds*. Some of the tweets which followed this column took this literally and assumed that the privatisation of half of the NHS's facilities would happen as soon as it became law.

A few days later, she used different language, suggesting that the government was 'fencing off 49% of NHS facilities to private practice', in a way that 'risks denying NHS patients their scans, services and beds'.[6] Now the 49% is no longer a theoretical maximum but a real minimum, a curtain which will be drawn around half the beds so that ordinary NHS patients cannot use them. We see again the *concentration* of the claim, the collapsing of a possible future into a certain present. And of course there can be no doubt about the intentions of the people who are closing the curtain: whatever they say, they are privatisers.

But meanwhile Shirley Williams was stoutly defending her efforts to, in her words, 'make a bad bill better'. She quoted Polly Toynbee's first article to delegates at the Liberal Democrats' spring conference, and went on to say:

> The so-called 49% is a myth or, to put it in non-parliamentary language, a lie. Either [Toynbee] just did not look at the detail and therefore is able to say that in the *Guardian*, or she did look at the detail and decided that tribalism should trump truth.[7]

And she went to offer this ringing denunciation, not just of her critics, but of the new forms of media that had apparently helped them: 'We are fighting an uphill battle for the truth, to be able to base people's opinions on facts, and not on the stuff they have presented on Twitter and tweet and, dare I say it, the new social network, which is known as Twist.'[8]

So what *is* the truth about the 49%? People often appeal for someone – the UK Statistical Authority, the BBC, one of those self-appointed fact-checking organisations, *someone* – to adjudicate definitively on arguments like this. But, although it sounds as if it should be objectively determinable, the meaning of the 49% is actually a matter of political opinion:

> 'When *I* use a word,' Humpty Dumpty said, in a rather scornful tone, 'it means just what I choose it to mean – neither more nor less.'
>
> 'The question is,' said Alice, 'whether you *can* make words mean so many different things.'
>
> 'The question is,' said Humpty Dumpty, 'which is to be master – that's all.'[9]

The case of the 49% is different from that of the 'death panel'. The desire of many Tories to see significantly greater commercial activity in the NHS was, and remains, real and the debate between the bill's opponents and the Lib Dems – on whether or not the other safeguards which the latter claimed to have won were or were not sufficient – was a question of political substance. For these reasons, to this day Polly Toynbee vehemently defends the language of the 49% as a legitimate way of bringing a real political issue to life.

She has a point. We can follow a more or less straight thread between the 49% and a hard knot of genuine political disagreement, and the arguments about the meanings of words turn out to a significant degree to be political arguments about fundamentals – above all, about rival philosophies on how best to run and protect public services. Unlike in the example of the 'death panel', the compression and maximality of the 49% are grounded in the kind of debate which policymakers have to engage in and where, in the absence of certainty of argument – or even of meaning (because intentionality is itself in question) – the listener must judge between the competing speakers on the basis of their assessment of the speakers themselves and their own orientation to the issue: *ethos* and *pathos*. We certainly encounter the imagery of the conspiracy theory – all those curtained-off beds – but at least the theme of the conspiracy, namely that the Tories want to see more commercial activity in UK hospitals, sits in the mainstream of the political debate.

Nonetheless, as a way of helping the public to understand the thrust of the Lansley bill, the 49% argument fails miserably. The imprecision of the 49% sits squarely within a wider ambiguity in the NHS debate which the opponents of the bill used ruthlessly to their advantage: woolliness about the meaning of the master-word *privatisation* itself.

Despite the strong public service spirit of the NHS, the reality has always been universal public *provision*, mixed public/private *supply*. In practice, the NHS has always relied upon supply from both publicly owned institutions and private contractors: the UK's army of general practitioners may well think of themselves as devoted public servants, but from a legal point of view what they run are effectively small businesses. In recent decades, numerous other services in the NHS have also been outsourced to private contractors.

Since the foundation of the NHS, no major British politician, let alone party, has proposed abolishing universal provision; what has been at issue is the question of supply and the mechanisms by which that supply can best be commissioned to deliver the universal provision. As we have seen, successive British governments have taken the view that supply could be improved both in terms of quality and value for money if the system of supply could be progressively *marketised*; if, for example, different publicly owned NHS hospitals were made to compete with each other (and sometimes with private providers) for NHS work; or if GPs could be financially incentivised to deliver treatments and services to their patients in a more cost-effective or qualitatively better way.

But over decades opponents of these reforms have tried to persuade the public that they are in fact preliminary steps towards the dismantling of universal provision itself, and the switching of some or all of the population from the existing tax-based system to a large-scale (presumably insurance-based) private system. These critics often use the word *privatisation*, politically charged since the Thatcher era, to mean either (1) market-derived competitive practices, or fully fledged 'internal markets', even when they do not involve private players; (2) a (further) switching of health-care supply from state-owned to private contractors; (3) the long-range perceived threat of the UK abandoning its commitment to universal access to health care regardless of income, in favour of a wholly private system, or a 'two-tier' one with high-quality private medicine for the better-off and impoverished state provision for the poor; or (4) some or all of the above. The use of the one word to bridge these different meanings implies that they are all necessarily connected and naturally lead on one from the other – even though experience from other European countries demonstrates that, at least in principle, that need not be the case.

How does the 49% fit into this NHS privatisation schema? In two ways. First and most obviously, it is an example of definition (1) above; the idea being that NHS hospitals should seek as many sources of income as possible and, if they have marginal spare capacity, should rent it out and use the resulting commercial income to invest in better facilities or services, or to offer lower unit charges to NHS commissioners for their 'public' work. In this sense, the 49% belongs clearly in the supply half of the equation. But the thought of a greater number of NI IS beds being filled with private patients can also spark a thought about provision – don't these extra private patients imply that the government secretly plans to make changes on the demand side and, specifically, that it intends to abolish or limit the right to universal health care? Nowhere in the Lansley bill is this even hinted at, but the thought of those 49% of beds and the vague spectre which the word *privatisation* conjures up, makes the claim credible to many.

What it doesn't do is to help the public understand the *actual* provisions and policy questions raised by the Health and Social Care Act 2012 – any more than the spectacle of an elder stateswoman and a distinguished journalist, both known for the seriousness of their thinking on social policy, trading insults about a number which does not even appear in the Act. It's worth noting that this was a bitter battle that took place not between left and right, but *within* the left and between protagonists who had previously been in ideological accord on many social issues.

Just as with Obamacare, there were two parallel debates about Lansleycare: a crude ideological one which proceeded with little or no regard to the specific proposals in the bill and which ended, as such debates almost always do, in an angry stand-off; and a sophisticated technocratic one which remained largely within policymaking elites and which ended, not with the view that some fundamental point of principle had been breached, but that the political process had so jumbled and weakened the legislation that it might now prove difficult or impossible to implement coherently, whatever its merits.

Some of their American counterparts had already begun to fear that the same might be true of Obamacare.

The Lansley bill was eventually passed in substantially amended form. But in some respects, the bill's opponents could be said to have won the rhetorical battle. Ipsos MORI found consistently low levels of public understanding of what was proposed – at no point did those claiming to understand the bill rise above 30%. By the spring of 2012 Ipsos MORI found that only 22% of respondents thought that 'the government has the right policies for the NHS', while the proportion of respondents who thought that the reforms were really about privatisation had grown from 3% in December 2010 to 15%.[10] That was always the word Andrew Lansley's opponents were trying to land. As for Lansley himself, he was shortly thereafter shuffled away from his post at Health. One failure, according to off-the-record briefings from party colleagues, had been his inability to communicate the rationale for the bill effectively to the public.[11]

We should note something else. Shirley Williams mounts a spirited defence of the Lib Dem position with some sharp catchphrases of her own, that alliterative and triadic 'tribalism trumping truth' line and her joke about the social network 'Twist'. But a rhetorical asymmetry has opened up: it is becoming harder to argue in favour of compromise than against it. In my time as a journalist and editor, I've seen the noun and verb *compromise* become a pejorative and the adjective *uncompromising* a compliment. To change one's mind is to execute a U-turn or, in the States, to flip-flop.

For some politicians in some situations, compromise is still possible. Everyone knows that formal coalition involves give-and-take, so David Cameron and George Osborne's numerous policy compromises and changes passed political muster. Even after the Conservatives achieved an overall majority in 2015, the two continued to enjoy some leeway in the adjustment or abandonment of policy. There was a price to pay, though, when the UK came to vote on the EU. And when ideological convictions run high – for many parties and for many activists in all parties, that means on *every* issue – to meet a political opponent halfway is treason. Anything less than utter certainty can sound – and I mean literally *sound* – weak or false or both.

So trying to 'make a bad bill better', though of course redolent of the give-and-take on which all democratic government is based, is now a risky thing to admit to in public. Surely the right thing to do with a bad bill is not to amend it, but to abolish it? In the case of Andrew Lansley's health reforms, this is exactly what the Labour Party is committed to at the time of writing – which probably means that the NHS can look forward to further waves of reform as far as the eye can see.

The Excluded Middle

Early in 2012, as the US presidential primary season got under way, one of Mitt Romney's advisers suggested that perhaps, if elected, he should only repeal the bad parts of Obamacare. The right reacted with savagery. Here's the blogger Erick Erickson:

> If a Republican gets into the White House and does not sweat blood trying to repeal Obamacare in its entirety (regardless of success), I predict the end of the Republican party legitimately . . . If the GOP takes back the White House, its voters will expect a real fight, not a half-hearted attempt.[12]

The most interesting words here are in the parenthesis – 'regardless of success'. Solidarity with one's own supporters is more important than improving a given piece of legislation. It is better to fail purely than only partly to succeed. Ranged against the language of nuance and compromise, the language of radical solidarity is simpler and more powerful.

But is this *really* a matter of language? Many people believe that what's playing out here is strictly ideological, and that the only reason why compromise is becoming increasingly difficult in Britain on topics like health, and is virtually impossible in America across much of the domestic agenda, is because of a gulf on policy fundamentals. But that, of course, is what an absolutist rhetoric makes one believe. For decades, the rhetoric of Northern Irish politics convinced all the parties that the substantive gap between Protestants and Catholics was unbridgeable; once the political leaders on both sides began to see a way of selling reconciliation to their supporters, the essential substance was settled in months.

In June 2014, Senator Lindsey Graham and Representative Eric Cantor were two of a number of Republican incumbents who were facing challenges from Tea Party insurgents in primaries. It was generally believed that the senator had a real fight on his hands, while Congressman Cantor was in no danger. In the event, Lindsey Graham saw off his challengers without much difficulty, while Cantor – who was at the time the second most senior Republican in the House and the heir apparent to the then Speaker John Boehner – lost badly in his Virginia district to a rival who was considered such a no-hoper that the main Tea Party groups had refused to back his campaign.

Cantor had been considered more of a hardliner than Graham, and analysts therefore initially struggled to explain why he had been ejected, while Graham had not; the result ran counter to the assumption that the more conservative a given incumbent was, the less vulnerable they were to rejection in favour of a Tea Party rival. Immigration reform was an important factor in the primaries but, at least on the face of it, that didn't make the result any easier to understand. Senator Graham had been an outspoken advocate of immigration reform, and had drawn plenty of conservative flak as a result, whereas Cantor's position had always been more cautious; he had never supported more radical measures like citizenship for illegal (or 'undocumented') immigrants and, though he *had* previously expressed muted support for more modest reforms, had ruled even these out by the time of the primary.

When Lindsey Graham was asked to explain why Eric Cantor had lost, he gave an answer which takes us clearly back to the world of rhetoric:

> You've got to take a firm stance one way or the other . . . The worst thing you can do on an issue like this is to be hard to figure out. And I am not hard to figure out on immigration.[13]

The same *New York Times* story which reported those words also included an interview with Frank Sharry, the executive director of a pro-immigration reform lobby group. He claimed that it was one of those issues where 'you're either for it 100% or you're against it'. According to Sharry, 'Cantor was trying to carve out a middle ground, but there really isn't one to be found, and he ended up speaking out of both sides of his mouth.'

This, I believe, is a better account of our dilemma than a simple tale of political extremism. A politician (admittedly one with solid conservative credentials in other policy areas) can carve out a maverick position on a given issue and, if he does so with sufficient conviction and consistency, can win the grudging respect even of voters who take a different view. A second can be both more doctrinaire and circumspect, yet can still come a cropper if his rhetoric suggests changeability. Cantor's crime was less about the policy itself, or about his position on the Republican political spectrum, than about 'speaking out of both sides of his mouth'.

What has been lost here is the possibility of uncertainty, of listening to others, of considering the evidence and the political realities and adjusting one's position accordingly. Ideology, values and policy differences are still critical to the story – though even they are more or less inseparable from the public language in which they are couched – but, to a significant degree, the radicalisation has taken place in the field of rhetoric. It is less that the policy centre ground has disappeared than that the zone of ambiguity and flexibility – that zone where almost all political progress takes place – has become rhetorically insupportable, not just between ideological orientations but within them, and not just in the traditional pragmatic political centre ground but towards the extremes as well. Now it's 100% or nothing.

7 How to Fix a Broken Public Language

> Most people who bother with the matter at all would admit that the English language is in a bad way, but it is generally assumed that we cannot by conscious action do anything about it. Our civilisation is decadent, and our language – so the argument runs – must inevitably share in the general collapse.
>
> George Orwell[1]

'Every February since 1940 I have found myself thinking that this time winter is going to be permanent', George Orwell wrote in 1946.[2] But the winter of that year was particularly bleak. The previous spring, while Orwell was in Germany covering the last gasp of the European war for the *Observer*, his wife Eileen had died during an operation. Now he found himself in a desolate flat in Islington with Richard, the toddler whom he and Eileen had adopted in June 1944. Richard was a consolation, but the responsibility of bringing the child up by himself was one of many cares weighing on Orwell. His own health was fragile, and that same February he suffered a haemorrhage. He was unbearably lonely. During the winter, he would approach no fewer than four young women with offers of marriage. All would be rejected.

The city outside his flat offered scant comfort. Last year's victory bunting was gone and now London was gripped in a long cold morning after. The fighting might be over, but rationing and the other domestic privations of war continued. Britain was exhausted and the fruits of victory were nowhere to be seen. The international scene was just as gloomy. The wartime camaraderie between the western allies and Stalin's USSR was a thing of the past: the struggle between democratic capitalism and communism resumed where it had left off before the war. In diplomacy's thermometer, the mercury was falling like lead.

In many ways, this is the world of *Nineteen Eighty-Four*: a numb, battened-down society, its people shivering indoors or huddled behind the steamed-up windows of smoky, overheated pubs: not yet recovered from the trauma of war, already fearful of the future. It is a world of impersonal and unstoppable historical forces, of communities turned into machines, of individuals who have been stripped of agency, yet left with an undiminished capacity to feel pain.

But as miserable as he was, this was George Orwell's hour. *Animal Farm* had come out in Britain in August 1945 and would be published in the US later in 1946. The book had turned Orwell into a major figure; soon no one would dismiss him as just one more voice on London's literary left. Here was a writer who resisted ideological classification (to his discomfort he would shortly be taken up by the American anti-communist right), and whose dark allegory seemed to transcend its time and political context. *Animal Farm* wasn't just about totalitarianism. It was about how we humans create and destroy societies.

For the first time in his life Orwell was famous. Publishers and editors had begun to compete for his services as an essayist and reviewer, and money – not a fortune, but more than he'd ever earned before – began to flow in. Perhaps with Richard's future in mind, perhaps to distract from his loneliness, perhaps because this really was his moment and the ideas and words just kept coming, he threw himself into writing. Between the springs of 1945 and 1946, he wrote well over a hundred articles, reviews and essays; he also began to plan the novel that would become *Nineteen Eighty-Four*.

One of those essays was 'Politics and the English Language'. Published in April 1946, it reads like an almost physical reaction to all that frantic reviewing; a cry of revulsion from someone who has consumed one atrocious piece of prose too many and, having sent the offending object flying across the room, is now intent on exacting revenge. But despite its brevity and informality, it is also the best-known and most influential reflection on public language written in English in the twentieth century.

The immediate reason for the essay's success is the fact that it ends with some practical advice on how to write well, or at least how not to write badly. Orwell advises against cliché, unnecessary use of long words, overwriting, excessive use of the passive voice, and pretentious foreign or technical terms. There were some then (and are many more now) who maintained that there are no 'right' and 'wrong' ways of speaking and writing, but a plurality of different practices each of which is as valid as the next. Orwell himself goes out of his way to insist that he is *not* proposing 'the setting up of a "standard English" which must never be departed from', nor even promoting 'what is called "a good prose style"'. And his final advice is not to take his practical hints too seriously – better to break the rules than to say something 'barbarous'.

But the overwhelming majority of readers of 'Politics' have cheerfully ignored both him and his critics. The essay became popular in schools and colleges precisely because parents and teachers believed that Orwell could indeed help young writers to develop a 'good prose style', and that an essay or job application, or even a simple email, written in the spirit of Orwell's advice would be more likely to find favour than one which flouted it. And they were right. Anyone who writes professionally or trains others to do so knows that – no doubt with all due health warnings – his principles are a good place to start.

But many people also believe that Orwell effectively nailed the subject of rhetoric and public persuasion, and that everything he wrote about language then is still true today. For them, if anything has happened in the meantime, it is that the fears which he expressed then have come to pass, and that the poor old English language, which he reported to be 'in a bad way' seventy years ago, is in an even worse state now. To them, and more than either *Animal Farm* or *Nineteen Eighty-Four*, 'Politics and the English Language' is prophetic.

What is certainly true is that George Orwell's take on public language in his essays and novels – and in particular his acute sense of its plasticity and the treacherous ease with which it can be commandeered and perverted by malign forces – remains astonishingly influential. It was no surprise that, when searching in December 2013 for the right words to condemn the NSA's extensive harvesting of phone data, US Appeals Court Judge Richard Leon should have settled on the phrase 'almost Orwellian'.[3] Sarah Palin's 'death panel' and 'level of productivity in society' owe a clear debt to *Nineteen Eighty-Four*. But couldn't a critic just as easily accuse the former Alaskan governor of an Orwellian use of language herself?

Some words will never escape the gravitational field of Planet Orwell. The use of the adjective 'big' always evokes Big Brother. Suggest that we all have a 'Big Conversation', as Tony Blair did, and many people will take it as final confirmation that you have decided to listen to no one but yourself. David Cameron murdered his own dream of a new era of community involvement by calling it the Big Society, a name which, thanks to George Orwell, immediately invokes its exact opposite – a Little Society with a bombed-out welfare state, and power and wealth in the hands of an elite. In *Nineteen Eighty-Four*, the regime insists that its citizens should accept that black is white, if that is what state priorities dictate; indeed it uses the term *blackwhite* for this reversal of reality and of the meanings of words in the official new language, Newspeak. No one who has read the novel can ever entirely dismiss the suspicion that, for purposes of their own, our political leaders have also secretly signed up for a similar programme of semantic inversion.

Across the West, whether debating national security or the welfare state or anything else, politicians look for ways in which they can invoke Orwell's master-narrative and claim that their opponents, or some other powerful group, are using language in some distorted and instrumental way to shut down a debate or advance a secret agenda. Everyone seems to agree that there is a language-conspiracy. The only disagreement is who is behind it.

Yet Orwell was prompted to write the two novels and 'Politics and the English Language' not by general cynicism about language or politics, but by a specific fear, which we should not allow our awareness of this wider influence to obscure. It was that Britain, and perhaps the entire western world, would succumb to Stalinist totalitarianism. In the case of 'Politics', his concern was that the language of public discourse would become so debased that it could not support healthy political debate or resist infiltration by the communist left and their fellow travellers.

One of the examples he quotes in the essay to illustrate atrocious prose is an impenetrable extract from an essay by the Marxist intellectual Harold Laski, based on a talk he gave at a PEN symposium held in 1944 to mark the 300th anniversary of John Milton's defence of press freedom, *Areopagitica*. ('I am not, indeed sure, whether it is not true to say that the Milton who once seemed not unlike a seventeenth-century Shelley had not become, out of an experience ever more bitter in each year, more alien to the founder of that Jesuit sect, which nothing could induce him to tolerate.') Orwell had attended some of the celebrations and for him they represented everything he despised about the British left: its woolliness and faddism, its disgraceful unwillingness to face up to the truth about Soviet Russia. As for Harold Laski, the revered professor and political theorist who had once advocated violent Marxist revolution, but who was now a leading light in the Labour Party: to George Orwell, he seems personally to have embodied the proximate anxiety of 'Politics' – that the communist left would use a smokescreen of euphemism and gobbledegook to hide their real intent, which was to turn Britain into a controlled society on the Soviet model. No wonder Orwell decided to pick on him.

But any appreciation of Orwell's essay must confront the awkward fact that these fears did not come to pass. The UK did not become a communist country. The Labour Party remained a democratic coalition of the left, even though Harold Laski became its chairman for a while. It was democracy and our messy, imperfect freedom which triumphed, and communism which collapsed almost everywhere.

Nor do we truly live in an 'Orwellian' world today, even though it often suits politicians and commentators to say so. The misinformation and confusion which surrounds us is not, for the most part, the result of a conspiracy by the government, Google or anyone else. In the West, neither governments nor private companies have an incentive to embark on such a risky enterprise; and although many controlled societies do still exist around the world, their ability to lie without being found out or to suppress dissent certainty isn't getting any easier. The thumbdrive and the smartphone are relentless subverters of the censor's craft.

But don't Edward Snowden's revelations in 2013 about the mass surveillance conducted by the NSA, GCHQ and other western intelligence agencies argue otherwise? Didn't they confirm at least one of Orwell's predictions, namely that technology would give future governments new ways of snooping on their citizens? Yes and no. When we read *Nineteen Eighty-Four* today, we realise that the telescreen in Winston's apartment, through which the Oceanic state controls him and everyone else, is an Internet-enabled interactive device with a webcam as well as a screen. It's a remarkable feat of prescience about the technology which now dominates our lives.

What Orwell did *not* foresee was that, in the real future, the most assiduous surveillers of Oceania's citizens would be the citizens themselves; that they would freely choose to record every intimacy of their lives in words, sound and pictures, and then use all available means to distribute them to as many strangers as possible. The real Winston is an exhibitionist. He wants to be watched. If his telescreen ever broke, his life would feel quite empty until he got it going again. Even the end of privacy has played out rather differently than Orwell predicted.

Yet that still leaves 'Politics and the English Language' standing squarely in our path. It was written at the threshold of modern mass communications and during an important pivot in our understanding of language: the outworkings of both would take decades to realise, but George Orwell is already asking all the right questions.

★

The argument of 'Politics and the English Language' is that modern public language has become stale, pretentious, confusing and vague. The effect is to 'anaesthetise' part of the reader's brain, making coherent thought and debate difficult or impossible. The difference between the debased prose of England and the sinister language of the totalitarian regimes is one of degree rather than essence and, if left unchecked, the first may lead to the second. But Orwell refuses to accept that the battle is lost. Although 'one cannot change all this in a moment', he calls for writers to abandon the second-hand and lazy and replace them with simple, clear, original prose.

Right at the start of his essay, Orwell argues (as I do) that language can be an agent, as well as a product, of change:

> Now, it is clear that the decline of a language must ultimately have political and economic causes: it is not due simply to the bad influences of this or that individual writer. But an effect can become a cause, reinforcing the original cause and producing the same effect in an intensified form, and so on indefinitely.

In other words, a feedback loop can allow negative changes in language to bolster the exogenous forces which originally caused them; those forces will in turn provoke a further deterioration in the language; and so the decline continues. But Orwell also believes it is possible for positive changes in the way we write not just to stop the cycle, but to throw it into reverse:

> one ought to recognise that the present political chaos is connected with the decay of language, and that one can probably bring about some improvement by starting at the verbal end.

The heart of 'Politics and the English Language' is Orwell's analysis of what has gone wrong with the prose of his time. He identifies two broad faults – 'staleness of imagery' and 'lack of precision' – and then lists four of the tricks by which weak writers 'dodge' the task of coherent prose composition: *operators, meaningless words, pretentious diction* and *dying metaphors*. His hope seems to be that eliminating these bad practices will not just improve 'the verbal end', but begin to address the wider 'political chaos' he sees around him.

Operators, or *verbal false limbs* as he also calls them, are roundabout ways of expressing a given thought when a simple word will do: *render inoperative* rather than *break, exhibit a tendency to* rather than *tend to*, and so on. He also deprecates the use of the passive voice rather than the active, noun constructions rather than gerunds (*by examination of* instead of *by examining*), and phrases like *in view of* and *on the hypothesis that*.

To illustrate what he has in mind by *meaningless words*, he points to two characteristics: first, the use of abstract words (he quotes an idiosyncratic list including *romantic, plastic, values, human, dead, sentimental, natural, vitality*) in contexts, like artistic criticism, where they 'do not point to any discoverable object' and are therefore 'strictly meaningless'; second, the fact that in political discourse, a number of key terms (his examples are *democracy, socialism, freedom, patriotic, realistic, justice*) have 'several different meanings which cannot be reconciled with one another'. This immediately leads Orwell to discuss the tendency of oppressive forces like the USSR or the Catholic Church to use words in *blackwhite* ways: 'The Soviet press is the freest in the world' is an example.

Pretentious diction means exactly what it suggests: the voguish preference, particularly in political and literary prose, for complicated and important-sounding words where simple ones will do. His examples vary from the apposite to the eccentric – one of the words he fulminates against is *predict*. Orwell segues from this to an attack on the peculiar jargon of Marxist–Leninist pamphleteering and speechifying: *petty bourgeois, lackey, hyena, White Guard*.

His treatment of cliché – he focuses on *dying metaphors*, by which he means the use of worn-out figurative expressions – illustrates both the power and the limitation of his account of language. He delivers his litany of tired phrases (*no axe to grind, hotbed, ring the changes*) with relish, though he declares victory too soon in the case of some 'recent examples'. He claims that *explore every avenue* and *leave no stone unturned* were 'killed by the jeers of a few journalists'. He would have been disheartened to learn that both would be not just alive but (here's another one) *in the pink* seven decades later.

But Orwell's perspective on metaphor and cliché is a narrow one. He lists *Achilles' heel* as a dying metaphor. Actually the phrase neatly expresses in two words a thought that would otherwise take a whole sentence to set out, and does not involve a clash of inappropriate images because its metaphorical use is so commonplace that it no longer evokes the image of a bipolar Bronze Age hero. Preferring a phrase like *iron resolution* – which he claims has lost its literal association and is therefore acceptable – to one like *Achilles' heel* is nothing more than a matter of taste.

Why do people use clichés? Orwell never offers a view, but 'Politics and the English Language' leaves one with the impression that it must be some combination of intellectual posturing, general laziness and communist subversion. Actually, clichés survive because they are handy, because other people understand them immediately and, yes, because you don't have to think about them too hard. They are an organic part of language rather than a cancerous excrescence. They certainly have a life cycle – from brilliant birth to intolerable old age – but they are more likely to be killed off by Darwinian competition from younger, fresher clichés, than because of conscious spring-cleaning exercises like this one.

The same is true of Orwell's other 'tricks'. We can all summon up examples of absurd circumlocution, pompous vocabulary, airy bullshit and unnecessary jargon. His advice – to use plain, concrete English and original and coherent linguistic imagery wherever one can – is obviously sound. Put as uncompromisingly as it is in 'Politics', however, it comes off as a counsel of perfection which is at odds with the way human beings actually speak and write. It's perfectly legitimate for writers to strive for nuance, for example, and to say you are *not unhappy* does not mean exactly the same as saying you are *happy*. Nor is all jargon the same. He quotes two German words in his rogues' gallery of pretentious diction: the first, *Weltanschauung*, has a perfectly good English equivalent, 'world view'; but the second, *Gleichschaltung*, refers specifically to the Nazification of German institutions in the 1930s, a meaning which is certainly not conveyed by the generic English translation, 'coordination'.

The dirty secret about 'Politics and the English Language' is that, despite his claim that his main concern is clarity, what George Orwell really cared most about was the beauty of language. Indeed, the imperative to write beautifully is the last and most important of his recommendations, though, as we saw, he disguises it by throwing it into the negative: 'Break any of these rules sooner than say anything outright barbarous.' This does not mean that the essay is really about aesthetics rather than politics. It is rather that Orwell associated beauty of language with clarity, and clarity with the ability of language to express rather than prevent thought and, by so doing, to support truthful and effective political debate. Whether he was aware of it or not, then, he had arrived at the classical understanding of rhetoric and, in particular, the ancient belief that the civic value of a given piece of rhetoric is correlated with its excellence as a piece of expression.

A Particular Picture of Language

It is consistent with Orwell's expansive view of the connection between language and politics that, of the five set-piece examples of bad writing which Orwell gives us, only one – a tedious Marxist harangue – should deal with politics head-on. Another is about psychology, a third about literature and religion, and two about language itself, including the following extract from the distinguished scientist Lancelot Hogben's *Interglossa*:

> Above all, we cannot play ducks and drakes with a native battery of idioms which prescribes such egregious collocations of vocables as the Basic *put up with* for *tolerate* or *put at a loss* for *bewilder*.

Despite its dotty and rather splendid dissonances (the 'ducks and drakes' crashing into the 'native battery' or the mouth-clatter of 'collocations of vocables'), many readers of Orwell's essay have probably glided over this sentence without the first idea of what Hogben is talking about.

Nor does Orwell give any indication that he is interested in the underlying substance. He machine-guns Hogben in a one-sentence burst which first mocks the scrambled imagery of playing 'ducks and drakes with a battery which is able to write prescriptions', then chides the writer for not being willing 'to look *egregious* up in the dictionary and see what it means', not that Hogben's use of that word is notably egregious.

But let's take a closer look. Lancelot Hogben was a zoologist and a political activist all his life, but he had another interest: the development of new languages. He was initially an enthusiast for Basic English, the 'international auxiliary language', which the linguist and philosopher C. K. Ogden had launched in 1930 to help with the teaching of English as a second language around the globe, but which many also hoped would contribute to world peace by fostering understanding between different peoples. Hogben came to believe that he could do a better job himself, however, and in 1943 he published *Interglossa: A Draft of an Auxiliary for a Democratic World Order*. Interglossa was also a new language which aimed to promote a harmonious world, but it was aimed, in the first instance, at the world's scientists:

> Because natural science is the *only* existing form of human co-operation on a planetary scale, men of science, who have to turn to journals published in many languages for necessary information, are acutely aware that the babel of tongues is a social problem of the first magnitude.[4]

Hogben based the vocabulary of Interglossa on classical root words, rather than English ones, on the basis that Latin and Greek already provided the world's scientists with a shared technical nomenclature. The bizarre sentence which Orwell quotes in 'Politics' is an attempt by Ogden to argue that Interglossa's richer vocabulary is superior to that of Basic English. A rough translation might go:

> One of the disadvantages of basing a universal language on English is that, when (to restrict the number of words novice speakers have to learn) you use a phrase made up of short simple words to substitute

for more complex ones which have been excluded from the language's restricted vocabulary, you are forced into clumsy idiomatic English usages. For example, Charles Ogden did not want to add the words *tolerate* and *bewilder* to the vocabulary of Basic English, and therefore ended up suggesting that speakers of Basic should use the phrase 'put up with' for the first and 'put at a loss' for the second.

On the face of it, Orwell could have chosen Hogben's sentence simply because it is so mangled, or because Hogben's leftish utopianism set his teeth on edge. But earlier, around 1940, Orwell had written an essay, 'New Words', published only after his death, in which he too proposed creating a new vocabulary to 'deal with parts of our experience now practically unamenable to language'[5]. In 1942, he produced a programme for the BBC on Basic English and corresponded with Hogben about it afterwards.[6] And Interglossa seems to lurk behind other parts of 'Politics', for instance Orwell's claim that a shift to a vocabulary based on Latin and Greek is already taking place:

> Bad writers, and especially scientific, political and sociological writers, are nearly always haunted by the notion that Latin or Greek words are grander than Saxon ones.

For Orwell, though, the result will not be an international peace movement led by the world's scientists, but 'an increase in slovenliness and vagueness' – and perhaps something worse. He goes on to give us a list of Latinisms to avoid, including *predict* as well as such other seemingly innocuous specimens as *expedite* and *clandestine*. Then, in a faintly loopy footnote, he claims that English flower names like *snapdragon* and *forget-me-not* are also being insidiously replaced by Greek equivalents. This is the flip side of utopian internationalism, a fear of deracinated* alien words crowding out native ones, like Asian longhorn beetle and other nasty foreign blights threatening our splendid English broadleafs.

But Orwell himself believed that public language was in urgent need of renewal. Indeed, the extracts he quotes in 'Politics and the English Language' themselves seem to represent a 'babel of tongues', to use Hogben's phrase, with social and political consequences which Orwell

---

* Another Latinate no-no according to Orwell.

believes add up to a problem 'of the first magnitude'. Having examined both Basic English and Interglossa, however, he seems to have concluded that these radical cures could be worse than the disease, and that there was nothing for it but to work with the language we've already got. Certainly the new language he created in *Nineteen Eighty-Four* is conceived as an instrument not of peace and understanding, but of oppression. Newspeak's vocabulary is restricted not to make it easier to learn or share, but to limit the range of ideas that can be discussed, or even thought.

★

Humanity is both rational and perfectible. At present, it lives in the darkness of ignorance and prejudice, the victim of political and religious oppression, and centuries of benighted tradition. Only show them reason, however, and men and women will walk out of their prison into the light. Much of this battle must be fought in the field of language. The forces of oppression rely on the frailties of traditional discourse to peddle their myths and lies. We must replace their compromised language with one founded solely on reason and evidence.

This, broadly, is the rationalist agenda for language and society which gathered momentum in the Enlightenment and was then transmitted to the nineteenth and twentieth centuries by thinkers like Auguste Comte. It found its strongest expression in philosophical positivism. According to positivism, true knowledge can only be derived from empirical observation and logical or mathematical deduction. Though he predates positivism as a movement, in 1748 the Scottish Enlightenment philosopher David Hume crisply set out the implications of positivistic rationalism for language and literature:

> If we take into our hand any volume; of divinity or school metaphysics, for instance; let us ask, Does it contain any abstract reasoning concerning quantity or number? No. Does it contain any experimental reasoning concerning matter of fact and existence? No. Commit it then to the flames: For it can contain nothing but sophistry and illusion.[7]

By the early twentieth century, some philosophers had come to believe that most, or perhaps all, of the problems of philosophy were actually problems of language. Once terms were clarified and all non-logical, non-empirical material was removed, the misunder-standings would disappear and what would be left would be unarguably valid. Perhaps the most famous statement of this position is Ludwig Wittgenstein's *Tractatus Logico-Philosophicus*, which was published in German in 1921, and in English a year later. At the end of the Preface to the *Tractatus*, the young Wittgenstein says: 'I therefore believe myself to have found, on all essential points, the final solution of the prob-lems.'[8] By 'problems', he means all of the answerable questions of philosophy.

C. K. Ogden, the inventor of Basic English, was an important figure in British positivism. He contributed to the translation of Wittgenstein's *Tractatus* into English and later, with I. A. Richards, wrote *The Meaning of Meaning*, which explored thought and semantics through a positivist lens and in turn influenced A. J. Ayer's classic of positivism, *Language, Truth, and Logic*. Basic English sprang from some of the ideas Ogden and Richards had developed in *The Meaning of Meaning*.

When applied to public language, the positivist approach implies that, within Aristotle's triangular model of rhetoric, logical argument (*logos*) is essentially all that matters, and that expressions of belief or other forms of subjectivity (*ethos*), and attempts to empathise with those listening (*pathos*), are distracting and potentially dangerous. Language associated with cultural practices which pre-date the Enlightenment may harbour superstition and irrationality and so is also suspect. Rationalism prefers philosophy and social science constructed anew from first principles: no wonder that it generally resonates more with the left than the right.

There are passages in 'Politics and the English Language' which show the unmistakeable influence of positivism. We've already encountered Orwell's passing remark that some of the words used in art and literary criticism 'do not point to any discoverable object' and therefore are 'strictly meaningless'. Meaning, Orwell implies, depends on a one-for-one relation between a specific object and the word which signifies it. Elsewhere he goes further. 'If you simplify your English,' he says, 'you are freed from the worst follies of orthodoxy': 'You cannot speak any of the necessary dialects, and when you make a stupid remark its stupidity will be obvious, even to yourself.' Simplification for Orwell entails removing words and phrases which are deceitful, meaningless or unnecessary. Like the positivists, he seems to be claiming here that the result will be a language so perspicuous that qualities like 'stupidity' will be immediately apparent. These striking claims hint at some underlying theory of language and, just before he moves on to his closing practical rules, Orwell duly offers us one.

Words, he says, are dangerous adversaries, echoing Lewis Carroll's Humpty Dumpty. To show who's in charge it's important to let 'the meaning choose the word, not the other way about'. He spells out what this entails:

> When you think of a concrete object, you think wordlessly, and then, if you want to describe the thing you have been visualising, you probably hunt about till you find the exact words which seem to fit it. When you think of something abstract you are more inclined to use words from the start, and unless you make a conscious effort to prevent it, the existing dialect will come rushing in and do the job for you, at the expense of blurring or even changing your meaning. Probably it is better to put off using words as long as possible and get one's meanings as clear as one can through pictures or sensations. Afterwards one can choose – not simply *accept* – the phrases that will best cover the meaning, and then switch round and decide what impression one's words are likely to make on another person.

In the case of a 'concrete object', one can just about make sense of this. I'm hungry and an image of a piece of fruit appears in my mind. I consult my inner encyclopaedia of fruits. Is it hard or soft? Is it round or some other shape? Is it green or orange or yellow? By a process of elimination, I come up with the entry 'banana' and discover that it fits the softish, curved, yellow object in my mind's eye perfectly.

But even this process feels quite unlike my actual experience of being hungry and thinking about a banana. Orwell's assertion that, when we see or think of concrete objects, we think 'wordlessly' and then go through some process of finding the right word to match the image, seems wrong. There is no sense of any kind of conscious search, unless for some reason we *can't* call the name of an object or a person immediately to mind; it is only then that we reach for our mental reference books. And the moment we turn to abstract concepts, Orwell's theory falls apart altogether. His advice here is to 'put off using words as long as possible and get one's meanings as clear as one can through pictures or sensations.' Take a Republican attempting to express their visceral objection to Obamacare. What would it mean for them to 'get one's meanings as clear as one can' by resorting to pictures and sensations?

The way in which our brains process conscious *meanings* feels intrinsically linguistic: the words spring to mind as quickly as the meanings and feel inseparable from them. Indeed, they sometimes seem to appear *before* the meanings and provide the material from which any new meaning has to be constructed. This is the very process which Orwell warns us to avoid. It is, however, the way our brains generally work.

By 1946, some former adherents had concluded that positivism was unsustainable. One of them was Ludwig Wittgenstein. *Philosophical Investigations*, his most important later work, begins with a passage from St Augustine which presents a theory of language more or less identical to the one Orwell offers us in his essay. St Augustine, Wittgenstein says, 'gives us a particular picture of the essence of human language':

> It is this: the individual words in language name objects – sentences are combinations of such names. – In this picture of language we find the roots of the following idea: Every word has a meaning. This meaning is correlated with the word. It is the object for which the word stands.[9]

But then Wittgenstein points to the limitation inherent in this scheme:

> If you describe the learning of language in this way you are, I believe, thinking primarily of nouns like 'table', 'chair', certain actions and properties; and of the remaining kinds of word as something that will take care of itself.

For Wittgenstein, language is self-evidently far more than a collection of words each of which have a single meaning which is derived from their relationship with a 'discoverable object'. In a series of deft thought-experiments, he demonstrates how the same word can mean different things in different circumstances. Wittgenstein argues instead that words derive their meaning from the context in which they are used by human beings. So, whereas a positivist might simply dismiss any talk about God as nonsense, Wittgenstein thinks of theological discourse as a *language-game* taking place within a social and cultural context in which words like *soul*, *God* and *sin* do indeed have meaning. As he says of religious teaching about the soul:

> Now do I understand this teaching? – Of course I understand it – I can imagine plenty of things in connexion with it. And haven't pictures of these things been painted?[10]

He is not claiming that one has to believe in the *existence* of the soul, merely that it is patently incorrect to suggest – as many positivists did – that the word *soul* is meaningless.

Wittgenstein's critique of positivism and his insistence on the importance of the lived social context of language was soon supported not just by other philosophers, but by anthropologists, psychologists and students of semantics, semiotics and the other new language-related disciplines which sprang up in the post-war years. The question of how we acquire and use language has not yet been settled, with rival approaches emphasising environment and social interaction, or biologically determined fundamental human linguistic faculties, or some combination of the two. But none of these theories, nor the most recent advances in neuroscience and developmental psychology, support Orwell's model of language or the positivist thinking that inspired it. But news that the purest application of rationalism to the question of language had been holed below the waterline never reached the majority of western intellectuals, let alone the wider public consciousness.

So where did George Orwell come to rest on the matter? As we have seen, in marked contrast to today's prevailing orthodoxy about language, Orwell was a prescriptivist who believed that there are better and worse ways of saying things; in other words, that different usages and styles of language can be objectively ranked. This is characteristic of the rationalist approach, as is his theory of language and the conviction that simpler prose will make the truth self-evident.

On the other hand, everything we know about him suggests that he would have found political correctness and other modern forms of linguistic repression repugnant and absurd. He was deeply suspicious of utopianism. Certainly by *Nineteen Eighty-Four*, he had come to associate the modification and simplification of language with dehumanisation and tyranny. In 'Politics and the English Language' itself, his theorising about language is followed not by a call for a new vocabulary and grammar, but by a set of modest and practical suggestions about how to improve our use of the language we already have.

The George Orwell of 'Politics' was drawn to the idea of rationalist purity in language, but there was something about it which scared him. It seemed to threaten the plain and humane English he grew up with and, worse, he sensed within it the potential for perversion and abuse. Like a window-shopper, he looked longingly through the glass at it, and then walked on.

Blood and Soil

But now let's eavesdrop on a completely different kind of public language. Here is Adolf Hitler addressing party and government leaders in September 1936:

> Once you heard the voice of a man, and that voice knocked at your hearts, it wakened you, and you followed that voice. For years you pursued it, without ever having even seen the owner of that voice; you simply heard a voice and followed it. When we meet here today, we are all of us filled with the miraculousness of this gathering. Not every one of you can see me, and I cannot see every one of you. Yet I feel you, and you feel me! It is the faith in our *Volk* that has made us small people great, that has made us poor people rich, that has made us wavering, discouraged, fearful people brave and courageous.[11]

This is not just an example of the beguiling rhetoric which brought Hitler to power and which, more than any other public language in history, gave oratory a bad name. If we read the passage carefully, we realise that Adolf Hitler was someone else eager to broadcast a theory of rhetoric – his own.

It goes like this: modernity is terrifying, its depredations and disruptions have left us all poor and frightened, it has crushed our sense of individual meaning and worth; yet it is still possible for these feelings to be expressed, confronted, perhaps even vanquished by a single 'voice' that can be heard by everyone.

The lesser miracle is modern technology: the microphone, the loudspeaker, the radio mast which enable Hitler to be heard even by people he cannot see and who cannot see him. The greater miracle is the sense of oneness between the unique voice and its audience, a union built on shared experience but also on the German people's collective faith in themselves as a community. What Hitler claims to be striving for is a melding of *ethos* and *pathos* into a shared state of mutual understanding and identity, almost a state of common being.

Vanishingly few politicians have Hitler's gifts in this department or, mercifully, his monstrous intent. But this bond of reciprocal trust and identity, or some approximation of it, is what people mean when they describe a given speaker or speech as *authentic*. Like rationality, authenticity sounds like an obvious virtue in rhetoric. Who wants *inauthentic* public speakers, after all? And yet, like rationalism, authenticism – by which I mean the single-minded belief that all that really matters in public language is the supposed authenticity of a given speaker – is an altogether more complex idea than it first appears, and a more dangerous one.

Adolf Hitler himself seems to have been a conscious authenticist, believing that the more 'authentic' rhetoric sounded, the more persuasive it would be. He used his own story – his *struggle* – as a narrative template which could encompass the story not just of the ecstatic crowds immediately in front of him, but of the whole of Germany. He took immense care, in what he said and how he was portrayed in newsreels and photographs, not to look like a member of the ruling elite, or even someone who wanted to join that elite, but to keep the aura of an outsider. Here was the veteran who won medals but never became an officer, the 'voice' which was somehow simultaneously on the rostrum and in the crowd. He constantly adapted his words and gestures to connect with the specific audience in front of him. 'For a minute he gropes, feels his way, senses the atmosphere', wrote his sometime friend Ernst Hanfstaengl, then 'suddenly he bursts forth'.[12] He even delayed marrying Eva Braun to the end, for fear that the presence of a wife might break the spell binding the lonely prophet to his people. Supposedly, authenticity is what is left when all artifice and instrumentality have been stripped away. In Hitler's case, it seems to have consisted of a weird mixture of natural resonance and icy calculation.

Adolf Hitler didn't invent authenticism nor, though it was much in the air, was it merely a product of Europe's traumatic interwar period. Like modern rhetorical rationalism, rhetorical authenticism is a child of the Enlightenment – indeed was a direct reaction to the rationalist school. Immanuel Kant's friend Johann Georg Hamann was one of the first to make the case that, when you take ideas and words out of their behavioural and cultural context, they lose meaning and relevance. For this reason, he is sometimes considered a precursor of the Wittgenstein of *Philosophical Investigations*. While Wittgenstein's objective seems simply to have been to understand language, though, Hamann had an agenda, which was to restore human belief – above all, religious *faith* – to its pre-Enlightenment primacy.

Hamann never fully developed his ideas, but they nonetheless entered the mainstream of European thought through a chain of influence, from Hegel and Kierkegaard to Nietzsche and Heidegger. Sometimes, as for Kierkegaard, religion – and the sense of what is lost when a society loses a language capable of expressing religious belief – is central to the picture. For Nietzsche, by contrast, authenticity consists of abandoning the false illusions of religion and the moral system which depends on it, and developing instead a new sense of what it means to be human. One of Hamann's contemporaries, the philosopher and poet Johann Gottfried Herder, had made the critical link between language, culture and nationhood, and increasingly the idea of authenticity of language became associated with another potent idea with roots in the Enlightenment: nationalism.

In Martin Heidegger's work *Being and Time*, published in 1927, human existence is understood to consist of different modes of being in a spectrum between the most *authentic*, in which *Dasein* – his term which encompasses both individual and collective human being – most clearly and deeply understands itself and its situation in the world, and the *inauthentic*, where *Dasein* risks losing itself in the crowd of *Man*, the undifferentiated human 'they'. Critically, language can also be divided into *Rede* and *Gerede*, pure discourse and the inauthentic and rootless rumour and gossip of the crowd.

Heidegger formally presents authenticity and inauthenticity as value-neutral but, even in *Being and Time*, the unspoken sense is that the authentic is superior to the inauthentic – something to be aimed at and admired, rather than merely described. And when it comes to Heidegger's politics, there is little room for doubt. By the early 1930s, the man who some consider the greatest philosopher of the twentieth century had reached the conclusion that Adolf Hitler was the embodiment of German *Dasein*, and that it was through Hitler and his revolution that the German people were now 'in the process of rediscovering their own essence' and an 'authenticity' grounded in 'blood' and 'soil'.[13] For a time Heidegger was both a Nazi Party member and an influential advocate for the regime. It's likely that he would have taken much the same view as Hitler himself about why his oratory was so potent: that its authenticity sprang directly from a shared sense of identity and being between the leader and his nation.

As we saw in Chapter 2, the association of authenticity of speech with authenticity of character and, in particular, the sense that 'rhetoric' (crafty, manipulative speech) is a reliable indicator of inauthenticity of character, goes back in English literature at least to Shakespeare. It was also alive in the literature of Orwell's own time. Here, for example, T. S. Eliot contrasts the *Logos* of St John's gospel – Christ as the 'Word' or ultimate ground of reason and order – with the crisis in modern secular discourse:

> Words strain,
> Crack and sometimes break, under the burden,
> Under the tension, slip, slide, perish,
> Decay with imprecision, will not stay in place,
> Will not stay still. Shrieking voices
> Scolding, mocking, or merely chattering,
> Always assail them. The Word in the desert
> Is most attacked by voices of temptation.[14]

The 'merely chattering' voices echo Heidegger's *Gerede*, the gossipy hubbub of everyday human life within which, but also against which, authentic *Dasein* must differentiate itself and find deeper meaning. The relatively recent neologism *chatterati*, a combination of *chatter* and *literati* which was intended to evoke a noisy, pretentious dilettantism, proposes the same conflict. *Our* thoughts about culture and politics are meaningful and profound, *theirs* vapid and irritating – but theirs still threaten to overwhelm ours. Authenticity surrounded by inauthenticity, fighting to be heard. Simple home truths battling against a sea of alien lies. This is the paradigmatic conflict the authenticist seeks to establish, and then proposes to resolve.

Like the rationalist, the authenticist prizes simplicity of language, not because he values reason but because he associates simple expression with honesty of emotion and at least the appearance of being willing to engage with the lowliest members of the chosen community. Whereas the rationalist venerates the facts to the exclusion of almost everything else, the authenticist often finds them suspect, calling them *factoids* or *statistics* – which in the anti-technocratic language of authenticity amounts to the same thing – to distinguish them from the bigger 'truths' he prefers to promote. Rationalism fetishises dialectic. For authenticists, what matters most is not argument, but story: their 'truths' are inextricably bound up with the narratives they tell about their community. The facticity of a given claim matters less than its fit with the narrative. If something *feels* true, then in some sense it must *be* true.

*

Authenticism is obviously at its most disturbing when considered in the context of twentieth-century totalitarianism. It takes many forms, however, and though it remains attractive to political and religious fanatics everywhere, it also underpins the rhetoric, tactics and strategies of many peaceful democrats. And today it's just as likely to be deployed by a left-wing party as a conservative one.

For many on the left, the privileged background of some conservative leaders makes them incapable by definition of identifying with and speaking the language of ordinary people. The Bushes were all born with silver spoons in their mouths, David Cameron went to Eton, Mitt Romney was a hedge-fund guy: don't listen to them because they cannot possibly understand *you*.

But the democratic right is just as capable of playing the authenticity game. A good number of Republicans decided that there was some aspect of Barack Obama's identity that they just didn't like. Was it, perhaps, the fact that he is black? Hell no, what do you think we are? But maybe he's a Muslim. Maybe he wasn't born in America. Convinced that *a person like that* shouldn't be in the White House, they have cast doubt on one part of his background after another in the hope that something would eventually stick and undermine public trust in what he said.

One of the many charges laid against President Obama was that he is a head-in-the-clouds intellectual – for true authenticists, all intellectuals are by definition inauthentic, notwithstanding the fact that the whole notion of authenticity was invented by intellectuals. Britain's conservative press did a brutally effective job in pressing that same charge home against Ed Miliband, whom they depicted as a weird and out-of-touch egghead. His own attempts at visible authenticity ended miserably. A video of him looking into a TV camera and trying various expressions, as a voice off-camera says 'OK Ed, look natural, no, look natural Ed, look natural', sums up the paradox of political authenticity today. Success comes not from *actually being yourself*, but from conforming to a standard of acceptable 'authenticity' – represented in this case by having the knack of relaxing in front of a television camera – which has been largely defined, not by the listening and watching public, but by political spin doctors and the media.[15] Indeed there's a standard-issue authenticity playbook for the mainstream politician: roll up your sleeves and lose the tie; show visible concern, maybe a controlled flash of anger; walk about a bit but remember the shot list – we always want to see the punters sitting behind you.

The public see through it in an instant, of course. Real authenticity is a sweaty shambles. Neither you nor your audience know what's going to happen next. Nobody's emotions are fully under control. The cameras have to follow it not like some deadbeat corporate marketing event, but like live sport. It's often an embarrassment. Once in a while it changes the course of history.

Authenticism surges through western politics in discrete waves and, in Britain, America and many continental European countries, we are living through a major wave right now. Brexit is a clear example, but only one of a chaotic series of authenticist assaults on rationalist elites which go beyond traditional party, ideology or interest. For anti-politicians like Donald Trump, pure rhetorical 'authenticity' – their ability to reject the entire public discourse of the established political classes – is their central point of differentiation.

But authenticism is playing out within conventional political structures as well. The Tea Party is, among other things, a rhetorical authenticist movement *within* the Republican Party. And yet it's hard to have it both ways. In the 2016 presidential race, the two main Tea

Party candidates, Ted Cruz and Marco Rubio, tried to insist that – despite the fact they were both Republican senators – they were outside the cosy power structures and dubious rhetorical habits of the Washington elite. But their authenticist rejection of the existing language of politics could never be *quite* as full-blooded as Donald Trump's; if victory was going to go to the candidate who could most clearly distance themselves from the whole world of professional politics, the race could only ever end one way.

On the left, there's some complexity. Since the days of Marxist–Leninist 'scientific socialism', the rhetoric of the radical left has aspired to a kind of utopian rationalism: evidence-backed revelation of the 'contradictions' within capitalism, dreams of the workers' paradise to come, a practical programme of how to get there. But after two decades of Third Way centrism and the global financial crisis, traditional full-blooded socialism has acquired a novel aura of authenticity. The fact that politicians like Jeremy Corbyn, Bernie Sanders and Alexis Tsipras have stuck to their principles through thick and thin has given them a credibility and iconoclastic power very like the insurgents of the right. Many people have forgotten, and the young may simply not know, that rhetoric of this kind was itself once considered hollow orthodoxy, or that seventy years ago, far from praising it for its truth-telling, George Orwell singled it out for its intellectual evasiveness and dishonesty.

Rationalists and authenticists find each other impossible to understand. Those few rationalists who could make any sense of the election of Jeremy Corbyn as leader of the Labour Party in 2015, or Donald Trump's campaign to be the Republican presidential candidate a year later, assumed that their appeal must have had something to do with the extremity of their policies. While many of today's 'authentic' politicians do indeed espouse radical policies, this analysis still misses the mark. To an angry public, what was appealing was not necessarily the radicalism of the policies as such, nor even their position on the spectrum of left and right, but the way in which the speaker's radicalism signalled a complete break with the status quo.

In Chevy Chase, Maryland in April 2016, I met an elderly black supporter of Bernie Sanders who was following the presidential race closely. He said he knew it was unlikely that Sanders would get the Democratic nomination, so I asked him who he would vote for if the choice came down to Hillary Clinton or Donald Trump. 'Donald Trump may be crazy, and he may even be a racist,' he said, 'but I can deal with that. At least Trump speaks his mind. When someone lies all the time, you don't know where you are.'

Although one shouldn't exaggerate the phenomenon, all over America reporters have encountered voters with similar instincts. When trust in politicians is low, perceived authenticity can be more important for some citizens than almost anything else – policies, ideological affiliation, even character flaws which in other circumstances would put them off entirely.

★

Given that the stated purpose of 'Politics and the English Language' is to warn the reader that weaknesses in language may result in a slide into totalitarianism, one might have expected George Orwell to devote some space to a consideration of the language of the totalitarian regimes of his time, namely the recently deceased fascist and militarist regimes of Germany, Italy and Japan, and his own bête noire, the USSR and its satellites. But that's not quite what we get. Orwell begins with frank speculation:

> When the general atmosphere is bad, language must suffer. I should expect to find – this is a guess which I have not sufficient knowledge to verify – that the German, Russian and Italian languages have all deteriorated in the last ten or fifteen years, as a result of dictatorship.

Even when he moves to particulars, he avoids the question of Hitler's oratory altogether, and concentrates instead on trying to establish the use of euphemism as a link between the deteriorating language of Britain and that of the Soviet Union. 'In our time,' Orwell writes, 'political speech and writing are largely the defence of the indefensible', from the horrors of war to continued British rule in India. Because the truth is too brutal to be shared with the public, politicians in many countries have resorted to euphemism: the bombing of civilians is called *pacification*, the mass execution and imprisonment of Soviet citizens during the Terror the *elimination of unreliable elements*, and so on.

But none of the examples of bad writing which Orwell quotes in his essay are in fact euphemistic. So he provides an imaginary quote (from yet another 'professor') which seeks to redefine – and thus cloak – murder and repression in the USSR as 'an unavoidable concomitant of transitional periods', which is 'amply justified in the sphere of concrete achievement'. He then attempts to pull this and the other real quotations together with a bold statement and a bravura metaphor:

> The inflated style is itself a kind of euphemism. A mass of Latin words falls upon the facts like soft snow, blurring the outlines and covering up all the details.

The image is arresting. We are in the Soviet Union, perhaps in one of the 'Arctic lumber camps' which Orwell mentions. There are a group of corpses on the ground, prisoners who have either died of abuse or been shot in the back of the neck. But snow has been falling and is making the corpses indistinct – the snow is euphemistic language. This is a masterclass for Professors Laski and others: an original, perfectly controlled and unforgettable picture which brings the thought to life in one short, simple sentence.

But then we pinch ourselves. Latin words? Are Latin words necessarily euphemistic in ways which words with other etymologies are not? Did they really sit up late into the night in the Kremlin, trying to devise fiendish new ways of infiltrating Latinate constructions into honest English prose? George Orwell clearly preferred words of what he takes to be native origin – presumably those derived from Anglo-Saxon and other early Germanic languages – to those he regarded as later foreign imports. He claims that the imports are less precise than the originals, but is the verb *to predict* really any less clear than *to forecast* or *to foretell*? Nowhere in his essay does he demonstrate the loss of precision which so exercises him.

He further asserts that words of Latin origin are more apt for euphemism. Modern bureaucratic euphemism thrives on abstractions, and English relies heavily on words of Latin origin for abstract nouns and verbs, so this feels like more promising territory for Orwell. But some of the most terrible euphemisms of history were rendered in resolutely native language. *Special handling*, half Latin half Saxon, is the English rendering of one of the terms the Nazis used to describe the process by which they murdered the Jews of Europe, but the German word *Sonderbehandlung* has nothing Latin about it. Nor does the policy objective it served: in English, *final solution* is Latin, but the German original, *Endlösung*, is again wholly Germanic. In the real world, the origins of our words are all mixed up. Is *climate change* a euphemism for *global warming* because it derives from Greek via Old French and Celtic via Latin and Old French, rather than French and Saxon? Etymology is interesting but, when it comes to politics and language, it is hardly determinative.

The truth is that George Orwell preferred words and customs which, rightly or wrongly, he took to be 'English', for instinctive rather than intellectual reasons: he was a cultural and emotional nativist. Once my people had a pristine language. Then foreign influences began to distort that language. Fancy words and complicated new ways of expressing thoughts entered our language so it became muddy and we could no longer distinguish honest speech from lies, or truthful speakers from false ones. Our task now is to purge our language of these impurities so that we can recover the straightforward and trustworthy way we used to talk to one another.

Orwell's appreciation of the English language was far more sophisticated than that crude programme of linguistic and cultural purification suggests. Nonetheless, it is what the instincts he expresses about foreign words in the essay would lead to, were they to be taken to their logical conclusion. The instincts themselves are ones that Herder himself would have recognised.

George Orwell is at least as drawn to authenticism as he is to rationalism. But it would be ludicrous to characterise him as a 'blood and soil' authenticist. Englishness defines him significantly, but Orwell's Englishness is itself a radically sceptical one – almost as sceptical about traditionalism's claims and the assumptions and institutions that underpin them as he is about Soviet Marxism. Insofar as he has a personal political agenda, it is a measured one: to reform England by stripping the tradition of its social and imperial injustices, but without losing the best of its values and attitudes; and to do this by winning the case within democracy rather than by violently replacing democracy with something else.

Nonetheless, it is hard not to conclude that he associates foreign-ness of language with a foreign intellectualism and foreign ideas – in particular those associated with Marxism – which he regards as a threat to everything he holds dear. Soviet rhetoric plays the same role for him that papal pronouncements and the language of Catholic theology did for the English Protestant firebrands of the Reformation. He can't quite rid himself of the fear that the foreigners may be right – a few years earlier he had seemed to accept the dialectical inevitability of revolution, musing that 'I dare say the London gutters will have to run with blood'[16] – but he still wants to fight to prevent it, or to die in the attempt. In 'Politics and the English Language', that means taking Harold Laski and the others on, above all, for their pretentious, over-intellectualised *inauthenticity*. They are fakes, he concludes, who use complicated gibberish to disguise their real purposes. The best way to defeat them is with some plain speaking.

This is unexpectedly close to the authenticist agenda of Donald Trump and the other anti-politicians. Authenticism is nothing like as present in 'Politics' as rationalism, but it's there. Had George Orwell been able to see the way the story would play out – communism defeated, democracy triumphant, a new sense of hollowness, and then once again the beguiling voices of authenticity – perhaps he would have devoted more space to it.

A Lost Balance

Argument without character is lifeless. The crowd drifts away. Character without argument is dangerous. Who can tell what that spellbinding figure would actually do if those cheers were ever parlayed into real power? Ignore the mood of your audience and they'll ignore you right back. Make it your lodestone and you risk sailing yourself and them straight onto the rocks.

A well-tempered rhetoric holds the demands of *logos*, *ethos* and *pathos* in balance to achieve its goal of critical persuasion – *critical* in that the speaker makes their case reasonably, confronting facts and arguments rather than bypassing them, inviting its listeners to reach a judgement using intellectual *and* emotional faculties. From

ancient times to the Renaissance and beyond, people studied rhetoric
to learn how to achieve exactly this balance. Like George Orwell,
they thought of it as an aesthetic challenge which was also a practical
political necessity. But Enlightenment rationalism held that traditional rhetoric was undesirable and unnecessary; the language of
pure reason would suffice. Academic and popular interest in rhetoric,
especially rhetoric as a useful skill, declined.

Yet the rationalists' alternative project for public language proved
impossible to implement. Over more than two centuries and around
the world, only a handful of attempts were made to impose elements
of the rationalist agenda on the language of actual human societies.
It would have been no surprise to George Orwell that these experi-
ments were all conducted by repressive regimes.

In due course even the political and philosophical underpinnings
of rhetorical rationalism would weaken. 'Scientific socialism' failed
everywhere it was tried. The Enlightenment programme to create
perfect systems of mathematics and logic was shown to be impossible
even in principle. Postmodernism challenged many of the other
assumptions on which the Enlightenment deification of Reason rested;
indeed some postmodernist intellectuals began to talk about rationalism as if it was nothing more than another variety of white male
European oppression.

Yet prescriptive rationalism still lurks in the background of
today's debate about public language. Rarely offered as a utopian
programme any more, it persists in many people's minds – nowhere
more so than among the educated elites who actually make policy
and run western governments and other institutions. Technocracy
is itself a product of the rationalist enterprise, so we shouldn't be
surprised when today's policy experts contrast *their* world of
evidence-based and hyper-rational discussion with the irrational
language-world of retail politics. Atheist public intellectuals discuss
the language of religion as if A. J. Ayer still ruled the roost and
Ludwig Wittgenstein had never been born. Political correctness is
inspired by the rationalist conviction that if you stop people saying
prejudiced or hurtful things, over time they will stop thinking and
acting prejudicially too – an unproven and psychologically
implausible conjecture which the fictional inventors of Newspeak
would have heartily endorsed.

In their eagerness to ensure that *ethos* and *pathos* were not over-looked in the pursuit of pure argument, the opponents of rhetorical rationalism went the other way. As we have seen, authenticism had its own philosophical underpinnings but, by the mid-twentieth century, these too had been compromised and were seen by many as an inde-fensible intellectual justification for demagoguery, bigotry and, in the case of Hitler and the other European dictators, the politics of murder.

Today authenticism is riding high again, but some of those old temptations – rabble-rousing, flagrant disregard for the truth, flirtation with out-and-out extremism – are back in earnest too. Its champions are as hostile to systematic, evidence-based argument as any of their forebears. They talk ceaselessly about the broken rhetoric of main-stream politicians, but their own remedy for the ills of our public language seems to consist of anger, vituperation and little else. They are at least as far as today's rationalists from seeing that an equilibrium has been lost, and that the only possible way of restoring our public discourse to health would be to begin to reintegrate argument, authen-ticity and empathy into a reasonable whole.

Seven decades after 'Politics and the English Language', the gulf of understanding between rationalists and authenticists is wider than ever and, while we may admire Orwell's determination to start 'at the verbal end' with practical advice for the reader, it seems unlikely that we can turn things around just by selecting short words rather than long ones. Populists like Sarah Palin and Donald Trump do indeed stick to short words, and they obey some of Orwell's other rules as well – active voice, lack of jargon, avoidance of words derived from Latin or Greek – but that hardly makes them part of the solution. The problems, and any possible remedies, lie deeper.

In later chapters, we'll explore how those problems play out in the discussion of science, war and of the values and beliefs which divide us. But before that, I want to turn to a branch of rhetoric which George Orwell doesn't mention once in 'Politics and the English Language', but which may have been the most influential of all in shaping the way we talk to each other publicly today.

8 Sentences That Sell

A good sales presentation should use as few words as possible. Any word that does not help to make the sale *endangers* the sale. Therefore, make every word count by using 'telegraphic' statements, as there is no time for 'letters'. Learn the MAGIC of making your 'selling sentences' sell.

Elmer Wheeler, 1937[1]

In the *Art of Rhetoric*, Aristotle identifies three genres of public language. The first two, *forensic* and *deliberative* rhetoric, are as familiar today as they were in his world. Forensic rhetoric is the language of the courts, deliberative rhetoric the language in which politicians set out their policy proposals and critique those of others, both within and beyond the walls of the Assembly or Parliament or Congress. Forensic rhetoric, Aristotle tells us, deals with past events – what happened and who is to blame? Its underlying purpose is justice. Deliberative rhetoric addresses the future: what *should* we do? Rather than seeking to condemn or exonerate individuals, it argues for or against different policies and opinions. Its purpose is to help citizens decide which would benefit the community and which harm it. Aristotle says that deliberative rhetoric is more challenging than forensic argument, because the future is unknowable. But it is also more worthy of the statesman because it deals with public issues rather than the actions and affairs of private citizens, and is less prone to partiality and sharp practice.

At first blush, Aristotle's third category of rhetoric is altogether less intriguing. He names it *epideictic* rhetoric. The Greek word suggests *display*, and it is sometimes called *demonstrative* rhetoric. This is the public language of a certain kind of formal occasion: a funeral oration (*eulogy*) for instance, or a speech in praise of a notable individual or institution (*encomium, panegyric*). Like forensic and deliberative rhetoric, demonstrative speech tries to *persuade* but, unlike them, does so without making an argument or getting embroiled in controversy. You may regard Pericles as an arrogant prig who has led Athens down the road to ruin, but the day of his funeral is surely not the right moment to bring all *that* up. Aristotle tells us that demonstrative rhetoric characteristically deals with the *present*, and that its focus and reason for existence is 'the beautiful and admirable'.[2] Its subject matter is praise and blame – though in practice praise tends to dominate.

Some kinds of demonstrative rhetoric have fallen out of favour in our world. For reasons we will explore later, we have become so conflicted about the meaning of war that we have more or less abandoned the millennia-old tradition of carving epitaphs and patriotic mottoes into memorials to the fallen. Often the only words visible on modern monuments are the names of the dead, the designers relying instead on the neutral geometries of stone, light and water to reflect and give body to our grief and gratitude. But other types of formal demonstrative rhetoric survive: the presidential tributes to lost astronauts we considered at the end of Chapter 3 are examples, as are those inadvertently hilarious speeches which incumbent US presidents give at the opening of their predecessor's official library, in which they are obliged to shower compliments on someone who is often a detested political enemy. Then there are the commencement addresses, the acceptance speeches at the Oscars, the remembrances of dead friends and relatives which, whether religious in flavour or not, remain a central part of our funeral rites.

But another very different form of demonstrative rhetoric has taken our world by storm. We wake up to it, eat and drink it all day long, then let it lull us back to sleep again. While it may not have been precisely what Aristotle had in mind when he defined this branch of rhetoric, it fits his definition like a glove. I'm referring, of course, to the language of marketing.

Marketing experts may well raise an eyebrow at the suggestion that marketing is a form of rhetoric, and that its many effects can be summed up by the word 'persuasion'. For instance, in their seminal

1999 survey of the academic field, *How Advertising Works: What Do We Really Know?*, Demetrios Vakratsis and Tim Ambler of the London Business School[3] identified what they called 'persuasive hierarchy' models of advertising which posited that consumers become convinced to buy a given product through the specific sequence of cognition (being informed and thinking about the product), followed by affect (consequently feeling good about the product) and finally behaviour (going out and buying it). But they also described alternate conceptual models in which affect and behaviour come before cognition, or make cognition unnecessary.

In their framework, the concept of 'persuasion' was reserved for those models which prioritise information and cognition. This is perfectly reasonable, but it should be clear by now that I think of persuasion as something that proceeds from cognition (or *logos*), and affect and experience (which we can compare to *ethos* and *pathos*), in any order and proportion. A wordless and purely emotional appeal on a given subject might be more *persuasive*, under my definition, than a closely argued one. The family resemblance between Vakratsis's and Ambler's schema for advertising and Aristotle's for rhetoric is itself striking. It might also be objected that advertising and other forms of marketing often achieve their impact in visual and other non-verbal ways. Again though, my definition of rhetoric extends beyond words to images and other sensory effects.

The impact of marketing on political rhetoric has already made a number of appearances in this book. So far, though, we have considered it as an exogenous force, acting upon and modifying the way politicians frame their language and how the media react to it. Now I want to examine the language of marketing from the inside.

*

Commercial messaging is not new – you can see proprietary phalluses helpfully pointing the way to brothels on the excavated streets of Pompeii – but the marketing that surrounds us today is a child of modernity. Mass production, distribution and communication meant that, for the first time, the same products and services could be offered to large numbers of prospective customers. It made sense for companies to give themselves and their products consistent names and visual liveries which they could then promote on posters and in newspapers. The naming and designing evolved into the discipline of *branding*, the billboard and newspaper promotion into modern *advertising*.

But of course rival companies were also able to brand and advertise *their* products, so companies began to look for ways of differentiating their offerings to make them more attractive than those of their competitors. A given product could offer the highest quality in its class, or the best value for money, or simply be the cheapest, or it could include innovations or other distinctive features which would be valued by customers in its target market.

To work well, differentiation needed to influence upstream decisions about product design and manufacture as well as downstream judgements about pricing, merchandising and advertising mix. Large firms – car manufacturers, for example, or makers of mass-market consumer goods – would soon find themselves with whole families of brands and sub-brands, all of which needed to be differentiated from each other as well as from their rivals. As technology accelerated product development, and competition drove market segmentation and product diversification, the advertising and PR channels multiplied and what had begun with a decent trademark, a few handouts and a bit of training for the sales force, became by the late twentieth century what modern generals call a three-dimensional battle-space.

It may transmit its messages through Snapchat or Pinterest, instant messaging or spectacular live events, but modern marketing still usually relies on persuasive public language to make its case. Like other forms of demonstrative rhetoric, it is an unashamed exercise in advocacy, its purpose generally being to promote the 'beautiful and admirable', and to convince its audience that the product or service in question exemplifies those qualities.

We came across Aristotle's term *amplification* in Chapter 2. It is an essential attribute in demonstrative rhetoric where it almost always means accentuating the positive. If you want to praise someone, Aristotle says, why not build him up by telling your audience how much braver, smarter, kinder and more modest he is than his contemporaries? Still worried you might sell him short? Compare him to the heroes of history and legend. The point is to choose whatever descriptions and comparisons show your subject in the best possible light. By the same token, if your man has serious rivals, it's best not to mention them at all; Aristotle suggests that the demonstrative rhetor should avoid negative comparisons, criticisms, qualifications or anything else that might weaken the positive portrayal of their subject. Marketing tends to follow this advice closely. If it mentions rival products at all – and it generally avoids this, especially if it wants to present the given product as a market leader – it is only to emphasise how far they fall short of whatever it is promoting.

It often also seeks to *decontextualise* its subject. At the supermarket, one packet of food tells us it 'contains 0% transfats', a second that it is 'sugar-free', a third that it is 'low sodium'. It all sounds admirably healthy, at least until we remind ourselves that a product which contains no transfats may still be loaded with sugar, while its sugar-free neighbour may turn out to be pure lard. The trade-offs and compromises involved in nutritional choices are not completely hidden, but they are de-emphasised as much as possible. The government insists on that 'Nutrition Facts' panel on the package precisely because it knows that, left to their own devices, many food manufacturers would omit these awkward facts entirely.

Not all marketing is like this. A firm dealing with a major safety failure, say, may decide to confront the problem explicitly with consumers to rebuild trust. Another may decide that full openness about ingredients, or the dangers of excessive consumption of the product, may itself be a valuable point of differentiation. Companies may embrace social or ecological responsibility in ways which involve messaging that goes beyond, perhaps even acts against, their commercial best interests. Nonetheless, in combination with amplification, decontextualisation is the norm in much of the marketing we see, and such regulation as there is – mandatory health warnings on cigarette packets, for instance, or the requirement in the US that the advertising of prescription drugs should be accompanied by suitably gruesome information about side effects – clearly recognises that.

Urgency has always been an essential element of commercial marketing. Buy this now. Offer must end soon. Click here for more information. Even messaging which appears to be about the distant future – have you made proper provision for your retirement? – typically concludes with an immediate call to action. Again, there are exceptions: some brand marketing is intended to change perceptions of a given company or product over time – an investment bank trying to repair its reputation in the aftermath of the sub-prime fiasco, for instance. But there is an impatience about most of the marketing we see and hear which distinguishes it from more stately forms of public language.

That impatience expresses itself in another way. In Chapter 2, we noted that orators are generally in more of a hurry than philosophers because they don't want to lose the attention of their listeners. How much more true is that of the marketeer whose contact with the consumer may only be fleeting and surrounded by noise and competitive distraction. So the *speed* with which the message can be delivered is also critical. That argues for brevity. Thus the imperatives of amplification and urgency operate together to dictate an *intensification* of every aspect of the communication: the choice and number of words on the digital banner ad, the pace of the TV commercial, the sales script in the call centre.

Amplification, decontextualisation, intensification: exactly the kind of long and ugly Latinate words which George Orwell warned us against. I've made marketing sound like a complex industrial refinery which uses these and other '-ations' to turn raw language into some other more purified and concentrated substance. Although there has always been more creativity to it than that suggests, I believe that this is essentially what it is.

In practice, marketing would prove to be a hit-and-miss affair, long on theory but sometimes short on results. As we shall see, marketeers have tended to recycle a handful of unchanging basic ideas in shiny new guises, in the light of new client needs, market conditions, or the opportunities afforded by new categories of data. Nonetheless, given its immense commercial importance, it probably shouldn't surprise us that its language should have been the first kind of public discourse to be the subject of large-scale systematic research to discover empirically how it works – and how it could be made more persuasive. Most people are aware that modern digital marketing relies heavily on data and analytics, but the theory and practice of scientific marketing began long before that.

Your First Ten Words

In 1937, the American firm Prentice-Hall published a book called *Tested Sentences That Sell* by Elmer Wheeler. It is both a practical primer and a kind of manifesto for what a methodical approach to the language of sales could achieve both for individual salespeople and the companies that employed them. It contains Wheeler's most famous piece of marketing advice, 'DON'T SELL THE STEAK – <u>SELL THE SIZZLE</u>!', by which he meant that you should always focus on 'the BIGGEST selling point in your proposition – the MAIN reasons why your prospect will want to buy'. But much of the book focuses on how even small adjustments to language can make a big difference to sales.

In the chapter 'FIVE LITTLE WORDS THAT SOLD A MILLION GALLONS OF GASOLINE', Wheeler recounts what amounts to a childhood marketing epiphany. This is how he begins:

> The selling word is mightier than the price tag. With words we govern people. A million people every week buy gasoline and oil because of certain tested words they hear from the Man at the Pump.[4]

The young Wheeler is helping at the pumps at his father's gas station in Rochester, New York when an unnamed salesman from Standard Oil asks him precisely what he says to sell fuel to motorists:

> I had no particular statement, so I told him: 'Sometimes I ask people if they want five or ten, other times I just say, "How many today?"' The salesman said, 'The next motorist who comes in, say this to him: "Shall I fill it up?"' I used the sentence, and the motorist told me to fill his tank. *I sold fifteen gallons instead of the usual five or ten.*
>
> What a sure-fire method of getting tanks filled up! The sentence worked, and has been working successfully now for twenty years.

More than half a century before behavioural economics gained traction, Elmer Wheeler had discovered the essential principle of 'nudge', in other words the use of subliminal cues to prompt individuals or groups to a desired response.

Wheeler spent years developing his ideas and employing them to help companies solve practical sales and marketing challenges. In due course, he founded the Wheeler Word Laboratory with the intention of researching the most effective selling language at scale. He claims in his book to have analysed over 100,000 sales words and techniques and to have tested them on no fewer than 19 million people. Both numbers sound like wild overstatements – *Tested Sentences* practises what it preaches about amplification – but it's clear that Wheeler had understood as early as 1937 that what we now call *big data* could play a central role in optimising marketing messages to the public. He quotes Sherlock Holmes saying that 'while individuals may be insoluble puzzles, in the aggregate they become mathematical certainties', and goes on to explain: 'This statement means that you can never foretell how one person will react to a given selling sentence, but that you can say with scientific accuracy what the average will do.'[5]

So what did all this data tell Elmer Wheeler about persuasive language? One of his most important findings is about that need for urgency:

> People form 'snap judgements'. They make up their opinions about you in the first ten seconds, and this affects their entire attitude toward what you have to tell them. Give them a brief 'telegram' in these first ten seconds so that their opinion will be in your favour. Make the wires 'sing' – so you will be given a chance to 'follow up'.[6]

By *telegram*, he means the shortest possible form of words to express your message. In the quotation at the start of this chapter, Wheeler distinguishes between *letters*, meaning normal prose or spoken English, and *telegrams*, by which he means compressed language that immediately reveals the unique selling proposition of the product in question. Whether it's the salesman, or Mom and Dad, or the preacher, and whatever it is that they're selling, 'their first ten words will be more important than their next ten thousand!'

The unblinking focus on the 'sizzle' implies decontextualisation – a spotlight is shone on the core selling point and everything else, including any awkward drawbacks or limitations, remains in shadow – but Wheeler says he is utterly against deliberate hood-winking. Better to play it straight and use his methods to make the best of what you've got. In fact, *Tested Sentences* is anything but cynical in tone; Wheeler has the innocent fervour of an inventor who has stumbled on a new technology which will benefit the whole of humanity, in this case by bringing great products and happy consumers together more effectively than ever before.

He also has some clear advice about argument. 'Never disagree with a customer who offers an objection':

If the customer says, 'It looks heavy to me,' don't say, 'Heavy? Of
course not.' Instead say, 'It does LOOK heavy, but feel how light it is.'
Seem to agree, but bring the prospect diplomatically around to your way of
thinking.[7]

This section – entitled 'WIN DECISIONS – NOT ARGUMENTS' –
shows just how radically this approach to language diverges from the
way we normally think about debate. Whereas philosophical dialectic
and deliberative rhetoric both strive to get to the bottom of arguments,
all a salesperson following Elmer Wheeler's advice has to do is to get
the prospect to focus on the 'excellence and beauty' of the product,
and the objections will simply disappear from view. We can see the
advantages of this approach in simplicity and impact. And the decision
to sidestep the whole painful process of adversarial dialectic means
that the speaker has much greater freedom about what to say and
how to say it. They achieve maximum persuasiveness not by honing
complex arguments, but by empirically testing many different possible
messages with customers, and using the results to select the most
promising one and optimise its expression.

We might not worry too much about this approach if the issue
facing the listener was nothing more serious than which vacuum
cleaner to buy. But supposing someone started applying it to philosophy or politics?

Two and a half thousand years before *Tested Sentences*, Plato claimed
that a group of people were doing just that in the Athens of his day.
His concern was about the itinerant teachers of rhetoric and philosophy known as *sophists*. In the *Gorgias*, he presents Socrates running
witty circles around one of the celebrity sophists. Socrates argues that,
whereas dialectical philosophy tries to reach true understanding of
the questions it considers, rhetoric – or at least the sophist Gorgias'
version of rhetoric – merely tries to 'flatter' its listeners:

[Rhetoric] seems to me, Gorgias, not to be a valid discipline among
the arts at all, just a matter of having the craftiness and the nerve to
pull a fast one on the public. If you want to give it a name, I'd call it
a form of *flattery*. Flattery comes in many shapes and sizes – one of
them is cookery, which may seem like an art to some but which as far
as I'm concerned is nothing more than a knack or routine. I say that

rhetoric is just another form of flattery . . . And if you ask me what *sort* of flattery, I'd say it's a sham version of a certain kind of politics.[8]

For Socrates, cookery is a 'knack' rather than an art, because all it requires is learning what ingredients or preparations people like. According to him, Gorgias does the same with words. The Greek noun Plato has Socrates use for 'knack', *empeiria*, is the word that gives us *empirical*: he is accusing the sophist of using trial and error to establish what people want to hear, and then of serving it up to them, regardless of whether it is true or insightful. Plato has had a premonition of the systematic use of data to optimise language – and has immediately realised the threat to proper, old-fashioned argument.

Despite his rival's disobliging portrait of him, however, Gorgias amassed enough of a fortune from his rhetoric classes to have had a gold statue of himself put up in a temple, and is said to have lived peacefully and prosperously to the improbable age of 108. It was not him, but the straight-talking Socrates who ended up in the dock.

A Few Key Takeaways

Today Gorgias' approach increasingly holds sway, not just in retail marketing, but in realms of public language which, until relatively recently, were considered too serious for anything other than evidence-based dialectical argument. A good example is that centrepiece of modern political, corporate and institutional life – the strategy presentation.

Much of this book is about how policy is discussed and debated once it's been formulated. Over the next few pages, we'll look at how the sausage is made – in other words, how the proposals which may eventually become policy are developed, shared and refined inside government departments, companies and every other kind of organisation *before* the moment of completion and adoption. And to help us, we're going to dip into another *how to* guide.

Are you 'terrified of speaking in front of a group'? Or 'simply looking to polish your skills'? Either way, the *Harvard Business Review Guide to Persuasive Presentations* is here to help. The front cover is itself a model PowerPoint slide: beneath the main title are three things the book promises to help you do, arranged in three punchy bullets: 'Inspire action, Engage the audience, Sell your ideas'. When we see that Aristotelian triad, we know we're on familiar turf. This is a book about rhetoric – and a state-of-the-art one at that.

Nancy Duarte, the author of *Persuasive Presentations*, begins by making the case, contra Socrates, that persuasion is indeed an art – and one that repays real effort:

> We work in a first-draft culture. Type an e-mail. Send. Write a blog entry. Post. Whip up some slides. Speak.
>
> But it's in crafting and recrafting – in iteration and rehearsal – that excellence emerges.
>
> Why worry about being an excellent communicator when you have so many other pressing things to do? Because it will help you *get those things done*.
>
> So, as you conceive, visualise, and present your message, don't skimp on preparation, even if you're giving a short talk. It actually takes more careful planning to distill your ideas into a few key takeaways than it does to create an hour-long presentation . . . And gather lots of feedback so you'll be all the more effective when you start the process again.[9]

We see at once how close this is to Elmer Wheeler's approach. The goal now is not the sale of some external object or service, but the selling of 'a few key takeaways' – in other words, the promotion of some of the important ideas in the presentation itself. But the method is very similar. At its heart is recursive empirical optimisation: 'crafting and recrafting' are required as the presentation is being prepared but, once it is delivered, the speaker should solicit 'feedback' and build that into the next presentation.

Amplification is the thread that runs through the book. 'Amplify Your Message Through Contrast' we are told early on, because 'a skilled communicator captures an audience's interest by creating tension between contrasting elements – and then provides relief by resolving that tension': the author adds a handy list of paired contrasts – past/future, stagnation/growth, need/fulfilment, etc. Amplification can make a point more memorable as well as more dramatic so, if possible, facts should be attention-grabbing: 'If statistics are shocking, don't glide over them – amplify them.' Where possible, language should be heightened:

Another example: If you say your presentation is about 'the Florida wetlands', that's also just a topic. Add your point of view and what's at stake. For instance: 'We need to restrict commercial and residential development in Florida's wetlands, because we're destroying the fragile ecosystem there and killing off endangered species.'[10]

People, Nancy Duarte tells us, 'will move from pain and towards pleasure', so you should 'prod them' with words like 'destroying' and 'killing' so that they feel uncomfortable staying in their current position.

Another chapter deals with sound bites. Because of their power and memorability, it's essential to 'embed well-crafted sound bites into every talk' – though it's also important not to deliver them 'with a lot of fanfare', because they should appear 'spontaneous'. She gives us the example of Steve Jobs using rhythmic repetition to drive one such formulation home. Jobs was holding an emergency press conference to deal with a problem with the iPhone 4 – namely that some consumers were finding that, if they held it in a certain way, the antenna didn't work. The message he wanted to convey, however, was not about the practicalities of the problem, but Apple's relationship with its customers:

> As social media scientist Dan Zarrella, at Hubspot, points out, Jobs repeated the phrase 'We want to make all our users happy' several times during his talk. Midway through, Jobs flashed a slide showing the antenna issue affected only a fraction of users. Soon, a message appeared at the bottom: 'We care about *every* user.' A few slides later: 'We love our users.' Then 'We love our users' appeared again on the next slide. And the next. And the next. 'We love our users, we love them', Jobs concluded. 'We do this [provide a free phone case that will solve the problem] because we love our users.' That 'love' was the message the press took away from his piece of 'crisis communication'.[11]

Duarte doesn't ignore dialectic completely – she advises careful research to identify any 'logical arguments' which could be used by members of your audience to resist the case you are making – but emphasises throughout the need to 'balance analytical and emotional appeal' and to 'add emotional texture'. And the central idea of the book is about 'STORY': 'use storytelling principles and structure to engage your audience', from the beginning which should set up whatever challenge or tension your presentation is intended to resolve, to the end which is 'where you describe how blissful their world will be when they adopt your ideas'.[12] The reader is left with the impression that in most situations story is safer and more effective than argument. PowerPoint itself, with its deck of separate slides that can be arranged in any order, encourages impressionistic storytelling rather than structured reasoning.

The Harvard Business Review Guide to Persuasive Presentations is a thoughtful piece of work by someone who seems familiar with Aristotelian as well as contemporary ideas about how best to persuade an audience. But that last mention of the 'blissful' world to which the speaker must beckon their audience emphasises just how far we are from the world of deliberative rhetoric. Like the language of marketing, like other forms of demonstrative rhetoric, the aim of *Persuasive Presentations* is the beautiful and the pleasurable. Conclusions are reached not through dialectical argument but as the punchline to an emotionally satisfying narrative. Elmer Wheeler told us to 'win decisions – not arguments'; now again, instead of offering our audience a series of logically connected propositions which can be tested and challenged, Duarte advises us to guide them smoothly through a dramatic and compelling story to a predetermined mood-state. Choices which in reality are painful or finely balanced will be presented as inevitable, obvious even. Interest and relationships will be reduced to elementary human instincts and those primal opposites: need/ fulfilment, sacrifice/reward, stagnation/growth.

To a large degree, policy formulation has moved from portrait to landscape, from prose to bullet point and graphic, from argument to story. If this is the way that policy is made, is it any wonder that a similar shift should have taken place in the way it is then communicated? We love our users, we love them. It wouldn't be right to ask them to think too hard.

It's Not What You Say, It's What They Hear

Politicians are instinctive marketeers and, given the competitive pressures they face, are always on the lookout for any innovation that might give them an edge in getting their message out. Crisp phrases intended to make headlines and help ordinary voters make sense of complex policy positions have been a feature of political communications since the early days of the mass media. Take the 'Cross of Gold', a phrase from an 1896 speech by William Jennings Bryan ('you shall not crucify mankind upon a cross of gold'), which immediately became a universal shorthand for opposition to the gold standard. Or 'He kept us out of the war', the central proposition of Woodrow Wilson's 1916 presidential campaign. That election saw such aggressive marketing by both parties that the following year Congress for the first time considered the regulation of political advertising.[13]

In 1930 *Advertising Age* was able to claim that 'a political campaign is largely an advertising campaign', and by 1940 the columnist Dorothy Thompson was on CBS radio criticising the infiltration of American politics by ad men intent on making a 'hard sell': 'The idea is first to create the fear, and then to offer a branded antidote.'[14] Thompson told her listeners that she would be voting for FDR because, unlike his Republican opponents, he had no advertising gurus helping him. Elmer Wheeler, by contrast, found himself praising 'Salesman Roosevelt' in *Tested Sentences*, for using 'word magic' during the 1936 campaign to gain the confidence of his prospect. He quoted a vintage Roosevelt passage:

> Four years ago the White House was like an emergency hospital. Businessmen came to me with headaches and backaches. No one knew how they suffered, except old Doc Roosevelt.
>
> They wanted a quick hypodermic to relieve the immediate pain, and a quick cure. I gave them both. They got action. In fact, we cured them so quickly and efficiently that now these same people are back, throwing their crutches into the doctor's face.[15]

Roosevelt, Wheeler concluded, 'knows that some words sell people and others do not, and he makes certain that he uses only language tested to stamp itself on the mind of his prospect directly and instantly, and to remain there forever'.

In the decades after the Second World War, political marketing became more systematic and endemic. Advertising agencies were brought in to offer strategic advice about messaging long before the time came to devise TV spots and posters. Increasingly, people from advertising and marketing backgrounds would be chosen as full-time staff members by presidents and other political leaders: no less than five members of the Nixon White House team, including his chief of staff, H. R. Haldeman, came from J. Walter Thompson. Meanwhile, political marketing became a campaign issue itself. At the Democratic Convention in 1956, the presidential nominee Adlai Stevenson claimed that the Republicans were about to unleash every trick in the marketing book: 'The idea that you can merchandise candidates for high office like breakfast cereal – that you can gather voters like box tops – is, I think, the ultimate indignity to the democratic process.'[16] He neglected to mention that the Democrats had just signed up a Madison Avenue advertising agency of their own.

By the second half of the twentieth century, political marketeers could draw on a rapidly growing body of theory and practical experience about the different needs and activities that made up the emerging discipline of marketing: market research, marketing strategy, brand marketing and positioning, direct marketing and customer-relationship management, advertising, public relations and corporate communications.

Ideas which had been developed at the start of the century in the fields of psychology and ethology had been rapidly applied to commercial and corporate problems. For instance, Edward Bernays, a critical figure in the development of modern public relations, borrowed concepts from psychoanalysis (Sigmund Freud happened to be his uncle) and Ivan Pavlov's theories about conditioning in animals and humans to create his own thesis about crowd behaviour and how a commercial organisation – or a government – could 'engineer consent' across a modern industrial society like the United States.[17]

Theorists in other branches of marketing also absorbed ideas and experimental findings from across the social sciences. Even in the early days, as we've seen in the case of Elmer Wheeler, they had a strong instinct that the deepest insights would rely on a combination of high-level conceptual pattern recognition, potent case studies, and vast quantities of statistical data: big ideas, compelling human stories and that alluring promise from the world's greatest detective of 'mathematical certainties'.

In due course, marketing would absorb many additional techniques and theories from the emerging disciplines of social psychology and social anthropology. These disciplines also claimed to base their theories on empirical evidence, but the nature of this evidence varied: the bias of the anthropologists was for long-term observational studies of relatively small groups of people (this would led to the marketing category of *ethnographic fieldwork*, in which researchers were immersed in the lives of consumers), while – especially in the growing overlap between social psychology and economics – the psychologists would often rely more on large-scale quantitative research and statistical analysis. None of these could claim to be exact sciences; the judgement and 'feel' of the researchers in interpreting the data was still held to be critical. But together they added depth and range to the insights which the marketeers could offer their clients.

To almost any democratic politician, it was an irresistible package. And so, slowly but inexorably, political marketing began to move upstream: instead of being brought in at the end of the process, to plan advertising campaigns to message pre-existing policies and personalities, marketeers started to be invited into much earlier conversations about political strategy, and even into the sacred realms of policy formulation. Now surveys, focus groups and other forms of market research would be used to help decide what the political agenda of a given party should be, rather than merely how that agenda should be sold.

Political leaders had relied on pollsters for decades to help them track the public mood, but the polls and the insights they offered were inevitably retrospective – they told you what the public were saying, or who they might vote for, last week or last month. The new marketing professionals claimed that they could build audience models which were sufficiently deep and sophisticated to be *predictive*. This is what this group really care about – announce that policy in that way and this is how they will react. In practice, reality would often stubbornly refuse to conform to the research and the public would reject policies and candidates which the data said they should embrace. But there were successes too – and the prospect of being able to test and fine-tune political ideas and messages in a marketing lab before letting them out into the world was too tantalising for many politicians to ignore.

One of the techniques the new generation of political marketeers introduced was *segmentation*. Shopkeepers and manufacturers have known since way back when that it often makes sense to divide prospective customers into different groups and to tailor the products you offer them accordingly: men and women, young and old, rich and poor, and so on. These high-level human differences remained important but in the 1950s, marketing experts began to develop a more sophisticated doctrine. Here is Wendell R. Smith writing in the *Journal of Marketing* in 1956:

> Market segmentation involves viewing a heterogeneous market as a number of smaller homogeneous markets in response to differing preferences, attributable to the desires of consumers for more precise satisfaction of their varying wants.[18]

In theory, a marketeer could divide a population into discrete groups of similar customers, each of which could be targeted with relevant products – and relevant messages about those products. Nor was it necessary to restrict these groups to traditional categories like age or gender. The marketeer could study the data and create entirely new segments based on shared interest, attitude or lifestyle: sporty singles, upwardly mobile families, thrifty savers. Unlike simple demographic categories, these new segments were imputed rather than real, and as a result they could feel artificial or tendentious. But they could bring an audience to life and inspire great work not just from advertising creatives but from product teams and even company executives.

If you could segment customers, then why not voters? In due course, political campaign managers and even the candidates themselves would be poring over segmentation models with the eagerness of the hungriest sales director. During the 1996 US presidential election, for instance, both the Bill Clinton and the Bob Dole camps decided to focus on a segment known as the *soccer moms*. The term literally meant a mother who drove her children to soccer matches, but it suggested a suburban wife and mother who was active in her community, had a hectic life to juggle and was ambitious for her family. Finally – and crucially for the parties – she was someone who cared about the issues but was a political moderate who could be persuaded to vote either Democrat or Republican.

The phrase became so salient that the American Dialect Society voted it the Word of the Year[19] but, although newspapers and TV companies found it very easy to locate and interview sample 'soccer moms', they were never a concrete category – like African Americans or the under-fives – but a concept constructed from a mixture of qualitative and quantitative data and intuition. Nonetheless, the concept had a crispness and humanity which a more precise but less resonant segmentation ('middle-class female moderates') would have lacked, and the parties knew they could use it as a creative touchstone for everything from political advertising to policy selection. In the event, insofar as they existed at all, the soccer moms made their own decisive choice in favour, not of saturnine, ill-at-ease Bob Dole, but the altogether more empathetic William Jefferson Clinton.

Deep understanding of qualitative and quantitative research and other marketing techniques would soon become a prerequisite for anyone who wanted to present themselves as a political consultant or manager. In America, the Republicans held a lead in the field through most of the 1990s and early 2000s, but then Barack Obama's campaign team took segmentation and audience-targeting to a new level. According to Ken Strasma – a Democratic political consultant with a firm tellingly named Strategic Telemetry – while some customers might still be looking for a 'silver bullet' and want to know 'is it cat owners or bourbon drinkers or some nice buzz phrase like that?', the truth depends on 'the interactions between hundreds of different data points – it's rare that you see one single indicator pop'.[20] Within a decade, categories like 'soccer moms' had become old hat, too imprecise for the micro-targeting of messages, too broad to be of much predictive use. So the Obama team abandoned the comfort blanket of the 'nice' phrases, and set off instead in pursuit of those myriad numerical intersections. The hope was that data science could lead them towards the holy grail of contemporary marketing – messaging fine-tuned not for a million people, or a thousand or a hundred, but an individual.

Like earlier advances in political messaging, the new marketing techniques made their way across the Atlantic. By the mid-1990s, the UK had in Tony Blair a prime minister who was open to what was then state-of-the-art strategic audience advice from Philip Gould and other professionals. And, as we have seen, when David Cameron walked into No. 10 after the 2010 general election, he brought with him Steve Hilton, someone else who'd shown an interest and aptitude for marketing throughout the course of his career as a political strategist, and who was now fizzing with ideas about how to use digital technology, social psychology and behavioural economics, not just to gain unprecedented understanding of the electorate and to use that knowledge in policy formulation, but also to form a closer relationship with them. The new breed of political marketing experts shared Elmer Wheeler's dream of a potent new persuasiveness based on empirical analysis and conceptual deconstruction of public attitudes and aspirations. Now they believed they had the technology and the know-how to make that dream come true.

Of all contemporary practitioners in this field, perhaps the one who has concentrated most closely on how to engineer the most effective political language down to individual words and phrases is the American political and business consultant Frank Luntz. The author of *Words That Work* and numerous other books aimed at politicians and business leaders, his contention has been, like Wheeler's, that successful public language need not be left up to chance or individual instinct but can be arrived at by exhaustive and recursive testing with audiences. Here he is, writing in the *Huffington Post* in January 2011:

> Words matter. The most powerful words have helped launch social movements and cultural revolutions. The most effective words have instigated great change in public policy. The right words at the right time can literally change history.[21]

On the basis of his research Frank Luntz goes on to offer his readers eleven key words and phrases that politicians and other leaders should use in 2011. Most are disarmingly simple. *Imagine* remains a very powerful word, apparently – so too, unsurprisingly, does *integrity*, especially in the phrase *uncompromising integrity*. He also strongly recommends the phrase *I get it*:

> This explains not only a complete understanding of the situation, but a willingness to solve or resolve [it]. It's short, sweet and effective – and too few leaders use it.[22]

Frank Luntz recommends *I get it* not through instinct but because he has seen and measured audiences reacting to its use. One of his techniques is the 'Instant Response Focus Group', in which a selected group of respondents listen to a speaker or some other stimulus and use handsets to continuously dial in their reactions which are blended to create a moving graph that advances in real time. Luntz has often used this technology – which bears a strong family resemblance to one of Elmer Wheeler's 1930s inventions, the splendidly named 'psychogalvanometer' – to help broadcasters rank the eloquence of different politicians. In 2005, we used both man and machine on the BBC *Newsnight* programme to observe how a particular group of voters responded to the Tory MPs who were then vying to become party leader. The politician who scored best on the handsets that night was David Cameron, who indeed went on to lead his party; it has sometimes been suggested that he owed that victory in part to his very visible success with the Instant Response Focus Group.[23]

For Luntz, finding the right words is a challenge in behavioural science. Because human beings are significantly driven by emotions rather than intellect, one way of expressing a given policy or political thought may be strikingly more persuasive and emotionally acceptable than another. A speaker who does *not* carefully test wording in advance may find that their audience reacts in radically different ways than he intended. Better to do the research first and find out what works best by systematic trial and error. Luntz's company motto is: 'It's not what you say, it's what they hear.'

Often, according to Luntz, the answer is the use of strong, simple English; like George Orwell and Nancy Duarte, he argues that jargon and technocratic language is always a mistake. And like Elmer Wheeler, he believes that the authenticity of the speaker and the integrity of what is said is key; he sees his methodology not as a dark art to help unscrupulous speakers mislead and bamboozle audiences, but as a means for politicians and CEOs to secure a bond of credibility and empathy between them and their listeners.

Although clarity is important, the intensity of a given expression is critical for Frank Luntz. As a pollster to Newt Gingrich in the mid-1990s during the *Contract With America** period, Luntz strongly promoted the phrase 'death tax', which had first been coined by the

---

* This was a Republican policy manifesto, released in 1994, written principally by Newt Gingrich and Dick Armey.

conservative activist James L. Martin, as a more emotive way of describing estate tax. His recommendation was not based on gut instinct, but on systematic testing in which audience reactions to the rival terms 'death tax' and 'inheritance tax' were measured side by side. The 'death tax' may have been an influence on Sarah Palin's 'death panel' a decade and a half later.

Sometimes, however, it's important to let the air out of the balloon rather than to pump it up. It was Frank Luntz who advised George W. Bush's administration not to talk about 'global warming' but the more neutral-sounding 'climate change': adjust the words even by millimetres and you change the terms of the argument, and without many people noticing. The compressed, cunningly turned political language which has featured repeatedly in this book is the product of many different trends and forces. We can also see it as the culmination of a new discipline – the optimisation of language by methodical empirical testing, which was invented in the last century to help sell commercial products and services, but which is now routinely applied to political rhetoric by specialists like Frank Luntz.

Neither he nor other practitioners would accept that their techniques necessarily privilege empathy and impact at the expense of systematic argument and explanation but, given the brutal reality of politics and modern media, that is often the result. Despite Plato's best efforts, it is Gorgias rather than Socrates who is currently winning the argument. No longer restricted to the Athenian marketplace, today the busy sophist divides his schedule between Madison Avenue, Silicon Valley, Washington, London and the world's other power centres.

But the technology which is now driving marketing makes even Frank Luntz's wired focus-groups look old-fashioned. Today a growing number of chief marketing officers sport a computer science degree and expect the majority of their decisions to be data-driven. Data scientists use machine-learning, a form of artificial intelligence, as well as more traditional statistical analysis to sift through server-farms full of information, looking for patterns of consumer behaviour which can be used to predict future actions and preferences. The testing of different marketing messages and executions on digital platforms no longer requires questionnaires or interviews, but is done and assessed in real time on a percentage of the user base. And once again it turns out that seemingly microscopic changes of expression – the exact wording used to encourage a consumer to buy, even the colour or font size in which the appeal is made – can significantly affect the outcome. A/B and multivariate testing – in which multiple variants of a digital site are shown to different groups of users and the results compared – were inevitably adopted by the politicians and their marketing specialists. Dan Siroker, a former engineer at Google Chrome, was Director of Analytics for Barack Obama's 2008 campaign. There Siroker used A/B testing and other types of Web optimisation to significantly increase the percentage of visitors to the Obama site who converted to becoming subscribers (by submitting their email addresses). This in turn led to a big jump in campaign contributions. Siroker later co-founded the tech company Optimizely, whose software has been used in the 2016 election cycle by the campaigns of Jeb Bush, Marco Rubio, Ben Carson, Bernie Sanders and Hillary Clinton among others.

The testing is more often used to optimise the broader user experience of a given site, determining whether it is better to have a video or a still image in the background, or how large and what colour a 'I agree' or 'Contribute' button should be. But some candidates also test which 'headlines', in other words which campaign messages or promises, resonate most with users and make them most likely to subscribe or donate. Sometimes rival ways of expressing a given political message are tested alongside each other. It is not clear how far these automated tests influence the broader rhetoric of the candidates – but it's hard to believe they have had no impact at all.

Nor do candidates have to wait for the results of traditional opinion polls, retrospective research and educated guesswork to gauge public reaction to their campaigns. Real-time *sentiment analysis*, based on data from social media and Web search, can show immediate and evolving reaction to a product launch or a presidential debate or anything else.

Meanwhile, social media is at hand to perform a kind of informal linguistic optimisation. Sarah Palin could have hired Frank Luntz to help her find the best possible phrase to attack Obamacare, but she didn't need to. The Internet and platforms like Twitter and Facebook have turned the whole of online humanity into a vast laboratory of political language. A commentator or political player can put out dozens of sentences and phrases a day. Most sink without trace, but every so often one of them is so eye-catching or thought-provoking or funny that within minutes it is being reposted and retweeted across an ever-widening pool of people. Over time, public figures learn what is most likely to work in each digital environment: thus the *death panels* and 'Don't Retreat, Instead – RELOAD!', Sarah Palin's own distillation of the art of rhetoric, which I quoted at the start of Chapter 1.

And, as we've discussed, newspapers and conventional broadcasters watch these platforms – especially Twitter – obsessively, and a tweet or posting can cross over and be further amplified through traditional media channels. There is a kind of Darwinian natural selection of words and phrases going on and, by definition, the only kind of language that emerges from this process is language that works. You hear it, you get it, you pass it on. The art of persuasion, once the grandest of the humanities and accessible at its highest level only to those of genius – a Demosthenes or a Cicero, a Lincoln or a Churchill – is acquiring many of the attributes of a computational science. Rhetoric not as art, but as algorithm.

A Question of Judgement

By now it sounds as if all the cards are stacked against the public. If the language of marketing becomes a decisive influence on the other forms of public language, and if Sherlock Holmes is correct and our collective response to it will approach 'mathematical certainties', are we doomed to become like Pavlov's dogs, salivating on cue? Or is there some way we can keep our critical distance and make up our own minds on the matter in question?

To answer that, let's begin with traditional commercial marketing. Why, given the persuasiveness of all the commercial messaging, don't we just buy every single product on the supermarket shelves? A professor of marketing might begin by offering two answers. The first is *competition*. Every marketing message has to compete with rivals. You see an advertisement for a car and for a moment become convinced that the best sports coupé in the world is a BMW. But a few seconds later you are confronted with an ad for a Mercedes coupé, then an Audi. Each makes different claims and, more importantly, evokes a different ambience: the Mercedes offering to say something about your success in life, perhaps, while the BMW might flatter your image of yourself as a skilled driver, and as for the Audi – well, precisely by *not* being either a Mercedes or a BMW, it might seem to confer on you an individualism and lack of conformity (at least compared to other buyers of expensive German cars).

The second is *empirical feedback*. When people consume products or use services, they are able to put marketing promises to the test. A movie studio may claim in its marketing materials that a given film is the funniest ever made but, if the opening-night audiences discover there isn't a laugh in it, by the following morning the grim truth will be there for all to see on Rotten Tomatoes and IMDb. Many products are what economists call *information goods* – you can only assess the quality of the product after consuming it – but if shoppers are unhappy with the product they bought they won't come back for more, and may well tell their friends to avoid it as well.

But both competition and empirical feedback depend on a human ability to subject consumer choices – and rhetorical claims – to a process of critical discrimination and to make an assessment, in the light of both the immediately available information and broader life experience, of which is the best or the most credible. The Greeks called this faculty *phronesis*, a form of practical wisdom or judgement which they came to distinguish from *sophia*, the wisdom they associated with scientific and abstract knowledge. Cicero called it *prudentia* in Latin and the English word *prudence* is an apt term for it.

It is prudence that arms us against unwarranted marketing claims, by allowing us to perform a sense-check on anything which sounds too good to be true, and the same goes for any other kind of persuasion. In mature and well-functioning political and rhetorical environments, awareness of the public's capacity for prudence encourages politicians who otherwise might be tempted to promise the earth to show some restraint.

But how strong a faculty is it? This was a point of contention in the classical world and remains so to this day. Many ancient observers emphasised the fallibility of *phronesis*, and the consequent vulnerability of the people to unscrupulous or misguided persuasion. For those who had witnessed the disintegration of political institutions and civil order, this inherent weakness in practical judgement was enough to reject the merits of democracy. Thucydides tells us how one day the firebrand Cleon, 'the most violent of the citizens', convinced the Athenian Assembly to respond to a revolt on the island of Mytilene by despatching a trireme to slaughter the population.[24] Within twenty-four hours, Diodotus had persuaded the Assembly to reverse its decision and send a second trireme to catch the first. Rival orators, racing ships, the crowd tipping first this way, then that, the fate of every soul on Mytilene hanging in the balance. That, Thucydides seems to say, is democracy for you.

Nor was this pessimism about the people's practical wisdom limited to the classical period. Thomas Hobbes, who had translated both Thucydides' *History* and Aristotle's *Art of Rhetoric*, and who had seen bitter religious and political differences pull England apart in the first half of the seventeenth century, came to believe that the private judgement of most individuals was so weak and changeable that they could add nothing useful to public discussion or decision-making. 'What can that large number of debaters contribute to policy with their inept views but a nuisance?' Hobbes asked.[25]

So where do attitudes towards practical judgement stand today? This issue is closely related to how we feel about rhetoric. If you have faith in the ability of the general public to apply common sense and powers of discrimination to what they are told by politicians, you're unlikely to believe that marketing-speak will conquer all or that the task of repairing our public language is hopeless. The famous dictum attributed to Abraham Lincoln (though there is no evidence he actually said it) expresses this attitude neatly: 'You may fool people for a time; you can fool part of the people all the time; but you cannot fool all of the people all the time.'[26] There is a correlation between critical faith in the practical wisdom of the public and a wider belief in the benefits of democracy. Trial by jury, so central to the justice system throughout the English-speaking world, also presupposes a belief in the faculty of prudence in the public at large.

But if you regard the average citizen as gullible and unreflective, then, like Plato and Hobbes, you may believe that it *is* possible for the politician and the marketing guru to fool all the people all the time, or at least so many of them that it makes no odds. At present, the indications of pessimism about practical wisdom are multiplying.

The fear of dumbing down in all its manifold guises is essentially a fear that others less wise or well-educated than yourself will, left to their own devices, prove unable or unwilling to ask the right questions or make the right cultural choices. Calls for censorship, of which we will hear more later, almost always betray a lack of faith in the ability, not of course of the would-be censor, but of the public at large to discriminate between worthwhile and meretricious or destructive ideas or opinions. And – *pace* Frank Luntz and many others – the urge to *simplify*, not to trust your audience with the complexity and ambiguity with which politicians and policymakers have to deal every day, is also a marker of disbelief in prudence.

You can believe in a universal faculty of practical judgement and still take the view that our rhetoric has taken a wrong turning. But unless you believe in human prudence, there is nothing which will convince you that there is a way back from here. When we come to consider remedies, this question of how far we are prepared to trust our fellow citizens will become central.

*

Over the past four chapters, we've explored the root causes of the crisis which has overtaken our public language. First, the changing character of western politics, with previous affiliations based on class and other forms of traditional group identity giving way, especially after the end of the Cold War, to a more complex and uncertain landscape in which political leaders struggle for definition and differentiation. Second, the widening gap between the world view and language of the experts who make modern policy and those of the public at large. Third, the impact of digital technology, and the disruption and competition it has brought, on journalists and politicians alike. Fourth, the battle between rationalists and authenticists about what constitutes good public language, a battle which has dragged on without resolution for more than two centuries, and which continues to confuse and distort the discussion of rhetoric to this day.

Finally, we have charted the way in which the language associated with sales and marketing has come to shape and colour public language as a whole and, at least in part, to replace traditional deliberative rhetoric. The effect has been to give political language some of the brevity, intensity and urgency we associate with the best marketing, but to strip it of explanatory and argumentative power. And against this and the many other pressures on public language, we have introduced the fragile notion that human beings are blessed with an innate faculty of prudence which they can use to decide who and what to believe.

Over the coming pages, we'll examine what a failing public language means for the discussion of the most important – and contentious – issues of our time. Those issues include the decision to go to war, and the boundaries of tolerance and freedom of speech. But let's begin with science and society.

9 Commit it to the Flames

I have a theory, and it's a theory that some people believe in, and that's the vaccinations. I mean we never had anything like this. This is now an epidemic. It's way, way up over the last ten years – it's way up over the last two years. And you know, when you take a little baby that weighs like twelve pounds into the doctor's office and they pump them with many, many simultaneous vaccinations – I'm all for vaccinations, but I think that when you add all of these vaccinations together and then two months later the baby is so different and lots of different things have happened, I really – and I've known cases.

Donald Trump, 2012[1]

In Stanley Kubrick's 1964 film *Dr Strangelove*, the rogue air-force general Jack D. Ripper attempts to trigger a nuclear exchange by sending his wing of B52s to attack Russia. Shortly before shooting himself, he explains his motive to RAF exchange officer Lionel Mandrake:

Ripper: You know when fluoridation first began?

Mandrake: No. No, I don't, Jack. No.

Ripper: Nineteen hundred and forty-six. Nineteen forty-six, Mandrake. How does that coincide with your post-war commie conspiracy, huh? It's incredibly obvious, isn't it? A foreign substance is introduced into our precious bodily fluids without the knowledge of the individual, and certainly without any choice. That's the way your hard-core commie works.

Mandrake: Jack . . . Jack, listen tell me, ah . . . when did you first become, well, develop this theory?

Ripper: Well, I ah, I, I first became aware of it, Mandrake, during the physical act of love.[2]

Fifty years later, many otherwise apparently sane people are gripped by a fear very like General Ripper's – that childhood vaccines, introduced like fluoridation in the name of better health, are in fact responsible for an epidemic of their own.

Like any drug, vaccines have side effects and it has long been known that a few of the millions of children who receive vaccines will react adversely to them, on rare occasions very seriously so. Unlike other drugs, vaccines are generally administered to disease-free as opposed to sick children and adults. The seeming unnaturalness of that – the doctor or nurse pressing a needle into a perfectly healthy baby and making him or her cry – has always prompted atavistic fears in the minds of some parents. There are numerous historical examples of opposition to vaccination programmes, especially when the authorities have attempted to make them compulsory. But the present panic about vaccination has an epidemiology of its own.

In 1998, a British medical researcher called Andrew Wakefield claimed in a paper published in the *Lancet* that he and his colleagues had discovered a link between the MMR vaccine (which protects against measles, mumps and rubella), a form of bowel disease, and autism. The overwhelming majority of experts in the field were sceptical about the Wakefield claims from the start, and other research teams were unable to reproduce his results. The obvious danger – that giving excessive credence to scientifically unsound concerns about the safety of the MMR vaccine might cause some parents not to immunise their children, with consequences for the health of the whole population – was also pointed out immediately.

But in the early years the story was often covered in the news in the UK and beyond as if the argument was evenly balanced. The BBC's agenda-setting morning radio programme *Today* covered the story assiduously, mounting a number of on-air debates in which non-expert representatives of vaccine pressure groups were given equal time with government scientists and doctors.[3] And the weight given to the Wakefield theory had its effect. A *Today* poll in 2001 discovered that – egged on no doubt by the programme's own tendentious coverage – no fewer than 79% of respondents thought there should be a public inquiry into the topic.[4] As predicted, rates of vaccinations fell not just in Britain but in other countries too, and some years later the incidence of measles in the UK and elsewhere began to rise.

The wheels of scientific and professional accountability grind slow but, in due course, Andrew Wakefield's paper would be discredited as not just erroneous but fraudulent. Another learned medical journal would describe it as 'perhaps . . . the most damaging medical hoax of the last 100 years'.[5] Wakefield himself was struck off the medical register in 2010 for serious professional misconduct. His co-authors had disowned both paper and theory years earlier.

And that, one might have thought, would be that. But long before the final damning verdict was delivered on the MMR/autism claim, the anti-vaccination movement had gathered a momentum of its own. Rather than abandon their belief in the link, anti-vaccinators advanced a host of conjectures about ways in which vaccines might be responsible for autism and other disorders and disabilities. One of them was the 'too many, too soon', or 'vaccine overload' theory. This is the theory to which Donald Trump is alluding (perhaps even claiming authorship for) in the excerpt from a phone interview with the Fox News morning show *Fox & Friends* which begins this chapter.

There is no medical or scientific evidence to support this theory, or even a conceptual model to suggest why it might be true. The childhood vaccine schedule has been, and continues to be, exhaustively monitored. We have no more reason to believe that infant vaccination causes autism than that eating Brussels sprouts does. But to true believers, these facts are not facts at all, but evidence of conspiracy and cover-up. Robert F. Kennedy Jr is one of many anti-vaccine campaigners to accuse the US government and the medical establishment of concealing the truth about the dangers, of holding 'secret meetings', of 'collusion' with Big Pharma, and – insofar as foreign aid encourages and funds vaccination in the developing world – of risking the world's condemnation for poisoning their children.[6] In a characteristic modern rhetorical inversion, the anti-vaccinators began to define that medical establishment itself as the 'anti-vaccine-safety lobby' and describe themselves, not as *antis* at all, but as campaigners *for* children's health. Look at a sample anti-vaccine site (childhealthsafety.wordpress.com), and you will find the defenders of vaccination described as 'cyber thugs and bullies'. 'These animals', says the site, 'are nasty, just nasty.'[7]

After the discrediting of Andrew Wakefield, most of the media adjusted their approach to the story, no longer granting vaccine scepticism equal time or equal treatment (in their interview with Trump, the hosts of *Fox & Friends* go out of their way to make it clear that most physicians do *not* believe there is any connection between vaccination and autism). But the fascination is still there, even if for reasons of journalistic and ethical safety the claims now tend to be followed by a question mark. Here's a 2012 headline from *Mail Online*:

> MMR: A mother's victory. The vast majority of doctors say there is no link between the triple jab and autism, but could an Italian court case reignite this controversial debate?[8]

One of the reasons for the continued media interest is the identity of many of the most vocal advocates of vaccine-scepticism: they are celebrities. Take the reality-TV star Kristin Cavallari:

> You know, at the end of the day, I'm just a mom. There are very scary statistics out there regarding what is in vaccines and what they cause – asthma, allergies, ear infections, all kinds of things. We feel like we are making the best decision for our kids.[9]

Then there's the model, film and TV actor and all-round personality Jenny McCarthy, who is perhaps the most prominent and persistent of the anti-vaccine celebrities:

> Us moms aren't treating autism, we are treating a vaccine injury. And when you treat the vaccine injury, the autism goes away, minimises or disappears.[10]

'In 1983, the shot schedule was ten,' she told *Good Morning America*: 'That was when autism was one in 10,000. Now there's thirty-six and autism is one in 150 . . . All arrows point to one direction.'[11] As General Ripper might say, it's incredibly obvious, isn't it?

The liberal comedian and chat-show host Bill Maher told his HBO audience that he did not believe that healthy people were vulnerable to the H1N1 (swine flu) virus and was against anyone – and particularly the government – sticking 'a disease into his arm'.[12] In point of fact there is no doubt that healthy children and adults *are* vulnerable to H1N1, that many have caught it, and some died from it. Nor do the vaccines that protect against it contain live virus, as Maher seems to think.

The intriguing question is why Bill Maher thought he had sufficient expertise to hazard a judgement about flu vaccination in the first place. Is it that he believed that virology is less specialist than other scientific disciplines, and that the issue of who will and who won't benefit from a given vaccine is a topic on which anyone, no matter how sketchy their grasp of the science or how limited their access to the data, can add something useful? He gave a clue when he posted a blog in response to the furore which his original remarks had provoked:

> I agree with my critics who say that there are far more qualified people than me – it's just that mainstream media rarely interviews doctors and scientists who present an alternative point of view.[13]

His argument seems to go like this. The powers that be (the government, the majority of the medical scientific community) are trying to stamp out heterodoxical – but quite possibly valid – perspectives on vaccine safety. 'Mainstream media' is cravenly complying with this exercise in suppression and, as a result, these alternative points of view just aren't getting aired. Yes I, Bill Maher, may be underqualified to speak about them but at least I have a platform from which I can raise them. And surely *some* conversation about vaccines is better than no conversation at all.

This is an appeal for open-mindedness and free speech, cast as a gallant David and Goliath contest between maverick but perhaps truth-telling 'scientists and doctors' (and of course Maher himself), and the faceless power-structures of the state and the pharmacological-industrial complex. The appeal transcends conventional left–right political orientation: conservative libertarians who have their own ideologically-grounded suspicions about such sinister federal institutions as the Centers for Disease Control might well find themselves rallying to the Maher flag.

The question which Bill Maher's argument provokes – to what extent, if at all, is it right to abandon the normal conventions of balance in debate and media coverage when medical or scientific findings are disputed by mavericks or non-scientists? – is an interesting one, and we will return to it. But that doesn't make his argument valid in this case. In the blog, he describes vaccination as a 'nuanced subject'. Actually, idiocy aside, it's notably unnuanced – the science and the statistics are clear-cut – and, insofar as there *are* nuances, they are ones which require scientific training to understand. And virtually none of the people who actually have that training believe there is any need to have the kind of debate of which Bill Maher seems to be in favour, one which would treat the inventions of Andrew Wakefield and the ramblings of a Jenny McCarthy as if they were to be taken as seriously as real science.

So what effect are today's vaccine sceptics having on public attitudes and parents' willingness to vaccinate their children? A paper published in the journal *Pediatrics* in 2011 (but referring to survey research conducted in 2009) suggests that the prudence we discussed in the last chapter is not dead.[14] The respondents (a representative sample of 2,500 parents) were asked who they would trust to provide them with information about vaccine safety: 76% said they would trust their children's doctor 'a lot' and a further 22% 'some'. Government vaccine experts/officials predictably got much lower, though still net positive scores: 23% said they would trust them a lot and 61% some, while 16% selected 'not at all'. As for celebrities, 2% said they would trust them a lot and a further 24% said 'some', though 74% or three-quarters of the respondents said they wouldn't trust them at all.

The celebrities, then, come a poor third to the family doctor. But that quarter of respondents who say they would trust the advice of celebrities on vaccine safety either 'a lot' or at least 'some' is still disturbing, given the potential impact of even a small percentage of parents refusing to allow their children to be vaccinated. And the same underlying survey suggested that broader – and unfounded – doubts about vaccines had taken significant hold: 25% of respondents agreed with the statement that 'some vaccines cause autism in healthy children' and 11.5% said they had actually refused a vaccine for their children that had been recommended by their doctor.[15]

These findings suggest that my *New York Times* colleague Frank Bruni was too pessimistic when he wrote in a column in April 2014 that 'whether the topic is autism or presidential politics, celebrity trumps authority and obviates erudition'.[16] The battle is not lost yet, at least not so far as vaccines are concerned. But why should there be a battle at all? Why should anyone pay any attention to what celebrities and other entirely non-expert voices have to say on the subject? Isn't there some way of changing the way subjects like vaccine safety are discussed so that the simple scientific truth emerges and the public are no longer duped?

Serious, Rational, Reasonable

Throughout the history of the West, almost everyone who has thought systematically about our acquisition of true understanding has accorded a special status to science. What is privileged is less the emerging body of scientific theories as such than the methodologies that underpin them: first the application of logic and deductive reasoning in the case of mathematics and abstract science; and second the 'scientific method', in other words the systematic use of empirical evidence to test hypotheses about the observable universe. David Hume's injunction that we should commit to the flames all propositions and claims that do not derive either from 'abstract reasoning concerning quantity or number' or 'experimental reasoning concerning matter of fact and existence' encapsulates these two special claims.

During much of the twentieth century, the majority of politicians and public intellectuals were prepared to defer to the prevailing scientific consensus when they discussed science-related issues, even though they knew that knowledge of science was typically low among the general public, and that it was easy – and could sometimes be politically advantageous – to stoke public confusion and fear.

There was generally less agreement between experts in economics, sociology and the other social sciences, and the politicians could therefore pick and choose experts whose take on a given policy area accorded with their own perspective or ideological preference. Nonetheless, these experts were also typically accorded – and showed each other – a significant level of professional and personal respect. All this was important because, as we noted in Chapter 6, public policy formulation became progressively more technocratic as the century progressed, and the standing of the scientists, doctors, economists and other experts who were helping to draft those policies was critical if the policies themselves were to command public support.

In the 1990s, as with so many other forms of rhetorical restraint, this set of conventions began to break down and is now in ruins. The controversy about vaccines is far from an isolated outbreak. The same phenomenon – a willingness to ignore or argue against science and the facts in pursuit of one's own point of view – is apparent in many other policy debates: climate change, genetically modified crops and energy policy are all prominent cases in point. In the social sciences, obfuscation and outright denial of even those facts which all the experts regard as incontrovertible is endemic. During the campaigns leading up to the 2014 referendum on Scottish independence and the 2016 vote on the UK's membership of the European Union, for instance, it proved impossible in the public debate to reach any common ground about what the economic and constitutional consequences of a *yes* or a *no* might be. Both sides dismissed the claims of academic economists with whom they happened to disagree, and categoric statements by such theoretically independent and impartial expert figures as the governor of the Bank of England were simply ignored by everyone who found them inconvenient. In the case of the referendum on Europe, constitutional experts who warned about the narrow framework for exit set out in the Lisbon Treaty were dismissed out of hand by those politicians who feared that the legal reality might frighten off the public, and who wanted instead to present the treaty provisions as non-binding and open to negotiation. It was as if there were no facts or laws, only opinions, and the public were free to believe whatever they lived.

It is plain that the way *authority* plays out in contemporary public language has become disordered – in how it is used in argument and, more importantly, in how it is heard and evaluated by the listening public. In this chapter, we will examine why. Science will be our main focus: its claim to objective authority is uniquely clear-cut and the failure of that authority to prevail is therefore uniquely stark. But what goes for hard science and medicine goes also for the social sciences, urban planning and the many other fields where specialist knowledge finds itself in collision with modern adversarial politics.

Let's begin by hearing a sophisticated example of the case *against* science – sophisticated, because it doesn't take issue with the authority of science in its own realm, but argues that, when it comes to public policy debate, science needs to learn its place:

Ladies and gentlemen, the climate change debate is much more than just a battle over scientific theories and environmental statistics. At its

core is the question of which approach our societies should take in
view of a serious concern that could possibly turn out to be a real
problem sometime in [the] future. What rational societies and policymakers need to ask is: what are the most reasonable and the most
cost-effective policies that neither ignore a potential problem that may
possibly materialise in the distant future nor the actual economic costs
of such policies here and now. Fundamentally these are social, ethical
and economic questions that cannot be answered by science alone but
require careful consideration by economists and social commentators.[17]

The speaker is a social anthropologist called Dr Benny Peiser. He
is the director of Global Warming Policy Foundation, a British think-
tank-cum-pressure-group chaired by the former Tory Chancellor of
the Exchequer, Nigel Lawson. Dr Peiser was introducing the
Foundation's annual lecture in 2011.

Let's take a close look at this passage. What comes across at first
is the judicious tone. Climate change is a 'serious concern' which
might turn into a 'real problem'. What 'rational societies and policymakers' have to do is to arrive at policy responses which are both
'reasonable' and also 'cost-effective'. *Serious, rational, reasonable.*

If we look closer still, we detect a little rhetorical filigree: within a
couple of sentences, that 'serious concern' is getting pushed linguisti-
cally away from us with a triad of qualifications – it turns out that
it's a *potential* problem that may only *possibly* happen in a *distant* future,
whereas staring us in the face is another triad which is only too immediately present – the *actual* and specifically *economic* costs which we
will have to pay *here and now*. These contrasting triads are a trope
which was well known and widely used thousands of years ago.

Having thus contextualised and 'fixed' climate change, Benny Peiser
then turns to science's role in formulating a response. Here comes
another triad: 'fundamentally' these are '*social, ethical* and *economic*
questions' which 'cannot be answered by science alone' but require
careful consideration by 'economists and social commentators'. That
word 'fundamentally' is important. What it implies is that the layer
of policy consideration which addresses social, ethical and economic
questions is somehow weightier or more critical than the scientific
layer. It's as if the science were a necessary but insufficient precursor
to the *real* debate. In support of this, let me quote some remarks Dr
Peiser made a few months before the passage I have just quoted:

> The global warming hysteria is well and truly over. How do we know?
> Because all the relevant indicators – polls, news coverage, government
> U-turns and a manifest lack of interest among policymakers – show a
> steep decline in public concern about climate change.[18]

There was considerable polling evidence to back Dr Peiser's contention that, by 2011, public anxiety about climate change was indeed
receding. But what this second quote again implies is that there are
two layers of discourse about climate change: a scientific layer whose
'relevant indicators' are atmospheric temperatures and so on; and a
separate layer of public perception, policy and politics with its own
quasi-scientific metrics – opinion polls, news coverage and that (presumably slightly harder to measure) 'manifest lack of interest among policymakers'. The good news, at least as far as Dr Peiser is concerned,
is that in this second layer the metrics are going his way. But of course
none of *that* tells us anything at all about the first layer. The planet
could be heating up even as public interest in climate change cools.

The subordination implied by that 'fundamentally' in Dr Peiser's
first quote seems to apply not just to the science of climate change
but to science as a whole. When it comes to policy discussions and
the assessment of possible responses and mitigations, whatever science
discovers will require 'careful consideration by economists and social
commentators'.

Now we all know who economists are, but what about these 'social
commentators'? What training and qualifications do you need to
become one? Or is *social commentator*, like that other modern media
standby the *community leader*, an office which involves an element of
self-election? If you read through the names on the board of trustees
of the Global Warming Policy Foundation and indeed some of the
authors of its reports, you're left with the impression that in practice
'social commentators' means retired politicians and civil servants,
academics in the social sciences and – there is no easy way of breaking
this to the reader – journalists.

Let's try substituting that in Dr Peiser's last sentence. *These are . . .
questions that cannot be answered by science alone but require careful consideration by journalists.* It doesn't work, does it? That's because of the stark
difference in authority between scientists and journalists. Ipsos MORI
tracks levels of trust expressed by members of the British public in

different professions. 89% of respondents to their 2005 survey said that they would generally trust doctors to tell the truth, while the number for scientists was 79%. But only 25% said they would trust journalists, while ministers and politicians as a class were trusted by only 22 and 21% respectively.[19] In a straight fight for credibility between scientists and journalists, then, journalists are going to be massacred, and retired politicians will fare even worse. Much safer to ask them both to kneel, receive a tap from the sword and arise as members of that splendidly new and untainted category of authority, the social commentator.

Dr Peiser's remarks are all about authority – and specifically about *which* authority takes precedence when it comes to weighing public policy choices. Indeed the Global Warming Policy Foundation's website is itself a kind of shrine to authority, or at least a simulacrum of it. The Foundation, the site tells us, is all about 'restoring balance and trust to the climate debate', which again sounds suitably measured and grown-up. Who, after all, can be against 'balance' and 'trust'? To someone like me brought up in a tradition of impartial journalism, the word 'balance' suggests an even-handed approach to a topic, but that certainly isn't what the founders of the GWPF have in mind. Their site is an anthology of straightforward and thorough-going climate scepticism, much of it from familiar voices. Let one author and one title stand for many: Christopher Booker and *The BBC and Climate Change: A Triple Betrayal.*[20] 'Only triple?', I want to say. Standards really must be slipping.

But in one sense, I think the GWPF really *is* an attempt to restore balance to the debate. Faced with the formidable scientific institutions backing the case that dangerous climate change is almost certainly taking place – the Intergovernmental Panel on Climate Change, or IPCC, the Royal Society, the American National Academy of the Sciences and so on – the Foundation is an attempt to put a heavy paw into the *other* scale by gathering together a group of committed climate sceptics, many with distinguished careers in government, business and academia. Dr Peiser's remarks are best seen as a demand that these other authorities should be taken as seriously, and when it comes to policy formulation, perhaps *more* seriously, than the scientists. When such important social and economic questions are at stake, isn't it both dangerous and politically unrealistic to leave science – and particularly the policy implications of science – to the scientists?

How best should we think about this gambit? Let me begin with myself. Like most non-scientists of my social and educational background, I accept that science is by far our best way of understanding the material world. When it comes to an argument, I almost always find myself instinctively on the side of mainstream science. I *don't* do that because I have personally checked the evidence which underpins *The Origin of Species* or worked through Schrödinger's equations: I haven't the expertise to do either. No, I back science because I find Karl Popper's account of the scientific method compelling* and because, at the level of common sense, the explanatory and predictive success of science is so overwhelming. And I've spent enough time with scientists to be convinced that the culture and practice of science genuinely aim at truth.

At the same time, I know that it's too simplistic to say that science is always and immediately right. Sometimes there's not enough data, or the puzzle of what the data means has yet to be cracked, or the whole thing is still a work in progress: the science is, or at least appears, *unfinished*. On other occasions, scientists disagree – there are rival explanations, or there's a candidate explanation which some scientists back but others oppose: in these cases, the science is *disputed*. On still other occasions, someone may call into question the good faith of the scientists – they're in the pay of the government or big business or committed to some cause and therefore their work may lack impartiality and thus reliability: we might call this *corrupted*, or at least *compromised* science. We also know that, on very rare occasions, there have been dramatic revolutions in the history of science when a consensus view has been overturned in favour of a radical new theory.

So as we listen to a given scientific debate, in principle any number of doubts can appear. Yes, of course we still believe in the authority of good, finished, honest science – but maybe in *this* case it's not quite ready; or maybe we're in the middle of a he-says-she-says wrangle;

---

* In *The Logic of Scientific Discovery* (1934) and elsewhere, Popper argued that what distinguishes scientific theories is that they are *falsifiable*, in other words they can always be challenged and, if necessary, rejected or amended in the light of new evidence. It is this permanent openness to inductive and deductive challenge (rather than a belief in the unshakable truth of any given set of theories or a belief in even the *possibility* of immutable scientific truth) that gives the scientific method its epistemological credibility.

or maybe there *is* something fishy about the way that report was paid for; or maybe that lone scientist I heard on the radio is right and it's the other 99% of physicists who will be proven wrong in the end. In an age of endemic suspicion and uncertainty, it doesn't take much for the weevils to get to work.

And there's something else. Let's imagine a conversation between two characters. We can think of them as stereotypes, though many of us will have encountered plenty of real-life examples of both. Let's call the first person the Executive. She doesn't dismiss the green agenda out of hand, but thinks there's a lot of nonsense and political correctness attached to it and is genuinely terrified about the cost and bureaucracy involved in some of the proposed solutions. To her, what the Global Warming Policy Foundation says probably makes a lot of sense. The second person I'll call the Environmentalist. He's someone who worries at every level – from the practical to the moral – about the damage he believes humanity is doing to our ecosystem. His fear is not that policymakers are doing too much, but too little and too late.

The conversation begins with climate change. Unsurprisingly, the Executive says she's got grave doubts about the so-called science behind global warming. Didn't those scientists in East Anglia do something wrong and didn't even the IPCC drop a clanger about Himalayan glaciers? Are you a scientist? asks the environmentalist. No? Then who are you to doubt the conclusions reached by the overwhelming majority of the world's climatologists?

Then the conversation switches to genetically modified food. Now it's the Environmentalist who voices doubts about the science: perhaps it's not ready and we don't yet understand the potential risks. Or perhaps, because of the commercial interests involved, the science isn't truly independent. And now it's the Executive who makes the case for simply backing the experts.

In other words, our preconceptions – our world view even – can be critical in determining whether we're prepared to accept the authority of science or to turn up the dial on all the available doubts. How can we predict whether or not someone is convinced by the scientific case for anthropogenic global warming? Is it how many years they spent studying science in school and college? Or does it depend on how much they've read or how many scientists they've heard talking about the subject? In fact, it turns out that a strong indication is how they vote. Numerous polls both in Britain and America suggest that people to the left of the political spectrum are more likely to believe the case than those on the right.[21] To take a single example, a Pew poll conducted in the US in January 2014 suggested that 42% of Democrat voters thought that dealing with global warming was a 'top policy priority', whereas only 14% of Republican voters did.[22] One's response to a piece of hard, technical science can, to a significant degree, be a matter of ideological taste.

We tend to view science, like everything else, through the lens of our own beliefs and prejudices. As we saw in the case of vaccine safety, and notwithstanding the fact that scientific uncertainty is itself a topic which requires scientific expertise to master, we can easily find ourselves treating the reliability of a given scientific claim as if it was like any other debate in which our own and other people's lay opinions are as good as anyone else's. And we arbitrarily shift our view about our own level of authority. We probably won't argue the toss when a dentist tells us that her X-ray of our mouth shows an abscess. But we may very well believe we have something useful to add – something we've read on the Web, the benefit of our common sense, a fond anthropomorphic memory of *The Wind in the Willows* – as a scientist explains the case for or against culling badgers.

*

When we consider this background – of preconception and expectation, fear and prejudice – against which science has to make its public case, the puzzle of why scientific evidence and judgement is so often treated as just one more opinion becomes easier to explain. But we need to add to this another factor which concerns the structure and character of argument itself.

Modern public debates about science often represent a messy clash between two, not just different, but diametrically opposed approaches to argument: *scientific argument* and *advocacy*.

Scientific argument – if we imagine it idealised in a perfect scientific paper – seeks to state its case not just as *clearly* as possible, but in a sense as *weakly* as possible. Every objection, every area of doubt should be flagged up. Suppose there is a rival theory, which our paper intends to argue against: it should be presented in its most compelling form.

All of its strong points should be set out before the evidence supporting the paper's own hypothesis is brought to bear.

Advocacy does the opposite. Advocacy prefers to ignore or skate over the weak points in its own case and to focus on those in its opponent's. It feels less of an obligation to clarity and comprehensiveness, and is quite happy to rely on rhetorical effects to win the day. Advocacy can itself be part of a systematic search for the truth – in the context of a law court, for instance, where each side can make their own case and challenge the other's – but it is a quite different *way* of seeking the truth.

So what happens when you mix science and advocacy? Let's take an example involving the UK's most distinguished scientific body, the Royal Society (RS). In 2007, Channel 4 broadcast a documentary called *The Great Global Warming Swindle* which, as its title suggests, aired strongly sceptical views.[23] It was the most high-profile part of a wave of scepticism which many scientists feared might be turning public opinion against the case for anthropogenic climate change. In June that year, the RS weighed in with a paper called *Climate Change Controversies: A Simple Guide.* It begins with these words:

> The Royal Society has produced this overview of the current state of scientific understanding of climate change to help non-experts better understand some of the debates in this complex area of science.[24]

Then it lays its cards on the table. The paper, it says, is not intended

> to provide exhaustive answers to every contentious argument that has been put forward by those who seek to distort and undermine the science of climate change and deny the seriousness of the potential consequences of global warming. Instead, the Society – as the UK's national academy of science – responds here to eight key arguments that are currently in circulation by setting out where the weight of scientific evidence lies.

Next the reader is treated to a series of punchy ripostes to eight of the arguments put forward by the climate sceptics on pages headed 'Misleading argument 1', 'Misleading argument 2' and so on.

This passage is almost a rhetorical mirror-image of Benny Peiser's introduction to the GWPF's annual lecture. Now the 'weight of scientific evidence' and 'the UK's national academy of science' in all their sober might are ranged against 'those who seek to distort and undermine the science of climate change'. The only real caveat offered is that the 'consequences of global warming' are only 'potential'. Note also the withdrawal of the assumption of good faith. This is not a debate between people of integrity but a battle between enlightened science and hostile forces who actively want to 'distort' and 'undermine'. The same claim can be found in a letter to the journal *Science* in 2010 from hundreds of members of the American National Academy of Sciences: 'many recent assaults on climate science and, more disturbingly, on climate scientists by climate change deniers are typically driven by special interests or dogma, not by an honest effort to provide an alternative theory that credibly satisfies the evidence'.[25]

We're told in neither case what the evidence is of this malign intentionality. The conclusion that the deniers have ulterior and dishonest motives was not arrived at through Hume's 'experimental reasoning': it's conjectural – and the kind of *ad hominem* point-scoring we normally associate with political rather than scientific discourse. This is how the RS guide ends: 'We must also prepare for the impacts of climate change, some of which are already inevitable.'[26] Not *probably* inevitable, but inevitable. As advocacy, this is forthright stuff. It uses the extraordinary authority of the Royal Society to full effect and it spells out its case in plain language and with far fewer conditions and qualifications than one would normally expect to see in a communication from scientists.

And that was the problem. What followed was predictable: forty-three members of the RS complained about the tone of *Climate Change Controversies*, in particular about its 'stridency' and failure to fully acknowledge areas of 'uncertainty' in the science. Accordingly, the RS commissioned a new guide which was eventually published in the autumn of 2010.[27]

The rhetorical flavour of this second guide is very different from the first. It is called *Climate Change: A Summary of the Science* and, at least to my layman's eye, it is exactly that. Now the question of scientific uncertainty is dealt with at length. Indeed the guide is partly structured along a spectrum of certainty in sections with titles like 'Aspects of climate change where there is a wide consensus but continuing debate and discussion' and 'Aspects that are not well understood'.

As far as I can tell, the underlying scientific evidence on which the two guides rely is almost identical. I've no doubt that the majority of the scientists who signed off on the second guide were just as convinced that the weight of the evidence points to a high probability of significant anthropogenic warming as the authors of the first. The difference between the two guides is in the character of the argumentation: the second draws back from the techniques and language of advocacy towards something which is much closer to straightforward scientific exposition.

But the publication of the second guide did not signal a withdrawal by the RS from the policy debate about climate change. Senior representatives – including successive presidents – of the Society have continued to play a lively part in that debate, urging governmental action at national and international levels while maintaining steady fire on the climate sceptics. That fateful transition from the dialectical and rhetorical zone of science qua science to that of advocacy has also occurred in the US. 'As scientists, it is not our role to tell people what they should do or must believe', the American Association for the Advancement of Science (AAAS) said in March 2014, but then proceeded to do exactly that, going beyond the dissemination of scientific knowledge to urge action on CO_2 emissions.[28] This is the exact boundary between science and politics – the boundary not just between two vocations and disciplines, but between two realms of discourse and argument – and both the RS and the AAAS have chosen to cross it.

As we noted, Benny Peiser's 2011 claim that the global warming 'hysteria' was over – or, to put it more soberly, that public and political interest and urgency on the topic was on the wane – was based on reality. In the UK, a Populus poll suggested that between the autumn of 2009 and the spring of 2010, the numbers of those who said they did *not* believe that global warming was taking place had jumped from 15% to 25%, and that of those who agreed with the statement 'man-made climate change is environmentalist propaganda for which there is little or no evidence' had risen from 9% to 14%.[29] In the US, the percentage of respondents who thought there was 'solid evidence' that any kind of warming was taking place fell from 70% in 2006 to 62% in 2014.[30] In 2013, when Americans were asked to rank global threats, climate change was cited by fewer (40%) than North

Korea's and Iran's nuclear programmes (59% and 54% respectively), not to mention 'international financial instability' (52%) and 'China's power and influence' (44%).[31] Scepticism is lower in other western countries and in much of the developing world, although the issue recently fell down the policy agenda in some of these places as well, especially after the global financial crisis drew the attention of both politicians and populations away from the environment and towards the challenge of restoring economic stability and growth.

Compare this with the overwhelming view of the world's climate scientists. One survey suggested that no fewer than 97% of atmospheric scientists believed that man-made climate change is happening.[32] Scepticism is not unknown even among climatologists, but is extremely rare. A study which looked at scientific papers published on global warming in peer-reviewed journals during 2013 and 2014 found that of 69,406 papers, only 4 came down against anthropogenic warming.[33] This piece of research was compiled by a campaigner against climate change scepticism, but many other studies support the conclusion that there is no meaningful 'scientific controversy' between the overwhelming majority of working scientists in the field that there is a very high probability, not just that the planet is getting warmer, but that industrial activity is a major cause and that the consequences for human life on earth will be serious.

This stark contrast between the judgement of the experts and the public at large led many scientists to conclude that the world faced an acute failure in the popular understanding of a critical scientific issue. This failure meant a lack of public consensus in favour of meaningful action on climate change and, because politicians are so influenced by the public mood, that in turn was undermining national and multinational progress on the topic. The problem, then, was not about our scientific knowledge as such, but about the *transmission* of that knowledge into the public realm. It was a problem of communication, in other words, and the scientists decided to address it as exactly that and with traditional rhetorical tactics. Stand up and be counted. State your argument with as few caveats as you can. Take the battle to the enemy. The campaigning 2006 documentary *An Inconvenient Truth*, a compendium of the scientific evidence of serious anthropogenic warming based on Al Gore's celebrated slideshow, was an influential example of this more aggressive approach.

It's easy to understand why, given what they believe is at stake, so many climatologists have felt that it is their duty to speak out on global warming, and why so many scientists who are *not* climate specialists have been emboldened to join them. Experts turn to advocacy when they fear that the facts may not be getting through, that they need to do something more to convince their audience – but how effective is it as a tactic? Not very, at least if climate change is anything to go by. Like any forthright manifesto, *An Inconvenient Truth* may well have rallied those who were already convinced that dangerous climate change was taking place, but there's little evidence it convinced many sceptics or even made significant inroads into the undecideds. Nor is it demonstrable that stronger language from the IPCC or national scientific bodies has significantly changed opinions. Advocacy and arguments about bad faith play into the hands of the climate sceptics who would much rather have that kind of debate than one about the facts themselves. The more a scientist sounds like a politician with an agenda, the less convincing they are likely to be.

The Pollution of Meanings

How does the media manage to make sense of this complex landscape? With great difficulty, is the honest answer. The headline reasons should come as no surprise: the subject is hard, life is short, impact and controversy usually beat evidence and explanation. In the case of science and the media, however, it's worth spending some time on the particulars.

First, with notable exceptions like *The New York Times*, there are far fewer specialist science correspondents than there were a generation ago – the deteriorating economics of news has seen to that. The generalist reporters, editors and commentators who end up covering science stories often have little more knowledge of the subject, or ability to distinguish between specialist scientific 'opinion' and the hunches of untrained activists or politicians, than an average member of the public. This loss of subject-specific expertise is true across the social sciences as well.

Second, both they and the readers are often trapped in clichéd narratives and cultural stereotypes about science, which make for easy headlines but impede rather than aid understanding. In their study of biotechnology and the popular press in Flanders, 'Knowledge, Culture and Power',[34] Pieter Maeseele and Dimitri Schuurman included an intriguing table of the 400 metaphors used in the Flemish popular press between 2000 and 2004 to describe the debate about different kinds of biotech:

> GMOs*: use of the 'Frankenstein' metaphor – 22 times.
> GMOs are pollutants – 4 times.
> The battle against GMOs is a crusade – twice.
> Cloning is *Jurassic Park* – 6 times.
> Cloning means eternal life – 26 times.
> Genetic manipulation is a Nazi practice – 10 times.
> Genetic manipulation is *Brave New World* – 6 times.
> Genetic manipulation is an activity pursued by Saddam Hussein – once.

And so on. Although a few are positive, the overwhelming majority of the metaphors are negative, and many nightmarish. The powerful and readily digestible narratives evoked by the use of words like *Frankenstein, Jurassic Park* or *Nazi*, all of them redolent of science gone wrong or perverted to evil ends, have the effect of setting up a journalistically potent air of jeopardy and panic, but hardly help a reader judge the objective evidence and the case for and against GMOs. Promises of 'eternal life' belong to another genre of science writing which chiefly trades in miracle pills and magic cures, namely the grotesque exaggeration of early-stage medical discoveries which in most cases lead to nothing at all. These kinds of myth and legend are widely disseminated, however, and their influence often crowds out science reality. In Flanders, Maeseele and Schuurman concluded that what they called 'the science-industrial complex' had either lost or was losing 'the interpretive struggle'.[35]

Even those science correspondents and columnists who are too sophisticated to play the Frankenstein card can still fall under the influence of deep narratives about humanity, science and nature. Rachel Carson's 1962 book about the use of pesticides, *Silent Spring*, set out a substantial body of empirical evidence, but what made the

---

* Genetically modified organisms (including food).

book resonate was its focus on industrial mankind's hubris as the central threat to the natural world, and its ominous, elegiac tone. In her 'fable for tomorrow', a dystopic description of an imaginary American town after nature has been ruined, she wrote that 'some evil spell had settled on the community'. This almost religious sense of the fragility of the natural world, of wanton human greed and a squandered stewardship, has coloured much of the reporting of environmental issues ever since.

The Club of Rome's famous 1972 report, *The Limits to Growth*, successfully created a paradigm about economic growth and the exhaustion of the world's natural resources which informs the reporting of these topics to this day, even though the simulation on which it was based remains controversial and many of its projections, which were taken by the media at the time to be predictions, have turned out to be wide of the mark.[36] What the press and public took from *The Limits to Growth* was a simple story, and that story stuck.

A third issue is that reporters and editors wrestle with many different kinds of authority. Doctors and scientists are clearly authority figures, and are generally treated as such. But we live in an era where victims are accorded a high level of authority as well: their pain and, in the case of the bereaved, their personal loss are understandably thought to give them the right to speak out without aggressive cross-examination. Thus the asymmetry of a dispassionate expert debating the safety of a given medical procedure with someone who has no specialist understanding, but who carries the immense human credibility of having been through the experience themselves – and the inevitable risk that the statements these two people make will be regarded as somehow equivalent.

We may not like it, but in media terms celebrities have a kind of authority too – rightly or wrongly, many people are genuinely interested in their opinions – and, as we saw in the case of vaccines, some celebrities either are, or at least know, victims of the thing against which they are complaining, and therefore enjoy some of that authority as well. Jenny McCarthy has an autistic son. Even Donald Trump tells us, 'I've known cases.'

At least from their own perspective, then, editors often find themselves trying to juggle and balance different *kinds* of authority within a story or a studio discussion. It is not that scientific authority is blatantly disrespected, rather that in much of modern media it is not granted the privileged status relative to other voices which most scientists – and plenty of thoughtful non-scientists – think it should be. In many ways, this is the heart of the media's conundrum of how best to integrate science, and the special language of science, into the general public discourse which is their stock-in-trade.

*

In July 2011, the governing body of the BBC published a report on the impartiality and accuracy of the way in which the BBC covers science, written by the eminent British scientist Professor Steve Jones.[37] It's a thoughtful and serious piece of work which was welcomed and accepted almost in its entirety by the BBC. But if you read it, you'll come across an argument – a rather civilised argument, it must be said, but an argument nonetheless – between Professor Jones and some of his BBC interlocutors which goes to the heart of the question of how we should think about authority in public argument.

When it comes to impartiality, to what extent should the BBC (and by extension the media as a whole) treat science like everything else – politics, religion, the arts – and to what extent differently because of science's unique epistemological claims? To caricature the two extremes, the first would suggest that science should climb into the boxing ring like every other interest and submit to all the usual rules of adversarial debate, the second that the role of the broadcaster when a scientist wishes to speak is to turn on the microphone at the start and to say thank you at the end. I know many scientists who fervently believe in the second position. To use the framework I introduced in Chapter 7, they are Enlightenment *rhetorical rationalists*, who believe that argument grounded in evidence and logic should always and immediately carry the day. They consequently find the many contemporary examples where this is manifestly *not* the case evidence either of a dysfunctional media or possibly of some kind of collective public madness.

Steve Jones claimed that some people in the BBC told him that the doctrine of impartiality implied 'equality of voice'. For a broadcaster or other news provider who strives for political impartiality, the concept of equality of voice is more or less obligatory for election coverage (where airtime to different parties may be allocated on the basis of electoral support and monitored with a stopwatch) and is likely to extend more loosely to all-party political debate, and perhaps even to discussions between politicians and members of the public on broad questions – immigration, euthanasia, same-sex marriage – where there are broad divisions of opinion.

But it doesn't make sense in all circumstances. The BBC's Editorial Guidelines in fact call for *due* impartiality, which I take to mean an approach to fairness in debate which takes account of the specific context of the argument. There are many moral questions where there is something close to unanimity among the public – about murder, terrorism and other serious crime, for instance – and where 'equality of voice' would be regarded by most people as inappropriate and offensive.

Nor is equal time or equal attention applicable in debates about facts, where those facts are incontrovertibly or substantially known. The dangers to health from smoking are so clearly established that it would not be impartial, but irresponsible to give a smoking enthusiast equal time with the Chief Medical Officer or Surgeon General; or fail to warn the audience about the very different background – minority perspective, lack of medical knowledge or corroborating evidence – against which to judge the interview. When it comes to climate change, the BBC has progressively shifted the balance of its coverage – and the access to the air given to the two sides of the debate – in the light of the growing scientific consensus about global warming expressed in successive findings of the IPCC and similar bodies. Despite errors in the early stages of the MMR/autism controversy, the same became true of coverage of that issue.

No responsible media organisation slavishly interprets impartiality as 'equality of voice' in every instance and, if any BBC editor told Steve Jones that such equality was appropriate in scientific controversies like that about climate change, they were wrong.

None of this of course will stop the sceptics demanding equality. In this chapter, we heard Bill Maher argue if not for that, then at least for *more* voice for vaccine scepticism on the basis that the science is less clear-cut than the orthodox view claims; as we saw, however, he was simply misinformed about the level of doubt about the science. Indeed, given the clarity of the science, vaccine-scepticism is probably still over- rather than underrepresented in terms of share of voice. Many climate change deniers similarly exaggerate the uncertainty associated with the science in order to argue for more airtime for their claims. The GWPF often does that, although, as we saw with Benny Peiser, they have a second, altogether more interesting claim – namely that the *policy implications* of climate change demand a much broader debate because they inevitably impinge on matters of wider social and economic significance.

This point is impossible to dismiss, and it illustrates how difficult a task it is for the media to do justice to a topic like climate change, while simultaneously maintaining due impartiality in every layer of the debate: at the level of the fundamental science, mirroring the balance of expert opinion and granting, say, less than 10% of airtime or words to the sceptical perspective; while handling a debate between political parties about the right policy response on the basis of 'equality of voice'. The task is made that much harder by the fact that it is in the interests of all the parties – and particularly those on the sceptical side – to constantly flit back and forth between questions of science and those of policy.

Let one example stand for many. When, in February 2014, the *Today* programme staged a discussion between Lord Lawson, the chair of the GWPF, and Professor Sir Brian Hoskins, the director of the Grantham Research Institute on Climate Change and the Environment, about the connection between climate change and a recent spate of floods and other extreme weather events in Britain, the BBC received numerous complaints. The complaints were at first rejected but then in June 2014 upheld on appeal, on the basis that the radio interviewer's failure to correct false statements by Lord Lawson on matters of science had failed to meet the Corporation's requirements for both accuracy and due impartiality. This is how one complainant characterised the case:

> It is very unfortunate that the BBC sought initially to justify the inter-
> view with Lord Lawson on the grounds that he had been invited on,
> as chair of the Global Warming Policy Foundation, a campaign group
> for climate change 'sceptics', to discuss the economics and politics of

climate change. However, as in previous interviews, Lord Lawson used most of his airtime to dispute the science of climate change. This interview is symptomatic of the confused and flawed approach adopted by some BBC programmes towards the coverage of climate change. A review by Professor Steve Jones for the BBC Trust in 2011 recommended that programmes should be more careful about creating a false balance between scientists and climate change 'sceptics'.[38]

'Confused and flawed' the approach may sometimes be, but in the real world of quotidian live media, the challenge of segregating science and policy debate is borderline impossible. Many scientists clearly believe that the best solution would simply be to exclude the sceptical viewpoint from the media altogether and some media organisations have adopted this approach. The *Los Angeles Times* no longer publishes letters which cast doubt on global warming[39] and the editors of the science forum subsection of Reddit have done likewise[40]. But these moves led to inevitable cries of censorship and may give credence to the very conspiracy theories on which the sceptics dine out.

One can sympathise with the frustration of the scientists and their supporters, and still doubt whether anyone has ever won an argument by stopping their opponent from being heard. If you are confident of your case – and science has every reason to be confident about climate change – you should welcome every opportunity to debate it. Censorship speaks instead of weakness – and perhaps of a kind of despair about whether the public are capable of discriminating between the valid claims of science and the essentially false prospectus of the sceptics.

But writing in *Nature*, Dan Kahan, a professor at Yale Law School who comments on the climate change debate, argues that the difficulty of successfully communicating information to the public about science lies not with the public's reasoning capacity (that practical wisdom we discussed in the last chapter), but with a divisive 'science communication environment'. He goes on to say: 'Overcoming this dilemma requires collective strategies to protect the quality of the science-communication environment from the pollution of divisive cultural meanings.'[41] So now we have an ecology of language itself and, instead of Rachel Carson's pesticides or those noxious vaccines, a pollution of 'divisive cultural meanings'.

Yet, although we may sympathise with Professor Kahan's frustration, surely those 'divisive cultural meanings' are an inevitable part of post-Enlightenment pluralism and open democratic debate and, even if we could imagine any 'collective strategies' which could protect us from them – Professor Kahan suggests that both psychology and anthropology might come in handy – would we really want to employ them? And in any event, just who would decide which of the cultural meanings were the divisive ones? That too might well turn out to be a source of division because, in a world which struggles to accept the special status of any discipline or expertise, an appeal to authority is likely to be a fool's errand.

Nonetheless Professor Kahan puts his finger on the problem. If you want evidence that our public language is heading into crisis, look no further than the climate change debate. Science is meant to be the decider, a species of knowledge that stands above the fray and whose pronouncements should be listened to and acted upon without delay. But instead it too is subject to the blurring of definitions and demarcations that we have encountered throughout this book.

And if the authority of science no longer carries the day, then why should we accept any other branch of specialist knowledge? Why should we believe what the economists and social scientists and other government experts tell us? Or accept the decisions of the courts? After all, if knowledge counts for nothing and everything is a matter of opinion, we're all experts and no one can persuade us otherwise.

10 War

_____

He handles great subjects in rhythmical language, and becomes
quickly enslaved by his own phrases. He deceives himself in the
belief that he takes broad views, when his mind is fixed upon one
comparatively small aspect of the question.
Lord Esher on Winston Churchill, 1917[1]

War is the greatest test of the rhetor. To convince a country to go to
war or to rally a people's courage and optimism during the course of
that war depends on your ability to persuade those who are listening
to you to risk sacrificing themselves and their children for some wider
public purpose. It is words against life and limb.

The need for length and detail as you explain the justification of
the war; the simultaneous need for brevity and emotional impact;
authenticity, rationality, authority; the search for a persuasiveness that
does not – cannot – sound anything like marketing given the blood
and treasure that are at stake: everything we have discussed so far in
this book comes together when we consider the rhetoric of war. The
scale of the challenge is the reason why so many of history's famous
speeches, from Pericles' oration for the Athenian dead to Lincoln's
Gettysburg Address to Churchill's speeches and radio addresses during
Britain's struggle for national survival in 1940–1, are concerned with
war – its necessity, its nobility, its terrible cost. So too many of the
best-known passages of rhetoric in fiction, from Henry V at Agincourt
to Aragorn in front of the Black Gate in *The Lord of the Rings*.

The wars we have fought in recent years may not compare in scale
to the cataclysms of the first half of the twentieth century, but they

have presented political and rhetorical challenges of their own. The justification for war has characteristically been more disputed and the wars themselves less decisive, early gains giving way to stalemate, recriminations at home and uncertain outcomes. Even relatively low-risk, initially popular interventions – no troops on the ground, aerial bombardment only – have had a habit of turning sour. Hospitals get bombed. The local good guys turn out to be not quite so good. And after all the time and money and heartache: success of a kind in a handful of cases; in others, anarchy and the metastasis of the very threat we went to war to eliminate.

Then there are the shadow wars, the wars and actions we didn't fight but which some claim we should have done: to halt the slaughter of innocents in Yugoslavia, Rwanda and Syria, to stop Iran getting the bomb, to help the Ukrainians fight off the Russians. Damned if you do, damned if you don't – the damnation sometimes coming from the same critics.

Protesters against a given military intervention often claim that their country's leaders have embarked on it for personal political advantage or vainglory – it's a charge which has been enthusiastically echoed in novels and movies at least since *War and Peace*. You'll have your own views about the leaders and wars of your lifetime. What we do know is that, with the exception of Margaret Thatcher and the Falklands and George H.W. Bush, John Major and the other leaders of the coalition which successfully fought the Gulf War in 1990–91, any western leader of the last thirty years who hoped that military action would improve their reputation has been sadly disappointed. In recent decades, war has been more likely to shred a leader's reputation than to rescue it.

So what role does our troubled public language play in this most fraught area of public policy? Let's begin with a benchmark:

> You ask, what is our policy? I will say: It is to wage war, by sea, land, and air, with all our might and with all the strength that God can give us; to wage war against a monstrous tyranny never surpassed in the dark and lamentable catalogue of human crime. That is our policy.
>
>   You ask, what is our aim? I can answer in one word: victory, victory at all costs, victory in spite of all terrors; victory, however long and hard the road may be; for without victory there is no survival.[2]

It's 13 May 1940. Winston Churchill has been prime minister of the United Kingdom for three days. This is his first speech to the House of Commons as the nation's leader. It is also day four of the German invasion of northern France. As Churchill speaks, the French defence is breaking at Sedan. Dunkirk is less than a fortnight away.

This passage of Churchill's speech has the structural clarity of a sonnet, or a prayer. There are two parts – stanzas I want to call them – the first asking and answering the question *what is our policy?*, the second the question *what is our aim?* The first is controlled by the repeated word *war*, the second by the repeated *victory*, though perhaps the most important word in the entire passage is the one to which everything else has been building: *survival*. The extract is rich in technical rhetorical effect: *anacoenosis* (rhetorical question); *alliteration* (*wage war*, that *God* can *give* us); *enumeratio* (the listing first of the ways in which the war must be fought, then of the challenges that must be faced before victory can be secured); *tricolon crescens* (those three *victory* clauses which progressively grow both in length and emphasis); and so on. Yet it never feels studied or contrived, but immediate, unforced, fluid; the repetition, alliteration and the short, spare clauses driving both the speaker and listener forward.

There's one phrase – the 'monstrous tyranny never surpassed in the dark and lamentable catalogue of human crime' – which reminds us of the orotundity which even Churchill's contemporaries found old-fashioned and pompous. In this context it is reassuring, Churchill the autodidact weighing the present threat in the scales of the past and assuring us that, on this occasion at least, the moral stakes are as clear as day.

And that's what strikes us most about this passage, and about the 'blood, toil, tears and sweat' speech as a whole. It is not, first and foremost, a moral call to arms. Churchill is rallying the Commons and the nation in the face of a real world emergency. The enemy is racing across France towards the Channel. Invasion and national destruction are not distant theoretical threats, but in imminent prospect. Yet the moral imperative is so congruent with the contingent emergency, the enemy so clearly in the wrong, that for once the language of *should* and *must*, of ethical and practical necessity, are one. It is a moment in time – Churchill, as we shall see, was no angel when it came to rhetoric – but it is magnificent.

What a long shadow that clarity casts. How difficult for any subsequent prime minister to stand at the Despatch Box to make a case for war that combines national self-interest and moral necessity so seamlessly. Let's listen to one trying. The location is again the House of Commons, the date is 18 March 2003, and Tony Blair is opening the debate into whether Britain should join the United States and other allies in invading Iraq:

> At the outset I say that it is right that the House debate this issue and pass judgement. That is the democracy that is our right but that others struggle for in vain. Again I say that I do not disrespect the views in opposition to mine. This is a tough choice indeed, but it is also a stark one: to stand British troops down now and turn back or to hold firm to the course that we have set. I believe passionately that we must hold firm to that course.[3]

There is a gracious tone to this, and indeed to the whole of the speech: an acknowledgement that, as Blair states a few sentences later, 'people who agree on everything else, disagree on this', while 'those who never agree on anything' find 'common cause'. In these opening words we hear moral argument at once: whereas the United Kingdom is a country where people have the right to question and debate everything the government proposes, the citizens of Iraq are not so lucky. Next, there is the recognition that this is a 'tough choice', not in the Churchillian sense of a decision which, while straightforward in itself, will require sacrifices in its execution, but a choice which is difficult to make. It is also a 'stark' choice: either to 'stand British troops down and turn back' or to 'hold to the course we have set'.

But who are *we*? Well, this first *we*, the *we* who have set the course so far, is clearly Tony Blair himself and his government. But then he goes on to say: 'I believe passionately that we must hold firm.' This second *we* includes not just his government but his listeners, everyone who will be voting in the Commons and, by extension, the nation. It's easy to miss the distinction and to hear the following meaning: *we-everyone must hold firm to the course that we-everyone have already set.* One way of persuading a reluctant audience to make a painful decision is to convince them that they have essentially already made it, and that to refuse it now would involve an illogical and dangerous climbdown. The blurring of *we-government* and *we-people* helps Tony Blair establish this implicit context.

The simplicity and power of the short sentence 'I believe we must hold firm' stand out, though. There's no hint of machismo: indeed the words 'hold firm' imply defence – of Britain and the world's security – rather than attack. The 'I believe' is important too. This is a statement by the leader of a government, but it is also explicitly a personal endorsement. Knowing how divided his party and the country are, Tony Blair lays his political judgement and reputation on the line. Like Churchill, Blair has practical policies and aims to lay out, but 'I believe we must hold firm' tells us that this is also a question of personal resolve or the lack of it, and a question of principle.

But the case he has to set out is far more complex and nuanced than Winston Churchill's. It's a tale not of a direct attack on British allies and forces and – who knows? – soon the British homeland, but a shaggy-dog story of UN resolutions and weapons inspectors and diplomatic manoeuvrings. The questions it seeks to answer are not as simple as *what is our policy?* or *what is our aim?* but *have we exhausted all diplomatic ways of ensuring that Saddam Hussein complies with Resolution 1441?* and *are the consequences of his non-compliance so serious that they justify the use of force against him?* Tony Blair, of course, will answer a firm *yes* to both of these abstruse questions.

Nonetheless in the midst of this painstaking exposition, the ghost of Churchill makes an appearance. Is Saddam Hussein another Adolf Hitler? Are those who oppose the war in 2003 like the appeasers of the 1930s? Tony Blair's answer is a subtle one. He protects himself by dismissing what he calls 'glib and foolish comparisons with the 1930s', and states explicitly that 'No one here is an appeaser', but then immediately goes on to talk about 1930s appeasement at some length. He claims that those arguing against military intervention today are different from their predecessors in an important respect: whereas the appeasers may not have realised how dangerous Hitler was, their modern equivalents have no such excuse, given Saddam Hussein's undisputed record of aggression and WMD development. Then he adds this Churchillian thought:

> the world has to learn all over again that weakness in the face of a threat from a tyrant, is the surest way not to peace but – unfortunately – to conflict.[4]

The reference to the 1930s is unmissable. But the present situation was quite different. The West had already fought one war against Saddam, and imposed stringent conditions and sanctions on him after it. There had certainly been a lively debate about those sanctions – with some arguing that they were too harsh, and others that they were unlikely to be effective no matter how hard they were made – but there had been no equivalent of the western inaction which greeted Hitler's remilitarisation of the Rhineland, annexation of Austria and invasion of Czechoslovakia. In the case of Saddam, it was impossible to argue that the forces of appeasement had had the upper hand in western policy. In any event, it's absurd to suggest that the 'surest way' to war is not to fight one. The surest way to war is simply to go to war, which is exactly what Tony Blair is now proposing.

Eighty years on, hindsight, revisionism and modern scepticism have done little to blunt or tarnish the impact of Winston Churchill's rhetoric. Around a decade and a half after he delivered it, it is impossible to read Tony Blair's speech in the way it was intended to be heard at the time. His argument rests centrally, indeed almost exclusively, on Saddam Hussein's weapons of mass destruction and the manifold dangers they pose: direct danger to his neighbours and the Middle East and, if the terrorists with whom he colludes get their hands on them, to us; and indirect danger, because if we don't take on Saddam and neutralise *his* weapons, other bad regimes will keep or acquire weapons of their own. The term 'weapons of mass destruction' appears fourteen times in the speech, and individual WMD – VX, anthrax, mustard gas, sarin, botulinum toxin, radiological bombs – many more times.

None of them were ever found. That is what we know now. And that knowledge eviscerates the speech. To us now, it is a speech without a foundation, a speech almost literally about nothing – but which nonetheless led to a war. This is *not* to reach a verdict about whether or not the speech was delivered in good faith – in other words, whether Tony Blair himself *believed* at the time that Saddam had WMD. It is simply to say that what we might call the *objective* moral justification set out for going to war has disintegrated utterly.

In his passage about the 1930s, Tony Blair suggested that we shouldn't blame the appeasers because it was only later that the scale of the menace of Hitler became clear. But now we have to confront the opposite revelation. In this case, it was only later that it became apparent how much *smaller* the threat of Saddam was than Tony Blair had claimed at the time. Once it became clear that the WMD didn't exist, other reasons for toppling Saddam Hussein would be adduced – that he was a tyrant and a mass-murderer, that he destabilised the region, that a democratic Iraq could be a force for good in the Middle East – but they do not form a significant part of the prime minister's case for going to war *at the point when the decision had to be made*. You may or may not believe that Tony Blair presented a knowingly false prospectus. There is no question that his argument rested on a false premise.

★

The most memorable peroration of that week was the resignation speech given the day before by Tony Blair's Labour colleague Robin Cook, who had decided to leave the Cabinet over the issue of Iraq. Cook laid out his argument drily enough, but the sadness in his voice and the foreboding in his face gave his exposition a tragic weight. This is how he ended:

> It has been a favourite theme for commentators that this House no longer occupies a central role in British politics. Nothing could better demonstrate that they are wrong than for this House to stop the commitment of troops in a war that has neither international agreement or domestic support. I intend to join those tomorrow night who will vote against military action now. It is for that reason, and for that reason alone, and with a heavy heart, that I resign from the government.[5]

At ten o'clock the following evening, the House of Commons voted to go to war with 412 votes in favour to 149 against. The invasion began two days later.

Despite the quality of the debate, the 'commentators' whom Robin Cook had been so keen to prove wrong had a point. To all intents and purposes, the question of Iraq had been decided long before the motion was laid before the House, and the principal rhetorical instruments which Tony Blair's government had used to make its case, and to satisfy itself that it had sufficient political and public support to proceed, were not parliamentary speeches but summaries of the intelligence in the government's possession about Saddam's alleged secret weapons. In the media, these summaries were called *dossiers*, a name which, at least in a British tabloid newsroom, conjured up a lost world of spies and stolen papers, Tintin and *The Riddle of the Sands*.

One of these had been published around six weeks before the parliamentary debate. This so-called 'February Dossier' was immediately discredited – part of it turned out to have been plagiarised from a PhD thesis which was itself more than a decade old. Commissioned by Tony Blair's communications director Alastair Campbell, it did the government's campaign to win support for the invasion no good at all.

But there had been an earlier dossier – the 'September Dossier' or, more soberly, *Iraq's Weapons of Mass Destruction: The Assessment of the British Government* – which had been published the previous autumn, and which was regarded at the time of the Commons vote as altogether more authoritative. MPs who voted in favour of the motion, and members of the public who supported the government's position, did so to a significant degree because they found this first dossier persuasive. Within a couple of months, though, they would be asking themselves if it was as suspect as the other, and if they themselves had been victims of a confidence trick.

On 22 May 2003, some nine weeks into the invasion, two men met for an abstemious drink (one Coke and one Appletiser) in the Charing Cross Hotel in central London. The first man was Dr David Kelly, a WMD expert working within the Ministry of Defence, the second Andrew Gilligan, a journalist from the BBC's *Today* programme. They'd met several times before; Kelly was the key source in an investigation Gilligan was carrying out into the British government's public claims about Iraqi WMD. Gilligan made some notes on the 22 May meeting in his electronic organiser:

transformed wk before pub to make it sexier

the classic was the 45 mins. mst thngs inndossier wre dbl sc but that was single-source. one source said it took 4 minutes to set up a missile assembly, that was misinterpreted . .

most people in intel werent happy with it, because it didnt refect the considere view they were putting forward

campbell

real info but unr, incl against ur wishes

not in orig draft - dull, he asked ifanything else cd go in.[6]

Most of Gilligan's digital shorthand is easy to translate. Dr Kelly told the journalist that the draft of the first dossier on WMD had been 'transformed' during the week before it was published to make it 'sexier', meaning more impactful and frightening, and therefore more persuasive. As we've seen, Aristotle's rather less steamy term for the same rhetorical impulse is *amplification*. An example was the suggestion that Saddam's chemical weapons could be deployed at only forty-five minutes notice and, because he also possessed medium-range missiles, could be used to attack British military bases in Cyprus in that time frame: this improbable claim had given some newspapers their headline when the dossier was published. The claim hadn't been in the original draft, Gilligan recorded Kelly as saying, because it was based on a single intelligence source and the experts were doubtful about it, but Alastair Campbell had thought that earlier draft to be 'dull' and had asked if anything else could be added to beef it up. During the subsequent inquiry into the affair conducted by Lord Hutton, Andrew Gilligan himself explained the densest passage: 'Campbell real info but unr, incl against ur wishes' means 'Campbell: real information but unreliable, included against our wishes'.[7]

Andrew Gilligan used this and other conversations with David Kelly as the basis for an interview and subsequent reports on the *Today* programme on 29 May, in which he made a number of specific allegations about the government and the dossier. He said that he had learned that the dossier had been changed 'at the behest of Downing Street'. As for that forty-five-minute claim,

what we've been told by one of the senior officials in charge of drawing up the dossier was that, actually the government probably, erm, knew that that forty-five-minute figure was wrong, even before it decided to put it in.

The 'erm' which follows the 'probably' – itself an attempt to take the edge off the accusation – is one of the most fateful hesitations in the history of journalism. Crazily, given the gravity of the charges that he was making, Andrew Gilligan was speaking in a live, unscripted radio interview with a presenter and was deciding how to express his story as he went along. He didn't *have* to allege that the government knew that the forty-five-minute claim was wrong, and seemed a little uncertain about whether he should do so, but ended up doing it anyway. Put together with his 'at the behest of Downing Street', the meaning was inescapable: Tony Blair and/or those immediately around him had knowingly distorted the September dossier to strengthen their public case.

The government reacted with fury to Gilligan's charge. Their response was couched in mangled English but it had a lawyer's vulpine precision: 'not one word of the dossier was not entirely the work of the intelligence agencies'. Although this sounds like a comprehensive denial, it in fact fails to answer the Kelly/Gilligan charge: Downing Street could have cajoled and bullied the authors of the dossier into radically altering the dossier, adding intelligence they thought was unreliable and insisting that caveats be removed, without adding a single phrase or new idea of their own.

The war of words had begun. David Kelly informed his bosses at the Ministry of Defence that he had met Andrew Gilligan, but said he did not believe he was the journalist's main source. They leaked enough information for the press to be able to identify Dr Kelly. He was then subjected to an ugly televised interrogation by a Select Committee of MPs. He told them he had not said the things which Andrew Gilligan had reported and they accepted his word. Nonetheless, he appeared extremely anxious. Shortly afterwards, he took his own life. Now the prime minister's own reputation – and quite possibly his job – was on the line, and the Kelly/Gilligan affair became the biggest running story in the UK, bigger even than the invasion of Iraq itself for many months.

To observers at the time, Kelly/Gilligan was a battle about politics and journalism. We can also see it as a battle about rhetoric. Andrew Gilligan's charge was that the first dossier was a piece of deliberately reckless rhetoric; that the government had been so eager to persuade the public that they had exaggerated what they knew, removing qualifications and presenting snippets of quite possibly erroneous intelligence as if they were facts – in other words, that they were guilty of doing to the first dossier many of the things I have claimed that contemporary politicians do to other expressions of public language.

But the government's counter-attack turned on a claim about rhetoric too. They effectively charged that Andrew Gilligan himself had been guilty of amplification, in that he had added an unsubstantiated accusation that they had knowingly falsified the dossier to make his story more impactful. Yes, it might be true that David Kelly and some of the other weapons experts in the MoD had had their doubts about the dossier, but establishing that did not prove the more heroic allegation that the distorting had been done on purpose. Like canny plaintiffs in a defamation action, they hoped to win the broader reputational fight by picking away at what they took to be the weakest point in Gilligan's story.

The government chose Brian Hutton, a senior judge who had made his reputation hearing terrorist cases in Northern Ireland, to hold an inquiry into the Kelly/Gilligan affair. Lord Hutton's inquiry soon zeroed in on the electronic record of that consequential meeting in the Charing Cross Hotel. Here is some of Andrew Gilligan's testimony:

> Q. Then there is the entry which is just a single word, 'Campbell'. Was there any question that gave rise to that entry?
>
> A. Yes, it was something like: how did this transformation happen?
>
> Q. Right.
>
> A. And then the answer was that, one word.
>
> Q. He said just 'Campbell'?
>
> A. Yes.
>
> Q. And what question led to the next entry?
>
> A. Well I was surprised and I said: What, you know, Campbell made it up? They made it up? And he said: No, it was real information but it was unreliable and it was in the dossier against our wishes.
>
> *Lord Hutton*: May I just ask you, Mr Gilligan, looking at the first paragraph, you put the question: Was it to make it sexier? And Dr Kelly replied: Yes, to make it sexier?
>
> A. Yes, to make it sexier, yes, so he adopted my words.
>
> *Lord Hutton*: Now are you clear in your recollection that you asked how was it transformed, and that the name Campbell was first spoken by Dr Kelly?
>
> A. Yes, absolutely.

> *Lord Hutton*: It was not a question by you: was Campbell involved
> in this?
> A. No, it was him. He raised the subject of the 45 minutes and he
> raised the subject of Campbell.[8]

So it was Gilligan rather than Kelly who had first used the word 'sexier',
although Gilligan claimed that Kelly had accepted it ('Yes, to make it
sexier'). On the other hand, Andrew Gilligan stubbornly maintained
that it had been David Kelly, rather than he, who had first mentioned
Alastair Campbell's name. Although Andrew Gilligan had not referred
to Tony Blair's right-hand man in his broadcast reports, the fact that it
was David Kelly who had first introduced Campbell's name was crucial
to his assertion in those reports that his source, that 'senior official',
had confirmed that the government had deliberately changed the dossier.

But here too there was a question about journalistic sourcing. David
Kelly had not witnessed Alastair Campbell asking for the dossier to
be doctored; in fact he had never met Alastair Campbell. Nor had he
been in the room for any of the discussions between senior officials
about its composition, nor seen any documentary evidence about it.
David Kelly was an authoritative source about attitudes to the
September dossier among WMD experts within the MoD. When it
came to how the government might or might not have changed the
dossier, he was just speculating. And of course – just like the government's unreliable claim about the forty-five-minute warning – Gilligan's
story was 'single source'.

Andrew Gilligan's allegation of deliberate distortion was in effect
a claim that he had found proof that the government had lied to the
British public and gained support for a war on the basis of that lie.
The implication of the allegation was lost on no one, and it explains
why the government reacted to it with such anger. But on this point
his source, so credible on other issues, wasn't really a source at all.

The BBC told Lord Hutton's inquiry that it acknowledged significant
shortcomings in its journalism. The government acknowledged
nothing at all. In his findings, Hutton came down entirely in favour
of the government but many, perhaps most, observers took (and still
take) a different view. Andrew Gilligan's journalism may have been
flawed, but the broad thrust of his story – that the political imperative
to present a compelling case had been allowed to influence the final

version of the dossier – has become received wisdom. In the matter of reputation, the government won the battle but lost the war.

In an era when people distrust politicians' words, the idea of presenting them with dispassionate bundles of facts – intelligence findings, satellite images, maps and diagrams – has a practical appeal. If they are likely to doubt your rhetoric, why not let the evidence speak for itself? But once you make that supposedly dispassionate bundle your principal means of persuasion, all the techniques and temptations of rhetoric at once suggest themselves to you. We may never know for sure whether the intelligence-community technocrats were cajoled or directed into sexing up the dossier, or whether the political purpose of the thing was so obvious that they didn't need to be told. What we do know is that, having made a show of taking rhetoric out of the picture, somebody somewhere decided to put it right back in again.

But rhetoric played a crucial role on the journalistic side of this story as well. Andrew Gilligan had an excellent and original story – one of the government's own WMD experts rubbishing the content of the crucial dossier – but it wasn't enough. There was a bigger prize: the possibility of delivering a full *ad hominem* blow by asserting that Tony Blair or someone very close to him had deliberately deceived the public by ordering that the evidence be distorted. Andrew Gilligan would later accept that his allegation – that the government probably knew that the forty-five-minute claim was wrong – was itself 'insufficiently supported', and that he hadn't used 'exactly the right language'[9]. He excused himself by pointing out that he had been speaking in a live broadcast (though he had repeated similar allegations in later scripted reports). But it is hard not to suspect that, whether consciously or not, he too was tempted to do just what he was accusing the government of having done with the dossier, namely to go with the stronger, clearer rhetorical line despite the gaps in the evidence.

I watched the Kelly/Gilligan drama unfold from the relative safety of Channel 4, but heard throughout from many of those involved on the BBC side, including the then director general, Greg Dyke. It was a brutal and depressing episode to watch even as a witness, marked by a gulf of incomprehension and, on the government side, a vindictive unwillingness to find a way out even at the end. At its heart was the wholly unnecessary tragedy of David Kelly – a decent man who followed his conscience, and was rewarded for his pains by being ground to destruction between the mills of the British establishment.

Of Pretexts and Contexts

A *pretext* is a false explanation or justification one gives for some course of action because the real reason for the action is illegal or embarrassing, or is judged to be insufficiently persuasive in some other way. It is an illegitimate rhetorical tactic in which the speaker replaces the truth with a 'better' argument.

To state the obvious, a pretext is only a pretext if the speaker is aware that the justification they are giving is false or seriously deficient. George W. Bush and Tony Blair would no doubt argue that their claims about Saddam's WMD were *not* a pretext because they and their governments genuinely believed them at the time. Their critics might reply, echoing Mandy Rice-Davies, well they would say that, wouldn't they? This is why controversies about pretexts usually drag on for years. A politician wrongly accused of using a pretext will naturally deny it. But a politician who is justly accused of using one will also deny it. Unless you can get inside a given politician's head, or find some documentary evidence which confirms whether she *knew* at the time that what she was saying was false or misleading, you'll be hard pressed to prove whether she is guilty or innocent.

If we step back, though, there's a wider question: which is why the discussion of pretexts, real or alleged, turns up so regularly in the modern rhetoric of war. This is not a new phenomenon. Medieval magnates usually found some territorial, dynastic or religious excuse, no matter how far-fetched, to justify a land grab or an attempt on the crown. Adolf Hitler routinely ordered 'false-flag' attacks against German targets – for instance against the German radio station in Gleiwitz in August 1939 on the eve of his assault on Poland – so that he could claim that the subsequent onslaught was defensive rather than aggressive.

Today an angry debate about 'pretexts' is the norm. It is telling that even such a flagrant act of unprovoked aggression as the al-Qaeda attack on the World Trade Center and other targets on 9/11 should now be the subject of multiple conspiracy theories which reinterpret the event as an act of mass murder which the US government, or the Israeli or Saudi government, or other shadowy forces allowed or caused to take place (LIHOP, let it happen on purpose, and MIHOP, make it happen on purpose, are the acronyms used for the two main schools of thought) as a pretext to justify the subsequent wars. Some theorists make similar claims about the 1941 Japanese attack on Pearl Harbor.

If people can claim, and some credulous readers believe, that the attack on the US Navy in Hawaii, which involved thousands of Japanese sailors and airmen, hundreds of planes and multiple aircraft carriers, was in fact a put-up job by the American government, it's hardly surprising that less clear-cut modern wars – wars which are not a reaction to a direct attack, but a response to aggression against an ally or an attempt to interdict a claimed future security threat – should be endlessly parsed for pretexts.

But deep suspicion and the hunt for hidden motives is only one of the challenges the modern war orator faces. TV and the Internet have brought the horror of war home to any western citizen with the stomach to watch. This is all the more true of today's 'asymmetric' wars, in which high-tech weaponry of immense destructive power is deployed against enemies in the developing world who operate in the midst of civilian populations. The inevitable direct and indirect human cost, not to mention casualties on our own side, only seems acceptable if the highest moral bar can be met. As a result, there is a tremendous temptation to focus on the strongest possible elements in the case for war. National security and self-defence are the aces. Noble ideals – peace, democracy, the protection of human rights – can also be high-value cards, though in practice are liable to be scrutinised closely for signs of double standards or cant. Other factors, including economic self-interest, geopolitics, obligations to allies or wider diplomatic considerations are downright dangerous. As a result, they tend to be underplayed or omitted entirely.

Once western leaders could discuss national self-interest openly. Here, for instance, is President William McKinley in 1898, presenting his justification for asking Congress to authorise US intervention to free Cuba from Spanish rule, an action which triggered a wider Spanish–American war:

> The right to intervene may be justified by the very serious injury to
> the commerce, trade, and business of our people and by the wanton
> destruction of property and devastation of the island . . . With such
> a conflict waged for years in an island so near us and with which our

people have such trade and business relations; when the lives and liberty of our citizens are in constant danger and their property destroyed and themselves ruined; where our trading vessels are liable to seizure and are seized at our very door by warships of a foreign nation.[10]

During the Suez crisis in 1956, it was still possible for Anthony Eden to cite economic interests as a justification for military action against Egypt's President Gamal Abdel Nasser, though by now the protection of these interests has come to be described as a form of national defence:

> I will now speak to you about the situation in respect of the Suez Canal dispute. Before we examine the political implications of this event I must record in plainest terms the economic impact upon our life in this country of any hostile interference in the free passage of the canal. It is no exaggeration to say that this is a matter of survival for us as a trading nation. It concerns the employment, the standard of living and the pay packet of every man and woman in the land.[11]

In recent decades, however, any western leader who majored on economic factors or any other national self-interest when trying to justify the need for war would risk being branded an imperialist or a war criminal or both.

National self-interest has not disappeared, of course. It continues to play a central role in every foreign-policy decision, including those about military action. But because it can sound instrumental and inhuman, it is seldom discussed as openly and honestly as it once was. That can in turn breed exaggerated suspicions that the real reason for a given war is hidden – that western military intervention in the Middle East, say, is always really about oil. Public distrust encourages rhetorical circumspection which only serves to stimulate more public distrust.

*

Late on the evening of 4 August 1964, President Lyndon Johnson went on television to address the American people. According to the president, earlier that day the American destroyer the USS *Maddox* had been attacked in international waters by North Vietnamese torpedo boats. It was the second such attack in the past three days, he said:

The performance of commanders and crews in this engagement is in the highest tradition of the United States Navy. But repeated acts of violence against the armed forces of the United States must be met not only with alert defense, but with positive reply. That reply is being given as I speak to you tonight. Air action is now in execution against gunboats and certain supporting facilities in North Vietnam.[12]

An act of open and unprovoked aggression and targeted military action to neutralise the attackers: self-defence, in other words, as sanctioned by the UN Charter and international law. But then, like a fencer's foil, the president's rhetoric starts darting. Forward and backward, feint and parry. America's response will be 'limited and fitting'; 'we Americans know, although others appear to forget, the risk of spreading conflict'. Lingering doubts? 'We still seek no wider war,' Lyndon Johnson assures the watching viewers. At that a sceptical citizen might be tempted to relax a little, but the president's rhetorical sword is still flashing. Now the thrust:

Finally, I have today met with the leaders of both parties in the Congress of the United States and I have informed them that I shall immediately request the Congress to pass a resolution making it clear that our government is united in its determination to take all necessary measures in support of freedom and in defense of peace in South East Asia.[13]

And suddenly everything – the map, the implications on the ground, above all the president's policy goals – widens. Now President Johnson is declaring that America must commit not just to a 'limited' immediate response, but at the same time agree 'to take all necessary measures'. The protection of the *Maddox* and the US Navy's right to sail the high seas has swollen to include support for 'freedom' in South East Asia, the word *freedom* in this Cold War context having the meaning of *freedom from communism*. And what began as the brave captain and crew of the *Maddox* exercising their right to self-defence has become the 'defense of peace'. How do we defend peace? The president doesn't spell it out, but as we've already discovered in the case of Tony Blair and Iraq, political leaders can find themselves arguing that we defend peace best by going to war.

It's an irony which is seldom lost on those on the other side of the conflict. As Tacitus has the Caledonian leader Calgacus ironically remark of the Romans: 'they turn a country into a wasteland and call it peace'.[14]

Three days later, Congress passed a joint resolution which author- ised the president to use military force without the need for further approval if any ally in the region asked for help against the commu- nist threat. In the months and years that followed, America's involve- ment in the Vietnam War grew and, although Congress continued to debate and vote support for the war, the 'Gulf of Tonkin Resolution' came to be seen as a key trigger for the escalation, and the president's use of the incident to bend Congress to his will as an example of ruthless over-reach by the executive branch.

But there was more. Almost from the start, questions were asked about the Tonkin incident and, the more that was revealed, the more suspicious it appeared. At the time of the attack on the *Maddox*, the US was itself engaged in multiple covert operations against North Vietnam. The USS *Maddox* had indeed been in international waters, but it had been conducting a signals intelligence operation against the North. But most troubling of all was evidence – confirmed in recent years – that the critical 4 August attack on the destroyer, which was the stated reason for President Johnson's broadcast and the justi- fication for his appeal to Congress, hadn't been a real attack at all but a case of panicky sailors misreading radar images and seeing imaginary enemy craft. Worse, senior members of the government, almost certainly including the Secretary of Defense, Robert McNamara, and perhaps even the president himself, had known at the time that the report of that second attack might well be false. Here, in *Naval History Magazine* in February 2008, Lieutenant Commander Pat Paterson, at the time of writing a serving officer in the US Navy, puts it all together:

> Questions about the Gulf of Tonkin incidents have persisted for more than 40 years. But once-classified documents and tapes released in the past several years, combined with previously uncovered facts, make clear that high government officials distorted facts and deceived the American public about events that led to full US involvement in the Vietnam War.[15]

For this reason, Lyndon Johnson and the Tonkin incident has become a classic subject for academic studies of political rhetoric. The key term which is almost invariably used in these studies is the word 'pretext'.

In 1978, Richard A. Cherwitz – who was then a doctoral student and is now a distinguished professor of rhetoric – wrote a paper called 'Lyndon Johnson and the "Crisis" of Tonkin Gulf: A President's Justification of War'.[16] In the section titled 'The Rhetorical Situation: Tonkin Gulf as a Pretext', Cherwitz methodically deconstructs Johnson's language and finds many of the rhetorical tactics I have drawn attention to in this book: the use of limited and 'dubious' facts; 'vivid and descriptive language' including 'powerful adjectives' to help dramatise and exaggerate the events; the building up of the authority of his office and his personal character or *ethos*; compression, as in the three short sentences Johnson used in his address to Syracuse University the day after the TV address:

> The attacks were deliberate.
> The attacks were unprovoked.
> The attacks have been answered.[17]

A further rhetorical device is the 'magnification' of what Cherwitz calls 'local events' to a global context: 'Although the Tonkin incident transpired thousands of miles from the United States mainland, the president was able to highlight the severity of the events, giving them a sense of international importance, by associating them with a broader doctrine striking closer to home.'[18]

But Professor Cherwitz's seminal paper needs a little rhetorical deconstruction of its own. His immediate verdict – that the Johnson administration had used one minor incident and a second non-existent one to secure congressional and public support for US military involvement in the war – is no doubt valid. But what was the political context – and the political motives which explain their actions? Cherwitz's answer to this question is not based on dispassionate rhetorical analysis, but relies on his own, quintessentially political verdict on American foreign policy at the time:

> United States foreign affairs in the 1960s were characterised by the
> expansion of presidential power used to support a policy of unilateral

military interventions into Third World nations. The president, acting
as commander-in-chief, on numerous occasions in the 1960s, embroiled
the US in conflicts with other nations.[19]

Cherwitz's language – 'expansion of presidential power', 'unilateral
military interventions' against 'Third World nations', 'on numerous
occasions', above all that adjective 'embroiled' – leave us in little doubt
about his own ideological position on American foreign policy. But,
whether you agree with him or not, his is a verdict reached with the
benefit of hindsight, rather than the political context *as it appeared to
Lyndon Johnson at the time.* That is the relevant context if we want
to understand why he said what he did. It is also the only context in
which we can consider intentionality and therefore reach a conclusion
about whether Tonkin really was a pretext and, if so, what kind of
pretext it was.

By way of contrast, let's first consider the political context for that
other alleged pretext, the UK government's claims about WMD in
the run-up to the invasion of Iraq in 2003. It was this: Britain had a
free choice about whether to join in the American-led military intervention or not. Other western allies stayed out. Secretary of Defense
Donald Rumsfeld made it clear that the US was prepared to proceed
with the invasion of Iraq with or without the UK, noting that there
were 'workarounds' in the event of British non-participation.[20] Nor
was the invasion itself the culmination of some inexorable long-range
strategic logic. After Saddam's attack on Kuwait, President Bush's
father had had both the justification and the troops in the theatre to
press on to Baghdad, but had decided not to do so.

This is why the question of the specific evidence offered to justify
the invasion is so crucial. Had Tony Blair's government *not* produced
its 'evidence' about Saddam's WMD, the UK would not have taken
part in the war. It's as simple as that. And, although it is less certain,
there is a good chance that there would have been no Iraq War at all,
had the Bush administration not presented their own equivalent of
the dodgy dossiers.

Tonkin was different. There was a war going on already, the Cold
War, a global struggle against the USSR and its allies which Professor
Cherwitz does not mention once in his paper. Cherwitz introduces
the global context for the Tonkin incident as another 'rhetorical device',

as if giving the security situation in Vietnam 'a sense of international importance' was nothing more than a deceitful trope. But connecting local flashpoints to the tense global stand-off between the superpowers was what everyone on both sides of the Cold War did. Specifically, America, the USSR and China all believed that Vietnam was a geopolitically important theatre in that wider struggle. Lyndon Johnson was a president whose main focus was domestic reform but, by the summer of 1964, his officials had concluded that the troops of the South Vietnamese government were losing their fight with the Viet Cong and that, without rapid and substantial American military involvement, the South would collapse.

Unlike Iraq in 2003, the proposal to intervene in Vietnam in 1964 fitted coherently into a political world view which enjoyed extensive bipartisan and popular support. The Johnson administration believed it was dealing with a crisis in a frontline state which was critical to its overall aim to contain global communism. In this context, it may well have been looking for a triggering event, some high-profile example of Viet Cong 'aggression' which could be used to fire up Congress and the American people and pave the way for escalation. Potential triggers were not hard to find. That first engagement with North Vietnamese torpedo boats on 2 August was probably genuine and, given the number of American military in the zone of conflict and the rate at which the situation was deteriorating, it's likely that another suitable incident would have presented itself soon enough.

It has often been asserted that, had it not been for Tonkin, the Vietnam War might never have happened. Having just rehearsed the Kelly/Gilligan story, we are familiar with the rhetorical temptation to go for the gravest possible charge: that Johnson lied that night, and tens of thousands of Americans and millions of South East Asians died as a result. A less emotive but more plausible verdict is that America's war was coming one way or another, not because of a piece of false rhetoric, but because of the internal logic of US Cold War foreign policy; that Tonkin was not a *material* pretext but a convenient trigger in a period which was likely to offer other such triggers.

Tonkin may have been handy for the president, but in many ways it suited Congress and the American public too. Public as well as private doubts about the incident were expressed quickly, but the president's policy gained widespread acceptance anyway. Many Democrats shared the party leadership's hawkishness on Cold War issues, and most Republicans took an even tougher line. The theory of an 'Imperial Presidency', which Cherwitz refers to several times in his paper, is a construct which has the advantage of making it possible to narrow the blame for Vietnam to a small elite; but the idea that the Gulf of Tonkin Resolution disarmed Congress and amounted to a constitutional coup is fanciful. In reality, the legislative branch continued to hold the purse strings and voted repeatedly to fund the war over the years that followed. The less conspiratorial but no less unsettling truth is that America went to war in Vietnam as a functioning democracy; that large majorities in both Houses supported the policy, not because they were the naïve victims of a lie, but because they supported the administration's broad policy stance on the Cold War and, despite the question marks over Tonkin, were prepared to give the president the benefit of the doubt. Political and popular support for the war only began to wane in earnest when it became clear that it was going badly.

And that's the rub. Congress and people acquiesced in the escalation, but the manner in which it happened – and the highly abbreviated justification Lyndon Johnson offered in making the case for it – gave both plenty of optionality when it came to future support. Had the escalation in 1964 led to rapid and decisive success, they would probably have thought of themselves as full partners in the enterprise. When casualties mounted and failure loomed, it became Lyndon Johnson's war. Within a few years it had broken him.

This is the problem with partial explanations and pretexts, even ones which play an incidental rather than a decisive part on the road to conflict. When it comes to war, modern audiences tend to want to have it both ways. Our assent is always qualified and, while we may overlook a short cut or even a deception on the speaker's part if we find their overall case convincing, we also reserve the right to use it as a pretext ourselves later on, to distance ourselves from the decision when things start heading south.

The Old Lie

In *Ulysses*, James Joyce has Stephen Dedalus say that history is a nightmare from which he is trying to awake. War, and war rhetoric, are like that. No matter how persuasive the case for military intervention, many listeners still find dark questions pressing in on them. The speaker may sound reasonable, but what if it turns out that he or she is wicked or mad? How can we be sure that this supposedly limited affair won't become a quagmire? Aren't all wars fundamentally futile? Are we on the brink of sending young men and women off not to victory and honour, but to slaughter – of themselves, their enemy and who knows how many innocent civilians?

This nightmare has a name. It is our received understanding of the First World War. More than the terrible but – for the western allies – altogether more intelligible conflagration that followed it, more than any other earlier conflict in history, the Great War has infected our understanding of war and looms like a dark question over each new call for military action. How can we be sure that *this* set of leaders won't turn out to be as murderous and irresponsible as the foolish and bloodthirsty old men who wrecked Europe in 1914?

The Great War master-narrative is necessarily concerned with rhetoric. Those wicked leaders didn't fight the war themselves, they persuaded millions of ordinary people to do it for them. How they used public language to convince the 'doomed youth' of Europe to take to the trenches, and how we can ensure they never do it again, is central both to the story and its message. Let's look at the end of the most famous poem by the most celebrated poet of the war, Wilfred Owen:

> If you could hear, at every jolt, the blood
> Come gargling from the froth-corrupted lungs,
> Obscene as cancer, bitter as the cud
> Of vile, incurable sores on innocent tongues,
> My friend, you would not tell with such high zest
> To children ardent for some desperate glory,
> The old Lie: Dulce et Decorum est
> Pro patria mori.[21]

Dulce et decorum est pro patria mori ('It is sweet and fitting to die for your country') is a motto from the Roman poet Horace which was often used in Victorian and Edwardian England to memorialise young men killed in war. As recently as 1913, it had been chosen to adorn a memorial in the chapel at the Royal Military Academy at Sandhurst.

Juxtaposed with the effects of a poison-gas attack – and by extension with the rest of the mindless, murderous experience of the trenches – this conventional piety is revealed as a lie. Owen never tells us anything about the *friend* who has been spreading the lie, but we take it that he means everyone – the military establishment, jingoistic newspapers, political, religious and educational leaders – who contributed to the culture that made the war possible. You told us that war was heroic and noble. Now we know what it really is.

'Dulce et Decorum Est' is a warning about rhetoric, but it is also rhetoric itself, indeed one of the most compelling pieces of anti-war rhetoric ever written. Its message is apparently timeless – the lie is not just any lie, but 'the old Lie' – although Wilfred Owen's poem is in fact a reaction to a specific war and its horrors. Its immediate subject, chemical warfare, was new, but so too was its utterly modern disenchantment and moral disgust. 'Dulce et Decorum Est' is a response to the coming of modern industrial war.

*

By the end of the American Civil War half a century earlier, it had become clear that industrialisation was changing the character of warfare. Vast machine-age armies armed with modern weapons were impossible to beat in a single battle, and had instead to be worn down through multiple attritional engagements. Victory in this new kind of war would depend less on inventive generalship than on social and economic factors – population size, manufacturing capacity, transport infrastructure, scientific and engineering capability – which, at the end of the long and bloody process of attrition, would leave the better-resourced side still standing after its opponent had collapsed.

But this new reality – war as a mincing machine into which two adversaries would feed their young until one side ran out of fresh meat – was, and remains, too terrible to contemplate. We can think of the original Victorian use of the *Dulce et decorum* tag as a rhetorical coping strategy, an attempt to focus not on the unspeakable actuality of industrial warfare, but on the motives and character of the combatants who could, in principle, be every bit as chivalrous and pure as those in previous conflicts. Thus First World War pilots in their newly invented flying machines became *knights of the air*. It is this rhetorical gambit which Owen dismisses as being impossible to sustain in the face of the actual experience of the trenches.

The battle between these two contrary reactions – the effort to render the war meaningful by associating it with romantic/religious transcendence, and the angry denial of that effort – raged on in the years after the Armistice. In the hymn 'O Valiant Hearts' (1919), the fallen follow 'the martyred Son of God' and having 'drunk His cup of sacrifice', are expected to rise with him victorious in the end. Similarly, in 'I Vow to Thee, My Country', written in 1918 and also sung to this day, the dead soldier's love of his country is compared to Christ's love 'that lays upon the altar the dearest and the best',

> The love that never falters, the love that pays the price,
> The love that makes undaunted the final sacrifice.[22]

But even then a rival rhetoric – a rhetoric of futility – was taking shape. Self-sacrifice was still central, but the altar on which that sacrifice took place was no longer an innocent quasi-religious one but an altar of arrogance and ineptitude. The war poets, and especially Owen and Siegfried Sassoon, were important contributors to this new rhetoric.* So too was Robert Graves, whose mordant and absurdist memoir *Good-Bye to All That* (1929) struck many readers as a confirmation of the version of the war painted by the poets.

So who was to blame? The generals and the politicians were the obvious targets. In the immediate aftermath of the war, the British commander-in-chief Douglas Haig and the other generals were feted. Haig was made an earl and his former troops elected him president of the Royal British Legion, which was set up in 1921 to help veterans of the war. Soon, though, a revisionist mood set in, driven not just by literary expressions of the bloody horror of the Western Front, but also by the age-old instinct of politicians eager to protect their own reputations by shifting the responsibility elsewhere.

This chapter began with a warning about Winston Churchill delivered by Lord Esher to Douglas Haig, at a point when the war was deadlocked and the politicians at home were growing restive. Esher's

---

* In his 'Statement of Defiance', published in *The Times* on 31 July 1917, Sassoon said that he had come to see the conflict as a 'war of aggression'.

1917 warning was prompted by recent events – a few months earlier Churchill had circulated a highly critical note about Haig's Somme offensive to the Cabinet – but it also presaged the future reputational assault the generals would face from the politicians.

In 1917, Churchill's own standing as a military strategist was at an all-time low after the ignominious end of the Gallipoli campaign which he had inspired and promoted. Characteristically, that did not stop him sharing his bitter criticism of the performance of the British commanders, and his own suggestions about what they should do instead, with anyone who would listen. The doctrine of attrition offended everything he believed about war and leadership, which is why, in Esher's words, he had taken to using 'rhythmical language' to tell himself an alternative story about the stalemate in the trenches, one based on his own strategic instincts.

The plain truth was that the new advantage which machine guns and more accurate artillery gave the defenders had baffled the most brilliant military minds on all sides in the early years of the war. It would take a long period of innovation and trial and error before they developed the tactics and weapons which would enable the decisive battles of 1918. But in Winston Churchill's simplified narrative, the answer had been obvious all along; it was only the dolts commanding the British Army who had been unable to see it.

After the war, he returned to the attack. In *The World Crisis 1911–1918*, he described the campaign on the Somme as 'from beginning to end a welter of slaughter'. He declined to take Haig on directly, but the malice was not far from the surface:

> The military profession reposed in him a confidence which the various fortunes, disappointments and miscalculations attendant upon three years of war on the greatest scale left absolutely unshaken. The esteem of his military colleagues found a healthy counterpart in his own self-confidence.[23]

Douglas Haig had the misfortune to fall foul of not one, but two of the most eloquent politicians of the century. David Lloyd George, who had been in the Cabinet which had taken the country to war and was prime minister for the latter years of the conflict, was as keen as anyone to deflect criticism about the conduct of the war towards the generals, and he was equally cutting. Haig, he claimed in retrospect, lacked the 'necessary breadth of imagination and vision to plan a campaign against some of the ablest generals of the war'. Indeed, he had never met a man in high position 'so utterly devoid of imagination'.[24] A more visionary and less smug British commander, he implied, could have achieved victory far sooner and at much lower cost. That self-serving and tendentious judgement soon became the received wisdom. But if the generals were so incompetent, why hadn't the politicians replaced them? And wasn't it the politicians, rather than the generals, who had started the thing in the first place? Despite their best efforts, Britain's wartime political leaders soon joined the generals in the dock.

The grip of this narrative – of lions led by donkeys, of a country betrayed by its political and military elites – only grew with time. It receded in the years before, during and immediately after the Second World War, a cataclysm which as we have seen was different enough from the earlier war to produce narratives of its own. But it soon returned and by the last third of the twentieth century had become normative. It is the gravamen of the groundbreaking BBC documentary series The Great War (1964), as well as the exuberant stage and screen musical Oh! What a Lovely War (1963 and 1969, respectively) – the knowing irony of the title revealing just how deeply the narrative had taken hold. Barbara Tuchman's The Guns of August (1962), about the beginning of the war, won a Pulitzer. Two decades later, in The March of Folly, she would generalise the First World War narrative of stupidity and betrayal to explain wars throughout western civilisation, from the siege of Troy to the abandonment of the US embassy in Saigon.

The first centenary of the start of the war has passed now with much new scholarship and fresh debate, but little change to popular conceptions about the conflict. It is not too strong to say that, if Dulce et decorum est represents the old lie, the simplistic narrative of betrayal and incompetence weaves a new lie which serves the same essential purpose as the first – to provide a comforting alternative to what would otherwise be an unbearable reflection on what our industrial inventiveness has wrought, and indeed on what we are capable of as human beings. This new lie makes much of dishonest rhetoric but in important ways is a piece of dishonest rhetoric itself. Yet it is so widely accepted that, whether we are conscious of it or not, it influences the discussion of almost every war, not just in Britain but across the West.

*

In April 2006, the British Defence Secretary John Reid spoke at a press conference in Kabul about the British Army's deployment into Helmand province. He hoped, he said, that this deployment – which was intended to focus on reconstruction, security and the building of strong local institutions – would be different from earlier phases of the war which America and its allies had begun in Afghanistan in the aftermath of 9/11:

> We're in the south to help and protect the Afghan people to reconstruct their economy and democracy. We would be perfectly happy to leave in three years' time without firing one shot.[25]

That last phrase, 'without firing one shot', would be quoted again and again over the next eight years as the British Army fought a long, bloody and fruitless campaign in Helmand against the Taliban. It's obvious what the phrase means in context – *we're here to build and we're not looking for a fight* – but, if you take that context away, you can easily make it sound like the ludicrous home-before-Christmas optimism that is said to have marked the first months of the Great War. Here's Simon Jenkins writing in the *Guardian* some eighteen months after the press conference:

> John Reid, the then defence secretary, even talked of completing the Helmand deployment 'without a shot being fired' . . . The whole Helmand expedition has from the start been a suicide mission.[26]

Note the inversion. *Without a shot being fired* means something quite different from *happy to leave without firing a shot*: instead of an assurance that the British Army didn't intend to fire first, now we have a prediction that there will be no fighting whatsoever. To my ear, even the word order seems to conjure up a plummy First World War general. Simon Jenkins can then contrast this mad prediction with the reality, which is that the deployment has turned out to be a 'suicide mission'. But the prediction is an artefact of his own misquotation.

For years now Dr Reid has energetically tried to convince the world that, in his words, 'I never at any stage expressed the hope, expectation, promise or pledge that we would leave Afghanistan "without firing a shot".'[27] He once phoned me at home when he heard someone on the BBC suggesting that he had, and I acted on the call. But once this kind of narrative takes hold, it is almost impossible to dislodge. At the start of this book, we discussed the way that compressed phrases can take over a debate. Dr Reid's problem was rather one of *meanings*: instead of his own original meaning, a new meaning had been imposed on his words – a meaning whose connection to national memory (or myth) was so powerful that it took on a life of its own.

In March 2012, the *Lancashire Telegraph* reported the death in action in Afghanistan of Sergeant Nigel Coupe from the Duke of Lancaster's Regiment. Here are some of the comments that were posted on the paper's website under that story:

> This now brings the total killed to 400. When he was Defence Secretary John Reid boasted that we would be in and out of Afghanistan without a shot being fired. I wonder [how] he can sleep at night.

> The military have done a fantastic job over there at great sacrifice. More than can be said for the politicians. The sad thing is there have never been any casualties amongst the Westminster regiment.

> I wear my poppy with pride every year and pray for those that don't come back . . . RIP good lads; I for one will not forget.[28]

We're very close to the First World War here. Dr Reid's comment has become a 'boast', and now it refers not just to the Helmand deployment but to the whole Afghan War. The phrase is now fixed in its inverted form. And there's that jibe, which could have come from any decade in the past century, about 'the Westminster regiment'. Here we have the paradigm of betrayal, which applies not just to one generation of politicians but to *every* generation, to politicians as a class.

Sophisticated writers can even claim that the fact that John Reid never said what is attributed to him is irrelevant, because the invented quotation in fact reflects a broader reality. Writing in the *Guardian*, again in 2012, Julian Borger acknowledged that Dr Reid had been completely misquoted, but then went on:

> the myth does nonetheless encapsulate a deeper truth about the blithe optimism with which the Blair government sent the first deployment of 3,000 soldiers into Helmand in early 2006.[29]

Thus a sentiment which began as an attempt by a British minister to assure the Afghan people that his government's intentions in Helmand were to do as little fighting and as much reconstructing as possible had morphed into a proof-text of incompetence and callousness. And the fact that he didn't actually say it means nothing – even to those who know he didn't say it. That is the deeper truth.

The Afghan campaign, meanwhile, would eventually remind the world of another disagreeable fact of life, which is that 'justified' wars can end just as unhappily as the 'unjustified' ones.

*

The arrival of industrial warfare had a second profound impact on the way we think about both the morality and the rhetoric of war. By the latter years of the Second World War, the Allies had a decisive advantage over the Axis powers in all areas of materiel and notably in aircraft. As a result, they were able to achieve air superiority and bomb the industrial heartland of both Germany and Japan against diminishing resistance. Hundreds of thousands of German and Japanese men, women and children died in these raids, even before the dropping of the two atomic weapons on Hiroshima and Nagasaki in 1945.

How should we think of such mass killing? The question is relevant not just because the bombing raids cast a question mark over the twentieth-century's most 'moral' war, but because the West still enjoys the same air supremacy and astonishing preponderance of weaponry over the nations it fights today.

In February 2015, the Archbishop of Canterbury, Justin Welby, gave an address at the Frauenkirche in Dresden as part of a service to mark the seventieth anniversary of the British bombing which killed some 25,000 people:

Walking together as friends requires talking together in truth. As Croatian theologian Miroslav Volf challenges us: 'To remember wrong-doing untruthfully is to act unjustly.'

Much debate surrounds this most controversial raid of the Allied bombing campaign. Whatever the arguments, events here seventy years ago left a deep wound and diminished all our humanity. So as a follower of Jesus I stand here among you with a profound feeling of regret and deep sorrow.[30]

But this 'talking together in truth' was too much for some British politicians and newspapers, and Lambeth Palace quickly denied that the archbishop's remarks were an 'apology' or that they touched on the 'question of blame': he had simply been bearing witness to the 'tragedy of war'.[31] But, while the regret which the archbishop expressed in his address may not have added up to an 'apology', his use of the quotation from Miroslav Volf does indeed appear to imply that he thought the British bombing raid was an example of 'wrong-doing'. The suggestion is so controversial because Britain – so quick to accuse other nations of being in moral denial about their actions during the war – has never got to the bottom of the debate about its bombing of the German civilian population during the war. Was it necessary and justified, indeed requiring a heroic sacrifice by the tens of thousands of killed and injured aircrews? Or was it a war crime?

Such a topic is too complex, too loaded with ethical abstractions and religious undertones, for it to be remotely comfortable territory for today's political leaders. As a consequence, the morality of contemporary military practice is insufficiently publicly debated: the use of drones and special-forces death squads to assassinate suspected enemy commanders with frequent mistakes and inevitable collateral casualties; the effect on civilians of the aerial destruction of a nation's infrastructure; military alliances by the West with groups and nations whose own conduct on and off the battlefield is known to fall short of the barest legal and human-rights standards, and so on. The West's adversaries may be guilty of far worse abuses but, as even the most gung-ho defence minister must reluctantly acknowledge, that is hardly an adequate excuse. Better to say as little as possible and leave it to people like the archbishop to wander into that minefield.

The past weighs heavily on us. The great conflicts of the twentieth century have left us with a hunger for the moral high ground but a bitter residue of cynicism and distrust. When we debate going to war, some of the real motives are unspoken, while the question of how our soldiers, sailors and aircrew should behave when fighting has been rendered so complex, and so disturbing, by the reality of modern warfare that we are liable to turn away for fear of seeing too much. We want our nations to be strong and safe. And yet we also want to be able to think of ourselves as good. As a result, our leaders end up contorting themselves like Cinderella's unfortunate sisters, struggling to fit the ungainly and hideous reality of modern war into the crystal slipper of moral simplicity.

Not In My Name

Of course, political leaders – and citizens – always have another choice. Some three years after Tonkin, Martin Luther King travelled to the Riverside Church in New York City to 'break silence' on the war in Vietnam. He praised the faith leaders who had invited him and said he had found himself 'in full accord' with the statement they had recently released which said: 'A time comes when silence is betrayal.' Then he launched into a carefully argued but fiery critique of the war. Here he is close to the apogee, the point just before he turned from his condemnation of America's war to the 'five concrete things' he proposed to bring the conflict to an end:

> Surely this madness must cease. We must stop now. I speak as a child of God and brother to the suffering poor of Vietnam. I speak for those whose land is being laid waste, whose homes are being destroyed, whose culture is being subverted. I speak for the poor of America who are paying the double price of smashed hopes at home, and death and corruption in Vietnam. I speak as a citizen of the world, for the world as it stands aghast at the path we have taken. I speak as one who loves America, to the leaders of our own nation: The great initiative in this war is ours; the initiative to stop it must be ours.[32]

In many ways we have returned to the power and simplicity we heard in Winston Churchill's voice back in 1940. The five *I speaks* take us through the religious, moral and political reasons for ending the war. King begins with an instinct ('Somehow this madness must cease'), and ends with a specific political call ('the initiative to stop it must be ours'), in an arc which starts and finishes with short, declarative statements but builds in the middle to more complex sentences. If Churchill's master-word was *victory*, King's central concept here is *destruction*: physical destruction ('laid waste', 'destroyed', 'death') and the destruction of aspirations and values (a culture 'subverted', 'smashed hopes', 'corruption'). He speaks more in sorrow than anger, but the rebuke is no less sharp-edged for that – and, although King uses the plural when he appeals to the 'leaders of our own nation', President Lyndon Johnson is clearly the main object of that rebuke. What Johnson is being rebuked for is Tonkin and everything that flowed from it.

By the late 1960s, the idea that war – and particularly modern industrial war – is 'madness', to use Martin Luther King's word, was no longer an iconoclastic revelation, but an unquestionable fact for many across the West. There was a brief period after the Cold War when it seemed that the era of wars involving the West – and thus the need for anti-war protests and songs and movies – might be over. But then the wars began again, and so did the protests.

Today's anti-war movement was inspired by opposition to recent western interventions in the Middle East, but its sense of itself and its language are heavily influenced by previous responses to war: ethical pacifism, particularly associated with Quakerism but also embraced by some other Christians and believers in other faiths, as well as by some humanists; the liberal internationalism which flourished in the aftermath of the First World War, and which sought unsuccessfully to make another such bloodbath unthinkable; the mass protests against atomic and hydrogen weapons from the 1950s through to the 1980s; and the opposition to the Vietnam War which radicalised so many previously apolitical Americans and introduced strong anti-war themes into popular culture. Important too is the coming together of two schools of ideological thought: the first a general theory about western capitalist countries and their taste for imperialism, the second a specific belief about a western tendency to fear Muslim peoples and culture (Islamophobia) and a consequential desire to attack and oppress Muslim countries.

One of the beliefs that binds anti-war protesters together is the certainty that *their* rhetoric (though they would of course dislike the term) is quite different from that of the political leaders whom they oppose. When they speak, they do so like Martin Luther King, as 'citizens of the world', aghast at the path their countries have taken or are about to take. Who can possibly be in favour of bombing children? Who can seriously argue for war rather than peace? We can acknowledge the good faith of the majority of those who campaign against war, without accepting that things are really quite as politically or rhetorically straightforward as that.

The largest grouping within the anti-war movement in the UK is the Stop the War Coalition (STWC). Founded soon after 9/11, with the Campaign for Nuclear Disarmament (CND) and the Muslim Council of Great Britain, it organised what is often said to have been the biggest public protest in British history: the February 2003 demonstration in London against the invasion of Iraq. As its name spells out, the STWC was intended to be a *coalition* which could rise above the ideological differences of its constituent members. Indeed, this coalescing of members of different political tribes is what gives any anti-war movement much of its moral force: it is much easier for the establishment to dismiss an ideologically homogeneous pressure group than something which looks like a cross-section of society as a whole.

Despite the packaging, however, and like almost all western anti-war groupings, the STWC is overwhelmingly a political formation of the left. Indeed, to a greater extent than many realise, it is a creation of the hard left and of people who have no love for either 'bourgeois democracy' or free speech. Several of the founders of the STWC were members of the (Trotskyist) Socialist Workers Party (SWP) and the Communist Party, and many of its current activists are members of these and other extreme left parties. The SWP in particular is famous for its energy and organisational skills, and it is given much of the credit, by friends and foes alike, for the impact which the STWC made in its early days. Some years later, it helped launch another consumer-friendly brand – the Coalition of Resistance, this time created to campaign against 'austerity' and government cuts – and it's hard not to conclude that the SWP, whose core ideology is regarded as beyond the pale by almost all voters, has developed these coalition brands as a political marketing tactic, hoping to build support and advance elements of its agenda under these more acceptable umbrellas.

Jeremy Corbyn – who most of the British media describe as an extreme left-winger, but in this company looks like a centrist – was chairman of the STWC from 2009 to 2015. His successor, Andrew Murray, is a former communist who has defended both Josef Stalin and North Korea. Another senior official is the chair of the CND. In its 'Ban the Bomb' heyday, CND was a relatively broad political church, but today it too has drifted well to the left and its chair is another former communist.

On 14 November 2015, the STWC website published an article with the headline 'PARIS REAPS WHIRLWIND FOR WESTERN SUPPORT FOR EXTREMIST VIOLENCE IN MIDDLE EAST'. According to the article, the real cause of the attacks (which killed 130 people and injured hundreds more) was 'Washington's decades-long, bipartisan cultivation of religious extremism':

> Without decades of intervention by the US and its allies, there would have been no 'war on terror' and no terrorist attacks on Paris.[33]

The article was promptly deleted, but not promptly enough to prevent an outcry. This and other statements after Paris convinced many in the Labour Party that their leader could not remain the chair of such an organisation, and Jeremy Corbyn stood aside shortly thereafter. The Green Party's Caroline Lucas also resigned as one of the vice chairs.

Then a group of human-rights activists wrote a letter to the *Guardian* a few weeks after the Paris attacks about a separate issue, namely what they saw as the STWC's bias towards the Syrian regime and lack of concern about its victims. The letter also alleged that the coalition routinely misrepresented Syrian anti-Assad groups and stopped them from speaking at rallies:

> As well as systematically ignoring war crimes committed by the Assad regime, STWC often misrepresents the opposition to Assad as being largely composed of jihadi extremists and agents of imperialism; marginalising the non-violent, secular, democratic, local community

and non-aligned opposition to his tyranny. It also misrepresents the call by Syrian civil society organisations for civilian safe havens and humanitarian corridors; claiming they are calls for western bombing, when they are actually bids to stop Assad's bombs and save lives. We urge STWC to take on board these constructive criticisms and change its stance to support the Syrian people's struggle against the war being inflicted on them by both Isis and Assad.[34]

The charge is that influential voices within the coalition want to impose the following narrowly doctrinaire view on the public stance which the STWC as a whole takes on the Syrian conflict. The conflict is the fault of western imperialism. Bashar Assad should be defended because he is standing up to this imperialism. Those rebelling against him are western stooges and, if they are persecuted or killed, they only have themselves to blame. Even so-called Islamic State is the fault of the western imperialists, because it was the West which fuelled religious extremism for years.

People are entitled to believe whatever they want to about Barack Obama, François Hollande and David Cameron, and to organise protests against them. My point is not to criticise a particular analysis of the Syrian civil war, or to deny a link between the attack in Paris and western military and diplomatic actions in the Middle East. It is rather that, whatever your views on the substance of the arguments, these two recent controversies make it clear that there is a lot more going on ideologically in the STWC than its headline rhetoric would suggest, and that some of its key members have a political agenda which goes far beyond, and in some respects flies in the face of, its simple anti-war message.

The STWC may be an extreme case, but all anti-war movements face similar pressures: the risk of entryism and exploitation, and of the endless splintering with which all most radical organisations seem to be afflicted; the inevitable arrival of difficult real-world choices and compromises.

Anti-war activists like to contrast their truth-telling with the bogus rhetoric of the warmongers. Indeed puncturing the false rhetoric of the other side is one of their main objectives. As we have seen, there can be moments – 'Dulce et Decorum Est' and Dr King's speech in the Riverside Church are two of them – when such a thing is possible, for an eloquent individual at a given point in time. For the most part, however, and certainly in its familiar form in western countries today, anti-war rhetoric suffers from most of the same faults it criticises in the rhetoric of its targets: a tendency to omit awkward arguments or to downplay unresolved issues, to pretend that difficult choices are easy, to talk straight past the other side in the debate, to oversimplify everything. Just like conventional political rhetoric, it has its fair share of hypocrisy and hidden agendas. Judge the argument against a given war as you would seek to judge any other policy question: on the merits of its case, not on some imagined superiority in the way it lays out its rhetorical stall.

One of the most resonant of all the many anti-war slogans is the cry of one of the groups who campaigned against the Iraq War, 'Not In My Name'. The idea is a simple one: governments are capable of some decisions which are so heinous that it is the moral duty of citizens to disown them. But of course the whole point of democracy is that the decisions reached by our representatives, even ones with which we disagree, *are* done in our name – indeed that democracy only works if those who lose a given debate agree to abide for the time being by the decision of the majority, even if they hope to get it overturned in the future.

Martin Luther King sought to change the US government's mind about Vietnam, not to challenge the democratic legitimacy of the decision to go to war or to leave the debating chamber altogether. At least rhetorically, 'Not In My Name' threatens to do both of those things. Many anti-war protesters are good democrats but, as we've seen, some of those who guide the anti-war movement embrace ideologies which regard western democracy as a capitalist snare and prefer the regimes of some of the world's most vicious dictators, though they generally try not to say that out loud when the children are listening. And of course wars which do not offer an easy opportunity to attack western leaders – like the largely ignored war in the Democratic Republic of Congo which may have claimed as many as 6 million lives, perhaps twenty times more than have died in Syria to date – are of little or no interest to them because they are less politically promising.

*

Many people hope that one day war will be abolished. But wishing for something does not make it so. When I became a journalist, it looked as if there was only one future war in which the UK was likely to be involved – a theoretical global conflict which few in their hearts believed would ever happen. In the event, during my time as producer and editor, British forces took part in four major wars, as well as numerous smaller military interventions.

The leaders we vote into power still often make and sometimes win the case for war. But our public language has yet to find a way of dealing adequately with the reality of what modern war means. Perhaps it is indigestible, indeed *should* be indigestible, because it is too monstrous to be put into words. As a result, we are likely to say too little or, like Winston Churchill in 1917, to comfort ourselves with 'rhythmical language' which suits our own finer feelings, whether we are a hawkish armchair general, a humanitarian interventionist or a selective pacifist.

Our inability to debate war honestly and in the round is a terrible weakness. Our governments grow evasive and reckless with the truth, the media by turns credulous and paranoid, the public ever more distrustful. Bitter, disunited, too confirmed in our prejudices even to bother to discuss them with those who disagree with us – woe betide us and our public language if we are ever truly tested.

11 The Abolition of Public Language

In closing, I tell you: if there is no check on the freedom of your words, then let your hearts be open to the freedom of our actions.

Osama Bin Laden[1]

Would you put an extreme right-wing political leader – a man who once denied the Holocaust and who has a criminal conviction for race hatred – on national TV so he could try to win the watching millions over to his party and its loathsome policies? I did.

In the autumn of 2009, I was told that the BBC's news division was proposing to invite Nick Griffin, the leader of the British National Party (BNP), onto *Question Time*. The panel invariably includes representatives of Britain's biggest political parties, but the producers vary the mix from time to time by including a speaker from a minor party – the Greens, say, or the SNP. Because of the prominence and potential political value of the platform, the BBC only includes parties which have achieved a certain threshold of actual electoral support; notoriety, journalistic currency, even a sudden rise in the polls are not enough. But by late 2009 the BNP had done as well at the ballot box as other smaller parties who had previously been invited onto the programme. Accordingly the editor of *Question Time* had decided that it was time to offer the BNP a seat on the panel.

Yet to many people – by no means just the left – the BNP was a special case. It had been founded in the early 1980s as a result of a civil war within an earlier British extreme right-wing party, the National Front. Its first leader, John Tyndall, and its initial policies were unashamedly racist. In an effort to widen its electoral appeal and perhaps match the success of far-right parties on the Continent like France's Front National, Nick Griffin had softened the BNP's rhetoric on immigration and ethnic minorities, though there was compelling evidence (for instance in the 2004 BBC undercover documentary, *The Secret Agent*) that the real attitudes of the party leadership had changed less than they claimed. Some feared, moreover, that the BNP was beginning to get political traction on issues which were known to be playing on many voters' minds. Immigration was palpably rising as a concern, especially in the blue-collar and lower-middle-class districts of England which were the natural hunting ground of the BNP. So too was anxiety about Islamist terrorism. And the next general election was only months away.

It's the Director-General's lot to be the final arbiter of editorial decisions before transmission. Once a story or a programme has been transmitted or posted or tweeted, other courts can sit to weigh up and pass judgement on the decision: the BBC's own governing body, the broadcasting regulator Ofcom, external inquiries, even actual courts of law on a few occasions. But until the moment of broadcast, the DG is the last port of call and – although any remotely sane occupier of that seat will seek advice from their colleagues – the BBC's constitution makes it clear that the responsibility rests solely on the DG's shoulders. It is a single point of accountability or, in the jargon of systems architecture, a single point of failure.

Around half the BBC's DGs have been dismissed or otherwise forced to leave, and more often than not because they were thought to have failed to discharge this duty adequately. In fact most major editorial controversies at the BBC involve decisions in which the DG played no part and which he was not even aware of until after the content was aired. That can still be curtains if the offending output is the latest in a series of alleged mistakes, or thought to be evidence of a systemic failure of editorial management, or if the aftermath and response to the uproar are badly handled. But set-piece judgement calls – where a tricky and high-stakes decision is brought into the DG's office on a silver platter, as it were – do still happen. The BNP and *Question Time* was a classic of the genre.

At least there was thinking time. I've already set out the case in favour of inviting a representative of the party onto the programme: their status as a legally constituted political party, their electoral success and the fact that the names of BNP candidates would soon be appearing on ballot papers. The case against allowing them to appear is summed up in its purest form in the title of a policy which was first adopted in the UK by the National Union of Students in the 1980s: 'No Platform for Fascists'. Here is the NUS's Aaron Kiely defending the policy in a blog posted in September 2012:

> This policy is rooted in the fact that <u>fascism stands for the annihilation of whole groups of people, the elimination of democracy and all freedoms</u>. Given this, there is no logical debate to be had with fascists. Providing them with a space to air their views strengthens them and in turn endangers many – Black, Jewish, LGBT, disabled people, women and all targeted by fascism across the decades. We should always remember that the millions of people who died at the hands of Nazis' slaughter [*sic*] did not die because their debating skills or arguments were not powerful enough. They died because once fascism had abused the democratic system to get its grip on power it soon closed down any freedoms to prevent any resistance. That's why I have always and will always defend NUS' [*sic*] No Platform policy.[2]

Fascism is so intrinsically repressive and anti-democratic, according to this argument, that there is no good reason to include it in conventional democratic debate, and every reason to exclude it. The fascists themselves only engage in the democratic process in order to undermine it and get their 'grip on power'. Giving them the space to air their views only 'strengthens' them. Quite why this should be so is taken as read, but let's spell it out: fascist ideas may be repellent yet opponents can still fear that they will find an audience, especially if the espousers are crafty enough to dress them up in an attractive package. Thus Mussolini and Hitler. Thus – who knows? – the modernising, apparently moderating Griffin.

In fact few mainstream politicians believed that the BNP, the English Defence League and other fringe groups on the extreme right posed a credible near-term threat to democracy. Despite a handful of victories in European and local council elections, they had never won a single seat in the UK Parliament. They had never been able to sustain the momentum of such victories and, besides, voters who hated the EU and lost sleep over immigration now had a rather more acceptable alternative in UKIP, a party which (despite its Little Englander policies and generous complement of cranks) seemed to share little with Hitler's Brown Shirts beyond an affinity for beer.

Nonetheless, many politicians of the left – and especially those with experience of them on the ground – detested the BNP, and almost all politicians on left and right regarded them with distaste. Even if you rejected the idea of *no platform for fascists* on libertarian and freedom of speech grounds, then, you might still not wish to appear in a televised debate with them. And you might have had a second reason for being against such an appearance. A *Question Time* including the BNP was bound to feature policy areas, especially around race, which the British political establishment regarded as intrinsically dangerous. In the past few years, a dam has burst and, under pressure from UKIP and the public themselves, the major parties have begun, not just to engage in a debate about immigration, but on occasion to bid against each other. In the 2016 Brexit debate, it burst out into the open. In 2009, however, there was still something of an agreement not to make it a major political battlefield. But with the BNP in the studio and a large cross-section of the public listening in, who could predict where the debate might lead?

So I knew that political reaction to a yes decision would be predominantly hostile. But I chose to extend the invitation anyway. My thinking went as follows. *Question Time* is an integral part of the wider system of democratic debate in the UK. Given the threshold of support the party had demonstrated, one could exclude the BNP from the programme only if one also held that they should be excluded from that wider arena of debate too. In other words, that their political views should be censored. But by what authority could I or the BBC decide to censor a political party? Because we ourselves disagreed with its policies? That would manifestly breach the BBC's commitment to political impartiality. Because other political interests told us we should do so? Ditto. I wrote an article for the *Guardian* at the time which argued that, while democracies *do* occasionally conclude that a given set of political ideas are so likely to lead to violence or communal discord that they should be banned, this is a job not for a broadcaster or any other journalistic body, but for those with the democratic mandate to do so:

> Democratic societies sometimes do decide that some parties and organisations are beyond the pale. As a result, they proscribe them and/or ban them from the airwaves. The UK government took exactly this step with specific parties and organisations in Northern Ireland in the 1980s. Many would argue that proscription and censorship can be counter-productive, and that it is usually better to engage and challenge extreme views than to try to eliminate them through suppression. My point is simply that the drastic steps of proscription and censorship can only be taken by government and parliament.
>
> Though we argued against it, the BBC abided by the Northern Ireland broadcasting ban in the 1980s, and, if the BNP were proscribed, the BBC would abide by that decision too, and the BNP would not appear on *Question Time*. But that hasn't happened, and until such time as it does it is unreasonable and inconsistent to take the position that a party like the BNP is acceptable enough for the public to vote for, but not acceptable enough to appear on democratic platforms such as *Question Time*. If there is a case for censorship, it should be debated and decided in parliament. Political censorship cannot be outsourced to the BBC or anyone else.[3]

The decision to invite the BNP onto *Question Time* was immediately and widely condemned. Peter Hain, the Labour government's Welsh Secretary and formerly a renowned anti-apartheid campaigner, described it as 'abhorrent' and 'unreasonable, irrational and unlawful'.[4] David Cameron, then leading the Conservatives in opposition, told a journalist from *The Times* that it made him feel 'uneasy'.[5] Many politicians claimed that Nick Griffin's appearance on the programme would give his party a new legitimacy and significantly boost their vote in the general election. The main parties deliberated whether to field panellists themselves – Labour had an explicit policy of not appearing on the same platform as the BNP – but ultimately decided to do so. The final panel was a strong one: for Labour, the Justice Secretary, Jack Straw; for the Tories, Baroness Warsi, a shadow minister of South Asian heritage; for the Lib Dems, Chris Huhne, another front-bench spokesperson; and Bonnie Greer, a noted African American writer.

There were hundreds of angry protesters outside Television Centre when the programme was finally recorded and broadcast. Inside the studio, Nick Griffin did indeed get his chance to speak, though he spent most of the evening under ferocious attack from his fellow panellists and from many members of the invited audience. Greer described sitting next to Griffin as 'probably the weirdest and most creepy experience of my life'[6] (but then, rather magnificently, went on to write an opera about it[7]). After the programme, she declared that Griffin had been 'trounced' and most observers agreed with her, though there was a minority who argued that the questions and audience had been stacked against him. Given the breadth and depth of revulsion towards him and his party, however, it is hard to see how it could have been otherwise. Virtually no one claimed that it had been a good night for the BNP. A few brave souls even went so far as to suggest that the BBC might have made the right decision.

Nor did the party reap any political benefit. Despite promising a political 'earthquake' and putting up a record number of candidates, the BNP once again failed to win a single seat in the 2010 general election. Popular support for the party dwindled, and in the 2014 elections for the European Parliament it lost its two seats, one of which had been occupied by Nick Griffin. Shortly thereafter Griffin was replaced as party leader.

It's impossible to know how significant his appearance on *Question Time* was in his and the BNP's subsequent eclipse; other factors, particularly the rise of UKIP, were also at work. But we can be sure in retrospect that the dire warnings of what would happen if Nick Griffin appeared on national TV were groundless. Some 8 million people watched the programme and the vast majority of British voters would have seen, heard or read coverage of it both before and afterwards. Far from increasing as a result of that, the BNP's political support collapsed.

Freedom of expression is often discussed as if it were solely a right conferred on the *speaker* to say or depict whatever they want. Defined like this, it can sound like a gift bestowed by a generous and tolerant society on an individual – a political agitator, say, or an avant-garde artist – to allow them to achieve a personal goal, whether ideological or aesthetic, through the expression of counter-cultural or 'offensive' views or art. And so it is, but it is also and more importantly a right of the *audience* to hear and see whatever they want to, and to form their own judgement about it. Freedom of expression is also the freedom of *impression* and it is a right which is to be enjoyed, not just by those with something public to say, but by everyone. By contrast, the compulsion to censor is rooted in the fear that the public cannot be trusted to reach sensible views about anything and that, if they are exposed to unwholesome political ideas or erotic art or whatever it is that the censor has latched on to, they will be seduced and corrupted by them. Those who call for censorship place little faith in the strength of their fellow-citizens' *phronesis*, that innate faculty of prudence which we discussed in Chapter 8.

We put Nick Griffin on *Question Time* because the public had the right to see him and listen to him responding to questions put to him by a studio audience itself made up of people like them. They did so and drew their own conclusions.

Pain Points

Except in cases which involve outright criminality (child pornography or incitement to violence, for instance), there is no evidence that suppressing ideas or cultural works of which you disapprove is a better way of defeating them in a modern democracy than confronting and debating them in public.

Those in favour of silencing fringe political views often cite fascism in Italy and Germany in the 1920s and 30s to illustrate the damage that can be done when extremists are allowed to exploit the privileges of democratic debate, but the circumstances were very different from our own. Civic structures were fragile, the political centre discredited, street violence and the prospect of outright revolution never far away.

And yet Mussolini's and Hitler's rise to power was marked not by a surfeit of open political debate and challenge but by a deficit of it, and by the failure of other political forces – in particular those parties who were genuinely committed to democracy – to unite against them. It's impossible to disprove the counterfactual proposition that censorship alone, or censorship and outright proscription, would have stopped them. When the government of Engelbert Dollfuss introduced these measures in Austria in the early 1930s, however, they failed to eradicate National Socialism in that country, just as they failed to contain many other radical and anti-democratic movements across Central and Eastern Europe in the twentieth century. Even in countries which have been wracked by war and economic crisis, and which lack a strong democratic tradition, it is not clear that silencing extreme political views ever makes them go away.

Attempts at official suppression of free speech in our own societies look universally malign or misguided in retrospect, from the clearing of library shelves in McCarthy-era America to the Thatcher government's prohibition on interviews with members of the IRA and other republican terror organisations, to which I alluded in Chapter 5. Centuries-long censorship of the arts in Britain and the US persisted into the 1960s but was then largely laughed out of the statute books by the *Lady Chatterley* and *Tropic of Cancer* trials and others like them. Few now regret its passing, or seriously claim that the world would be a better place if we were still prevented from reading the works of D. H. Lawrence or Henry Miller.

And yet, despite this history and the protection which freedom of expression enjoys under the law in all western democracies, would-be censors are growing in confidence and ambition, nowhere more so than on US and British university campuses. A characteristic example is the case of Erika Christakis, a specialist in early-childhood education, who until December 2015 was also Associate Master of Silliman College, one of the halls of residence at Yale University. A few weeks earlier, Yale's Intercultural Affairs Council had issued guidance to students warning them of the offence that could be caused to minorities by the wearing of inappropriate Halloween costumes. Christakis had the temerity to respond with an email of her own in which she asked aloud whether there was still room for 'a child or young person' to be 'a little bit inappropriate or provocative or, yes, offensive?'

The answer from some members of Yale's student body was an emphatic no. There were angry protests and, in early December, Erika Christakis decided to stop teaching classes at Yale. She said her decision was a response to a climate at Yale which was 'not conducive to the civil dialogue and open dialogue required to solve our urgent societal problems'. Her husband, Nicholas Christakis, who is Master of Silliman College, also got embroiled in the controversy. On

6 November 2015, one Silliman student posted an article about an encounter between the Master and a group of protesters:

> Today, when a group of us, organised originally by the Black Student Alliance at Yale, spoke with Christakis in the Silliman Courtyard, his response once again disappointed many of us. When students tried to tell him about their painful personal experiences as students of color on campus, he responded by making more arguments for free speech. It's unacceptable when the Master of your college is dismissive of your experiences . . . He seems to lack the ability, quite frankly, to put aside his opinions long enough to listen to the very real hurt that the community feels. He doesn't get it. And I don't want to debate. I want to talk about my pain.[8]

Those striking last two sentences ('I don't want to debate. I want to talk about my pain') sum up an uncomfortable conflict about free speech and cultural sensitivity – and between two forms of discourse, the *dialectical* and the *empathetic* – which is playing out on campuses on both sides of the Atlantic.

Earlier in 2015, students at Cardiff University had mounted a fierce campaign to stop the noted feminist Germaine Greer from giving a lecture there, her crime being that of 'misgendering', which in her case meant expressing doubt that transexuals who identified themselves as female should be treated as if they had been born women. But Greer has fought many of her own battles against the establishment; she not only turned up and gave her lecture, but used it as a platform to defend her and everyone else's right to state their opinions. 'I don't believe a woman is a man without a cock', she said with textbook clarity, though perhaps a fraction less cultural sensitivity than the student protesters had in mind. 'You can beat me over the head with a baseball bat. It still won't change my mind.'

On campus after campus, visiting speakers and senior academics are challenged either because their stated opinions are considered politically or culturally unacceptable, or because some students associate them with 'micro-aggression', a freshly minted term for veiled racist behaviour. Racism and other forms of prejudice and oppression persist and still blight lives: for those who are the victims of it, the pain is real. Nonetheless, one can acknowledge the persistence of overt and covert racism and its terrible human cost, and still be struck by the irony that the response to micro-aggression, by the angry young people who say they are victims of it, should itself involve so much intimidation.

Many public figures now refuse invitations from universities or, if the announcement that they are coming triggers a hostile campaign, cancel their appearance. In the graduation season of 2014, for instance, the former Secretary of State, Condoleezza Rice, pulled out of the commencement speech at Rutgers University, while IMF managing director Christine Lagarde withdrew from the same duty at Smith College. The objection to Rice was her involvement, as a member of George W. Bush's Cabinet, in the Iraq War. Students objected to Lagarde because she is the head of an organisation (the IMF) which they held responsible for 'the failed developmental policies implanted in some of the world's poorest countries'.[9]

That same season, Brandeis University took the even more drastic step of revoking its offer of an honorary degree – and the opportunity to address students that went with it – to the Somali–Dutch women's rights activist, Ayaan Hirsi Ali, because her 'past statements' about Islam were 'inconsistent with Brandeis University's core values', as the official news release puts it. Objections from a minority of students had frightened an American university into gagging a black female human-rights activist in the name of sensitivity to minorities. Aware that the university would be accused of limiting freedom of expression, Brandeis said Ayaan Hirsi Ali would be 'welcome to join us on campus in the future to engage in a dialogue', but no one expects her to take up that invitation anytime soon. At Brandeis and many other universities, the intimidation is working, and the range of opinions which students are permitted to hear has shrunk.

One of the most frequent – and most abject – excuses universities use when they exclude unpopular speakers is the safety of the wider student body. It's as if free speech were a dangerous indulgence which, like smoking, could have deleterious effects on passive bystanders. In fact, free speech is a fundamental human right which needs to be defended, not just in theory but in practice, if necessary with the police in attendance in riot gear. People have the right to protest against everything, including freedom of expression, but universities should take such protests in their stride. Caving in because somebody threatens violence speaks not of responsibility, but of cowardice.

This is how the former mayor of New York, Michael Bloomberg, who had himself survived a student-led campaign to disinvite him, characterised the situation when I heard him speaking to the graduating class at Harvard on 29 May 2014:

> This spring, it has been disturbing to see a number of college commencement speakers withdraw – or have their invitations rescinded – after protests from students and – to me, shockingly – from senior faculty and administrators who should know better . . . In each case, liberals silenced a voice – and denied an honorary degree – to individuals they deemed politically objectionable. That is an outrage and we must not let it continue. If a university thinks twice before inviting a commencement speaker because of his or her politics, censorship and conformity – the mortal enemies of freedom – win out.[10]

As Michael Bloomberg noted in his remarks, the recent spate of formal and informal acts of censorship on American campuses are invariably the result of campaigns by left-wing students – and subsequent cave-ins by predominantly liberal faculties – against speakers of the right, or those associated with institutions which the left claim are part of the power structures of the political and economic establishment.

Most attempts to silence opponents in the political realm are also associated with the radical left, but it's a different story when it comes to arts and culture. After it was announced that the New York Metropolitan Opera was proposing to stage John Adams' work *The Death of Klinghoffer* – which depicts the murder of the disabled Jewish American tourist Leon Klinghoffer during the 1985 Palestine Liberation Front hijacking of the liner *Achille Lauro* – there were vociferous calls from some generally conservative Jewish groups for the production to be abandoned. Morton Klein, the president of the Zionist Organization of America, described the piece with glorious hyperbole as 'an operatic Kristallnacht'.[11] The Met agreed to call off an international simulcast of the opera, but otherwise held its nerve. Attendees of the premiere (including myself and one of my sons) were greeted by angry but peaceful crowds shouting 'Nazi-lovers! You'll be in the water next!'

In the UK too, as we shall see, conservative religious groups have done their best, sometimes successfully, to prevent the public from making up their own minds about other artistic works which the protesters deem offensive, while elsewhere the self-proclaimed defenders of the Prophet Muhammad have resorted to outright murder to silence some 'blasphemers' and terrify the rest.

The urge to shout down or silence those whose creative work or opinions you hate transcends left and right. Its wellspring is an over-powering sense of victimhood (or victimhood by proxy) which convinces those in its grip that conventional public discourse and traditional notions about open debate and free speech have failed them utterly, and that they can only achieve understanding and justice by taking extraordinary measures. This is how the oppressed become would-be oppressors.

*

But if you want to encounter the most pervasive use of intimidation to discourage contrary opinions and drown out reasonable debate, you need look no further than your smartphone. Idealists had hoped that, in addition to offering users limitless information and valuable services, the Internet would nurture a new kind of participative debate in which ideas and opinions could be freely exchanged and discussed by people who had lacked any real voice in the analogue age. Such sites and discussion groups exist, but those who moderate chat rooms or comments about the news know that, for every poster and tweeter who wants to participate in a courteous dialogue, there is another – sometimes a multitude – with something darker in mind.

Hatred and rage take many forms on the Web but all share a contempt for traditional dialectical argument and a desire, where possible, to disrupt and supplant it with insult and categorical assertion. Extreme groups, from anti-western terrorists to white supremacists, now have an almost entirely unregulated and cost-free form of global distribution which they have embraced with enthusiasm and, in some cases, sophistication, especially in the use of social media. The impact on mainstream debate is no doubt less dangerous, but still deeply depressing. Arguments which would have once been conducted with a reasonable level of mutual courtesy now often quickly descend to the crude, the personal and the downright ugly.

Women are a particular target. In 2013 Caroline Criado-Perez and other campaigners convinced the Bank of England to put Jane Austen on a £10 note. That was enough to provoke a storm of social media abuse and threats of rape, violence and murder. Mary Beard, the classics professor and broadcaster, often speaks publicly on TV and radio about the issues of the day. Like prominent women in many western countries, she too has found herself pursued by trolls and, to use her phrase, 'generic, violent misogyny' on Twitter and other supposedly social platforms. Beard has treated the trolls to some of their medicine, naming and shaming them – though astonishingly also helping a few of them out on occasion with advice and job references.

Quite understandably, few women want anything to do with the male (and sometimes female) digital Calibans who try so relentlessly to intimidate and humiliate them. But the demonic anomie which the facelessness of the digital conversation has unleashed knows no bounds of gender, class or topic. Celebrities and the new stars of social media are probably most vulnerable, but the ugliness has crept into the discussion of politics, culture, ideas and social science, and can be directed at almost anyone. To pick one example from a sea of possibilities, for several years the Nobel Prize-winning economist Paul Krugman and the historian Niall Ferguson have maintained a lively argument about a number of economic questions, much of which has played out in the blogosphere. Both of these academic silverbacks are tough customers, and the language which has flown between them has often been sharp to say the least. Their argument has nonetheless been one of intellectual substance.

Now brace yourself and listen to some of the voices of the digital crowd following this heavyweight fight:

> Fuck Paul Krugman and the liberals that love citing this douchebag but can't seem to provide any rebuttal when I answer his talking points they throw at me. Utter hypocritical douche.

> He should be pinned down and shaved like a shiny baby's butt. It would be easier to see the shit coming out of his mouth.

the manky scottish cunt ferguson is a rothschild stooge and eyes wide shut rape party guest. a masonic of the scottish rite so this shit is just war between jewish families or silly in house acting.

So one piece of shit calls out another piece of shit for not being 'civil' – and this is Internet Epic?[14]

Poisonous, infantile, dehumanised and dehumanising: the tone of these comments is not exceptional by the standards that now obtain in the no-man's-land of digital debate. This is an assembly of rage which all are welcome to join – left and right, rich and poor, pro-lifers and pro-choicers, Islamophiles and Islamophobes, Zionists and anti-Zionists. The only qualification necessary for admission is unreasonable fury.

The Rhetoric of Conscience

A critical indicator that our public language is in crisis is the fact that so many people have in so many different ways given up listening to those they disagree with, preferring instead to prevent them from speaking or, if that's not possible, to put their fingers in their ears or abuse or intimidate them.

The thought process is clear: there comes a point when someone's values are so contrary to mine that further discussion is futile and I should treat them not as an interlocutor worthy of hearing out, or even as an intellectual adversary to be overcome through argument, but as a moral outcast who, if possible, should be prevented from speaking at all. Whether one agrees with it or not, one can easily see how a democrat in 1930s Germany might have reached exactly that conclusion about Adolf Hitler: the question which should concern us is how a measure which might be justified in such a political and moral extremity could possibly seem appropriate for something as arguable as a claim about 'failed developmental policies'.

As a first step towards answering this question, I want to explore what it is that makes debates which involve disagreements about values more fraught and seemingly irresolvable, despite the fact that we are sometimes told that we live in the most tolerant and broad-minded culture in human history. In his book *After Virtue*, the moral philosopher Alasdair MacIntyre has this to say about today's arguments about moral questions:

> The most striking feature of contemporary moral utterance is that so much of it is used to express disagreements and the most striking feature of the debates in which these disagreements are expressed is their interminable character. I do not mean by this just that such debates go on and on and on – although they do – but also that they apparently can find no terminus. There seems to be no rational way of securing moral agreement in our culture.[15]

MacIntyre suggests three characteristics of these debates which might explain why this should be so. The first is that the different views are incommensurable. The arguments of those in favour of and those against abortion rights may each flow logically and consistently from a coherent moral world view, but the world views represented on the one hand by *the unborn child's right to life*, and on the other by *a woman's right to choose*, start from such radically different premises that neither can be satisfactorily adjudicated from the perspective of the other. Each party can argue back to its own premises but, when they do, argument gives way to pure assertion and counter-assertion. As we saw with the 'death panel' and other examples in this book, this clash of incommensurable perspectives can make resolution impossible not just in strict 'values' debates, like that about abortion, but in any argument which one or both of the parties decides to view through an absolutist lens. Today that can include almost any political, social or cultural question.

The second characteristic MacIntyre notes is that these rival moral world views are usually presented not as if they were merely a matter of personal preference, but rather as *impersonal* and, in some sense, objective frameworks of values and standards, each of the antagonists claiming of course that *their* framework is the valid one. Furthermore, we tend to want to have our cake and eat it: we treat our moral utterances as both fully personal to us and as independently grounded – or, to put it in terms we have already discussed in this book, to believe that they exhibit both *authenticity* and objective *rationality*.

Finally MacIntyre claims that the language in which these world views are expressed is itself in a state of disorder because of the immense cultural and social change that has taken place in recent centuries. Looking back, we realise that critical terms like *virtue* or *justice*

> were originally at home in larger totalities of theory and practice in which they enjoyed a role and function supplied by contexts of which they have now been deprived.[16]

Divorced from the structures of moral thought and behaviour which originally shaped them, the meaning of these words is no longer secure. Our debaters may discover not only that they cannot agree with each other what the word *justice* means, but – and despite the apparent simplicity of the word – that they do not have a coherent definition of it themselves, and thus no certainty that the way they use it is consistent with their other ideas about morality.

Taken together, MacIntyre's observations help explain why arguments which touch on values and ethics can prove so intractable and why the participants so often conclude that further dialogue is pointless, and that they should resort instead to shouting louder or refusing to listen, to anonymous abuse on the Internet or, in some cases, to violence.

It's worth spending a little more time examining MacIntyre's second characteristic, that tendency to believe that *what feels true and right to me* is also necessarily *what is true and right for everyone*. One of the oldest ways of understanding this instinct was to interpret it as the voice of *revelation* and *conscience*: directly or indirectly, God has revealed to me the truth which I am now imparting to you. The name for the special kind of public language which results is *prophecy*. To state the obvious, the Bible and Qur'an are full of it. Someone who believes that God has spoken to them in this way is more or less compelled to believe that their message is categorical and universally applicable. So what happens when others disagree?

*

London, 1642. England is more than a century into the Reformation and, after decades of heroic efforts to control the centrifugal religious and political forces, the centre can no longer hold. Having failed to find and arrest five radical Members of Parliament, King Charles I decides personally to confront the Corporation of London. But a young ironmonger called Henry Walker has decided to do some confronting of his own, not with a sword or pistol, but with the help of a friend's printing press:

> Walker's invention being mounted on the Altitude of mischiefe, he plotted and contrived with a Printer, the said night before to write and print a perillous Petition to his Majesty, and borrowed the Printers wives Bible, out of which he took his Theame out of *Kings, Chap.12, vers.16* part of the verse; *To Your Tents O Israel.* There was writing and printing all night, and all the next day those Libels were scattered, and when his Majesty had dined, and had taken Coach to returne to *White-Hall*, Walker stood watching the Kings comming by amongst the Drapers in *Pauls church-yard*, and having one of his pamphlets in his hand meaning to have it delivered it to his Majesty, but could not come at him by reason of the presse of People, insomuch as *Walker* (most impudently sawcy) threw it over the folkes heads into his Majesties Coach.[17]

King Charles is an absolute monarch, Henry Walker a 29-year-old London tradesman, but the combination of Walker's religio-political confidence, new media technology (a pamphlet written and printed in a night and distributed the following morning), and the already tumultuous atmosphere in the capital lend the ironmonger and Charles a new equality of expression and give Walker the chutzpah literally to throw his argument at the king's head. Civil war wasn't far away.

Many of those who lived through it, including the political theorist Thomas Hobbes, came to believe that a significant cause of that war was the way in which Puritan dissent, preached from the pulpit by Protestant radicals and spread far and wide in pamphlets and tracts, undermined the authority on which the social order depended. The consequence was effectively a regression to the terrible natural condition of mankind which Hobbes famously described in *Leviathan* as a war 'of every man against every man'.[18]

The religious extremism of the time, and the terrifying certainty that the public statements you make are underwritten by God himself, was not of course restricted to radical English Protestants, or to the

Protestant side in the Reformation alone. Catholic zealots across Europe played their own part in stirring up rebellion and civil war, and at the start of the seventeenth century famously attempted, in the words of the ringleader Robert Catesby, to blow up 'the Parliament howse with Gunpowder . . . in that place have they done us all the mischiefe, and perchance God hath designed that place for their punishment'.[19] Hobbes' argument with the Protestant dissenters is one instance in the much wider Early Modern struggle between the forces of religious absolutism and those of secular pragmatism.

Hobbes' own pragmatism had a steely edge. The American political scientist Bryan Garsten notes in his magisterial defence of rhetoric, *Saving Persuasion*, that by the time Hobbes wrote *Behemoth*, his idiosyncratic history of the Civil War, he had come to wonder if it wouldn't have been better if the 'seditious ministers, which were not perhaps 1000, had been all killed before they had preached'.[20] Some of the uses of public language are so pernicious, Hobbes suggested, that it may be preferable to suppress them and their authors altogether than to allow them to tear the state limb from limb.

Hobbes was sceptical about the value of all rhetorical dialectic, observing that debaters seldom win arguments as such and warning that, without some absolute authority to arbitrate between them, all debates must 'either come to blowes, or be undecided'.[21] But he had a central fear of what Garsten calls 'the dogmatism of conscience', and the claim by the radicals that *their* arguments had a special and unanswerable status because of their divine inspiration. He argued instead that in their private lives everyone is entitled to believe whatever they want about conscience and prophecy but, when it comes to public argument, the statements that would-be prophets make should be regarded as opinions like any other and should not enjoy any special privilege. Further he held that, like all other private opinions, they should be subordinated to the judgement of a sovereign, whose 'Publique Reason' becomes in effect the collective conscience. It is the sovereign's job to decide then, not just who has made a good argument, but who has heard the authentic word of God. Only thus can anarchy be avoided.

By 'sovereign', Hobbes meant either an absolute monarch or an institution. Over the centuries that followed, the institution which the public would recognise as sovereign was liberal democracy which, especially in Britain, France and America, had a strongly secular flavour. In an open society, where anyone can say anything and public norms are too diffuse to form easy targets, the prophet can find him or herself struggling for an audience and for relevance: tolerance is a gracious but unrelenting leveller.

The case against the special privilege of prophecy was won so comprehensively that the argument itself was largely forgotten. By the late twentieth century, Hobbes' warning about the political danger of public language inspired by religious enthusiasm would have felt to most people like a transmission from some long-dead world with no possible meaning for the enlightened inhabitants of modern-day Earth. But appearances can be deceptive.

Should I be Charlie?

On 14 February 1989, the supreme leader of Iran, Ayatollah Ruhollah Khomeini, issued a fatwa, or religious ruling, calling for the death of the novelist Salman Rushdie. Rushdie's 'crime' was to have written *The Satanic Verses*, an exploration of identity and exile which drew in part on the life of the Prophet Muhammad. Many Muslims had come to believe – in a few cases because they had read it, in most no doubt because they had been told – that the novel was an assault on the honour of the Prophet and was blasphemous in its treatment of Islam.

The story didn't come out of nowhere. By the time the ayatollah promulgated his fatwa, *The Satanic Verses* was already a cause célèbre, and demonstrations and book-burnings had taken place in several countries. A familiar limits-of-free-expression debate had also already broken out in the UK – the rights of the artist versus the rights of a minority not to have its religion denigrated.

But the fatwa changed everything. And today, more than a generation later, everything remains changed. The moment lacked the horror and drama of 9/11 or the high emotion of the fall of the Berlin Wall, but in my years in journalism it stands as the third genuine world-historical inflection point: the third of the days I have lived through when the world looked like *this* when I walked into the newsroom, but irrevocably like *that* by the time the late shift went home.

Not that we understood at the time quite what *that* was. For me and my team – I was editor of *The Nine O'Clock News* – it was first and foremost a breaking story that needed to be teased out into its constituent strands. First, there was Salman Rushdie's safety. Would the British authorities protect him, and how? Where was he? Would he speak? Then there was the domestic and worldwide political reaction – a British author and a British book were now a global story and the debate about the rights and wrongs of the matter would become an international talking point. And what about the reaction of British and other Muslims? Would they back the fatwa? Would any of them support Rushdie? Finally, what was the ayatollah's true intent: was this really just a *theological* matter or, as some had already begun to suggest, an essentially *political* attempt by the most important Shi'ite leader to assert wider moral leadership in the Muslim world?

This reflexive slicing and dicing is what reporters and editors do, so much so that the process can feel strangely dissociated from the story in question. Harder to express, let alone report, was the collective incredulity. Could the ayatollah actually *mean* it? Could a world leader in 1989 really be calling for the murder (for that in secular terms was what it would be) of someone for writing a *novel*, and offering a cash reward into the bargain? It was tempting to interpret the fatwa principally as a piece of empty rhetoric, something said to achieve a certain effect but not to be taken any more seriously than most of the dire warnings routinely made by western politicians, words which might sound important when first said, but which soon fade into obscurity.

But the ayatollah meant exactly what he said. And murder duly followed – not of Salman Rushdie himself (he was spirited into hiding) but, because the ayatollah had also called for the killing of 'all those involved in its publication', of Hitoshi Igarashi, his translator in Japan, with further failed assassination attempts on his Italian translator and the publisher of *The Satanic Verses* in Norway. In 1993, after Friday prayers in the city of Sivas in central Turkey, a crowd of Sunni Muslims attacked a hotel which was hosting a cultural festival to which the writer Aziz Nesin, who had translated and published extracts of *The Satanic Verses*, had been invited. The crowd set fire to the hotel and thirty-five people died in the subsequent blaze. Perhaps 200 people died overall in protests and other incidents connected with the outcry about the novel.

There were some who knew exactly where they stood on the very day that the fatwa was issued. One was Rushdie's close friend, Christopher Hitchens:

> I felt at once that here was something that completely committed me. It was, if I can phrase it like this, a matter of everything I hated versus everything I loved. In the hate column: dictatorship, religion, stupidity, demagogy, censorship, bullying and intimidation. In the love column: literature, irony, humour, the individual, and the defence of free expression.[22]

Hitchens recognised at once that the fatwa represented a fundamental assault on western values: 'No more root-and-branch challenge to the values of the Enlightenment (on the bicentennial of the fall of the Bastille) or to the First Amendment of the Constitution, could be imagined.'

The British authorities spoke out against the fatwa and pledged to protect Rushdie, but with far less enthusiasm. Ministers emphasised their distaste for the offence which the novelist had caused and one of them, Norman Tebbit, went further: Salman Rushdie was a man, he said, whose 'public life has been a record of despicable acts of betrayal of his upbringing, religion, adopted home and nationality'.[23] The sense of irritation that a novelist who had not even been born in the UK could have had the effrontery to stir up so much trouble was widespread among politicians, religious leaders and others at the time. I remember the novelist P. D. James, who was then a BBC governor, relishing the image of Rushdie the great *provocateur* reduced to playing canasta night after night with members of the Special Branch.

For the critic John Berger, there was an equivalence between Salman Rushdie and what Berger took him to stand for – unbridled freedom of expression – and his Islamic opponents. Unless there was some restraint, he warned,

> a unique 20th-century holy war, with its terrifying righteousness on both sides, may be on the point of breaking out sporadically but

repeatedly – in airports, shopping streets, suburbs, city centres, wherever the unprotected live.[24]

Here the exercise of free speech has become a matter of 'terrifying righteousness', and Salman Rushdie is a soldier in a war which risks bringing death or injury to 'the unprotected'. Berger's appeal for the safety of the 'unprotected' – for which we can read 'innocent non-combatants' – implicitly identifies Rushdie as someone who is *not* innocent, but rather one of the perpetrators of the war.

The former US president Jimmy Carter took much the same line, though now the context is not the immediate threat of terrorist reprisal but of the amity between nations and cultures:

> Ayatollah Khomeini's offer of paradise to Rushdie's assassin has caused writers and public officials in Western nations to become almost exclusively preoccupied with the author's rights. While Rushdie's First Amendment freedoms are important, we have tended to promote him and his book with little acknowledgment that it is a direct insult to those millions of Moslems whose sacred beliefs have been violated and are suffering in restrained silence the added embarrassment of the Ayatollah's irresponsibility. This is the kind of intercultural wound that is difficult to heal. Western leaders should make it clear that in protecting Rushdie's life and civil rights, there is no endorsement of an insult to the sacred beliefs of our Moslem friends.[25]

Jimmy Carter's claim that the 'writers and public officials' in western nations had been 'almost exclusively preoccupied with the author's rights' may have been true of some of the writers, but it was patently untrue of most of the 'public officials'. And by no stretch of the imagination was *The Satanic Verses* a *direct* insult to anyone; it was a novel after all – a work of literature with imaginary characters set in an imaginary world. Jimmy Carter calls Ayatollah Khomeini's call to murder an 'added embarrassment' as if the imam was guilty of nothing more than a minor social faux pas, and as if his crime – solicitation to murder – was somehow equivalent to Salman Rushdie's. It's hard not to conclude that the embarrassment which President Carter feels most acutely and is most anxious to expunge relates to those lamentably unfettered 'First Amendment freedoms'.

We can think of freedom of expression as an absolute right and defend it stalwartly as such, offering like Voltaire to lay down our lives to defend the right of people to say and do things which we ourselves regard as hateful and false. Or we can think of it as something relative, a right which needs to be balanced with other duties and obligations if our societies are to remain tranquil. To propose, as President Carter and many other politicians implicitly did at the time of the *Satanic Verses* controversy, that we can magically do both – doff our caps to the absolute freedom envisaged in the First Amendment and the UN Declaration of Human Rights, but simultaneously tell everyone that the moral thing to do is to behave as if it were relative – is an uncomfortable middle position which is ultimately unlikely to satisfy anyone. Indeed a secure and settled answer to the dilemma has eluded western societies ever since: it remains an unresolved dissonance at the core of the modern liberal project.

But let's now fly twenty-six years forward to the day in early 2015 when a pair of heavily armed Islamist extremists stormed into the offices of the satirical magazine *Charlie Hebdo* in Paris and murdered eleven people inside, including those who had drawn and published a series of provocative (and often obscene) cartoons featuring the Prophet Muhammad. There had been other outrages in the years between. In Amsterdam in 2004, a Dutch–Moroccan man stabbed to death the author and director Theo van Gogh, who had collaborated with Ayaan Hirsi Ali on a controversial film about the oppression of women in many Muslim countries. The following year, death threats and violent protests greeted the publication of an earlier set of cartoons depicting the Prophet in the Danish newspaper *Jyllands-Posten*. Nonetheless, the murders of the *Charlie Hebdo* cartoonists and their colleagues (six more people would die in related incidents) came as an electrifying shock not just in France but across the western world – and the unfinished argument about the proper limits of freedom of speech returned with a vengeance.

On the night of the murders, the BBC's evening radio news programme, *The World Tonight*, asked Arzu Merali, who is the director of research at the Islamic Human Rights Commission, to take part in a discussion about the attack. This is how she characterised the wider debate:

You know there's been an awful lot of clamour and upset and this trope that's been going on for nigh on thirty years now about religious people, particularly Muslims, feeling offended and how this is an unacceptable affront to free speech, which for many of us coming from the human rights community is really a distraction from what really affects people, when this term is used as a stick to beat them as it often is with the Muslim community . . . Where things have been going wrong and people have been protesting and things like this it's tended to point to areas where the discourse itself is very demonised, it's very disempowering, it's marginalising and it works within the framework of structural racism, so what we have with the idea of free speech is it would be a fantastic idea, if there was equality of access to all the forums where we can speak. But marginalised communities, of which Muslims in European and westernised settings are certainly one, don't have that access.[26]

This statement reduced the other party to the discussion, the muscular journalist and free-speech advocate David Aaronovitch, to something near spluttering speechlessness: 'I have absolutely no idea what the last speaker was talking about,' he said. 'As soon as someone uses the word "discourse", it's a bad sign because it means that you'll find yourself dealing with something other than the subject.'[27]

In fact, Arzu Merali's remarks are not hard to understand. Like Jimmy Carter, she refuses to consider freedom of speech in the abstract and casts it instead in a political and cultural context in which Muslims feature first and foremost as victims. Unlike him, though, she offers a coherent theory about why the case for regarding freedom of expression as an absolute right is wrong.

Unpacked and elaborated, it goes like this. There is a 'framework of structural racism' in western societies which intentionally disadvantages ethnic minorities. Attitudes to minority religions are part of this framework and are exacerbated by the fact that secularisation has left the controlling elite with little religious belief or knowledge of their own. As a result, they treat Islam and the beliefs of other minorities with a contempt that alienates and separates them further. Within the vicious circle of this 'demonised' discourse, you shouldn't be surprised if words or images which are taken to be notably provocative trigger an extreme response. You can think of the response as a 'last straw' reaction by groups who already suffer immense social and economic inequality. The debate about free speech is a distraction. It is specious to talk about it as a universal right because it is not distributed fairly across society. It is a luxury enjoyed by the rich and powerful who then have the nerve to use it as a stick to beat those who have no voice at all. The argument for treating freedom of expression as sacrosanct is thus not a valid argument at all but a 'trope', a convenient rhetorical artefact that needs to be deconstructed (like this) if it is to be correctly understood.

If we politely ignore the looming shades of Karl Marx, Jacques Derrida et al., Arzu Merali's central point is a simple one: don't take freedom of expression too seriously. In the pantheon of human rights, it matters far less than essential economic, social and cultural needs that are currently denied to minorities. To endlessly emphasise it serves only to widen the gap between those minorities and the majority. She takes a harder line than Jimmy Carter then. She pays almost no lip service to the First Amendment and its equivalents; she makes no attempt to have it both ways. Her fundamental case is the same.

There's much that could be said about Arzu Merali's comments on *The World Tonight*. Is it really adequate to refer to the events at *Charlie Hebdo* as *things like this* (as in 'when things have been going wrong and people have been protesting and things like this'), as if mass murder is just another kind of protest and really only to be expected given the provocation? Isn't religiously inspired hostility to freedom of expression a feature not only of the cultures of Muslim minorities in the West but of countries in which Muslims have enjoyed powerful majorities for decades or longer? To put it more plainly, can the hostility be explained in its entirety as a response to modern-day 'structural racism'? Does it not in fact pre-date and, to a significant degree, exist independently of it? And does Arzu Merali truly believe that free speech is a 'fantastic idea', even in principle? She sounds less than enthusiastic.

But the essential challenge still hangs in the air, as it has since the ayatollah's fatwa: that, abstracted from cultural and social realities, a blind insistence on freedom of expression is self-indulgent and, because of the way it can reinforce alienation and inequality, potentially divisive and hegemonic. So how should we think about this right in relation to other desiderata like inter-communal respect and harmony?

Let's begin with the question of restraint. The Enlightenment understanding of free expression has always included a right to offend, but that doesn't mean that everyone has a mission to offend, or a moral obligation to publish everything. It is perfectly reasonable for a given media organisation to take care not unnecessarily to offend people, particularly when those people are members of an ethnic group who already feel isolated and vulnerable. Even with the majority population, there is a strong case for proportionality when it comes to offensive material – is the editorial or creative benefit of inclusion likely to outweigh the offence caused? – and for restraint if the answer to that question is no.

But a free society necessarily contains a plurality of audiences and editorial opinions, and different editors will make different judgement calls about the weight to give to different considerations and about the boundaries of acceptability for *their* audience. It is the right to make these independent editorial judgements that sits above any one individual's or group's assessment of the considerations. It cannot be relativised. It should never be undermined. To attempt to impose, or even to argue for some kind of normative 'restraint', to fail full-bloodedly to support the legitimacy of editorial choices which differ from those you would have made yourself, is to call into question that diversity of voices and opinions. It can be made to sound statesman-like and even-handed. It is in fact a betrayal of one of the foundations on which democracy and freedom stand.

Next, anyone who thinks that outrage at murderous attacks on freedom of expression is nothing more than a 'trope' and a 'distraction from what really affects people' is missing a fundamental truth about this right. History shows us that it is invariably the state and the powerful in society (including religious elites) who suppress free speech and minorities who often suffer as a result. In the real world, freedom of expression – and the freedom to report oppression and victimisation – is one of the few protections minorities have. Arzu Merali says she comes 'from the human rights community', and seems to propose a tension between freedom of expression and other, presumably more important rights. On the contrary, the almost universal experience in both western and developing-world societies is that this human right goes with all the others. In countries where it is recognised, it helps sustain other freedoms, promotes good government, discourages state violence and other abuse. Where it is denied – as it is in many countries including more or less all with a Muslim majority – other fundamental human rights suffer too.

Sensitivity about other people's beliefs is often both prudent and admirable. But nobody has an absolute right not to be offended, or to retaliate with violence if they feel offended. Freedom of religion is the right to follow your faith without molestation or persecution; in a free society it cannot extend to the right not to have your religion criticised or mocked. If you fear that you or your family may find a book or movie offensive, don't look at it and tell your children to ignore it too. This was precisely the advice given to Sunni Muslims with regard to the *Charlie Hebdo* cartoons, in the aftermath of the Paris attack, by Al-Azhar University, one of the leading centres of Islamic theological scholarship in the world:

> Ignore this unpleasant trifle, because the Prophet of mercy and humanity (peace be upon him) is on too great and high a level to be affected by drawings that lack ethics.[28]

That judicious piece of advice should be the end of the matter. But in 1989 Ruhollah Khomeini's fatwa made a far more radical demand: it was not that Muslims should not read *The Satanic Verses* but that no one should, that it and its author should cease to exist.

It's a demand which once again brings us face to face with the rhetoric of conscience and the dilemma which Thomas Hobbes identified in seventeenth-century England – how can the state and society deal with the injunctions of the divinely inspired? There's nothing to be gained by arguing the point, because the counter-party doesn't recognise the legitimacy of anything other than the truths which they believe have been disclosed to them. Triangulation – the *plague on both your houses* approach which John Berger, Jimmy Carter and many others adopted during the Salman Rushdie affair – doesn't resolve anything. You have to decide. Either you must (explicitly or implicitly) accept the special claim of the voice of prophecy, or you must reject it.

To accept it – to concede that *The Satanic Verses* should never have been written and all future editions of *Charlie Hebdo* should be removed from every news-stand, and that legislation should be passed to prohibit all future such occurrences – is impossible. Our Publique Reason, to put it in Hobbes' terms, is plurality and tolerance and, paradoxical as this may sound, it must be enforced. This is not because western liberal values are self-evidently superior to others. It is because reasonable as well as unreasonable people can disagree on what constitutes the good life or a good society, and it is only through the exercise of freedom of expression that their proposed answers can be weighed against each other and choices made and, if circumstances change, revoked. This is the right which makes the debate about all the other rights possible. It should be limited only in an immediate and absolute emergency. We must reject the ayatollah's demand not just in part but in its entirety.

★

Inevitably other religious groups in Britain and elsewhere sought (albeit in less violent ways) to ape the tactics used to attack Salman Rushdie and *The Satanic Verses*, or to argue that they too should enjoy the same deference which they claimed Islam now enjoyed because of the violent reaction to the novel.

In late 2004, the Birmingham Repertory Theatre cancelled its run of the play *Behzti* (or *Dishonour*). The play, which was written by the British Sikh woman playwright Gurpreet Kaur Bhatti, included the depiction of rape and murder in a Sikh temple and provoked an outcry in the Sikh community. On opening night, there was a violent demonstration outside the theatre in which several police officers were hurt and a number of arrests made. Attempts were made to find a compromise – could the scene in which the rape and murder occurred be moved from the (imaginary) temple to some other location? – but a couple of days later, after advice from the police and the Commission for Racial Equality, the theatre decided to abandon the production altogether.

At more or less the same time, I found myself in the middle of a similar controversy involving Christianity. The controller of BBC2, Roly Keating, had decided to televise the stage production of *Jerry Springer: The Opera*, a rambunctious piece of satirical musical theatre written by Richard Thomas and Stewart Lee. *Jerry Springer* is a fantastical account of the life and imagined death of the well-known US TV talk-show host. The first half of the show is a comically exaggerated version of the talk show complete with a series of bizarre and sexually deviant 'guests'. At the end of this first half, 'Jerry Springer' is shot by one of the other characters and the rest of the performance is set in the afterlife with Satan and God battling over his soul – and hoping to use his unique talents to solve their own problems. In this second half, the guests from the opening reappear as divine figures: a pervert in a nappy, for instance, now playing the role of Jesus.

Jerry Springer had been extensively performed on stage before the decision was made to televise it, and had attracted little attention for its content. But news of the planned broadcast was greeted with fury by several Christian groups, and particularly by some Protestant evangelicals. The BBC received around 50,000 communications, most of them emails, demanding that the satire should not be shown, and there were demonstrations outside Television Centre and other BBC facilities. The addresses of several BBC executives were published and anonymous threats made against them. Stephen Green, whose Christian Voice was the most active and vociferous of the protesting groups, got hold of my phone number and rang several times to lobby me personally. He was extremely angry and persistent but, it must be said, hardly threatening.

I am a Catholic myself, and am sensitive to extreme or grotesque depictions of the central religious figures of my faith. Absurd though it will seem to some, I have never watched *The Last Temptation of Christ*, *Life of Brian* or *The Passion of the Christ* as a result, though I would have done had the professional need arisen, and certainly do not believe that anyone who does not share my beliefs should be prevented from seeing them. In a free society, we can all make our own choices in such matters.

In fact, and without having registered in advance that it included depictions of Christian religious figures, I had attended the opening night of *Jerry Springer* in the West End some months before the controversy erupted, and hadn't been upset or offended in the slightest. It was obvious to me that the piece was a satire not about Christianity, but about the shallowness and insincerity of a certain kind of television. The figures who appeared in the second half of the piece were clearly intended to be seen not as actual portraits of God the Father, Jesus and Mary but, within the overarching conceit, as the characters who had already appeared in the earlier Jerry Springer 'show'.

When the protests began, the largest Christian denominations – Anglican, Catholic and Methodist – all had to decide where they stood on *Jerry Springer*. They contacted the BBC and we arranged for their representatives to discreetly attend the stage production so they could decide for themselves whether or not it was likely to give grave offence to Christians. They saw it and had much the same reaction as I. For understandable reasons, the major churches did not express any enthusiasm for the broadcast, but they didn't publicly oppose it either.

As I've already said, publishers don't have a duty to publish everything and have the right to take the sensitivity of their audience and other factors into account before deciding whether to publish or not. A few months before *Jerry Springer* came up, I'd taken a more finely balanced decision that the BBC should *not* broadcast *Popetown*, a satirical adult cartoon series set in the Vatican, because I did not consider it creatively strong enough, or indeed funny enough, to justify the offence it was likely to cause if we showed it. The programme was subsequently released on DVD in the UK and shown in many other countries. A few years after *Jerry Springer*, I decided controversially not to air a charity appeal aimed at helping the (overwhelmingly Palestinian) victims of an intense period of conflict in Gaza, lest it led some viewers to doubt the BBC's commitment to impartiality in the coverage of that war. Another British broadcaster (BSkyB) took the same view, but others disagreed and the appeal was widely seen.*

Each case has to be judged on its merits and different editors may come to different conclusions. This is what pluralism of expression looks like in reality. The multiplicity of outcomes, and the debate before and after publication about who is right and who wrong, are not evidence of a contradiction in the western conception of pluralism, but its essence and its virtue.

---

* My own approach to impartiality was pretty hard line throughout my career at the BBC. As DG, I turned down a request to erect a statue to George Orwell, a writer who I admire greatly, at Broadcasting House. I worried that we'd have to find an equivalent literary lion from the right and then representatives of other political persuasions, so that in the end the BBC's headquarters would come to resemble St Peter's in Rome.

Jerry Springer: The Opera had received a number of awards and the creative significance of the piece was not really in question. We planned to transmit the programme late at night when children would be unlikely to watch it, and to place explicit warnings in front of it to alert everyone else to its content. I could be confident then that we could keep the viewers who might stumble upon it to a small number, and thus reduce the *direct* offence which the programme would cause to a minimum.

But this calculation (artistic merit versus likely offence) was of no interest to the protesters. Like the ayatollah, their argument was an absolute one: even if every Christian avoided the transmission and no direct offence resulted, they believed that the national broadcaster should *still* not broadcast *Jerry Springer* because of its blasphemous nature. Some of them argued moreover that it was a matter of fairness: the BBC, they claimed, would never broadcast such a programme if it featured similar treatment of Islam or the Sikh religion (*Behzti* had recently been in the news). Why should Christians not be treated with equivalent respect?

In fact, the BBC *had* broadcast programmes which both Muslims and Sikhs had found offensive – for instance, the television comedy *Goodness Gracious Me* which I commissioned in the mid-1990s. But even if one accepts the underlying premise – that the BBC was likely to treat minority religions with more sensitivity than Christianity – I did not find this line of reasoning persuasive. As I have argued, no one has an untrammelled right not to be offended, and there is therefore no right to which different religions are entitled to demand equal access. Differential sensitivity – greater to religions associated with ethnic minorities, less to the established and fully socialised religion of the land – is not a moral requirement but, given the wider sense of isolation and prejudice which such minorities often feel, it is certainly a reasonable position for an editor to adopt.

For all these reasons, I decided that the broadcast should go ahead and *Jerry Springer: The Opera* was duly shown on BBC2 on 8 January 2005. And with that, the controversy promptly vaporised. The public watched the programme and formed their own view about it. The caravan of protest broke camp and moved off in search of the next enormity. The security guards departed and the rest of us got back to life as normal.

But *Jerry Springer* did leave me two personal legacies. The first was an attempt by Stephen Green and Christian Voice to prosecute me and Jon Thoday, the producer of the piece, for the crime of blasphemous libel. In the event, magistrates refused to allow the private prosecution to go ahead and the High Court confirmed that decision on appeal in 2007. The common-law offence of blasphemous libel (which extended 'protection' only to Christianity) was centuries old, but the judgement in the High Court about *Jerry Springer: The Opera* had the consequence of effectively abolishing it in the context of plays, films and television in England and Wales. The abolition was extended to all other forms of expression in the Criminal Justice and Immigration Act of 2008. Not much more than a legal footnote – the last person actually to be sent to prison for blasphemy was John William Gott in 1921 – but a small victory all the same for freedom of expression. In many other countries, blasphemy laws are being extended, not repealed.

The second legacy is the rather elegant iron railings and electric gate which were put up outside my home in the aftermath of the *Jerry Springer* controversy, and which still stand there today. *Jerry Springer* was no *Satanic Verses* or *Charlie Hebdo*, and none of the handful of threats I have received over the years has ever seemed remotely as serious as those I have recounted in this chapter. But the security people recommended them nonetheless. After all, if you're pursuing almost any kind of free expression in the early twenty-first century, you never know when things may take a personal turn.

The Enemies of Free Speech

As we saw, Hobbes' reaction to the radical threat was to argue for a 'sovereign' to whose Publique Reason individual citizens could submit themselves, restricting their own private reasons to purely personal affairs. He also came to believe that some forms of dissent were so dangerous that they should be prohibited altogether.

In fact British history took a different course. Over the next century or so, the country moved not towards absolutism but to a constitutional monarchy with a strong emphasis on parliamentary and public debate and a remarkably free press. The result was not anarchy and civil war, but a more cohesive and successful society. During Hobbes' lifetime, other philosophers (notably John Locke) began to develop the ideas on which modern principles of human rights – including the right to free expression – are based. In what became the United Kingdom, in other Northern European countries and in the colonies in America, radicals began to use the growing freedom of political debate and of the press to argue for the practical implementation of those rights: for the right to self-determination, the abolition of slavery, the emancipation of minority religions and of women, and so on. Disputed, delayed, incomplete and, as the twentieth century and our present tribulations demonstrate, no guarantee that human societies necessarily always move from lower to high levels of openness and respect for rights – but a vindication over hundreds of years of the ability of democratic institutions, public debate and the practical judgement of individual citizens to advance policy and drive progress.

Hobbes' pessimism was misplaced, in other words. A way was found, not merely to accommodate dissent without political violence, but to harness its power to stimulate reform. Alas, in the early part of the twenty-first century, many sovereign governments are proceeding on the basis not that Thomas Hobbes was wrong, but that he was fundamentally correct: that freedom of expression *is* a threat to effective government and destructive of social harmony, and that those 'seditious ministers' should indeed be silenced or killed.

Many westerners harbour a naïve assumption about the manifest destiny of freedom of expression, believing that some combination of modernity, capitalism and the apparently unstoppable momentum of the Internet mean that the barriers to the free exchange of ideas must inevitably collapse everywhere, and soon. It was widely hoped, for instance, that when the younger generation of Chinese leaders led by President Xi Jinping came to power in 2012, they would liberalise the controls on free speech. Exactly the opposite happened. President Xi's government has proved to be even more repressive than its recent predecessors. The Chinese authorities have arrested dissidents, blocked foreign news sites, harassed both foreign and domestic journalists and now explicitly seek what they call (using an appropriately Hobbesian term) *cyberspace sovereignty*, by which they mean complete control over what the Chinese public can see and do in the digital realm. Perhaps theories about the ineluctability of freedom of expression will turn out to be right. Beijing is having none of it.

In Russia, a very brief period of relative press freedom in the 1990s has been largely eroded by a combination of intimidation, violence (including the murder of some notable journalists) and the progressive purchase or expropriation of that nation's media organisations by interests aligned with the Kremlin. The government of President Recep Tayyip Erdogan is using harassment, arrests and repressive new laws to stifle dissent in Turkey while, in their 2016 report *Freedom in the World*, Freedom House reports issues in Ukraine, Moldova, Georgia, and in several Balkan countries. Classic state repression is the story in Iran and in much of Central Asia. Other than in Israel, freedom of speech and debate is more or less unknown in the Middle East and uncertain in much of Africa and Asia. Journalists are being killed, injured and imprisoned in unprecedented numbers in numerous countries, from the monstrous on-camera beheadings of western journalists by so-called Islamic State to the less reported but extensive slaughter of local journalists and stringers in conflicts and failing states around the world. Wherever freedom of the press is denied, political dissidents are persecuted and minorities put at risk.

Can we comfort ourselves with the thought that it's different in the West? The response by European and American leaders to the *Charlie Hebdo* massacre was far more robust than that to *The Satanic Verses* had been twenty-six years earlier. By the time of the attack, almost all mainstream politicians could see the extremist Islamist threat to freedom of expression for what it was and were prepared to speak out clearly against it. Yet here too there is cause for concern.

When European interior ministers met to discuss the *Charlie Hebdo* incident, they issued a joint communiqué expressing their disgust and the determination to bolster the principle of free speech. But they also added this paragraph:

> 3/ We are concerned at the increasingly frequent use of the Internet to fuel hatred and violence and signal our determination to ensure that the Internet is not abused to this end, while safeguarding that it remains, in scrupulous observance of fundamental freedoms, a forum for free expression, in full respect of the law. With this in mind, the partnership of the major Internet providers is essential to create the conditions of a swift reporting of material that aims to incite hatred

and terror and the condition of its removing, where appropriate/possible.[29]

In France, the controversial comedian Dieudonné M'bala M'bala was arrested soon after the attack and charged with condoning terrorism for saying on Facebook that he *felt like Charlie Coulibaly*. The phrase cleverly blends the widespread slogan *Je Suis Charlie*, which had appeared on thousands of posters and T-shirts to show support for the murdered cartoonists at *Charlie Hebdo*, with the surname of the killer in the siege at the kosher supermarket two days later, Amedy Coulibaly. I won't join your pious marches and vigils, he seems to say, I have more sympathy with the other side. Dieudonné M'bala M'bala was one of more than seventy people arrested in France in the immediate aftermath of the *Charlie Hebdo* attack for 'hate speech'.[30]

In the UK, the Home Secretary Theresa May was already attempting to pass legislation to make it illegal for extremists to speak at British universities. Who would decide who was an extremist and who wasn't? 'The organisations subject to the duty will have to take into account guidance issued by the Home Secretary', May announced.[31] Even democratic and broadly benign sovereigns can find themselves giving in to the temptation to police public language: to gag the Islamic firebrand, to take a heavy hand to the peaceful protester, to prosecute the troll.

But it's absurd to believe that you can defend freedom of expression by suppressing it. And to try to pick and choose, to declare (in retrospect) that the *Charlie Hebdo* cartoonists are heroes of free expression who must be celebrated, while Dieudonné M'bala M'bala is a villain who must be silenced, smacks of favouritism. If it is permissible to make fun of the Prophet Muhammad, then why not the dead cartoonists? If you deny the second on the grounds of taste, or even of national security – on the basis that Dieudonné M'bala M'bala is a recruiting sergeant for the terrorists rather than the attention-seeking prankster he so patently is – you risk making a mockery of your own claims about tolerance, and turning an unjustified claim of unequal treatment into a justified one. If western governments under-reacted to *The Satanic Verses* and sent mixed signals about free expression by relativising the issue, their successors risk making the opposite mistake;

by over-reacting and denying free expression to one group in the name of protecting it for another.

Or perhaps you believe that Internet courtesy can be made compulsory? In the UK, the legislation which enables prosecutions against the cyber bullies makes it a crime to 'send by means of a public electronic communications network a message or other matter that is grossly offensive or of an indecent, obscene or menacing character'. Indeed it is an offence to send any message which you know is false 'for the purpose of causing annoyance, inconvenience or needless anxiety to another'.[32] No one can be in favour of 'false' statements, but it's hard to imagine a lower bar than 'inconvenience' as an excuse for limiting free speech. Using the police and the courts to stop people lying on the Internet is the kind of policy normally pursued by dictators, yet in Britain it has led to many convictions. Some other European countries have similar legislation. Even if the routine vitriol of the Web fills you with foreboding, this is a cure which is worse than the disease.

One of the things that links the *sovereign* threat to freedom of expression in the West with many of the *non-sovereign* threats we have explored in this chapter is that potent term *hate speech*, another miniature gem of contemporary rhetorical compression. We hear it in the news so frequently that we may never ask ourselves exactly what it means – assuming that it has an exact meaning.

We know what a hate *crime* is. It is a crime – an assault, say, or a murder – which is carried out because of the perpetrator's hatred for the group represented by the victim. Someone lynched because of the colour of their skin, a gay man beaten up simply because he is gay. Our courts quite reasonably regard it as an aggravating factor in a given crime. But the crime itself would still be accepted as a crime even if it was proven in court that racial or anti-gay hate was not the motive.

Hate speech is a more diffuse term. It includes speech-acts which have always been considered criminal – direct and personal threats of murder, rape or other violence, for example. If such threats are made in the context of racist, sexist, anti-gay or some other form of prejudice, they too can be considered hate crimes. Hate speech also sometimes refers to kinds of speech which have been made criminal in some western countries relatively recently in order to prevent incitement to racial hatred and other kinds of hostility towards minorities.

But the use of the phrase *hate speech* extends far beyond these laws. It can refer to genuinely vicious and prejudicial language used against an individual or a group, or it can be nothing more than a playground insult thrown by one side in a given argument into the face of the other. Often false syllogisms are at work: if any criticism of the state of Israel is anti-Semitism and anti-Semitism is hate speech, then anyone who criticises Israel is guilty of hate speech; or by the same token, if any criticism of Islam or a Muslim society is Islamophobia and Islamophobia is hate speech, then anyone who criticises either is guilty of hate speech. Used like this, hate speech is, to borrow Arzu Merali's word, a 'trope' – a rhetorical device employed to isolate and shame an opponent – and it often has a contemptuous, bullying quality itself. Many of the groups we have discussed in this chapter use it in just this way.

Because of its imprecision and the cavalier way it is often used, hate speech is a slippery and dangerous concept. Dangerous both in the hands of the agents of the sovereign – the police, the prosecutors, the judges – and in those of the self-appointed vigilantes who seek to banish their particular bête noire from their chosen domain or from society as a whole.

The right to free speech includes the right to say hateful things. Those who want to say them should be allowed to say them and be protected by the state when they do so. Trying to discriminate between different kinds of hate – to outlaw anti-Semitic remarks but to overlook anti-Islamic ones or vice versa, for instance – is self-contradictory, no more coherent or defensible than deciding that, alone among all political parties, the BNP should not appear on *Question Time*. And where do you stop? If you want to criminalise all hate, you might just as well make it a crime to be a human being.

If modern governments, both repressive and liberal, are tempted to play the Hobbesian sovereign, the part that secretly appeals to many of the groups we have studied in this chapter is that of the Puritan radicals. Even those who claim to be secular still tend to adopt the rhetoric of conscience and to divide the world into a right-thinking elect (themselves), and opponents whose arguments have already been revealed to be false and who therefore need not and should not be heard. Like those seventeenth-century radicals, they are prone to factionalism and atomisation, turning the rhetoric which was once aimed at an external enemy on former comrades and friends. These groups share the importunate certainty of the prophet, the same lack of empathy with the other. But they can have an effect disproportionate to their numbers. Weak leaders, whether in the faculty club or the halls of power, are particularly vulnerable to them, some entranced by their evangelical singleness of purpose, others simply cowed.

The way to defeat them and the real extremists is not to gag, but to out-argue them. Let the mullahs sermonise. Let the cartoonists and the comedians do their worst. Let more or less anyone come to the universities. Let the hard right march. If you disagree with them, get out there and march too. Expose the fanatics to the light and laugh at them. Abolish those well-meaning laws which seek to suppress some kinds of antisocial speech but not others. Use the law only to gag speech which meets the American legal definition of *fighting words* – words which are intended to provoke immediate actual violence or directly intimidate, or to recruit violent extremists. Use it more broadly and you won't starve the fanatics, you'll feed them.

History or specific cultural challenges can understandably lead some countries to take special measures – the banning in Germany of the swastika and other symbols associated with Nazism is an example – though such bans should be limited in both time and scope. As for individuals, they should have legal redress in the case of malicious defamation and should also be protected from the kind of internet trolling which adds up to personal bullying and intimidation. But the law should always err on the side of free expression. Living in an open society means taking the rough with the smooth up to the point where, if it was a face-to-face encounter, a court would judge the troll's abuse to add up to threatening behaviour.

Free speech isn't a panacea. Protecting it means that the world will still be full of hateful words and ideas, though there's no need to add to them or to fight fire with fire. Nor is free speech a guarantee that bad things won't happen – that extremist rhetoric won't seduce some credulous young people, or even that another monster like Adolf Hitler won't emerge in one of our liberal democracies. Cultures and societies can go wrong for many reasons, and free speech won't stop all of them. But don't let that fact convince you that the suppression of free speech is any kind of an answer. It seldom achieves anything. In the end, it poisons everything.

The enemies of free speech are gathering. From politically correct students to Cabinet ministers, from the darker denizens of the Twittersphere to the Chinese politburo, they are an ill-sorted crew but they have more in common than at first appears. All are sure they are right. All harbour Hobbesian doubts about untrammelled public language. None of them trust the rest of us. The many good reasons they give for gagging their opponents are all bogus and should be dismissed out of hand. But against the tide of expectation, they are gaining ground. We are living through a long war for the freedom of expression and it is going badly.

12 Keep Calm But Don't Carry On

You must strive to know all things, both the unshakable heart of reality and the opinions of mortals which reveal their lack of understanding. You should get to know their opinions all the same, for only then can you make sense of the impressions and attitudes which human beings take to be the truth.

The Goddess, in Parmenides' *Poem*[1]

The time is out of joint. Short-wave radios once had the names of capital cities etched into their dials. Today, as we turn the knob and tune in to the world, from Damascus to Brussels to Moscow to Washington, the news is almost unrelievedly grim. The problems and differences that confront us may not yet be as catastrophic as those our parents and grandparents lived through, but they can feel more insidious and intractable.

Intolerance and illiberalism are on the rise almost everywhere. Lies go unchecked. Free speech is denied and state repression is returning in countries which even recently seemed on the path of openness. In the Middle East and Africa, and in the streets and suburbs of European cities, the murderous idiocy of religiously inspired nihilism can prove more persuasive than the milk-toast promises of secular democracy. We hear politicians talk. Children drown, starve, are blown to smithereens. The politicians go on talking. At home, boundaries – of political responsibility, mutual respect, basic civility – which seemed relatively secure a mere decade ago, are broken by the week. Often it feels as if there's a nihilistic spirit at work here too, a politics with no positive agenda of its own which seeks only to divide. A hectic rages in our blood.

These disheartening trends have any number of causes. In this book I have argued that the way our public language has changed is an important contributing and exacerbating factor. We've traced how a series of developments in politics, media and technology have combined with advances in our understanding of the levers of linguistic persuasion to boost the immediate impact of political language at the price of depth and comprehensibility. And we've explored how an unresolved battle between two post-Enlightenment instincts – naïve and overbearing *rationalism*, and the contrary tendency to over-emphasise identity and community, which I called *authenticism* – has distorted how we think about the language of the public realm.

In the face of this array of negative forces, I pointed to two beacons of hope. The first was the ancient notion that human beings are born with a faculty of practical wisdom or *prudence* which should enable them to discriminate between valid and dubious public language. The second was the prospect of a rhetoric which might one day achieve a new balance of argument, character and empathy. I used the phrase *critical persuasion* to describe it – 'critical' in that it would consciously address, and submit itself to, its audience's prudential scrutiny. It would seek to be reasonable rather than rigidly rationalist and, in its proportionate response to the legitimate demands of emotion and identity, would strive for actual truthfulness rather than rhetorical 'authenticity'.

But how to get there from here? In Chapter 7, we heard George Orwell hoping it was possible to 'bring about some improvement by starting at the verbal end'. What could that mean for us?

Language and Trust

On the face of it, the crisis in our public language is a crisis of trust in public words and the people who say them. Trust is the foundation of all human relationships, and most of us know what it feels like to lose someone's trust, or our trust in others. We also know how hard trust is to regain, once lost.

But there's more here than meets the eye. First, this falling off in trust in public language is only relative. As I noted in Chapter 1, people *never* trusted politicians that much. When the Palace of Westminster burned down in 1834, the writer Thomas Carlyle was one of several observers to note the cheers and applause from the large crowd of onlookers – 'There go their *hacts* [acts]!'[2] In 1944, just after the success of D-Day, and at a time when the UK was being governed by a government of national unity led by Winston Churchill, Gallup conducted a poll in which they asked respondents whether they thought that British politicians were first and foremost out for themselves, for their party, or for their country; 35% said they were out for themselves, 22% that they put their party first, and only 36% that they cared most about their country[3]. When it comes to distrust, there is little new under the sun. Nor is every kind of distrust necessarily harmful. It's hard to imagine a serviceable form of human prudence which didn't have healthy scepticism at its core.

Some have cast doubt, moreover, on whether the recent 'crisis of trust' is all that it is cracked up to be. When the philosopher Onora O'Neill gave her 2002 BBC Reith Lectures on the subject of trust, she pointed out that, in their daily actions and choices, people routinely demonstrated practical trust in the same institutions and professions which they told the pollsters they *distrusted*.[4] They might claim to have less faith in the medical profession, for instance, but that had hardly stopped them going to the doctor. 'We may not have evidence for a crisis of trust,' O'Neill concluded, 'but we have massive evidence of a culture of suspicion.' Although in her view certain institutional and cultural practices actively encouraged or spread *distrust*, the public had so far proven significantly immune to it, and that talk of a 'crisis' was somewhat overdone.

Things have changed significantly in the years since Onora O'Neill gave her lectures. In many western countries, levels of trust have fallen much further. When YouGov asked members of the British public that same Gallup question about self, party and country in 2014, seventy years after the original poll, a mere 10% of respondents said they believed that politicians put their country first.[5] More importantly, the distinction O'Neill drew between low levels of stated trust and high levels of functional trust no longer feels secure.

The public are voting with their feet. Their distrust in traditional politicians has caused many to support anti-politicians and radical alternatives. In the UK in 2026, it drove much of the vote to leave the EU. Instead of claiming not to trust mainstream media, a growing number of people no longer consume it. A significant minority of parents, as we saw, have ignored the settled advice of that distrusted medical establishment, and have refused to have their children vaccinated.

The 'culture of suspicion' diagnosed by O'Neill has spread from opinion polls to voting, political activism and civil unrest, and to private choices about everything from privacy to food safety to financial services. No doubt most people still end up functionally trusting most public services and institutions most of the time, but it is hard to deny that distrust – and the fury and sense of betrayal associated with it – is having a tangible and growing impact on our world. The word *crisis* does not seem too strong a description.

Some of the causes are so deep-seated that it might take decades, or longer, before our public language returns to full equilibrium and utility. But what, if anything, could the various players we have encountered in this book do now to stop further erosion, and perhaps even to begin the task of restoration?

*

Let's begin with the professional politicians. The first point is the most obvious. If you say one thing and do another, the public will lose their trust in you. They may let an anti-politician get away with murder – in the US, UK, Italy and elsewhere, election campaigns have become like celebrity pro-am golf tournaments where the amateurs are almost encouraged to miss shots and goof around – but not you. When it comes to the biggest decisions, above all the question of war, they will regard deceit, even recklessness with the facts, as a hanging offence.

Don't try to fool the public about who you are. If you look like a senator and talk like a senator, only the loopiest antics – Senator Cruz, please step forward – will convince them that you are not a member of that hated elite. And if voters are bound to view you as a professional politician, common sense suggests that you should think carefully before pouring buckets of ordure over your colleagues and yourself. Judges and doctors and generals don't do it. Indeed they take care – especially when a scandal raises wider questions about competence or ethics – to talk *up* their calling. All are trusted more than you are. Modern politics is like the last scene of *Reservoir Dogs*, with everyone aiming a gun at everyone else. Recognise that you can't shoot without getting shot yourself, and leave your more suicidal peers to finish each other off.

Treat the public like grown-ups. Share some of your *actual* thinking about policy, including the painful and finely balanced trade-offs you face, with the people you want to vote for you. There's no need to talk down to them; most of the citizens you serve do not have qualifications in economics or planning or public health, but that doesn't mean that they're stupid or incapable of understanding evidence or argument. If you can understand it, perhaps they can too.

Almost all modern public policy decisions are finely balanced. The evidence is uncertain, there are arguments and risks on both sides and the decision-makers must weigh probabilities rather than certainties. Admit it. Take the public into your confidence. They're unlikely to trust you if you're not prepared to trust them. And admit mistakes too, clearly and quickly.

Don't brush reality under the carpet. If you're on the left and discover that income equality is *falling* rather than rising (as it has done in the UK after the crash), or if it turns out that inequalities between generations may be more significant than those between classes, don't deny the facts for ideological convenience Get to the bottom of them – then go on to point out why they nonetheless raise issues of social justice or may lead to future problems.

Distilling complex public policy into plain language is difficult, but it must be done. In large measure, modern government *is* communication, yet the communications departments in most ministries and arms of government are full of frazzled time-servers. Clear them out and find a few actual writers. Throw in some graphics artists, videographers and multimedia producers to boot. And while you're at it, insist that the army of technocrats on whom you rely also take some lessons in lucid, unpatronising expression. Then, whether they like it or not, get them out in front of the mikes and the cameras. Give your focus groups and your A/B testing platform a break from the search for the best phrases for party political attack, and ask them instead to find the clearest way of laying out public policy choices.

Democratic politics is intrinsically and necessarily adversarial, and party (and sometimes personal) political advantage will be front and centre in much of what you do. But consider what the evolutionary biologists call *reciprocal altruism* when it comes to public policy discussion. Your bold new ideas about the environment, or how to address the pension burden, will never get a proper airing unless there's a political and media climate that provides space for serious discussion. If you use every trick in the book to stop your political opponent from getting a fair hearing for *her* ideas, you can hardly object when she does the same to you. There are risks in trying to break the vicious circle, not least that your own colleagues – who are themselves quite inured to it – will accuse you of naïvety or cowardice in the face of the enemy. Voters, on the other hand, might actually find it refreshing. And if you make the leap, you might be lucky enough to find one or two brave souls on the opposing side of the House prepared to take a chance on that old-fashioned thing called statesmanship.

This is not a plea for compromise as such. The two sides in even a constructive and courteous debate may end as far apart as they began, and the public may be faced with a stark alternative as a result. That's as it should be: we shouldn't fall into the trap of assuming that optimal public policy choices always sit in the middle of any given political battle. It's rather that no matter how deep the political divisions, it's always better to unearth the fundamentals of the argument and to expose them to the public. As we've seen repeatedly in this book, awkward policy areas which are ignored or reduced to the status of props in the pantomime of party politics, seldom solve themselves. Instead they return to haunt the politicians who tried to bury them. Immigration, inequality, the aspirations and concerns of ethnic, cultural and national minorities are all pressing current examples of this.

Spin has always been a part of politics and probably always will be. Have a care all the same. Machiavellian news management can still be effective in controlled societies where even outright lies may never catch up with you – thus the apparently never-ending political success story that is Vladimir Putin – but in the 360-degree digitally connected West, deniability is not what it used to be. As successive political leaders on both sides of the Atlantic have learned to their cost, what your attack dogs say 'unattributably' to further your cause with words and ways to which you yourself would never publicly stoop, always ends up being tracked back to you. Your people leave your fingerprints wherever they go and their character – their cruelty, their intimidation, their hypocrisy – soon becomes continuous with your own. Spin worked best when it was nameless and when almost everyone inside politics and the media colluded in it. Once it was given a handle, and the media started to report on it as a story in itself, its best days were over.

Don't always listen to communications advice from those who are politically closest to you. You may well agree with their verdict on the moral character of the gang who face you across the aisle, but think carefully before you give your own side the red meat they crave. In the run-up to the 2015 British general election several friendly commentators urged Ed Miliband to look and sound more 'angry' about the Tories and their policies.[6] No doubt anger was what Labour's heartland supporters wanted to hear, but was it really the right emotion with which to sway the unaffiliated, undecided voters on whom election victory actually depended? You need of course to do enough to keep your own troops motivated and united, but they are not your principal audience – not, that is, if you want to get into power.

Aristotle was right: amplification is a necessary implement in the politician's rhetorical toolbox. Life is short, you need to focus your audience's attention on your key message, to accentuate the contrast between your view of the world and that of your opponent. Conditional clauses and qualifying adjectives and adverbs are all very well in legal documents and policy discussions behind closed doors. Out in the open, the public want clarity and crispness, and the news media crave short headlines. So there will be occasions when amplifying and simplifying your point – your diagnosis, your attack, your promise – will make good political sense.

But constant exaggeration is dangerous. Initially, it can seem to win you a kind of respect. Adult policy debate can sound pernickety or just plain boring to the uninitiated, and politicians who break out of the charmed circle and offer simple, vivid judgements and single-sentence solutions, can initially sound adventurous, honest, inspiring. But for how long?

Exaggeration is a drug. It delivers an instant high but can have deleterious long-term effects. Every word you say can and will be taken down and used in evidence against you, and one day you may come to rue that sweeping generalisation or vicious put-down. Indeed, exaggeration can become your trademark so completely that the media will always expect it of you and, unless you say something essentially unreasonable, will not report what you say at all. Before you know it, you will find yourself playing a stock role in a stale political soap-opera, and your ability to be heard on matters of substance will be gone forever.

Nor will the language itself emerge unscathed. When Margaret Thatcher died, several leading lights of the left said that she had 'wrecked' Britain. Not 'damaged', not 'took in the wrong direction', not 'implemented divisive economic policies', but 'destroyed', 'wrecked', 'ruined'. I once walked into a hut in the highlands of Ethiopia during that country's civil war. It was full of women who had been extensively burned with phosphorus bombs dropped by the regime of Mengistu Haile Mariam. There was no pain relief for the women, nor any medicines as far as I could see, nor any prospect of medical attention. If the UK is a wrecked land, what words are left for these women and their plight, or for countries like Syria and Libya and Somalia, where wrecked means bombed and burned-out cities, slaughtered children, lawlessness, despair?

Given the character of contemporary politics and media, it requires almost superhuman self-control to refuse to give in to indiscriminate exaggeration – especially if your opponents have already abandoned all restraint – but it's still the wisest course. Exaggeration wins fewer elections than its devotees imagine and, even when it does, things usually unravel rapidly. Let's see if that proves true of the UK's headstrong 2016 Brexit vote. For political parties, there's a further risk: once begun, an internal competition for who can sound the most radical or the most ideologically pure can quickly become unstoppable. Parties who succumb to this temptation – the modern Republican Party is a splendid current example – lose control not just of collective discipline but of any coherent sense of their own identity.

So learn the right, rather than the wrong lessons from the anti-politicians. Steer clear of their bogus simplicity and instead acknowledge the complexity of real-world policy. 'There must be times', opined the *Daily Telegraph* in early 2014, 'when David Cameron envies Nigel Farage':

> The simplicity of the UKIP's message obviates any need for subtlety or nuance. His position is easy to articulate: he wants Britain to leave the EU – no ifs or buts.[7]

In the end David Cameron lost his job and his political career in the face of Nigel Farage's vaunted 'simplicity'. Yet the truth is that Britain's exit will be anything but simple – if the country still wants access to European markets and continued influence in European affairs – and the Leave camp's wild promises on immigration, tax and unfettered sovereignty may all have to give.

Throughout his career, Boris Johnson's quasi-anti-political persona – he presents himself as a postmodernist Bertie Wooster, flamboyant and pawkily self-aware – has allowed him to revel in gaffes and political gyrations that would have flattened a more straight-laced colleague. The Brexit referendum posed a problem for him, however. Without strong political convictions on the matter, he could have joined either camp, and argued for a time that the UK should vote to leave *and* negotiate to stay (he's fond of saying that his policy on cake is pro having it and pro eating it too). Eventually he summoned the media to a flash mob press conference. 'Let me tell you where I've got to . . . which is, um, I am, um, I've made up my mind,' he told them. Out it was.[10]

Deep social and political forces were at work in the referendum, but Johnson's arrival energised the Leave campaign and helped them to victory. Millions of disadvantaged Britons were persuaded to cast a protest vote against the country's elites by a man whose own CV (Eton, Oxford, the *Spectator*, the *Daily Telegraph*, MP for Henley, then Uxbridge) spoke of nothing but power and privilege. But, having never thought he would actually win, Boris looked more perplexed than pleased by the result and it was clear that there had never been a plan about what to do next. Within days, his lack of consistency and scruple had scuppered his hopes of becoming prime minister. Eccentricity and 'character' are fun. They can even look like trustworthiness for a time. Real leadership calls for something more: substance.

But counter-cultural zaniness is not restricted to British politics. Here is the veteran Italian satirist Dario Fo eulogising the comedian and latter-day party leader Beppe Grillo as a descendant of the mediaeval *guillari*, wandering entertainers who juggled with 'words, irony and sarcasm' as well as with clubs:

> He is from the tradition of the wise storyteller, one who knows how to use surreal fantasy, who can turn situations around, who has the

right word for the right moment, who can transfix people when he speaks, even in the rain and snow.[8]

Putting aside the ominous history of magicians and mountebanks in modern Italian politics, the business of leading a party, let alone running a country, requires rather more than that admirable gift for 'surreal fantasy'. In the 2013 general election, Grillo's Five Star Movement (or M5S) won a quarter of the national vote – and then promptly began to descend into infighting and factionalism that left 'the wise storyteller' telling the media he was feeling 'pretty tired',[9] and being accused by some of his closest colleagues of remoteness and autocracy. Grillo and M5S may still be an attractive home for anti-establishment voters (their anti-EU stance helped them perform well both in the 2014 European elections and in more recent regional and mayoral elections), but the thought of them ever actually getting into power is scary.

No, the lesson to learn from the anti-politicians concerns *ethos*. They look and sound like human beings. They lack the polish and control of the conventional politician. Their anger and impatience is not a carefully focus-grouped and calibrated rhetorical gambit but something they palpably feel. They make mistakes, change policies without warning and sometimes for no apparent reason, say things which would be regarded as deeply offensive if they had been uttered by a mainstream political leader. And yet – for at least as long as the anti-politician is an outsider – the public are disposed to forgive and forget. Their arguments (*logos*) may be simplistic, but at least they're not automata. That can be enough, even for sophisticated voters, to bridge the gap of persuasion.

It's something which precious few politicians from the established parties can pull off. Most have been schooled never to depart from their talking points, never to concede error, never to lose it. For them media interviews are a stylised game: difficult questions are greeted with non-answers or an answer to a quite different question, the one which the politician has been coached to give. The effect is evasive, brittle, alienating. Perversely, the heroic effort put into not making mistakes means that mistakes are the only thing the media end up pursuing.

I once spent an hour with Hillary Clinton when she was Secretary of State. In private conversation, she came across as exceptionally intelligent, thoughtful, open-minded, self-deprecating, human, mischievous. My colleague at *The New York Times* magazine, Mark Liebovich, had a similar experience when he was interviewing her off the record. Indeed, the encounter was going so well, and she was speaking with such personality and eloquence, that he suggested that they go on the record. At once, he says, the armoured visor came down and she shifted to the tried-and-tested defensive boiler-plate of the stump speech and the official press release. Her fault? Our fault? Those questions don't help much. Collectively we've managed to get to a place where it is almost impossible for the public to get a sense of what leading public figures are like beyond the embattled public persona. Between us, we need to figure out a way of demilitarising.

Finally, *pathos*. It is easy for politicians to convince themselves that they truly understand the public; that the sum of audience information to which they are exposed – quantitative and qualitative data, taken with their own inevitably rather random interactions with voters – adds up to a complete picture of the public mood; and that the models and segmentations which the marketing specialists construct for them are firm enough to bear the load of everything they want to build on them – the policies and the political tactics, the key words and tag lines, the stories and the narrative shapes.

In truth, audiences are like the sea, infinitely diverse and change-able, and this morning's conditions are a very imperfect guide to this afternoon's, let alone tomorrow's. The great rhetor is like a great sailor, their skill lying less in the way they turn the wheel than in their ability to read the sea ahead and to respond to it fluently and intuitively. It's not that data and instruments are useless – the sensible sailor consults satellite radar images and the GPS as well as their instincts – but that they are a complement to talent and the lessons learned from long experience rather than a substitute for them.

We live in the age of data science, and some straightforward human behaviours – patterns of buying consumer goods or browsing through online content – can be predicted across a given population with striking statistical success, as Elmer Wheeler foretold. But the higher-order questions with which the public language of policy and politics necessarily concerns itself involve matters of identity and morality, of a sense of individual and collective self, and an ever-changing and ever-disputed picture of what the good life consists of. None of these will be amenable any time soon to tracking pixels or algorithmic optimisation, or even to the most inspired polling guru.

The relationship of any politician with their public is ultimately a strictly human affair. It's you and them. That well-heeled band of experts no doubt have their use, though you should never forget that the segments and types they trade in – that 'new' generation you must win over, the soccer mom and white-van man – are abstracted versions of reality rather than reality itself. And once you're up there on the podium or staring down the barrel of the camera, they'll be nowhere to be seen. The only empathy your audience will be able to judge is yours.

Human beings are by nature social animals; they have an astonishing capacity to tell whether your openness to them is genuine or sham. The ability to truly listen is every bit as important to the rhetor as any gift in the speaking department – it is in fact a part of the same gift. Without it, *pathos* and *ethos* inevitably clash or drift apart and *logos*, the argument you wanted to make, the reason you stood up in the first place, falls on deaf ears. So listen.

*

Politicians are not solely responsible for the crisis in public language, and nor are journalists and editors. But that doesn't mean that the media are innocent bystanders either. So what can my trade do to respond to the issues raised in this book? What steps could we take as an industry, an academy, or even just as individuals to stop the rot?

First let's reject *perspectivism*, the notion that everything is point of view, that 'truth' is a meaningless concept: those who say that generally do so because reality doesn't suit them. There are such things as facts and it is still the job of journalists to report them. But this does not mean that we should be naïve in our realism. We can recognise that conscious bias is a commonplace in journalism, and that even journalists who strive to be impartial can be in thrall to unconscious narratives and prejudices. We can acknowledge the undertow of political and social power-structures and accept, to dilute Marshall

McLuhan, that the medium always influences the message and that changes in the form, length, velocity and interactive potential of media all affect the meaning it conveys. That is part of the burden of this book.

By all means be a critical realist, then, recognising that the way in which human beings perceive, make sense of and express reality is always mediated and subject to distortion. But accept too that there is a difference between the reasonable observation that, given the way history is recorded, we may never fully understand the rise of al-Qaeda and the attack on the World Trade Center, and the crackpot suggestion that Jerusalem and Washington were really responsible for 9/11.

Nothing that has happened to our world politically or technologically has made the need to find and expose the truth less pressing. If anything, the world has become harder to understand, and the tools and techniques available to the world's many liars more formidable. So we should ignore calls for journalism to become less hostile or adversarial, if that means any reduction of scepticism or unwillingness to pursue a story to its conclusion. Interviews with politicians should be courteous but they should be tough and, if the interviewee refuses to answer the question or obfuscates in some other way, toughness is more important than courtesy.

But don't restrict your toolbox to the instruments of inquisitorial torture. Allow space not just for policy debate but for policy explanation, and keep your finger off the scales until you get to the opinion pages. Perhaps a heavy editorial hand once sold newspapers or reassured doubtful readers. Today it may put many potential users off, including those younger customers you (and your advertisers) are so desperate to attract.

Give the politicians the space to set out their stall in their own words. Avoid the temptation to drop the initial political statement or policy announcement after its first few outings in your eagerness to move on to reaction and argument, forcing new readers or viewers to infer what the first speaker must have said from the angry response to it. It is a civic duty of serious journalism to allow politicians to be read or heard by the public at reasonable length in their own voice, and to debate with each other in paragraphs rather than ten-second pre-recorded bites. Then hear from everyone else – your own experts, the academics and pundits, members of the public – and let battle commence.

Our world is deafened by bogus revelation, venom and speculation dressed up as proven scientific fact, but true investigative journalism, grounded in evidence and presented cogently on its merits, can still make the whole room fall silent. The public need for it is greater than ever – and at every level, from parish council to city hall, up to governments and multinational institutions – and yet the supply is faltering. That's because investigative journalism breaks most of the rules of modern media economics. It is expensive and time-consuming, has a high failure rate and often involves the kind of intricate detail which contemporary readers are said to have no time for. Do it anyway.

Great investigations have a restorative power, not only over the institutions and injustices which are exposed, but over trust in journalism itself. And for brave news organisations, investigations offer another potential benefit: in a desert of undifferentiated and listicated journalistic packaged goods, they can present a valuable point of distinction, a parcel of high ground that can be seen for miles around.

This is something of a golden age when it comes to the journalism of analysis and contextualisation. Backgrounders are not a new thing: mid-twentieth-century newspaper readers followed battlefronts and moon shots and round-the-world solo sailors with the aid of maps and diagrams. As we saw, *brief expositions* or *bexbos* as we called them – secondary video or studio packages which aimed to put the initial piece of reportage into context – arrived at the BBC in the 1980s. By 2012, *The New York Times* was showing with its feature 'Snow Fall', the story of a complex and tragic skiing accident in the Cascades, how journalists could weave words, still images, videos and animating graphics and maps into a narrative whole-cloth which would tell the story better than any one medium could ever do.

But analytical journalism can go beyond the essentially descriptive and contextual and, especially in the field of public policy, burrow deep into the fundamentals of a story. Is Obamacare working or failing in practice? Do migrant workers help or hinder a given economy? The answers to these and similar questions typically come not from a Deep Throat in the shadows of an underground car park, but from the careful study of often publicly available data. We are still in the foothills of analytical journalism; greater public access to data and advances in machine learning and other forms of artificial intelligence should soon enable it to go further and deeper than it does today. This is one aspect of contemporary journalism which doesn't need to be changed, but reinforced. And cultural pessimists in the media please note: many of those citizens, who you think of as craving nothing but digital prolefeed, are eager to make sense of a complex world and are lapping it up.

You probably have your own views about whether good reporting and political partisanship can ever coexist. There are many reporters and editors who argue that their political view of the world gives their journalism a passion and an explanatory cogency unavailable to the cold-eyed impartialist. To me, real news journalism always strives for objectivity and political impartiality – everything else is special pleading. Call it opinion and we can all sit back and agree or disagree with it. Just don't claim that it's news: jumbling the worlds of *what is* and *what should be* is as incoherent and misleading as confusing astronomy with astrology.

But even politically committed journalists should keep a proper professional and social distance from the people on whom they report. Trying to have it both ways – bosom pal one minute, seeker after the truth the next – is impossible and often leads to the kind of collusion and trading of stories and people which gives journalism a bad name. Junkets like the White House Correspondents' Dinner replace the proper relationship between politicians and the press with a kind of mutual masturbation, jokey, false, politics as celebrity comedy with bouncers on the door to stop any ordinary voters getting in. Our democratic leaders know that their own mode of public discourse is tainted, so they're eager to borrow those of journalism, the entertainment industry and digital culture. If you get too close to them, within a heartbeat they'll be trying to sound and look just like you.

And beware another threat. The balance of power between press and advertisers has shifted in favour of the advertiser and there's good evidence that many old and new media organisations are bowing to pressure to soften their reporting so as not to offend commercial partners and thereby lose revenue. Allowing your reporting to descend into self-censorship or outright commercial marketing is as great a betrayal of journalism as any – and particularly pernicious because it can be so hard for readers to spot. There is a simple fact to be faced here: whatever they say in their annual corporate social responsibility review, few companies are in favour of 'transparency' when it comes to themselves. They may try to bury bad news by hiding it and obstructing legitimate journalistic inquiry; or, if that fails, by using threats and commercial leverage.

If it is clearly labelled to distinguish it from newsroom output, advertorial and its digital cousin 'branded content' are fine, but police that border carefully. The public language of politics has become a self-interested form of marketing-speak. Don't let the same thing happen to the language of journalism.

But the greatest threats are also the most fundamental. If the cardinal rule for politicians is not to say one thing and do another, that for journalists is not to lie. Very few professional reporters or editors deliberately perpetrate categorical untruths in their work, but many have become habituated to practices which, day by day, generate a legion of little lies: the twisted or 'improved' quote; the omission of facts or context which might spoil a given story; the use of the question mark not to ask a question but to present a wild claim or speculative smear as if it were a matter of legitimate debate; the out-of-context addition of photos or other images from a different time and place to suggest a mood of guilt, stupidity or inappropriate smugness in relation to the present story. This is mendacity as subliminal habit. Each little lie may seem trivial, but they add up.

Yet perhaps the most serious moral risk facing the modern journalist is the sin which the medieval theologians called *accidie*. It's the least discussed of the seven deadly sins – 'sloth' is how it is usually rendered in English, but what it really means is the fault of *going through the motions*, of losing a grip on the real meaning of words or actions. In journalistic practice, accidie leads a reporter to twist reality beyond recognition until it vaguely resembles one of his limited repertoire of routine narratives, and to exaggerate and demonise less out of malice than because that too is standard operating procedure, what the story 'needs', and definitely what his editor and – who knows? – perhaps even his readers have come to expect.

Have the digital insurgents managed to branch away from these old and deeply rutted paths? Politicians would like to think so and sometimes go through phases of ostentatiously offering interviews to

BuzzFeed and the *Huffington Post* rather than the *Wall Street Journal* and the BBC to underline the point. And it's perfectly true that great leaps have been made in multimedia, user experience, audience development, syndication. Journalism has never been more effectively packaged or efficiently distributed.

But more often than not the content which pops out at the end of this shiny digital tube bears an uncanny resemblance to the endlessly repeated and reused stories which people have been reading in the tabloid press for a century and more. Although there have been advances in analytical reporting, innovation in story shapes and the narrative tricks and tropes of everyday journalism itself has been surprisingly limited.

The result is a special case within the wider crisis of public language: that of a tribe whose discourse no longer has the breadth or the adaptability to reflect reality, but whose befuddlement is such that, even if they are aware of the dilemma, they are more likely to blame reality than themselves. Perhaps this is the real reason that the beast so often appears feral. It knows no better, is too set in its ways, too invested in the belief that anger and bile always get the biggest audience, in the end too frightened to try anything different. The real question about much old-fashioned journalism is not whether it *can* survive as a profession, but whether it *deserves* to – and whether anyone would miss it if it disappeared.

Language and Institutions

None of this will be solved, or even ameliorated, without meaningful progress on the economics of media. Silicon Valley engineers taught us to believe that news is atomic, in other words that consumers are chiefly interested in catching up with headlines and summaries of individual stories, that they don't really care who provides these units of news, and therefore that nothing is lost if they are aggregated from many different journalistic sources by an algorithm (Google News), or some combination of algorithm and human editor (*Huffington Post*). Perhaps third-party aggregation might even prove superior, because it could offer the individual user a wider choice of sources and, by tracking their consumption, predict and prioritise which stories they were most likely to find 'relevant'.

To the man with a hammer, everything looks like a nail. It's easy to see why computer scientists who were adept in the parsing, organisation and distribution of information but who had little expertise or interest in content as such, should have thought like this. Nor, particularly at the level of headlines and home screens, is the idea entirely wrong-headed. If someone *never* clicks on a sports story, over time it probably makes sense to drop sport down the list of stories on their home screen, even if you are a news provider with an aspiration to be a 'journal of record'. It is nonetheless a woefully impoverished view of how real human beings interact with news and other forms of journalism.

A great newspaper, news programme or digital news site does not churn out news like a pile of individual bricks, which can be laid by any passing stranger in combination with bricks from any number of other brickworks, and turned into whatever shaped house that stranger wants to build. It has a signature, a point of editorial view. It reaches out to a prospective audience with the offer of a relationship which transcends the mechanical transmission of new facts – a relationship which is cultural, political, emotional, communal.

Most 'stories' are not reports about one-off news events, but instalments in long-running, and often slowly developing political and social transitions and conflicts. They relate to what has gone before and what is to come, and the reader or viewer gets both informational value and a kind of comfort from coming to understand the approach of a given reporter, or columnist, or news brand. Consistency matters. Provenance matters. Trust – earned the hard way, through diligence, professionalism and high standards over years and decades – matters most of all.

A brick is a brick. Journalism is a complex cultural artefact. Indeed, in its deep and synchronous connectedness with politics, society and the wider culture, it is probably more complex than most other forms of literature or, dare I say, art. Journalistic organisations are not lookalike factories producing the same undifferentiated commodity. They are cultural institutions.

Alas, across the developed world the majority of them are *failing* cultural institutions. The slow-motion collapse of their business models, and the defeatism and resentment that go with it, are no doubt partly responsible – as Tony Blair claimed in his 'feral beast' speech – for the ethical and behavioural weaknesses in contemporary journalism we discussed a few pages ago. But it now looks as if causality runs the other way as well: that, once robbed of its transient distributive advantages, bad, unambitious journalism produces a bad business.

The easy profits that media companies once enjoyed bred a wide-spread complacency about quality. In their different ways, newspapers and television companies both enjoyed privileged access to users and were able to charge advertisers handsomely for the right to put their messages in front of them. High-margin advertising became their main source of revenue. Economically, advertisers were their real customers, readers and viewers a means to an end. In many news-rooms, the result was an instrumentality that could sometimes border on contempt.

Today across the West that model is unravelling, rapidly in the case of physical newspapers, more slowly but still relentlessly when it comes to broadcast TV. And in digital, it essentially doesn't work. Despite vast headline audiences, Web advertising is a problematic revenue stream for almost everyone other than global platforms like Facebook and Google. A vicious circle has set in: publishers responding to low advertising rates by overloading their pages with too many ads, readers retaliating by turning away or installing an ad-blocker. On smartphones, the problem is even more fundamental – there is no adjacent 'white space' to sell.

A few publishers, like *The New York Times*, are reinventing digital advertising. Rather than relying on the principles of adjacency and stolen attention, we're working with commercial partners to develop advertising messages which – while clearly labelled to distinguish them from our own journalism – are compelling enough to command interest and consumption on their own in our main content feed.

It's a demanding model, however, which requires far more brand equity, investment and creativity than most publishers can muster, whether they are legacy players or digital newbies. And, even for the lucky minority, advertising on its own will not be enough to pay for news. Membership, freemium models, e-commerce and events will not be enough either. There's nothing else for it: if high-quality journalism is to survive, the public will have to pay for it.

At *The New York Times*, we have the largest and most rapidly growing digital pay model for news in the world. We let 100 million people sample our journalism for free every month, but we still believe that every story and summary and video we create *should be worth paying for*.

It's a high bar. No one needs to pay for scandal, paparazzi shots, celebrity news, listicles or hate-filled prejudice and slander on the Internet. You can eat as much as you want of that free of charge. A pay model for news only works if you offer journalism which is genuinely distinctive and which delivers real utility and value to those who consume it. The real reason most western newspapers have failed to get digital pay models to work is not because of some deficiency on the part of their readers. It is because their journalism isn't compelling enough to sell.

I've made the case for serious, ambitious, well-funded journalism in this book for civic reasons. If you are a publisher of digital news, new or old, you should embrace this agenda for reasons of survival. The same goes for your counterparts in TV and radio, where radical disruption is only just around the corner. If enough players act now, there could actually be *more* first-class journalism in the future than there was in the days of easy money.

But many legacy news organisations are too set in their ways to change, and will probably go to their graves blaming everyone else for their sad demise. In the meantime, particularly in the UK and Europe, they will likely place more faith in lobbying for regulatory easement than in fundamental business reinvention. Where they can, they will use their political muscle to attempt to gain local protection from Silicon Valley, and to disembowel the public broadcasters.

Given the level of commercial disinvestment in journalism, we might expect political support for the BBC and other public broadcasters to be strengthening. The opposite is the case: across Europe, in Australia, Canada, Japan and elsewhere, governments are laying siege to the only institutions which could guarantee universal access to at least some high-quality serious journalism during this long and difficult digital transition. Their civil servants – tax-supported themselves – are still wedded to 1980s free market theories about the coming age of media choice which have turned out not to be true. Their political leaders are in hock to commercial media owners who have a selfish interest in the destruction of the public broad-casters.

Few modern politicians have the courage to acknowledge it, but the BBC and its sister broadcasters around the world are far more than state-owned purveyors of information, education and entertainment. Byzantine and fallible, chaotic, often maddening, they are full of creativity and public-spiritedness – not obsolescent throwbacks, but bulwarks of modern civilisation.

Scrutinise them. Reform them. Hold them to account. But recognise what is at stake. If abolished or hollowed out, they will be impossible to rebuild. The commercial interests who are lobbying for their margin-alisation or abolition are likely to fail in any case. And once the public broadcasters have been neutered, and subscription is the main way of funding journalism, what will happen to those citizens unable to afford journalism of real quality?

*

For good or ill, institutions – not just those involved in broadcasting and media, but institutions across public life – are critical to the future of our public language. Indeed, institutions are systems of public language themselves. They originate and then preserve the conventions under which a given community addresses issues, reaches decisions, defines and polices the boundaries of the sayable. When the way they use language becomes decadent, the damage is felt everywhere.

If things are to improve, our institutions must change fundamentally. First they must accept that their favourite language – the contemporary jargon of 'accountability' and 'openness' – is a busted flush.

During the global financial crisis of 2008, the systems of governance, accountability and compliance which were supposed to ensure proper oversight of individual banks and financial institutions, and of the financial system as a whole, were shown to be a farce. In the aftermath, instead of an honest acknowledgement of how far the interlocking safeguards of corporate governance, financial regulation, central bank oversight and the law had failed, the authorities simply pulled the same levers harder. If 5,000 pages of banking regulations didn't work, why not try 10,000? Treated with weariness and contempt by those to whom it is meant to apply, incomprehensible to the rest of us, why should the public place an ounce of trust in any of it? This too is accidie, the sin of pretending that empty words are really full of meaning.

The culture of compliance is a false god, a failed rationalist attempt to turn the quintessentially human qualities of honesty, integrity and trust into a regulatory algorithm. Abandon it. Start from scratch. Fit your rules around the central anthropological reality which is that trust is central in all our affairs and that trust is a subjective business. Shared values and peer pressure to do the right thing are more likely to prove effective before the fact than officious attempts to codify good behaviour – attempts which in themselves do nothing to change hearts or improve organisational culture, and which always seem to generate perverse incentives and outcomes.

What goes for financial regulation goes for lawmaking more widely. In books like *The Rule of Nobody* (2014), the American lawyer and writer Philip K. Howard has chronicled the vast waste and paralysis associated with an over-complex, contradictory and obsolescent legal code. To the wider economic and social cost, let's add public incomprehension and alienation. Law is a primordial and paradigmatic form of public language – Moses descending from Mount Sinai with his tablets. Turn it into a cacophony of technocratic babble and don't be surprised if the tribes of Israel grow restive.

Institutions must decide what they stand for. If you stand for scientific objectivity, don't squander that by lending your authority to political advocacy. If you run a university and claim to stand for intellectual and creative freedom, get off your backside and defend them. Extremism, including both Islamophobia and anti-Semitism (often skulking behind the term 'anti-Zionism'), is rising on many western campuses, while the leaders of universities and other institutions sit in a funk of liberal cognitive dissonance, or hide behind spurious claims about public order and responsibility. Who ever said it was going to be easy? High principles usually require risks and sacrifices.

You should of course seek to understand and empathise with everyone. I hope you will combine that empathy with clarity and courage about the sovereignty of free speech and the right of everyone to hold and express divergent views. But whatever you decide, it's time to get off the fence. Don't, by your example, teach a generation of young people how to equivocate and cower.

When an inexperienced pilot finds themselves in a spiral dive, their instinct is to tug the stick back. In a normal dive, that would restore the aeroplane to level flight, but in a spiral dive it simply serves to tighten the corkscrew and seal your fate: to return to level flight you have to straighten the wings and only *then* raise the nose. But with the ground hurtling towards you, the false survival instinct to pull back can be ungovernable. Many of today's institutions are in the grip of exactly this psychology. Take a deep breath. Look calmly at the instruments. Straighten the wings.

Teaching the Oily Art

And what of the public themselves, that audience which is no longer just an audience and for which we have no entirely satisfactory word in the English language? We media executives oscillate between affect-less terms like *user* and *consumer* and *customer*, while politicians typically talk about *voters* or *the electorate*. All these terms betray an underlying instrumentality: they are definitions of our listeners based on what we want to get out of them. The word *citizenry* would perhaps fit the bill if one didn't feel the need to don a tricorn hat and brandish a flintlock as one said it. So let's stick with *the public*, which at least has the advantage of directing our attention to the space which this group of people occupy when they step out of their private lives and congregate, and where they listen to, and sometimes speak, the language which is the subject of this book. What benefits would a healthy, high-functioning public language deliver to them? And what first steps could they and we take now to establish the conditions for it?

We can agree that broad public *deliberation* is central to the idea of democracy – the people at large weighing up the issues and deciding which proposal to back or which party and which leader should govern – but what does deliberation involve? In the English-speaking world, the simplest and most influential model is trial by jury. The jury hear all the evidence and arguments and then go away to consider their verdict. Consideration in this case means discussion and debate between the individual members of the jury and an attempt to reach unanimity.

When we think of idealised popular *political* deliberation, it is tempting to think of the jury room writ large, of a dialectical process to which every single citizen should in principle contribute, leading to a decision in which all – even the dissenters – played a part. We know of course that the issues are more complex and the jury vastly more diffuse, but we can still think *the more the merrier*: the more engagement, the more argument, the more personal commitment the better.

But is that realistic? Being in a jury puts every individual juror on the spot. Isn't the truth that, in the absence of that kind of specific public duty, most people prefer not to advance their own opinions or critique those of others? Only a small percentage of those who read a given online news story decide to share it with their friends, and only a small percentage of *them* add a comment. In those countries where membership of a political party is voluntary and doesn't offer any social or career advantage, most people prefer not to get involved at all. We may want to encourage and applaud the activists and cheerleaders, the bloggers and controversialists, but the legitimacy of democracy has always depended less on them than on the 90% or more of the population who take part in none of those things, who watch and listen and who, if they discuss politics at all, do so in a purely private setting.

The Athenians understood this. The *demos* was sovereign – the public was boss, there was no question about that. But they exercised their sovereignty in practice by doing little more than turning up, listening, and making a collective decision. The juries who reached a verdict in trials were very large and their deliberation did not involve asking questions of the witnesses or the rival rhetors, or even conferring with each other. Each citizen was expected to use their own practical wisdom independently to reach a conclusion and cast their lot accordingly. Justice depended not on unanimity or the ability of the more outspoken jurors to persuade their peers, but simply on the aggregation of the mass of individual opinions.

Public deliberation *can* mean modern citizen-juries, panels of voters debating the goals and trade-offs which the politicians are grappling with, but it certainly needn't. And it is probably unrealistic to imagine that more than a minority of voters would ever want to devote the necessary time to such a process, even if technology made it straight-forward.

Contemporary representative democracy does not depend, any more than Athenian direct democracy, on every citizen becoming actively involved in policy debate or routine political decision-making. It depends on a public who are willing and able to absorb the facts and listen to the arguments and, on the basis of that, to decide every few years who should govern on their behalf.

Perhaps that sounds too modest, too inert. In a democracy it is everything. In fact, more than political parties, more than leaders, it *is* democracy. But it is the argument of this book that the way today's political leaders and media speak to the public at large is making this essential democratic duty harder to discharge. As we have seen, the result is that some citizens are consciously or unconsciously opting out of their constitutional role altogether, while those who do take the trouble to participate often do so on the basis of a distorted view of reality and of the choices in front of them. If we are to do anything to address this in the short term, it will be the politicians and the media who will have to bear much of the burden. But is there anything that the public *themselves* can do to better prepare them to be a good sovereign?

Rhetoric has always been controversial – if he could have done, Plato would have gladly strangled it at birth. But, as we've discovered repeatedly in this book, ignoring it or pretending that it's possible to abolish it only makes things worse. Better to listen to the words of the Goddess in Parmenides' *Poem*, quoted at the start of this chapter. At least in my reading of this frankly baffling fragment,[11] the Goddess acknowledges the distinction between *true understanding* and *opinion* but argues that we must pay attention both to the real heart of any question, and to the often erroneous opinions of other human beings, because they too are intrinsically important. Rhetoric is the language in which those opinions are conceived and shared.

What the Goddess implies in her injunction is that opinion and the rhetoric of opinion will always be with us. There is no magic wand or programme of beautification which can transport us from our world to one in which the only words which are ever uttered are ones of perfect truth, or perfect authenticity, or perfect anything else. That is not our nature as human beings and it cannot be the nature of our language either.

So let's put public language at the heart of the teaching of civics. Constitutional history, the structure of the different arms of government, how a bill becomes law, the way our courts work – these should all have their place in the curriculum, but none of them is as important as the mastery of public language. Few citizens will ever be directly involved in the legislative process. Nor is detailed knowledge of the workings of the House of Commons or the US Senate likely to help a wavering voter make up his or her mind. But they will encounter rhetoric everywhere – every time they read or look at the news or hear a speech, open up an app or look at an advertisement. The dream of rhetoric as the art of reasonable, critical persuasion depends more than anything on the emergence of a *critical audience*.

We need to teach our children how to parse every kind of public language, from marketing-speak to the loftiest political utterances on TV and radio, the Web and social media. Young people should learn the history of political rhetoric and advertising, explore case studies, create their own public language in the form of text, picture and video.

The media, and especially mission-driven media institutions like the BBC and *The New York Times*, have an important part to play, as do all organisations – museums, think tanks, foundations – devoted to advancing the public's understanding of science and other policy areas. We all have a duty, not just to red-flag the tendentious and the suspect, but to help our audiences build their own mental model in each major policy area – economic, geopolitical, social, scientific – into which that day's statistics or political claims can be placed in a context of proportion and probability. They need to learn too how to challenge each model and to adapt it in the light of changing circumstances.

This is not the way rhetoric is generally taught today. The humanities as a whole stand at low tide, judged less economically valuable, less worthy of research grants than the sciences, an indulgence for privileged kids or those who don't know what to do with themselves. And even within the humanities, in most schools and universities rhetoric is well-nigh forgotten. If Cicero were alive today, he'd probably become an economist or a computer scientist. The last subject he'd choose to major in would be rhetoric.

But if anything can hold our brittle public realm together, it is more likely to be the right kind of rhetoric than a clever new piece of code. Let's remember that, like the other humanities, like all great art, the question which it wrestles with – how are we to live with each other? – is the most important question which confronts any human society. Let's teach our children rhetoric.

The Trump Test

Imagine a test. It may be invidious to name it after one individual – Donald Trump is, after all, a symptom rather than the cause of the disease – but at least the title should make my intention clear. The Trump Test is a measure of the health of a public language. To pass it, the language must enable ordinary citizens to distinguish at once between matters of fact and those of opinion, between grown-up political discourse and outright nonsense.

At present, not just in the US but in Britain and some other western countries, our public language is manifestly failing the test. Over the past few pages, I've proposed some steps we could take to stop the decline, but I'd be the first to warn against relying solely on them. Even if they were widely embraced, their effect would probably be modest. And too many of the actors are trapped in the downward spiral themselves for even that to be certain.

No, if our rhetoric is ever to return to health, we must look not just to near-term changes in behaviour, but to the fundamental social and cultural forces that play on our language. When will their balance change and start to favour regeneration rather than disintegration? Are there any early signs of that shift beginning to happen?

*

The seeds of renewal of a public language germinate in unexpected places, and where the cultural pessimists least expect them: out of the mouths of immigrants and refugees; in the border towns and on the jagged edges of our societies where people have less to lose and more to say because they have more to be angry about; in forms and contexts which are apparently removed from the supposedly serious business of politics and journalism.

The critical reception of Salman Rushdie's *Midnight's Children* (published in 1981) confirmed a growing sense that creative momentum in English literature was moving from its heartlands in Britain and America towards former colonies and countries where English was one language among many, and from the white heterosexual majority population to ethnic and sexual minorities. Immigrants and those whose biographies included long stretches of life in different cultures or marginalised communities turned up with increasing frequency in the prize shortlists.

All of this unsettled some conservatives, who worried that the focus on minority literature was driven by political correctness, and that this kind of cultural globalisation and relativisation risked turning English itself into a mongrel tongue. We could debate the first assertion. History suggests that the second is wholly fallacious and that, on the contrary, exposure to different cultures thickens the plot, introduces new vocabularies and new perspectives, and challenges the status quo in unsettling but ultimately fruitful ways.

There are other fresh shoots. Satire has been enjoying a comeback on television and the web in both Britain and America. Satirists have always been public language's street sweepers, brushing away bogus rhetoric in all its forms – the false, the fawning, the idiotic. Although satirical magazines and websites like *Private Eye*, *The Onion* and *Charlie Hebdo* play their part, this is especially true of today's TV satirists, Chris Morris and Armando Ianucci in the UK, Jon Stewart and John Oliver in the US among them. Programmes like *The Day Today*, *Have I Got News For You!*, *The Thick of It*, *The Daily Show* and *Last Week Tonight* have often done a better job of deconstructing the language of politicians, and helping viewers make sense of what is really going on, than the majority of straight news sources. Indeed, many people now rely on them not just for laughs, but for the most trustworthy commentary on current events.

People sometimes talk about satire as if it were just another expression of the wider cynicism and negativity which they detect in both media and politics, but it isn't. The best satire is a fusion of anger and creativity. It's a purgative and its purpose, like great journalism and great aspirational politics, is not to hurt but to cure.

Anger also powers the language of hip hop. While mainstream white rock and pop have never strayed far from the solipsistic world of personal feelings, hip hop is almost always socially situated and politically aware, and often conscious of itself as rhetoric: 'My words are weapons,' rapped Eminem in the song of that name.[12] This is scarcely news – Public Enemy were announcing that Elvis was a racist, and US history nothing but four centuries of rednecks back in 1989[13] – but hip hop has gravitated to the main stage in the decades since then without losing any of its indignation or linguistic inventiveness.

In hip hop, the personal is political and the political personal. Beyoncé's 2016 album *Lemonade* is a cycle of songs about betrayal, fury and redemption which places her own emotional life artfully within the wider struggle of black women for respect and love: the mothers of three young black men killed in law enforcement incidents appear in the film which accompanies the album. In response to one of those deaths, that of Michael Brown, who was shot and killed by a policeman in Ferguson, Missouri, the hip hop artist Killer Mike wrote this on his Instagram account:

> No matter how u felt about black people look at this mother and look at this father and tell me as a human being how u cannot feel empathy for them . . . These are not THOTS, niggas/niggers, hoes, Ballers, Divas . . . They are humans that produced a child and loved that child and that child was slaughtered like Game and left face down as public spectacle while his blood drained down the street . . .[14]

This is heartfelt and powerful prose. But compare it to the coiled outrage of the artist's song 'Pressure':

> Liberation costs more than a damn dollar
> It costs what Christ gave
> King gave
> X gave

A billion dollars don't make you an ex-slave
Nigga With an Attitude since fifth grade
I never behave
Rather be a dead man than a live slave[15]

Lin-Manuel Miranda's 2015 hip hop musical *Hamilton* tells the story of the American founding father Alexander Hamilton with the sophistication of a political science treatise and the musical and verbal wit of a Mozart/Da Ponte opera:

How does a bastard, orphan, son of a whore
And a Scotsman, dropped in the middle of a forgotten spot
In the Caribbean by Providence, impoverished, in squalor
Grow up to be a hero and a scholar?[16]

Hamilton deals with the ironies and disappointments of democratic politics not with weary cynicism but fascinated zest. The Thomas Jefferson who jokes about his slaves is played, like many other cast members, by a black actor. George III begins as an absurd caricature but is then allowed his own mordant critique of the brave new political world which Hamilton and his friends are building. Hamilton's idealism and sense of honour leads to a senseless death at the hands of Aaron Burr, but by then they have defined, not what American political culture was, or is, but what it might aspire to. With its sprung rhythm and switchback language, *Hamilton* itself hints at what a new political rhetoric might sound like, one which can acknowledge the disputatiousness and cynicism which are endemic to democracy, but never accepts that they are the whole of the story.

*

If we look hard, we can also see some promising new buds within political discourse itself. The language of *fairness* is one of them.

On the face of it, fairness is bitterly disputed in modern political discourse. Often rival definitions sit on both sides of a given argument. Can it possibly be fair if women and minorities earn less than men? But if it involves hiring and promoting people because of their gender or skin colour rather than purely on their professional ability, is positive discrimination (or affirmative action, as it is generally called in the US) fair?

The disputes that arise from these questions can leave listeners wondering whether *fairness* has any objective meaning at all, or whether it is one of those words that can be twisted to fit any side of any argument. But in modern pluralist societies, almost everyone agrees (at least in principle) that fair treatment is both a universal right and a moral duty, so any case that convincingly evokes fairness is likely to carry force. A battle to define what is fair, or which of two rival perspectives on fairness should prevail, is therefore a battle of substance – and, as we shall shortly see, sometimes there are clear-cut winners and losers.

Fairness has been a long time coming – politicians had been arguing about fairness at least since King John's barons forced him to sign Magna Carta in 1215, though the decisive advances in the theory and language of social justice were made from the late seventeenth century on. By 1948, when the United Nations made its Universal Declaration of Human Rights after the horrors of the Second World War, the argument for a global framework of fairness for all was carried *nem. con.* Forty-eight countries voted in favour of the declaration and none against. The eight countries which abstained (the Soviet bloc, Yugoslavia, South Africa and Saudi Arabia among them) had no intention of upholding the rights contained in the declaration, but it is telling that even at that time none of them thought it politic to vote against.

In the decades that followed, they and plenty of the countries which *had* voted in favour would betray the declaration in practice. The rights to equal treatment under the law, to freedom of expression and of association, to education and a basic standard of living – all would be routinely flouted around the world. Western countries too would fail to live up to the declaration, with flagrant abuses at home and abroad; even today, no one can look at the lives of the poorest members of our societies and believe that they enjoy equality before the law or that higher education is 'equally accessible to all'. The world's constitutions and political leaders talk the talk about equality and fairness, then, but frequently treat them with contempt in practice. No one is free from hypocrisy.

But this should not blind us to the progress that has been made. Certain universal values have been publicly asserted and only the most benighted and deranged political forces dare publicly to deny them. The innocent still get murdered, but almost everyone acknowledges that it is a crime and the regimes that are responsible know they risk economic, diplomatic and even military punishment, not to mention being put on trial in the International Criminal Court. The right to asylum, which is guaranteed in the Declaration, is profoundly awkward for the many countries who regard it as immigration by another name, and who would rather think of the taking in of refugees as something voluntary, rather than the moral and legal duty it is. But though the right is routinely honoured in the breach, at least it can no longer be denied in principle. As a result, it reveals the inhumanity of those who flout it, or equivocate about it, for all to see.

Public words about justice and humanity are far from a complete solution, but they count for something. So too, despite the piousness and self-regard that inevitably attends them, do the rock concerts and celebrity endorsements of the fight against poverty and oppression. They too have helped generalise the sense that, even though our societies may fall woefully shy of it, there is a universal set of minimum standards which should apply to the way human beings treat each other everywhere. Words and music are the softest kind of soft power but, like water eroding stone, over time they can wear away adamantine opposition.

Playing the fairness card doesn't necessarily make issues easier to resolve. Is it fair to deny a woman the right to have an abortion or fair to her unborn foetus to allow the abortion to go ahead? When fairness can be invoked by either side to a dispute with plausibility to their own supporters at least, it can postpone resolution indefinitely. But even here there can sometimes be unexpected breakthroughs.

Take same-scx marriage. Opponents of allowing gay people to marry each other did so largely for reasons of religion, believing first that homosexuality was sinful and second that marriage was intended by God to be the union of a man and a woman, not just to consummate their love for each other, but also to produce children. But even in as religious a country as the United States, it is widely accepted that matters of faith are a private affair. The advocates of reform, moreover, took care to make their case not on the basis that those opposed to homosexuality were wrong or bigoted but rather that marriage is a civil as well as a religious institution and that, in the civil realm, the exclusion of gays raised a simple matter of fairness: if one pair of consenting adults is allowed to get married, why not another? Western societies had long ago decided to make divorce legal, even though many of their citizens considered it to be wrong. These societies don't force anyone to get divorced or even to condone divorce in principle. But they argue that Citizen A doesn't have the right to prevent Citizens B and C from getting divorced if they so choose.

The effect was to drive a rhetorical wedge into the opposing camp. Sticking to religious and moral principles effectively meant retreating from the policy debate to the comfort of the pulpit, allowing the faithful to remain true to their convictions but ceding most of the active political ground to the reformers. The alternative was to confront the reformers on their own terms, but that meant abandoning religio-moral arguments for rather less certain sociological ones – which largely seemed to boil down to the proposition that heterosexual marriage is an ancient institution which you interfere with at your peril. Few of the vast uncommitted majority found that line of reasoning compelling. Many other 'time-honoured' institutions, like the historic privileges and power which men enjoyed over women, had already been successfully challenged and the result had not been Sodom and Gomorrah but social progress.

The decision to promote the term 'same-sex marriage' rather than 'gay marriage' was also an astute move by the proponents of reform. 'Same-sex' points the listener's mind towards matters of gender fairness and broader tolerance rather than gayness as such. Pragmatic, but also justified: the case was always equality before the law rather than a plea for any one sexuality.

For a long while it looked as if same-sex marriage was going to be another of those interminable values debates which never get resolved. But at some point the opposing party simply ran out of words. And so in the United States and a growing number of other countries, what had looked like a lengthy struggle gave way to something approaching a walkover.

In the Catholic Church, Pope Francis had opposed same-sex marriage when he was a cardinal in Argentina, claiming that the true inspirer of the proposed reform was 'the father of lies'. Since then, though, Francis has used the language of fairness to signal, if not a shift in his position on the specific issue, then at least a different approach both to the broader topic of homosexuality and to the role of the pope. Asked in July 2013 about gays inside the Vatican, he replied, 'If someone is gay and he searches for the Lord and has good will, who am I to judge?' *Who am I to judge?* manages to crowd humility, respect, orthodoxy (popes are indeed *not* meant to judge) and a characteristic touch of mischief into a handful of words. It's a sentence which contains more meaning – and more controversy – than all but a handful of the encyclicals that have been handed down by popes over the past 2,000 years.

Pope Francis has used the language of fairness and respect in other contexts as well, in particular in relation to the environment, global income disparity and the refugee crisis. It is not so much that he has abandoned the traditional authority of papal discourse, but rather that he has found a new way of expressing that authority *through* the language of fairness.

The progress to which these examples point is tentative and partial. The legalisation of same-sex marriage doesn't mean that hostility to gay people is disappearing; as the history of racism in western countries demonstrates, hatred and bigotry can survive long after overtly prejudicial language is moved to the margins of public discourse. Moreover, sometimes brave talk can be an excuse for the avoidance of tough practical decisions.

Still, the emergence of a powerful and widely accepted moral language gives the lie to some of our darkest fears about our public discourse. Though it is often spoken by the weak and dispossessed, there is something unstoppable about the language of fairness. The barriers it faces remain formidable, but we know that in the end the sea can wear down even the stoutest of coastal defences.

*

None of these proposals or examples guarantee that our public language will pass the Trump Test any time soon. The forces of political fragmentation and digital disruption are still playing out. Many of the players are trapped in habits and responses which they will find hard to break, even if they wanted to. Perhaps, to put it simply, too much has been said in this frantically prolix world of ours, too many hateful, mad, duplicitous words – and what is needed now is a period of forgetting, or a kind of general amnesty, before we can even hope for a recovery.

But let's not despair. Public language has come back to life before, as it did in England in the decades after the Civil War, sometimes even as the last rites were being read over it. Revival depends not on the victory of one ideology over another, nor any deliberate call for reform, but on a turning of the tide of culture and society. We're commonsensical creatures and we know that our life together depends on our being able to resolve our differences, at least most of the time. Sooner or later a new language of reasonable persuasion should emerge. We just don't know when.

So what can you do in this long uncertain interim? Open your ears. Use your own good judgement. Think, speak, laugh. Cut through the noise.

Afterthoughts and Acknowledgements

When the wealthy Boston merchant Nicholas Boylston died in 1771, he left Harvard University £1,500 to establish a new chair in rhetoric and oratory. The university accepted the money, but then inertia set in. Eventually, after three decades had passed without any visible action on the part of the university, Boylston's nephew Ward Nicholas Boylston filed a suit to recover the bequest. He only abandoned it after Harvard agreed to fill the chair at once – and consented to appoint his cousin John Quincy Adams, a US senator and future president, as the first professor.

Asking a non-academic with practical experience of public language and politics to lecture on the subject of rhetoric was an intriguing idea. But the potential downside must also have been obvious. When Adams eventually stood up in Harvard Hall in 1806 to deliver his inaugural oration, he began with a kind of apology:

> In reflecting upon the nature of the duties I undertake, a consciousness of deficiency for the task of their performance dwells upon my mind; which, however ungraciously it may come from my lips, after accepting the appointment, with which I am honored, I yet cannot forbear to express. Though the course of my life has led me to witness the practice of this art in various forms, and though its theory has sometimes attracted my attention, yet my acquaintance with both has been of a general nature; and I can presume neither to a profound investigation of the one, nor an extensive experience of the other.

Well, I know how he felt. In early 2012 Mark Damazer, the former Controller of BBC Radio 4, the present Master of St Peter's College Oxford and one of my closest friends, rang me to ask if I would consider becoming a visiting professor of rhetoric and 'the art of public persuasion' at that university. Certainly not, I thought at once.

Nonetheless that November, having convinced myself and the organisers that I might have something to say on the subject, I gave three lectures at St Peter's, followed by a public discussion which was moderated by Andrew Marr and included the government minister David Willetts, and the journalists Polly Toynbee and Will Hutton as well as myself. This book has grown out of the talks and some of the ideas which were raised and discussed by the panel and audience.

The publisher George Weidenfeld came up with the idea of the Oxford visiting chair as part of his Humanitas programme of visiting professorships, and this book wouldn't exist without him. George, who once had a desk at the BBC a few yards from that other 'George', Eric Blair or George Orwell, was at home in most of the political and cultural worlds I reflect on in this book and glided amusedly between them. He knew many of its leading characters personally. At the time of the lectures, I was about to move from my job as Director-General of the BBC to become chief executive of *The New York Times*. Before the first lecture, George sat me down on a sofa in the Master's lodgings at St Peter's and gave me the first instalment of what he called his 'Proustian' guide to New York. I last spoke to him at dinner on the Upper East Side three years later, a little reduced inside the pin-stripes, but still presiding puckishly. He died a few months later in early 2016 at the age of 92.

The lectures were dedicated to Philip Gould, a brilliant and kindly man who appears several times in this book as one of Tony Blair's political advisers. I know, because I discussed it with him, how passionately Philip cared about the relationship between the politicians and the media, and about the future of the BBC in particular. I hope he would have agreed with at least some of what I have had to say. I am sorry he is not here to tell me how wrong I am about the rest. The lectures were sponsored by Philip's last employer, Freud Communications. I am also grateful to Matthew Freud, another old friend, for his support of them.

But let me return to John Quincy Adams and the inconvenient but unavoidable facts about my own inadequacy as a guide to public language. Although I too have witnessed 'the practice of this art in various forms', and read a little about its 'theory', I am by no stretch of the imagination an expert in rhetoric. I'm familiar with a decent amount of classical literature, but that hardly makes me a classicist. This book doesn't claim to be a work of philosophy but it does deal with the history of ideas, so I should probably confess that I am not a philosopher either, and have no training in any of the many other disciplines which the book touches on – modern history, political science, social psychology, linguistics, marketing and so on – though I have bumped into most of them, one way or another, over my career.

So I must apologise to professionals in all these disciplines for crash-landing on their fields. I hope that the critical faculties and pockets of knowledge and experience that I *can* bring to bear have compensated to some degree for these deficiencies and that, while my congenital intellectual overconfidence may have frequently led me astray, it may also have allowed me to bushwhack my way to a handful of insights which might be hard to make out from any one of these established academic paths.

This is the age of data, and of the quantitative analysis of language; yet, while not quite data-free, my book is firmly rooted in the qualitative – in examples, personal experiences, criticism and opinions. In this, as in other respects, it falls well short of contemporary scholarly norms. I have spent the past twenty-five years of my life trying to understand the tidal wave of digital innovation that has transformed our world. But I was brought up in the humanities.

My school, Stonyhurst College in Lancashire, was originally founded by the Society of Jesus in the late sixteenth century in Northern France. The *Ratio Studiorum*, the early modern Jesuit system of education – itself based on the medieval *Trivium* which had introduced the student to the liberal arts by teaching grammar, logic and rhetoric – still influenced teaching at the school. Even in the 1970s, each year group was named after a given stage in the learning of Latin, 'Lower Grammar', 'Upper Syntax' and so on. The final year, which I entered in the autumn of 1975 to prepare for the Oxford entrance exam, was called 'Rhetoric'.

In truth, rhetoric wasn't much taught at Stonyhurst. It had gone into decline almost everywhere in the nineteenth century. In due course, that Boylston professorship at Harvard became a chair in literature rather than rhetoric, and today is always occupied by a leading poet. By the 1970s, and despite a modest mid-twentieth-century revival, rhetoric was a fairly obscure branch of the humanities and scarcely the stuff of sixth-form studies. But studying Latin and Greek made it unavoidable. Indeed, when I finally opened the Oxford exam paper I was confronted by a passage of English rhetoric – I think it was a gobbit of wartime Churchill – which the candidate was invited to turn into Greek in the style of his or her favourite Athenian orator.

Even back then, most educationalists would have dismissed this not just as elitist – how many candidates from state schools could compete with this kind of demented hot-housing? – but worthless from any conceivable perspective, economic, social or cultural. Many readers of this book may well agree with them. All I can say is that by this point, the *Ratio* had rolled up its sleeves and got down to serious business inside my 18-year-old head, and the interwovenness with which all the arts were taught – classical and modern languages, literature, history, philosophy, theology – meant that I began to feel a connectedness between all of them, and between the deep past and the present. This tendency was further encouraged by the two men who most influenced my education, Peter Hardwick at Stonyhurst, and John Jones at Merton College Oxford. Both taught me English literature, but much else besides.

Despite all of the digital talk then, I discover that I have written an old-fashioned essay. Many people have helped me in the course of its development. Professor Abigail Williams, who teaches English at Oxford, was the academic advisor on the lectures and was encouraging and inspirational throughout. Her Classics colleague, Professor Matthew Leigh, also added many insights and suggestions as well as casting an eye over my tendentious and rusty renderings of the Latin and Greek. Both Abigail and Matthew have kindly offered advice on this book as well. In addition I received helpful guidance on the lectures from Ben Page of Ipsos-MORI and Deborah Mattinson, who has played such an important part over the years in the Labour Party's strategy for reaching out to and convincing the public. Sebastian Baird supported me during the development of the lectures with research and fact-checking.

I have also received a great deal of help in expanding the ideas in the lectures into a book. Michael Sandel, the political philosopher and Harvard professor, suggested reading to me during the course of my research. Patrick Barwise, a thoughtful and indefatigable defender of public service broadcasting, who is Emeritus Professor of Management and Marketing at the London Business School, gave me valuable advice for the chapter on the role of marketing in the development of modern public language. Former Senator Bob Kerrey gave me several ideas in a series of conversations about rhetoric. Dr Frank Luntz, who features in the book and is a kind of P. T. Barnum when it comes to public language, has also talked to me about his take on the subject. Svetlana Boym, a playwright and novelist who was, until her death in 2015, Professor of Slavic and Comparative Literatures at Harvard, help me understand a little about the rhetoric of Vladimir Putin. My sister-in-law, Dr Rossella Bondi, added some fascinating suggestions about modern Italian political language. Rhys Jones helped with some research and fact-checking.

I also received advice and support from many past and present colleagues. At the BBC, David Jordan and Jessica Cecil provided ideas and comments on the lectures and read early versions of the book. They were part of the team who routinely helped me think through difficult editorial questions and controversies at the BBC. I can't mention everyone who influenced my development as an editor and the approach to journalism, free speech and impartiality which is set out in this book, but I am also particularly grateful for the good judgement and fast reactions of Mark Byford, Alan Yentob, Caroline Thomson, Ed Williams and Helen Boaden, as well as wise counsel from successive BBC chairmen, governors and trustees.

I've also received plenty of support for the project at *The New York Times*, including from Diane Brayton, Eileen Murphy, Joy Goldberg, Meredith Kopit Levien and Dorothea Herrey. Both Diane and Licia Hahn read the whole manuscript and provided ideas and comments. Amanda Churchill and the team in the DG's office at Broadcasting House helped greatly with the logistics of the 2012 lectures. My executive assistant at *The New York Times*, Mary Ellen LaManna, has supported me and my book with astonishing 24/7 dedication. I also want to thank my literary agent, Caroline Michel; Stuart Williams, Jörg Hensgen and their colleagues at the Bodley Head in London; and George Witte, Sarah Thwaite and all of their colleagues at St Martin's Press in New York.

I want to thank everyone on this long list for their great generosity, and to absolve them from any responsibility for any error or offence which the book may contain. The case of Mark Damazer is different. It was he who got me into this business in the first place, and it seems only fair that he *should* take his fair share of the blame for it. But in the unlikely event of there being any credit, he should take most of that as well. He has been an unfailing enthusiast, stern critic, gracious host, sympathetic therapist and devoted friend throughout.

Lastly, my family. In Jonathan Dorfman, I am lucky enough to have a brother-in-law of astonishingly wide reading in politics, literature and culture. Many of Jonathan's suggested quotations and astute observations have made it into the book. And I have received colossal intellectual and moral support from my wife, Jane Blumberg, who is not just my academic senior but the best literary critic I know, and from my three strong-minded children, Caleb, Emilie and Abe. Thanks to these four above all, for their backing and for their ideas.

*

There is a vast literature, ancient and modern, taken up with the themes of this book and I have no doubt only scratched the surface of it. But even a list of the works I have consulted would run for pages. Rather than a bibliography, let me mention some of the books I have found most useful – and which a reader who wants to pursue the subject further might enjoy. To this list, the reader should add the works cited in the notes.

The ancients are easy to find. You can enjoy them all for nothing on Perseus, Tufts University's excellent classics site (http://www.perseus.tufts.edu/). I've tended to use the Loeb and Penguin Classics editions, mainly for old times' sake. If you are not familiar with them and can only face one ancient work, read Thucydides. *The History of the Peloponnesian War* isn't a book about rhetoric as such, but about the collision of politics, public language, deep national culture and transient public mood. Somehow it manages to be a compelling commentary, not just about the war between Athens and Sparta and their respective allies two and a half millennia ago, but about every western war that has taken place since then. *The Landmark Thucydides* (edited by Robert B. Strassler, Simon and Schuster 1988,) is a good edition because of its many helpful maps.

You Talkin' To Me? by Sam Leith (Profile Books, 2011) is an excellent general introduction to rhetoric ancient, modern and contemporary. I also enjoyed Brian Vicker's more academic but still eminently readable *In Defence of Rhetoric* (Oxford University Press, 1998). *Saving Persuasion: A Defense of Rhetoric and Judgment* by Bryan Garsten (Harvard University Press, 2006) is a masterly and original analysis of the main lines of argument for and against rhetoric and perhaps the most persuasive defence of persuasion that I read. I also found Adam Adatto Sandel's *The Place of Prejudice* (Harvard University Press, 2014) interesting and valuable. Kenneth Burke was one of the mid-twentieth-century's most influential writers on rhetoric. I read *A Rhetoric of Motives* (Prentice-Hall, 1950) and sections of other works but – though this is no doubt more of a reflection on me than on Burke – rather struggled with his approach. *Contemporary Rhetorical Theory: A Reader* (The Guilford Press, 1999) was one of several collections of essays I examined to get a sense of academic thinking about rhetoric at century's end. Though it is only indirectly a book about rhetoric, I found *Dictionary of Untranslatables: A Philosophical Lexicon* (edited by Barbara Cassin, Princeton University Press, 2014; originally published as *Vocabulaire européen des philosophies: Dictionnaire des intraduisibles*, Éditions de Seuil, 2004) alarmingly moreish.

Kathleen Hall Jamieson's *Eloquence in an Electronic Age* (Oxford University Press, 1988) is an important and engaging study of how mass media influenced political speechmaking. I also benefitted from Stephen Fox's classic *The Mirror Makers: A History of American Advertising & Its Creators* (Morrow, 1984 – though I read the 1997 Illini Books edition).

On George Orwell, in addition to the great man himself, I looked at Christopher Hitchens (especially *Orwell's Victory*, Allen Lane, 2002), and *Orwell and the Politics of Despair* by Alok Rai (Cambridge University Press, 1988). Masha Gessen's *The Man Without a Face: The Unlikely Rise of Vladimir Putin* (Riverhead, 2012) is a white-knuckle introduction to the man and the system he has created.

There is a groaning bookshelf of tomes analysing the various ills which afflict our politics, media and public language, and new works arrive by the week. I've only read a tiny fraction of them and, in any event, have relied more on transient digital sources for evidence and contemporary commentary. But, in addition to the several titles mentioned in the body of this book, I read *Blur* by Bill Kovach and

Tom Rosenstiel (Bloomsbury USA, 2010) and *unSpun: Finding Facts in a World of Disinformation* by Brooks Jackson and Kathleen Hall Jamieson (Random House, 2007), both of which deal with information overload, facts and spin. *Unspeak* by Steven Poole (Little, Brown, 2006) is an angry, compelling complaint about the way politicians and others twist apparently straightforward words – *nature, community, abuse* and so on – to mean whatever they want them to mean and, as a result, deliver highly partisan messages through seemingly neutral language.

I quote John Lloyd's *What the Media Are Doing to Our Politics* (Constable, 2004) in this book. In fact, I have found his muscular take on the media during his years at the *Financial Times* unfailingly inter- esting – and often convincing. I could say the same for David Carr, who was a media columnist at *The New York Times* when I arrived in 2012 and who became an informal mentor to me, as he did to many others, somehow combining the need for strict journalistic impartiality with a passionate enthusiasm for what the *Times* could be at its best. David died suddenly at the *Times* in 2015. Writing on media by Lloyd and Carr, as well as by Emily Bell, Margaret Sullivan, Jim Rutenberg, Jeff Jarvis and Steve Hewlett, is well worth seeking out on the Web.

'Much have I travelled in the realms of gold,' John Keats claims at the start of 'On First Looking into Chapman's Homer'. I've returned from my own journeys in the realms of the Internet to confirm what you already know: it is not all 24-carat. Yet, more than anywhere else, it is where our public discourse is happening, and where it must be studied. The reader must and will find their own way. But let me finish with a word of praise for Wikipedia, that inevitably imperfect but – especially for a project like this – invaluable resource, a neural network for the world and the start of so many cultural and intellectual departures. This is people power (*demokratia*) at work in aid not just of opinion but of true understanding, another modest cause for hope in a troubled time.

Notes

1 Lost for Words

1 http://twitter.com/sarahpalinusa/status/10935548053.
2 Fredthompsonshow.com, interview archives, 16 July 2009.
3 Fox News, *The O'Reilly Factor*, 17 July 2009.
4 MSNBC, *Morning Joe*, 31 July 2009.
5 http://www.facebook.com/note.php?note_id=113851103434.
6 http://pewresearch.org/pubs/1319/death-panels-republicans-fox-viewers.
7 http://nypost.com/2015/07/12/end-of-life-counselling-death-panels-are-back/.
8 http://www.creators.com/opinion/pat-buchanan/sarah-and-the-death-panels.html.
9 Edelman Trust Barometer, 2016 Annual Global Study. See www.edelman.com.
10 Thomas E. Mann and Norman J. Ornstein, *It's Even Worse Than It Looks: How the American Constitutional System Collided With the New Politics of Extremism* (Basic Books, 2012), 196.
11 Amy Gutmann and Dennis Thompson, *The Spirit of Compromise: Why Governing Demands It and Campaigning Undermines It* (Princeton University Press, 2012), 214.
12 *The Times*, 28 February 1975.
13 Tony Blair, speech to Reuters, 12 June 2007.
14 BBC Pulse, National Representative Sample 2011.
15 Ipsos MORI, BBC News Economy Research for BBC Audiences 2012.
16 House of Commons Treasury Committee, *The economic and financial costs and benefits of the UK's EU membership*, May 2016.
17 BBC News, 27 May 2016. See http://www.bbc.co.uk/news/uk-politics-eu-referendum-36397732.
18 Thucydides, *History of the Peloponnesian War*, III, lxxx, 4.
19 Sallust, *The War with Catiline*, LII, xi.

2 That Glib and Oily Art

1 Quoted in Arturo Tosi, *Language and Society in a Changing Italy* (Multilingual Matters, 2001), 129.
2 Anthony Zurcher, 'The strange Trump and Carson phenomenon explained', BBC News website, 15 November 2015.
3 Thucydides, *History of the Peloponnesian War*, II, xl, 2.
4 Ibid., I, cxxxix, 4.
5 Aristotle, *Art of Rhetoric*, I, ii, 12.
6 Later in the *Rhetoric*, Aristotle also uses the term 'enthymeme' more generically to mean dialectical argument.
7 Aristotle, *Art of Rhetoric*, I, ii, 12.
8 Reported in http://www.bbc.co.uk/news/uk-politics-22025035.
9 Ibid.
10 Aristotle, *The Nicomachean Ethics*, IV, vii.
11 Interview with the *Wall Street Journal*, 22 September 2015, http://www.wsj.com/articles/full-transcript-interview-with-chinese-president-xi-jinping-1442894700.
12 All quoted in Josh Rogin, 'Europeans Laugh as Lavrov Talks Ukraine', *Bloomberg View*, 7 February 2015.

3 There You Go Again

1 Ronald Reagan, news conference, 12 August 1986.
2 http://germanhistorydocs.ghi-dc.org/docpage.cfm?docpage_id=3194.
3 Winston Churchill, election broadcast, 4 June 1945.
4 Letter from Eisenhower to William Phillips, 5 June 1953, Box 25, Ann Whitman Files, Eisenhower Presidential Library.
5 See Thomasina Gabriele, *Italo Calvino: Eros and Language* (Fairleigh Dickinson University Press, 1996), 40ff.
6 Nelson Mandela, 'I Am Prepared to Die' speech, 20 April 1964, www.nelsonmandela.org/news/entry/i-am-prepared-to-die.
7 http://www.washingtonpost.com/wp-srv/politics/daily/may98/goldwaterspeech.htm. It is still widely believed that the words are a paraphrase of a passage in one of Cicero's *In Catilinam* speeches, but no such passage exists. There is a passage in one of Cicero's letters to his son Marcus, which is itself a paraphrase of Aristotle, which might have indirectly inspired the speechwriters.
8 Denis Healey, House of Commons, 14 June 1978.
9 http://www.margaretthatcher.org/document/104078.
10 TV-am interview with David Frost, 30 December 1988, http://www.margaretthatcher.org/speeches/displaydocument.asp?docid=107022.
11 Margaret Thatcher, Conservative Party Conference speech, 10 October 1980.

12 Ibid.

13 Ibid.

14 Holli A. Semetko et al., *The Formation of Campaign Agendas: A Comparative Analysis of Party and Media Roles in Recent American and British Elections* (Lawrence Erlbaum Associates, 1991), 119.

15 Ronald Reagan, 'A Time for Choosing', 27 October 1964, http://www.reagan.utexas.edu/archives/reference/timechoosing.html.

16 Ibid.

17 http://www.theatlantic.com/national/archive/2012/01/doomsday-speeches-if-d-day-and-the-moon-landing-had-failed/251953/.

18 Presidential debate, Carter/Reagan, 23 October 1980.

19 Ronald Reagan, remarks at the Brandenburg Gate, 12 June 1987.

20 http://www.theatlantic.com/national/archive/2012/01/doomsday-speeches-if-d-day-and-the-moon-landing-had-failed/251953/.

21 Ronald Reagan, TV address on the *Challenger* disaster, 28 January 1986.

22 http://www.gallup.com/poll/116677/presidential-approval-ratings-gallup-historical-statistics-trends.aspx.

23 http://politicalticker.blogs.cnn.com/2013/11/22/cnn-poll-jfk-tops-presidential-rankings-for-last-50-years/.

4 Spin and Counter-Spin

1 http://www.lefigaro.fr/flash-actu/2011/01/05/97001-20110105FIL WWW00493-chatel-defend-le-style-oral-de-sarkozy.php.

2 George C. Wallace, first gubernatorial inauguration address, 14 January 1963.

3 Donald Trump, campaign speech in Dallas, 14 September 2015.

4 https://twitter.com/realdonaldtrump/status/703257866820415488.

5 Speaking in the fourth Republican TV debate in Milwaukee, 10 November 2015.

6 http://www.pbs.org/wgbh/pages/frontline/shows/clinton/interviews/morris2.html. Quoted in Taegan Goddard's Political Dictionary, http://politicaldictionary.com/words/triangulation/.

7 Tony Blair, 8 April 1998. See http://news.bbc.co.uk/2/hi/uk_news/politics/3750847.stm.

8 Anthony Seldon with Peter Snowdon and Daniel Collings, *Blair Unbound* (Simon & Schuster, 2007), 339.

9 Arturo Tosi, *Language and Society in a Changing Italy* (Multilingual Matters, 2001), 110.

10 Ibid., 116.

11 Ibid., 119, 120.

12 Quoted in 'Italy's Silvio Berlusconi in his own words', http://www.bbc.co.uk/news/world-europe-15642201.

13 http://www.theguardian.com/world/2009/aug/28/silvio-berlusconi-sues-sex-scandal.
14 http://www.lefigaro.fr/flash-actu/2011/01/05/97001-20110105FILWWW00493-chatel-defend-le-style-oral-de-sarkozy.php.
15 Vladimir Putin speaking at a press conference in Astana, Kazakhstan, 24 September 1999.
16 Rémi Camus, 'Language and Social Change: New Tendencies in the Russian Language', *Kultura*, October 2006. See: http://www.kultura-rus.uni-bremen.de/kultura_dokumente/ausgaben/englisch/kultura_10_2006_EN.pdf.

5 Why Is This Lying Bastard Lying to Me?

1 Speech to Reuters on public life, 12 June 2007.
2 Paul Ricœur, *Freud and Philosophy: An Essay in Interpretation*, trans. Denis Savage (Yale University Press, 1970), 32–3.
3 David Foster Wallace, 'E Unibus Pluram: Television and US Fiction', in *A Supposedly Fun Thing I'll Never Do Again* (Little, Brown, 1997), originally published in *Review of Contemporary Fiction*, 1993. I am grateful to Miguel Aguilar for drawing my attention to it.
4 Christopher Dunkley, '*The Nine O'Clock News* Goes Serious', *Financial Times*, 16 November 1988.
5 John Birt, 'For Good or Ill: The Role of the Modern Media', Independent Newspapers Annual Lecture, Dublin, February 1995.

6 An Unhealthy Debate

1 Speech to the Labour Party Conference, September 2013, http://press.labour.org.uk/post/62236275016/andy-burnham-mps-speech-to-labour-party-annual.
2 Report of the National Commission on Terror Attacks upon the United States, July 2004, http://govinfo.library.unt.edu/911/report/index.htm.
3 Mario Cuomo, interview in the *New Republic*, 4 April 1985.
4 Health and Social Care Bill, Clause 163, page 159.
5 http://www.guardian.co.uk/commentisfree/2012/mar/08/nhs-bill-lib-dem-defining-moment.
6 http://www.guardian.co.uk/commentisfree/2012/mar/16/who-right-on-nhs-polly-shirley.
7 Quoted in the *Observer*, 11 March 2012.
8 Ibid.
9 Lewis Carroll, *Through the Looking Glass* (1871; Vintage edition, 2007), 254
10 Ipsos MORI, Public Perceptions of the NHS tracker survey, 14 June 2012.

11 For example, Analysis column by Branwen Jeffreys, BBC News health correspondent, 4 September 2012, http://www.bbc.com/news/health-19474896.
12 'Romney Advisor: No Obamacare Repeal', http://www.redstate.com/erick/2012/01/25/romney-advisor-no-obamacare-repeal/.
13 Ashley Parker, 'Cantor's Lesson: Hedging on Immigration is Perilous', http://www.nytimes.com/2014/06/12/us/politics/cantors-lesson-hedging-on-immigration-is-perilous.html.

7 How to Fix a Broken Language

1 George Orwell, 'Politics and the English Language', *Horizon*, April 1946. Quoted throughout this chapter.
2 George Orwell, 'Some Thoughts on the Common Toad', *Tribune*, 12 April 1946.
3 Quoted in 'Judge Questions Legality of N.S.A. Phone Records', *The New York Times*, 16 December 2013.
4 Lancelot Hogben, *Interglossa: A Draft of an Auxiliary for a Democratic World Order* (Penguin Books, 1943), 7.
5 George Orwell, 'New Words', believed to have been written in 1940, first published in *The Collected Essays, Journalism and Letters of George Orwell*, vol. II (Secker & Warburg, 1958); quoted in Alok Rai, *Orwell and the Politics of Despair* (Cambridge University Press, 1988), 123ff.
6 Alok Rai, *Orwell and the Politics of Despair*, 125.
7 David Hume, *An Enquiry Concerning Human Understanding* (1748), Section XII.
8 Ludwig Wittgenstein, *Tractatus Logico-Philosophicus* (1921; first English edition 1922; Routledge and Kegan Paul, 1961), Author's Preface, 5.
9 Ludwig Wittgenstein, *Philosophical Investigations* (1953; Basil Blackwell, 1976), Part I, i, 2.
10 Ibid., Part II, iv, 178.
11 Adolf Hitler, Appeal to Political Leaders, 11 September 1936. See http://nsl-archiv.com/Buecher/Fremde-Sprachen/Adolf%20Hitler%20-%20Collection%20of%20Speeches%201922-1945%20(EN,%20993%20S.,%20Text).pdf.
12 Ernst Hanfstaengl, *Unheard Witness* (J. B. Lippincott Co., 1957), 266.
13 Martin Heidegger, address to the Freiburg Institute of Pathological Anatomy, August 1933. Quoted in Emmanuel Faye, *Heidegger: The Introduction of Nazism into Philosophy*, trans. Michael B. Smith (Yale University Press, 2009), 68 (German text at 351, n. 35).
14 T. S. Eliot, 'Burnt Norton' (1935), V.
15 https://www.youtube.com/watch?v=8mqFsVUIQrg.
16 George Orwell, 'My Country Right or Left', *Folios of New Writing*, autumn 1940.

8 Sentences that Sell

1   Elmer Wheeler, *Tested Sentences That Sell* (Prentice-Hall, 1937), 7.
2   Aristotle, *Art of Rhetoric*, I, iii, 5.
3   'How Advertising Works: What Do We Really Know?', *Journal of Marketing*, Vol. 63, No. 1, January 1999.
4   Wheeler, *Tested Sentences That Sell*, 110.
5   Ibid., 25.
6   Ibid., 7.
7   Ibid., 62–3.
8   Plato, *Gorgias*, 463–4.
9   Nancy Duarte, *HBR Guide to Persuasive Presentations* (Harvard Business Review Press, 2012), xv.
10 Ibid., 28.
11 Ibid., 59–60.
12 Ibid., 73.
13 Stephen Fox, *The Mirror Makers: A History of American Advertising and its Creators* (University of Illinois Press, 1997 edition), 307.
14 Ibid., 308.
15 Wheeler, *Tested Sentences That Sell*, 129–30.
16 Quoted in Fox, *The Mirror Makers*, 310.
17 See Edward Bernays, 'The Engineering of Consent', *Annals of the American Academy of Political and Social Science*, 1947.
18 Wendell R. Smith, 'Product Differentiation and Market Segmentation as Alternative Marketing Strategies', *Journal of Marketing*, July 1956. See https://archive.ama.org/archive/ResourceLibrary/MarketingManagement/documents/9602131166.pdf.
19 http://www.americandialect.org/woty/all-of-the-words-of-the-year-1990-to-present#1996.
20 Quoted in *Salon*, 16 July 2008. See http://www.salon.com/2008/07/16/obama_data/.
21 http://www.huffingtonpost.com/frank-luntz/words-2011_b_829603.html.
22 Ibid.
23 See, for example, Nick Cohen, the *Observer*, 10 December 2006, http://www.theguardian.com/commentisfree/2006/dec/10/comment.conservatives.
24 Thucydides, *History of the Peloponnesian War*, III, xxxvi.
25 Thomas Hobbes, *On the Citizen* (originally published in Latin as *De Cive*, 1642; Cambridge University Press, 1998, ed. and trans. Richard Tuck and Michael Silverthorne), 123.
26 See David B. Parker, *You Can Fool All The People: Did Lincoln Say It?*, History News Network: http://historynewsnetwork.org/article/161924.

9 *Commit it to the Flames*

1   Donald Trump in a telephone interview with Fox News, *Fox & Friends*, 2 April 2012.
2   *Dr Strangelove Or: How I Learned to Stop Worrying and Love the Bomb*, 1964. Co-written and directed by Stanley Kubrick; http://www.lexwilliford. com/Workshops/Screenwriting/Scripts/Adobe%20Acrobat%20Scripts/ Dr%20Strangelove.pdf.
3   BBC Radio 4, *Today*, 4 February 2002.
4   ICM Research/Today MMR poll August 2001, http://www.icmresearch. com/pdfs/2001_ august_today_programme_mmr.pdf.
5   *Annals of Pharmacotherapy*, http://www.theannals.com/content/ 45/10/1302.
6   Robert F. Kennedy Jr, 'Vaccinations: Deadly Immunity', article posted on rollingstone.com, July 2005, quoted here: http://www.globalresearch. ca/vaccinations-deadly-immunity/14510.
7   http://childhealthsafety.wordpress.com/2011/08/26/new-survey- shows-unvaccinated-children-vastly-healthier-far-lower-rates-of-chronic- conditions-and-autism/.
8   http://www.dailymail.co.uk/news/article-2160054/MMR-A-mothers- victory-The-vast-majority-doctors-say-link-triple-jab-autism-Italian- court-case-reignite-controversial-debate.html.
9   Bravo, *Watch What Happens Live*, 18 March 2014.
10 Fox News, *On the Record*, 6 June 2008.
11 *Good Morning America*, 4 June 2008, http://abcnews.go.com/GMA/ OnCall/story?id=4987758.
12 HBO, *Real Time with Bill Maher*, 9 October 2009.
13 Bill Maher, 'Vaccination: A Conversation Worth Having', blog posted 15 November 2009. See therealbillmaher.blogspot.com/2009/11/ vaccination-conversation-worth-having.html.
14 'Sources and Perceived Credibility of Vaccine-Safety Information for Parents', *Pediatrics*, first published online 18 April 2011, http://pediatrics. aappublications.org/content/127/Supplement_1/S107.full.pdf.
15 'Parental Vaccine Safety Concerns in 2009', *Pediatrics*, first published online 1 March 2010, http://pediatrics.aappublications.org/content/ early/2010/03/01/peds.2009-1962.full.pdf+html. It is worth noting that the survey was conducted before the final official verdict was delivered on the Wakefield MMR/autism paper and before the first outbreak of H1N1 (swine flu).
16 Frank Bruni, *New York Times*, 21 April 2014.
17 Benny Peiser, Introduction to Global Warming Policy Foundation Annual Lecture 2011, October 2011.

18   Benny Peiser, 'Climate Fatigue Leaves Global Warming in the Cold', Global Warming Policy Forum website. See www.thegwpf.com/benny-peiser-climate-fatigue-leaves-global-warming-in-the-cold/.

19   Ipsos MORI Trust in Professions Opinion Poll, 22 January 2016.

20   Christopher Booker/GWPF, 7 December 2011, http://www.thegwpf.org/christopher-booker-the-bbc-and-climate-change-a-triple-betrayal/.

21   See, for example, Pew National Survey, 15 October 2012, Guardian/ICM poll, 25 June 2012.

22   Pew Research, 'Top Policy Priorities', January 2014, http://www.pewresearch.org/key-data-points/climate-change-key-data-points-from-pew-research/.

23   Channel 4, 8 March 2007.

24   Royal Society, *Climate Change Controversies: a simple guide*, 30 June 2007.

25   Reported in the *Guardian*, 6 May 2010, http://www.guardian.co.uk/environment/ 2010/may/06/climate-science-open-letter.

26   Royal Society, *Climate Change Controversies: a simple guide*, 30 June 2007.

27   http://royalsociety.org/uploadedFiles/_Society_Content/policy/publications/2010/4294972962.pdf.

28   AAAS, *What We* Know, March 2014, http://whatweknow.aaas.org/wp-content/uploads/2014/07/whatweknow_website.pdf.

29   http://news.bbc.co.uk/nol/shared/bsp/hi/pdfs/05_02_10climatechange.pdf.

30   Pew Research, 2006 and 2014 polls, http://www.pewresearch.org/topics/energy-and-environment/.

31   Pew Research, international survey conducted March to May 2013, http://www.pewresearch.org/key-data-points/climate-change-key-data-points-from-pew-research/.

32   John Cook et al., 'Quantifying the consensus on anthropogenic global warming in the scientific literature', *Environmental Research Letters*, Vol. 8, No. 2, 15 May 2013.

33   Research by James Lawrence Powell, http://www.jamespowell.org/methodology/method.html.

34   Pieter Maeseele and Dimitri Schuurman, 'Knowledge, culture and power: biotechnology and the popular press', in Sigrid Koch-Baumgarten and Katrin Voltmer (eds), *Public Policy and Mass Media* (Routledge, 2010), 86–105. The table I refer to is Table 5.1 on page 101.

35   Ibid., 102–3.

36   *Foreign Affairs*, Vol. 91, No. 4, July/August 2012, 24ff.

37   Steve Jones, *BBC Trust review of the impartiality and accuracy of the BBC's coverage of science*, July 2011.

38   Bob Ward, policy and communications director, Grantham Research Institute on Climate Change and the Environment, http://www.lse.

ac.uk/GranthamInstitute/news/response-to-decision-by-bbc-editorial-complaints-unit-about-interview-with-lord-lawson-on-climate-change/.

39 http://www.latimes.com/opinion/opinion-la/la-ol-climate-change-letters-20131008-story.html.

40 http://grist.org/climate-energy/reddits-science-forum-banned-climate-deniers-why-dont-all-newspapers-do-the-same/.

41 Dan Kahan, 'Why we are poles apart on climate change', *Nature*, 15 August 2012.

10 War

1 A warning from Lord Esher to Field Marshal Douglas Haig about Winston Churchill (who was about to visit General Headquarters), 30 May 1917. Quoted in William Philpott, *Three Armies on the Somme: The First Battle of the Twentieth Century* (Knopf, 2010), 517.

2 Winston Churchill, House of Commons, 13 May 1940.

3 Tony Blair, House of Commons, 18 March 2003.

4 Ibid.

5 Robin Cook, House of Commons, 17 March 2003.

6 From BBC evidence to the Hutton Inquiry (*BBC 7/57*), quoted in http://news.bbc.co.uk/2/hi/programmes/conspiracy_files/6380231.stm.

7 Andrew Gilligan, evidence to the Hutton Inquiry, 12 August 2003, http://webarchive.nationalarchives.gov.uk/20090128221550/http://www.the-hutton-inquiry.org.uk/content/transcripts/hearing-trans05.htm.

8 Ibid.

9 Ibid.

10 William McKinley, address to Congress, 11 April 1898.

11 Anthony Eden addressing the Conservative Party Conference in Llandudno, 14 October 1956.

12 Lyndon Johnson, TV address on the Tonkin incident, 4 August 1964.

13 Ibid.

14 '*Atque, ubi solitudinem faciunt, pacem appellant*', literally 'and, where they make a desert, they name it peace'. Tacitus, *Agricola*, 30.

15 Pat Paterson, 'The Truth About Tonkin', *Naval History Magazine*, Vol. 22, No. 1, February 2008.

16 Richard A. Cherwitz, 'Lyndon Johnson and the "Crisis" of Tonkin Gulf: A President's Justification of War', *Western Journal of Speech Communication*, 42:2 (1978), 93–104.

17 Lyndon Johnson, address to Syracuse University, 5 August 1964, quoted in ibid.

18 Ibid., 99.

19 Ibid., 93.

20 Donald Rumsfeld, Pentagon briefing, 11 March 2003, quoted by UPI: http://www.upi.com/Business_News/Security-Industry/2003/03/12/ Rumsfeld-remarks-hint-at-differences/48271047454230/.

21 Wilfred Owen, 'Dulce et Decorum Est', from *Poems*, edited by Siegfried Sassoon and Edith Sitwell (Chatto & Windus, 1920).

22 Cecil Spring-Rice, 'I Vow to Thee, My Country' (1918).

23 Winston Churchill, *The World Crisis*, Vol. III: 1916–1918 (Bloomsbury, 2015), 10.

24 David Lloyd George, *War Memories*, Vol. II (Odhams, 1937), 1366.

25 John Reid, press conference in Kabul, 23 April 2006, quoted by Reuters, http://www.channel4.com/news/articles/uk/factcheck%2Ba%2Bshot %2Bin%2Bafghanistan/3266362.html.

26 Simon Jenkins, *Guardian*, 12 December 2007.

27 John Reid, House of Commons, 13 July 2009.

28 http://www.lancashiretelegraph.co.uk/news/9574114.UPDATED_ Soldier_from_Duke_of_Lancashire_s_Regiment_killed_in_ Afghanistan_named/.

29 Julian Borger, *Guardian*, 23 April 2012.

30 Speech by the Archbishop of Canterbury on the seventieth anniversary of the Allied bombing raid, 13 February 2015.

31 https://www.churchofengland.org/media-centre/news/2015/02/ statement-from-office-of-archbishop-of-canterbury-on-dresden.aspx.

32 Martin Luther King, 'Beyond Vietnam – A Time To Break Silence', speech at Riverside Church, New York, 4 April 1967.

33 Stop the War Coalition website, 14 November 2015 (now deleted), https://archive.is/du1n5#selection-637.0-637.78.

34 Letter to the *Guardian*, 9 December 2015.

11 *The Abolition of Public Language*

1 Osama Bin Laden, from the video statement *May Our Mothers Be Bereaved of Us if We Fail to Help Our Prophet (Peace be Upon Him)*, released on 19 March 2008. Republished in *IntelCenter Words of Osama Bin Laden*, Vol. 1 (Tempest Publishing, 2008), 194.

2 Aaron Kiely, *Redefining NUS' No Platform Policy would weaken fight against fascism*, 19 September 2012. See: https://www.facebook.com/notes/ aaron-kiely/redefining-nus-no-platform-policy-would-weaken-the-fight- against-fascism-how-it-/10152085722835580/.

3 Mark Thompson, *Guardian*, 21 October 2009, http://www.theguardian. com/commentisfree/2009/oct/21/question-time-bbc-bnp-griffin.

4 http://www.theguardian.com/politics/2009/oct/19/peter-hain-bnp- question-time. Peter Hain's claim that it was 'unlawful' was based on a

legal technicality concerning the BNP's registration as a political party. The BBC was advised that this issue did not affect the BNP's fundamental status nor its ability to field candidates at the next election – the key questions for us.

5   Janice Turner, 'No Garlic and Silver Bullets are Needed for Nick Griffin', *The Times*, 17 October 2009.

6   http://www.standard.co.uk/news/when-bonnie-greer-met-nick-griffin-6768790.html.

7   http://www.theguardian.com/music/2011/nov/23/bonnie-greer-nick-griffin-opera.

8   *Yale Herald*, 6 November 2015. The article was removed from the *Yale Herald* website apparently at the author's request shortly after it was posted, but is viewable here: https://archive.is/cOYdV.

9   http://www.ipetitions.com/petition/reconsider-the-smith-college-2014-commencement.

10 Michael Bloomberg, remarks at Harvard University's 363rd Commencement Ceremony, 29 May 2014, www.mikebloomberg.com/index.cfm?objectid:4D9E60A5-5056-9A3E-D07D6B773CAD46E4.

11 See Zionist Organization of America website: zoa.org/2014/10/10263133-reminder-huge-klinghoffer-protest-at-lincoln-center-today-at-6-p-m-press-conference-at-5-p-m/.

12 Quote given to Sara Eisen of Bloomberg TV and broadcast on Bloomberg, 6 March 2013.

13 Email to *Business Insider*, quoted by Joe Weisenthal, *Business Insider*, 6 March 2013.

14 Assorted comments on Tyler Durden's guest post 'Niall Ferguson Shatters Paul Krugman's Delusions', Zero Hedge, 23 October 2013.

15 Alasdair MacIntyre, *After Virtue: A Study in Moral Theory* (University of Notre Dame Press, 2nd edn, 1984), 6.

16 Ibid., 10.

17 John Taylor, *Works of John Taylor, the Water Poet*, Vol. 1 (Spenser Society, 1870), 4. Italicisation reversed.

18 Thomas Hobbes, *Leviathan* (1651), XIII, 8.

19 Jenny Wormald 'Gunpowder, Treason, and Scots', *Journal of British Studies*, No. 2, (University of Chicago Press, 1985), 141–68.

20 Bryan Garsten, *Saving Persuasion: A Defense of Rhetoric and Judgment* (Harvard University Press, 2009), 30, quoting Hobbes' *Behemoth* (1681).

21 Ibid., 37, quoting Hobbes' *Leviathan* (1651; Cambridge University Press, 1996), 33.

22 Christopher Hitchens, *Hitch-22: A Memoir* (Atlantic, 2010), 268.

23 Norman Tebbit, *Independent on Sunday* magazine, 8 September 1990.

24 John Berger, *Guardian*, 25 February 1989.

25 Jimmy Carter, *New York Times*, 5 March 1989.

26 BBC Radio 4, *The World Tonight*, 7 January 2015, http://www.bbc.co.uk/programmes/b04wwgzh. I have condensed Arzu Merali's language very slightly (her remarks were made in the course of a live radio discussion), but without changing the meaning.

27 Ibid., again with minor condensing of David Aaronovitch's response.

28 Quoted in *The New York Times*, 'New Charlie Hebdo Cartoon Stirs Muslim Anger in Mideast', 14 January 2015.

29 Joint declaration of interior ministers, Paris, 11 January 2015.

30 Associated Press, 27 January 2015.

31 Theresa May, quoted in the *Guardian*, 24 November 2014, http://www.theguardian.com/politics/2014/nov/24/terror-bill-requires-universities-to-ban-extremist-speakers.

32 Communications Act 2003, Section 127, http://www.legislation.gov.uk/ukpga/2003/21/section/127.

12 Keep Calm But Don't Carry On

1 Parmenides, *Poem*, Proem, II, 28–32.

2 *Letters of Thomas Carlyle, 1826–1836, Volume 2* (Macmillan, 1888), 227.

3 See: http://yougov.co.uk/news/2014/10/29/political-disaffection-not-new-it-rising-and-drivi/.

4 Onora O'Neill, *A Question of Trust: The BBC Reith Lectures 2002* (Cambridge University Press, 2002).

5 See: Yougov website above.

6 See Jane Merrick, *Independent*, 'Labour needs an angry leader: it's time for Ed Miliband to go to war', I February 2015. Also Polly Toynbee, *Guardian*, 'As Osborne plans more austerity, it's time for Labour outrage', 17 March 2015.

7 *Daily Telegraph*, 28 February 2014, http://www.telegraph.co.uk/news/worldnews/europe/eu/10668242/Europe-David-Cameron-cant-match-Nigel-Farages-simple-message.html.

8 Quoted by Tom Kington in the *Observer*, 2 March 2013.

9 Quoted in *The Economist*, 9 December 2014.

10 Remarks by Boris Johnson reported by the *Guardian*, 21 February 2016. See http://www.theguardian.com/politics/blog/live/2016/feb/21/cameron-marr-boris-johnson-eu-referendum-camerons-interview-on-the-marr-show-as-boris-johnson-prepares-to-declare-his-hand-politics-live.

11 See Leonardo Tarán, *Parmenides: A Text with Translation, Commentary, and Critical Essays* (Princeton University Press, 1965), p. 210ff. Interpretations

of the passage vary widely and, in cases like mine, probably tell you more about the intentions of the translator than they do about what Parmenides himself had to say. In the lecture series he delivered about Parmenides at Freiburg in 1942–3, Martin Heidegger translated this same extract as follows: 'There is, however, a need that you experience everything, both the stable heart of well-enclosing unconcealment, as well as the appearing in its appearance to mortals, where there is no relying on the unconcealed.' This translation from the German appears in *Parmenides* by Martin Heidegger, translated by André Schuwer and Richard Rojcewicz (Indiana University Press, 1998).

12 Eminem, 'My Words Are Weapons', first released as part of the Mix Tape, Volume IV by Funkmaster Flex (2000).

13 Public Enemy, 'Fight the Power', released as a single by Motown Records in 1989.

14 https://www.instagram.com/p/rkrM8xS1Mk/?modal=truc.

15 Killer Mike, 'Pressure' from the album *I Pledge Allegiance to the Grind II*, 2008.

16 *Hamilton*, music, lyrics and book by Lin-Manuel Miranda. *Hamilton* premiered in February 2015.

Index